THE RICH

THE RICH

From Slaves to Super Yachts:
A 2000-year History

John Kampfner

Little, Brown

LITTLE, BROWN

First published in Great Britain in 2014 by Little, Brown

Copyright © John Kampfner 2014

The moral right of the author has been asserted.

A CIP catalogue record for this book
is available from the British Library.

Hardback ISBN 978-1-4087-0426-4
C format ISBN 978-1-4087-0427-1

Typeset in Bembo by M Rules
Printed and bound in Great Britain by
Clays Ltd, St Ives plc

Papers used by Little, Brown are from well-managed forests
and other responsible sources.

MIX
Paper from
responsible sources
FSC
www.fsc.org   FSC® C104740

Little, Brown
An imprint of
Little, Brown Book Group
100 Victoria Embankment
London EC4Y 0DY

An Hachette UK Company
www.hachette.co.uk

www.littlebrown.co.uk

To my parents Betty and Fred

Contents

PART TWO

Now

Prologue

No man is rich enough to buy back his past.
                                   Oscar Wilde

This wasn't any old lobster. It was super-sized, a giant crustacean strug-gling to fit onto my bone-china plate. Opposite me the wife of a British diplomat smiled nervously, sharing my anxiety about how to tackle this dead monster. This was 1992, my first social engagement with a Russian oligarch. Vladimir Gusinsky and his wife Lena had invited a small group for dinner to their Moscow apartment, just down the road from the city's largest sculpture of Lenin at October Square. The wait-ers in their bowties hovered around us with excessive courtesy, constantly refilling our glasses with Chablis premier cru.

Russia was changing before my eyes. A tiny slew were getting rich beyond their wildest dreams. Only a year or two earlier, the roles were reversed. Although the best I would offer guests was a can of Heineken, from a foreigners-only hard-currency shop, I knew that as part of a small band of comfortable Western expats I was the object of envy. By the middle of that decade, by now back in London, I watched the gradual invasion of the first generation of New Russians. Some of those same friends of mine would pick disdainfully at their food at Gordon Ramsay, leaving most of it on their plate for show. Or they would drop into conversation about their most recent long weekend in Cap Ferrat.

Thus began my personal fascination with the global super-rich, their lifestyles, but more their psychology. First things first: we should admit that we are obsessed with the super-rich. We envy and abhor their lifestyles. We say we loathe what they have done to society, but we love to read about them in glossy magazines and to chart their success on lists.

How have these people achieved their success – if success is the right term for the sudden appropriation of wealth? Why are they so blessed? Are they smarter, more determined or just luckier than the rest of us? Is the present crop of wealthy any different from those who have come before? The people who are blamed for the economic crisis and for widening inequality are still living in their parallel worlds, raking in the bonuses, taking their private jets to their private islands, while doling out the odd scrap known as philanthropy. We think in the second decade of the third millennium AD that we are living through a uniquely divisive and unequal era. But are we? I decided to investigate, to delve into the past – two thousand years in fact – in search of answers.

Starting with ancient Rome, moving on to the Norman Conquest, the Malian kingdom, the Florentine bankers and the great European commodity traders, this story culminates with the oligarchies of modern Russia and China and the elites of Silicon Valley and Wall Street. From ancient times to the present day, from periods of stability to those of hubris and decline, they have more in common than we realise. For every Roman Abramovich, Bill Gates and Sheikh Mohammed there is an Alfred Krupp and Andrew Carnegie. The twenty-first-century super-rich are not an oddity of history. They can thank their predecessors for teaching them the lessons.

How do people become rich? They do so by fair means and foul, by entrepreneurship, appropriation and inheritance. They make markets and they manipulate them. They defeat the competition or they eliminate it. They gain or buy influence among the political leadership and the cultural and social elites. For more than a century American politics has made no secret of the link; indeed, it celebrates it. The more lavish the fundraiser, the more politicians feel obliged to attend. One such example is the Alfred E. Smith memorial dinner, a white-tie affair at New York's Waldorf Astoria hotel, in memory of the country's first Catholic presidential candidate. Nobody aspiring to the White House would dream of missing it. In October 2000, George W. Bush only half joked: 'This is an impressive crowd – the haves and the have-mores. Some people call you the elites; I call you my base.' The remark had the merit of honesty, and could be applied to many a global leader around the world in many an era.

This is the topography of the global nomads – they mix with a narrow group of similar-minded people, sparring with each other at the same auctions, fraternising on each other's yachts. They compare themselves only against each other, which often leads to dissatisfaction with their lot, to the belief that they are not wealthy or powerful enough. They pay as little back to the state in tax as they can get away with. They reinforce each other in their certainties, convinced that their acquisition of wealth, and spending of it through charitable enterprise, have earned them their place at the apex of global decision-making and moral supremacy. Lloyd Blankfein, the chairman and CEO of Goldman Sachs, spoke for many of his group when he famously quipped that he was 'doing God's work'.

Most of all, they are compulsively competitive – in the making of money and the spending of it. The first stage after the acquisition of wealth is the flaunting. Opulence has been manifested differently over the ages, but the psychology underlying it has rarely changed. For slaves, concubines, gold and castles of ancient and medieval times, read private jets, holiday islands and football and baseball clubs of the contemporary era. For some that is enough. They shun the limelight, hiding behind the high walls of their mansions, indulging themselves and their small coteries of friends and hangers-on in discreet luxury.

At an early stage the laws of gravity intervene. The richer you are, the richer you become. Equally, the poorer you are, the easier it is to fall further. Investment advisers say that making the first ten million is the hard part. Once you've reached that milestone, beneficent tax regimes, lawyers and regulators will do the rest for you. The best brains follow the money, so the regulators earning a fraction of the incomes are no match for them. The plutocrats exhort the state to get off their backs and yet when the going gets tough the state is invariably their best friend, bailing out banks and other institutions deemed 'too big to fail'. Profits are privatised, debts are socialised. As the American economist Joseph Stiglitz puts it: 'Much of today's inequality is due to manipulation of the financial system, enabled by changes in the rules that have been bought and paid for by the financial industry itself – one of the best investments ever.'

Now, as in centuries past, status symbols are not enough. Once satiated by wealth, they want more. Some (though not many) seek political office. One might think of Silvio Berlusconi. He has followed in the footsteps of Marcus Licinius Crassus. A safer, more plied, route is the businessman/banker who wields influence at one step removed – not in secret, but not fully in the open either. Think Cosimo de' Medici; think pretty much everyone who has acquired wealth and public profile in the modern day, from bankers to entrepreneurs to internet moguls. A seat on a government commission or cultural institution provides them with the respectability they crave, but also an assumption of vindication for their work.

Wealth rarely buys peace of mind. The super-rich are consumed by what happens next. They fear for their legacies and for their children. Will the money they have made be safe in their hands? Will the standing they have acquired in society be frittered away? Will statues be cast in their image?

They want to be remembered for more than making a fortune.

What matters most to them is reputation. The contemporary wealthy employ a veritable army to look after their brand, to wash away inconvenient facts about their past. The boundaries between predatory and productive activity, between the legally corrupt and the morally corrupt, are often hard to define. Lawyers are hired to slap libel writs; public relations agents massage the message. Crisis PR is a booming business, helping to divert attention from the antics of wayward offspring and gold-diggers. Academics and friends in the media spread the gospel. 'Thought leadership' comes with a price tag. The shadier the road to wealth that is taken – from the use of cartels and discreet pressure to outright violence – the more determined is the billionaire to become a pillar of the new establishment, emulating the manners and the lifestyles of those who became rich before them. In ancient times, it was important to fund an army. In medieval Europe, the papacy was the key route up the social ladder. Now? Anyone who is anyone is at Davos, or the secretive Bilderberg conferences, or at a society wedding in the English countryside, preferably with a junior royal in tow. Art galleries and charities will swoon at the munificence of the wealthy. Social success is all but guaranteed. The new elite merges with the established one. Old money was new money once.

With every lever at their disposal, the few who land up in jail or are otherwise shunned can be considered spectacular failures. To get on the wrong side of the law or the mutually reinforcing power elites takes some doing. At least that is the case in life. Managing reputation in death, the historical legacy, is a far more complicated endeavour. But with some advance planning that too is usually achievable.

What do I mean by 'the rich'? The word derives from the same Indo-European root that produced the Celtic word *rix*, the Latin *rex* and the Sanskrit *rajah*, which means 'king'. In many cultures over the ages the concept of wealth has been associated with royalty. The formal structures of society may vary between eras and cultures, but this link between money and rank has not. Being rich is a comparative term and quite a few achieve that status. At different times in history they have belonged to the court, the trading class or the twentieth-century professional class. Their lives are more comfortable than most, but they tend to be fully assimilated in society. The people I focus on in my study of the past two millennia are those who have, through their accumulation of wealth and lifestyles, set themselves apart from the rest. These are, to use the fashionable modern term, the super-rich.

Pretty much every country in the world has a 'Rich List'. Some countries have several. Some lists are international. They evoke mixed reactions among the general public, and among participants. Yet all of them – from the best-known, such as the *Sunday Times'* Rich List in the UK, to *Forbes'* in the US, to the Hurun Report in China – arouse fascination. Bloomberg has a daily online list of the world's Top 200. Movements are tracked in the same way as share prices. Some people are delighted to appear in the lists and take umbrage if they drop a notch. Others pay consultants fat fees to keep them out of the public eye, and regard any mention of their wealth as a sign of failure. The shy and retiring, it should be noted, are an ever-diminishing minority. It is so much harder now to live a life of anonymous fortune, but also why would one forgo the benefits that accompany it?

It is relatively straightforward to rank within a specific time frame – at least those parts of the income or assets that are known and declared. It is far harder to compare between generations. Giving a value to coinage many centuries old is hard enough. It is important to factor in not just the raw figures, but what the money could buy in terms of both material goods and power and influence, which are tougher to enumerate. Most lists relate to absolute wealth, as distinct from relative wealth – in other words an individual's purchasing power within countries and globally.

This book is not a numeric rich list for the past or the present day. Many, but not all, of my subjects were among the richest of their era, but they were not necessarily the number one. They each tell a different story about how money is made, how it is spent, and how reputations are manufactured and moulded. They also shine a light on the societies of their time and their own reactions to wealth.

The tale is divided into two parts, a larger 'then' and a shorter 'now'. Each historical chapter tells a story that can be read on its own, identifying themes that link the super-rich of that moment with those in successive centuries and, of course, with the present day. Some chapters focus on a single individual; others combine figures from their own time, or near contemporaries, or make comparisons with those from another millennium.

The contemporary chapters are designed to be different. They focus on groups: the sheikhs, the oligarchs and the Silicon Valley tech geniuses, otherwise known as the geeks. Finally come the bankers, hedge funders and private equity bosses, the pantomime villains accused of causing the financial crash of 2007–8 but still raking in the bonuses. By the time readers get to the modern subjects, they should recognise a pattern emerging – nothing that has occurred over the turbulent past few years is unique to its time. History, when it comes to the rich, has a habit of repeating itself.

I begin my journey in the first century BC. Marcus Licinius Crassus made his money in ways that would make the dodgiest property dealer proud. With the help of his slaves, he would watch as buildings caught fire, rebuild them and pocket a tidy profit. Such was his success in real estate speculation (think property bubbles, think foreclosures), Crassus went on to become the richest man in the Roman Republic. He re-invested his gains to buy power. He became a pillar of society, forming an alliance with Pompey the Great and 'discovering' Julius Caesar before coming to a sticky end.

A more extensive example of the land grab came a thousand years later. One of the wealthiest Englishmen of all time was Alan Rufus, a.k.a. Alain Le Roux, a man largely forgotten by history. As one of William the Conqueror's trusted henchmen, he took part in the Battle of Hastings and the Harrying of the North – the massacre of much of the population of north-east England. For his pains he was rewarded with land that stretched from top to bottom of the country. Rufus's story tells of the supplanting of one elite by another and the rewards that were available for loyalty. The systematic use of violence and ethnic cleansing, in which Rufus played a key role, redrew the map of England, creating an entire political and economic establishment that survives to this day.

For a single event that projected wealth, nothing can beat the Hajj of Mansa Musa. The leader of the Malian Empire took thousands of lavishly dressed foot soldiers and slaves with him on his great pilgrimage to Mecca in 1324. He dispensed so much gold en route that he trig-gered a global crash in its value. Musa's reign married ostentatious riches and public displays of piety. Wealth and power were inextricably linked. Yet, within two centuries of his death, his kingdom had been destroyed, his name erased from history by Europeans who couldn't imagine a black African to have presided over such treasures.

Few remember Cosimo de' Medici for his less than ethical banking practices. His place in history was secured instead through his spon-sorship of great artists and writers, and the construction of glorious churches in early Renaissance Florence. The practice of lending money, usury, is condemned in the Bible. Yet Cosimo de' Medici and the var-ious popes he sponsored struck a deal to get them all off the hook. The bank and the Vatican needed each other and both raked in the profits, just as banks and politicians have done in the twenty-first century. Power relationships and reputation management are the themes of this fourth chapter.

The Spanish *conquistador* Francisco Pizarro was an example of a self-made man, the illegitimate son of an infantry colonel and a servant, who achieved great wealth, but not status, through the acquisition of land and resources in the New World of what is now Latin America. Chapter 5 is about violence in the service of wealth creation, but also about the tense relationship between old and new money.

Chapter 6 takes two subjects, more than a millennium apart, to focus on the hereditary wealth of kings. Such was the monopoly of power and riches enjoyed by France's Louis XIV and the ancient Egyptian king Akhenaten that they built palaces and cities to venerate their rule. In the Pharaoh's case he even constructed his own religion. The supremacy of these semi-divine sun kings was total in life, but their legacies unravelled immediately on death. They both inform the story of the present-day Gulf sheikhs.

The Dutch East India Company was the first example of shareholder capitalism, with small investors back home enjoying the spoils of lucrative trade – the seventeenth-century equivalent of a successful Initial Public Offering of the modern day. The company directors found the tactics of their Governor General, Jan Pieterszoon Coen, a little too brutal and vulgar for their taste. But the enjoyment of riches such young adventurers brought outweighed any ethical concerns they might fleetingly have had. A little over a hundred years later, Robert Clive turned the East India Company into a dominant force in global trade, enshrining British rule over the subcontinent for two centuries. Clive's fondness for the baubles of wealth and his failure to show contrition in Parliament when events transpired against him were his undoing. The parallels with twenty-first-century bankers are uncanny.

Alfred Krupp, the subject of Chapter 8, was the quintessential entrepreneur, turning a family firm into a global corporation at the height of the Industrial Revolution. His steel business traded with anyone – the Russians, the British, the French – but when it needed to shore up its credentials back home in Germany it pandered to the patriotic demands of the Kaiser. Krupp built a corporate city around his mills, controlling his workers from cradle to grave. He was one of the earliest practitioners of the theory of trickle-down. All would benefit from the company's success, but some deserved to benefit more than others.

It is easy to understand why the robber barons are seen as the precursors of today's super-rich. By carving up the railroads, steel and oil industries and banks, they created monopoly empires and untold wealth for a few. Their parties and mansions form the backdrop to debate about twenty-first-century excess. More intriguing are the ideological similarities, which is why I focus on Andrew Carnegie in Chapter 9. His Gospel of Wealth, which brings together the notions of genetic superiority, free market and philanthropy, has become required reading for the turbo-charged billionaire of the modern age.

What of the period that came after Carnegie, between the end of the Second World War and the collapse of communism? There are few great examples of the super-rich from the 1950s, 60s and 70s, a period of state intervention and a brief bridging of the divide between the rich and the rest. There was one somewhat bizarre group worth dwelling on – a cluster of kleptocrat leaders who, under American or Soviet protection, were given free rein to plunder. From this horror list of bejewelled dictators, I could have turned to Haji Muhammad Suharto of Indonesia or Ferdinand Marcos of the Philippines, or perhaps Nicaragua's Anastasio Somoza. Instead, I focus on Zaire's Mobutu Sese Seko. As his country fell apart, he built a runway for his private jet and palaces of marble. Mobutu is a prime example of reputation failure among the super-rich. His modest rehabilitation in recent years suggests that even the most rapacious among the wealthy have their adherents.

The narrative moves from the twentieth-century eccentrics into the contemporary era, the convergence of globalisation, technology and the hegemony of Anglo-Saxon free markets that began in the 1990s. Instead of telling the stories of specific individuals, I focus on groups and their links to history.

If you have the money, why not create your own cultural paradise, enticing the Louvre and the Guggenheim to the desert? That is what the sheikh running Abu Dhabi has done. In Qatar, they are also focusing on art, but their model is simply to buy as many works by Grand Masters as they can lay their hands on at auction, throwing in the

Football World Cup for good measure. Dubai, more brash than the other two sheikhdoms, has opted to outdo its neighbours with the tallest, glitziest and most garish buildings in the world. Underlying some of these follies is intense ambition. Like Louis XIV and Akhenaten, the leaders of these three Gulf states inherited the wealth of a nation. Their goal is to use that to shift power and prestige. They have already gone a long way to achieving that aim, but the near collapse of Dubai in 2009 demonstrates the fragility of the model.

I next focus on the pacts drawn up by the newly emerging class of super-rich in Russia and China as well as the autocrats who rule those nations. The Russians, many of whom established their fortunes in the wild 1990s, when their country's natural resources were privatised on the cheap, were forced into an accommodation by President Putin. Under the unwritten terms of engagement, the oligarchs can make as much money as they like as long as they do not interfere with politics and ensure that the leadership cliques and other important officials are given a share of their immense profits. In China, the Communist Party's control over the new capitalists is more formal. Those who play the game can enjoy untrammelled luxury at home and abroad, commanding a new level of obeisance from estate agents, lawyers and financial advisers in London and New York.

The most romantic stories of instant wealth creation surely belong to the geeks. The awkward squad of American computer scientists and mathematicians have become a who's who of innovative entrepreneurialism, aided by sharp elbows and assorted chicanery as their companies moved from the chaotic start-up to the venture capitalist boardroom. The corporate tax avoidance schemes are rooted not just in the desire to maximise profit. Like the robber barons, present-day billionaires have come to believe that they are best placed to spend the money they have decided not to give to state coffers, always meticulously legally. The titans of the internet believe that the same brain power that produced technological invention can be transferred to solving some of the world's most intractable health and poverty problems.

The last stop on this tale of the super-rich down the ages is devoted to the pantomime villains – the bankers. Not only have many of the protagonists been found wanting in their day jobs; they have also shown remarkable ineptitude in managing their reputations. To end up lower down the ethical pecking order than oligarchs is some achievement. The arrogance and greed that led to the global financial crash were quickly replaced by self-pity. While some have been forced to quit, the blow softened by the extraordinary wealth they accrued, few seem blessed with the self-knowledge required to explain their actions. And yet, all may not be lost. A number of figures in the banking world are back at presidential and prime-ministerial top tables. As for public opinion, history suggests that this too will soften as economies recover and memories fade. No matter what the wrongdoing, the rich can usually secure rehabilitation . . . if they focus hard enough on the task.

The choices I alight on can be read on their own as individual stories. But they are also case studies designed to link the present with the past. They each represent both an era and a theme – from the appropriation of property and its use in self-veneration, to the roles played by religion, art and philanthropy in delivering benediction, to notions of class, conquest and acceptance, to cartels, industrialisation and good old-fashioned theft. So why did I select these subjects and not the many alternatives on offer?

Readers may have their own list. I would be intrigued to see whom they would have included and why. Among historical figures, the wealthiest monarch is said to have been Russia's Tsar Nicholas II. By the time the Romanov dynasty was overthrown in the Russian Revolution, the family's wealth was estimated at $45 billion (in today's prices). Theirs was, for sure, considerable and flamboyant wealth, but it was more hoarded than projected for a bigger purpose. I opted instead for Louis, the Sun King, because of the parallels with ancient and contemporary times.

As for bankers, a sixteenth-century German, Jakob Fugger, could have provided an alternative for a medieval money man and philanthropist, building the world's first social housing project. I could have opted for Thomas Guy, a wealthy wharf-owner and coal dealer who was miserly to his workers even by the standards of seventeenth-century London yet left a large bequest for the poor and sick, including for a hospital that still bears his name. Another alternative might have been

Alfred Nobel, the Swedish chemist who, after making his fortune by inventing dynamite, left it to endow the eponymous prizes. For longevity, I could have opted for the Rothschilds. But none, in my view, can match Cosimo de' Medici for his reputation-laundering brilliance.

In the discussion about money and power, there is no shortage of candidates among super-rich emperors and kings. For sheer brutality, Genghis Khan takes some beating. Among the ancients, Crassus is sometimes confused with Croesus, the King of Lydia and inventor of coins in the sixth century BC, from whom the term 'rich as Croesus' derives. But Crassus' greed as property magnate, politician, networker and schemer presents too many modern parallels to be ignored.

I have not produced a chapter on the scions of twentieth-century business, such as Henry Ford or the other great motor manufacturers, or Richard Branson, who made his first billion in aviation. Ford's support for Hitler was a terrible blot on the family name, but the relationship between wealth and dictatorship is covered thoroughly in the chapter on the Krupp dynasty, and in the mentions of assorted despots elsewhere in the book. There could have been a place for the shipping magnate Aristotle Onassis, or the oil tycoon who funded one of the largest private art galleries in the world, John Paul Getty. Nor have I covered some of the colourful multi-millionaires of post-war Britain, such as 'Tiny' Rowland, Robert Maxwell and Mohammed al-Fayed. No matter how colourful and controversial figures such as these have been, no matter the influence they might have wielded on individual politicians, they did not penetrate into every corner of public decision-making in the way contemporary bankers, oligarchs and internet giants have done.

Moving on to the present day, I could have dwelt on celebrity footballers or pop stars, a special category whose astronomic contracts and advertising deals are indulged by the public, as are their out-of-hours troublemaking antics. I could also have discussed any of the big retail chief executives, such as the Koch brothers or Sam Walton of Wal-Mart fame in the US. Their contributions to wealth creation – pulling political strings and enforcing low unit-labour costs to increase profit margins – are detailed elsewhere, not least in the story of Amazon. As for investors, George Soros appears in passing, while Warren Buffett's generous approach to philanthropy forms part of my consideration of Bill Gates and the creation of his foundation.

I have focused less on hedge funders and private equity and more on the banks because of their more visible role in the financial meltdown. One 'hedgie' who doesn't make it into Chapter 14 should be given an honourable mention here. John Paulson's decision to buy credit-default insurance against billions of dollars of sub-prime mortgages before the market collapsed in 2007 earned him almost $4 billion personally and transformed him from an obscure money manager into a financial legend. He found the scrutiny unnerving, particularly when it all went wrong (for some) in the crash. Paulson took umbrage when it was noted that his annual income was the equivalent of the salaries of eighty thousand nurses. 'Most jurisdictions would want to have successful companies like ours located there. We choose to stay here and then, you know, get *yelled* at. I'm sure if we wanted to go to Singapore, they'd roll out the red carpet to attract us,' he noted. That point is crucial. Almost all governments are in a race to attract the super-wealthy, and their lucrative micro-economy. If not New York, London or Singapore, why not Mumbai, Rio de Janeiro or Dubai – or Mexico City, for that matter, which is moving fast to become a welcoming venue for the super-rich?

Which brings us to Carlos Slim. The recent elevation of the Mexican telecoms mogul to world's richest man belongs in the book's conclusion, which asks why we tolerate some forms of wealth and not others. For many in Western countries that have suffered during the recent recession, hostility towards the super-rich is laced with a certain snobbery or even racism (just as it was towards Mansa Musa and the Malian kingdom). The sight of Russians, Chinese, or Mexicans living it up is, to many in the West, an affront. It challenges established notions of entitlement. A striking aspect of this present era is not the existence of the super-rich, but the fact that they exist in almost every country. They are a truly global phenomenon. The divide is growing not between societies but within them.

Finally, this narrative contains not a single woman. Among the ancients, I could have chosen Cleopatra or any of several medieval queens. In the present day, I could have opted for the heiress Liliane

Bettencourt, of L'Oréal fame; Australia's richest woman, Gina Rinehart, a mining heiress, might have made a good candidate. Or I could have gone for Queen Elizabeth II, who always makes it on to the global rich lists. It is sad but necessary to acknowledge that the vast majority of women who might be considered super-rich in history have acquired wealth through either marriage or inheritance. For the past two thousand years it is men who have made, and hoarded, wealth in societies that have been exclusively patriarchal. Therefore, I decided to stick with my male-only list in order to send a deliberate message. I am convinced that if a future version of this book is written, perhaps even in five or ten years' time, this imbalance will begin to be corrected. Indeed, the speed of change is accelerating. It is from the technology sector that prime candidates are most likely to emerge. Sheryl Sandberg of Facebook and Marissa Mayer of Yahoo (who have minor parts in this narrative) are fast becoming major figures among the rich and power- ful of the internet corporate world. A number of women are also moving quickly up China's rich lists. According to *Forbes'* 2014 bil- lionaires list, of the 268 newcomers, 42 are women – a single-year record. Yet it notes that only 32 billionaire women – or a meagre 1.9 per cent of all the globe's billionaires – had a meaningful hand in build- ing their own fortunes, as opposed to inheriting wealth. Other new billionaires to watch are Nigeria's Folorunsho Alakija, who moved from fashion design to oil prospecting, and Denise Coates, a Briton who runs an online betting company.

In September 2012, the left-wing French newspaper *Libération* ran the following front-page headline: '*Casse-toi riche con!*' This translates roughly as 'Get lost, rich jerk.' The object of its opprobrium was Bernard Arnault, France's richest man, who had just declared he was leaving for Belgium in protest at the 75 per cent tax rate imposed by the Socialist government. Arnault, who runs the LVMH luxury goods group, finally withdrew his threat, but only after threatening to sue the paper for insulting his honour.

What is so remarkable about this is not that the wealthy seek to domicile themselves and their businesses in low-tax havens, but that criticism of them has been so ineffective. Just a hop across the Channel,

British governments of all hues have taken the opposite approach, doing everything they can to attract the rich. They have deployed two arguments, the principled and the pragmatic – wealth creation is good (no matter how it is created), and some largesse in the form of taxation is better than none. British politicians have made a huge bet on the super-rich and the trickle-down effect of their wealth.

The French approach is exceptional. The Anglo-Saxon model has been adopted across the rest of the world, where countries compete to lower 'barriers' to self-enrichment. In so doing, they are following the path of history. The period between 1945 and the Thatcher–Reagan reforms of the early 1980s was a rare moment in which the state sought to intervene to smooth out some of the rougher edges of inequality. At the same time, the rich retreated from an active role in politics as – initially at least – this more egalitarian approach was seen to be fairer and more economically efficient. There is no shortage of statistics to highlight the extraordinary changes that have taken place over the past thirty years. Here is a small selection:

According to the US Congressional Budget Office, in the period between 1979 (the eve of Ronald Reagan's election) and 2007 (the start of the crash), American incomes increased overall by 62 per cent – allowing for tax and inflation. The bottom 20 per cent, however, received only an 18 per cent increase. The figure for the top 20 per cent was 65 per cent, while the top 1 per cent saw their incomes rise by 275 per cent. Three decades ago, the average American chief executive made 42 times more than the average worker. By the mid-2000s, that ratio had risen to 380:1.

The fabled top 1 per cent of earners (the principal targets of the Occupy movement) now own 40 per cent of the United States' wealth. The top 300,000 Americans have amassed almost as much income as the bottom 150 million. Yet the biggest shift in wealth has not occurred in this group, but in the top 0.1 and 0.01 per cent. The smaller the group, the more exponential is the rise. The wealthiest 16,000 families in the United States now enjoy an average income of $24 million. Their share of national income has quadrupled in the past three decades from just over 1 per cent to nearly 5 per cent. That is a bigger share of the national pie for the super-rich than in the first Gilded Age in the late nineteenth century. Oxfam noted that the 2012 income of the world's richest hundred billionaires was $240 billion – enough to wipe out extreme global poverty four times over.

In America, progressive taxation started to make a dent into inequality in the 1930s. In Europe, it did not kick in until the late 1940s or early 1950s. The Gini coefficient, the statistic that measures inequality, reached a low of 0.3 in the mid-1970s. Now it has climbed back sharply to a global average of around 0.4, a rise of a third overall. These decimals might seem minor, arcane even, but they cast a sharp light on the relationship between rich and poor, within countries and between countries. Anywhere below 0.3 is considered strongly egalitarian (Sweden and the Nordics go below the line, as does Germany). Anything above 0.5 is considered dangerous and divisive. The United States hovers around the high 0.4s. Chinese inequality has risen by 50 per cent since Deng Xiaoping's reforms, and now stands at 0.48. Statistics like that tell one part of the story, a dry part.

In the few years since the crash has anything changed? Rules and regulations have tightened, a little. The Gini has barely shifted. A few of the super-rich have seen their investment portfolios tumble. Some have fallen by the wayside, humiliated and resentful at their treatment. Yet nobody of any significance in the banks or elsewhere has faced prosecution. Politicians showed no appetite for bringing those responsible for the crisis to book, hiding behind legal complexities designed for (and often by) the wealthy. The vast majority have weathered the storm with consummate ease. Indeed, there is considerable evidence to suggest that in the recession, while the vast majority had to tighten their belts, the super-rich did better than ever. As economies shrank and people lost their jobs (and thereby stopped paying tax), the share of all income tax paid by the richest increased. And so did governments' dependency on their 'generosity'. In 2010, Alan Greenspan, the former chairman of the Federal Reserve, who after the crash admitted that he had misunderstood the behaviour of unbridled free markets, noted: 'Our problem basically is that we have a very distorted economy, in the sense that there has been a significant recovery in our limited area of the economy amongst high-income individuals.'

The Mayor of London, Boris Johnson, was much criticised for a speech he made in November 2013 in which he looked at the role played by the super-rich in the broader economy. In 1979 the top 1 per cent in Britain contributed 11 per cent to total income tax revenues. Now they contribute almost 30 per cent. The top 0.1 per cent, just 29,000 people, contribute fully 14 per cent of all taxation. Johnson concluded: 'Some measure of inequality is essential for the spirit of envy and keeping up with the Joneses that is, like greed, a valuable spur to economic activity.' Behind the infelicitous message lay a stark, and unarguable, point: all politicians are at it, fawning at the wealthy for a small splash of cash.

The difference between this contemporary generation and past eras lies not in the gap between rich and poor. It revolves around the relationship between the super-rich and a middle class that has dramatically lost out. This is a relationship laced with aspiration, envy and a growing sense of injustice. Often these groups hail from the same socio-economic background, comfortable but not wealthy – Medici, Coen and Clive serve as examples from centuries past, just as Jeff Bezos and Fred Goodwin do today. But through career choice, luck and in some cases skill, they end in very different financial circumstances. Will that middle-class resentment have any effect? The signs over the last few years suggest not. The problem lies not just in economic models and power, but in psychology. Newspaper editors know that there is no better way to arouse interest among readers or increase sales than to publish lists of the wealthy and stories about their lavish homes and their yachts. Politicians know that the public has a confused approach towards tax. They know it is a social good, but when the opportunity arises to pay less to the state – particularly when passing money on to the next generation – it is seized with alacrity. Whether or not they admit it in polite society, for many people the allure of bling remains as strong as ever.

That is why the wealthy invariably win. If history serves as a guide, it illustrates that, while some fortunes disappear and dynasties die, the super-rich have proved remarkably adept at not just preserving their economic and political power, but laundering their reputations. No matter how they made their money, they have created legacies that are often kinder to them than they deserve.

PART ONE

Then

CHAPTER 1

Marcus Licinius Crassus –
Scandal, fire and war

As long as the music is playing, you've got to
get up and dance.
Charles 'Chuck' Prince, CEO, Citigroup

He may have been the richest of them all. Marcus Licinius Crassus was
the ultimate oligarch who used the nexus of wealth and politics to
become one of the most powerful figures in the Roman Republic. He
was a man of his times, when corruption was an art form, when violence, politics and profit were rolled into one. This was an era of rapid
economic growth, with wealth flowing in from newly conquered lands.
Friendships and enmities, loyalties and betrayals, could be bought and
sold. The elite were all at it, but some were more successful than others.
His skills have proven transferable through the ages. He would have felt
right at home in the Russia of the past twenty years, or in other societies in which ruthlessness and greed were regarded as inevitable parts
of public life.

'The Romans, it is true, say that the many virtues of Crassus were
obscured by his sole vice of avarice.' Who would dare gainsay Plutarch,
the great moral philosopher and chronicler of ancient generals and
statesmen? 'For at the outset he was possessed of not more than 300 talents, and still, when he made a private inventory of his property before

his Parthian expedition, he found that it had a value of 7100 talents. The greatest part of this, if one must tell the scandalous truth, he got together out of fire and war, making the public calamities his greatest source of revenue.'[1]

Crassus could spot a business opportunity from miles away. As soon as a building was seen burning, he would send in his expert-slaves to deal with the dangers. That his teams might have caused the fire was of no particular concern. As the building went up in smoke, Crassus would buy out the hapless inhabitants, who knew that even the pittance he offered them was better than nothing. If no deal were done, the slaves stood aside and watched the house burn down. Then they would take the vacated and scorched land anyway.

Crassus used his cash to make himself indispensable. He would house senators and fund armies. In so doing, he managed his reputation to the top – one of the first examples of a goal that has obsessed the super-rich for the past two millennia. Through cunning and endeavour, rather than any particular skill, he came to dominate Rome, alongside his long-time rival, Pompey, and the precocious Julius Caesar. These three would later be known as the First Triumvirate.

Crassus was a better entrepreneur than he was a military general, but the glamour of the battlefield was hard to resist. After one successful campaign, he tried his luck against the Parthians. His death was humiliating and painful, his enemies pouring molten gold into his mouth as a symbol of revenge for the brutal quest for wealth that had defined his life.

Marcus Licinius Crassus was born into a leading Roman senatorial family around 115 BC – the exact date isn't known. His father Publius Licinius Crassus was the embodiment of a successful noble. In 97 BC he held the consulship, the highest political office in the Roman Republic, governing 'Further Spain' for three years. Publius returned home to a triumph, the supreme military honour, for his role in subjugating Lusitania (which approximates to modern southern Portugal and western Spain). He was then elected a censor in 89 BC, overseeing public morality and administration of state finances.

Crassus' upbringing was modest by the standards of the nobility. He was raised in a small house with his two brothers, Publius and Gaius,[2] achieving the required grounding in rhetoric and a polite interest in history and philosophy.[3] In his teens and early twenties, he served under his father on military campaigns in Spain and Lucania (in the south of Italy). As the second son, Marcus Licinius Crassus would have expected a solid senatorial career but no guaranteed inheritance.

Hopes of a steady and conventional rise in politics were shattered in 88 BC. Rome's first civil war erupted when the Marians, under Lucius Cornelius Cinna and Gaius Marius, seized the city in a coup while their rival Sulla was out of town fighting in the east. The city resisted for some time, but when it ultimately fell, Marius and Cinna exacted revenge, massacring their political enemies. Many of Rome's leading senators were murdered along with their families, their heads exhibited in the Forum. Crassus' brother Gaius was among them. His father committed suicide before his pursuers could get to him, an act deemed selfless and noble. His other brother, Publius, had died two years earlier in the first Social War and it seemed only natural then that 'Crassus took the widow to wife'. Pretty much everything was transactional in the Rome of the time; everyone had a value. He had two children by Tertulla, 'and in these relations also he lived as well-ordered a life as any Roman'.[4]

Suddenly Crassus had become head of the household, inheriting a modest fortune of seven million sesterces (this bronze and silver coinage was the currency of the time – the talents cited by Plutarch relate to the currency most commonly used by the Greeks). The family estates had been seized; his hopes of a political future in Rome were bleak. His first task was survival. With the Marian purge in full swing, Crassus escaped and fled to Spain, his father's old seat of power, with three friends and ten servants. His relative youth (he was still under thirty) may have helped him avoid proscription and a gory death.

Plutarch observed that from an early stage, when faced with adversity, Crassus was not over-endowed with courage. Once in Spain, he 'plunged into some fields along the sea shore belonging to Vibius Paciacus', a local lord. There he found a 'spacious cave', where thanks to Vibius he was brought abundant meals by a man who was, on pain of death, not allowed to look at him. Crassus was hardly sleeping rough. The cave 'opens out to a wonderful height, and at the sides has recesses of great circumference opening into one another'. That was not the end of the luxuries, as befitting a noble of his station: 'Vibius had made up his mind to pay Crassus every sort of friendly attention and it even occurred to him to consider the youth of his guest – some provision must be made for the enjoyments appropriate to his years.' And so 'two comely female slaves' were brought, no doubt helping alleviate the boredom during his eight months of self-imposed isolation. It must be said that Plutarch, on whom the record is disproportionately dependent, was not averse to embellishing a story or two. But even if some of the colourful detail may be a matter of retrospective decoration, the Crassus story stands up to historical scrutiny.

Although, in keeping with the times, the tale is based around military valour, Crassus had broader designs. In early 84 BC he heard that Cinna had been killed, and he quickly came out into the open again. He raised an army of 2500 men, recruited from his father's veterans who had settled in the area. Displaying an early flair for a predatory style of business, he then used this army to extort money from neighbouring Spanish cities to pay for his campaign. That was his way of expressing gratitude for their hospitality. He gathered ships and made his way via North Africa, finally joining Sulla in Italy in his war against the Marians. Sulla welcomed Crassus as a trusted lieutenant in his army, on the understanding that he wished to avenge 'thy father, thy brother, thy friends, and thy kinsmen, who were illegally and unjustly put to death'.[5] At the same time, an uppity young general called Gnaeus Pompeius, ten years younger than Crassus and known as the 'teenage butcher' by his enemies, arrived with three legions. This man was Pompey and he was to be a lifelong ally – and rival.[6]

When Sulla invaded Italy in 83 BC, both Crassus and Pompey were at his side. The outcome of the first Civil War was decided at the Battle of the Colline Gate, just outside Rome, in late 82 BC. Sulla's army had been facing possible defeat, but Crassus' forces triumphed on one wing, causing the enemy forces to flee. Crassus had broken through into the elite. He was praised as a public and patriotic figure who had proven critical in helping Sulla take back Rome. He did not go unrewarded for his pains.

After formally assuming power, Sulla rid Rome of anyone with

Marian sympathies. A list of those to be punished was produced; nobody in the Marian leadership was spared. But Sulla went much further than that, purging hundreds of fellow travellers whose links with Cinna and Marius were tenuous at best; they were condemned to death, their properties seized, their sons and grandsons barred from standing for office. This was regime change, the annihilation of a political class ruthless even by Roman standards, leaving vacancies aplenty in the ruling Senate and huge financial gains to be made from patronage.

The method of retribution was gruesome – and profitable. Proscriptions formed the basis of the real estate empire upon which Crassus built his fortune. Vanquished soldiers were cut down on the spot as they retreated from the battlefield; their severed heads were brought back to Rome to be exchanged for the promised bounty. Their widows and widowed daughters were forbidden to marry. At the heart of the proscription system was denunciation. If you could help get rid of someone, you stood a reasonable chance of gaining some of his assets. This story sums up the practice:

> One Thoranus, an ex-praetor [governor], had been denounced. He pleaded with the centurion, come to slay him, to delay until his son, a favourite of Marcus Antonius, could beg him for mercy. 'He has already appealed,' laughed the officer, 'but on the other side.' The son, in other words, had sought the reward offered the betrayers of the proscribed. The old man called for his daughter, begged her not to claim her share of the inheritance after he was dead, or her brother would ask for her life too. He then submitted to his doom.[7]

Crassus must have enjoyed exacting vengeance on those responsible for the death of his father and brother (although he was quite satisfied with the inheritance). What mattered to him most, however, was securing the land of his family's foes. Their confiscated property was auctioned off to pay the costs of the demobilisation of the victorious soldiers. As Sulla's right-hand man, Crassus was in the perfect position to reap the rewards. He and his agents identified what they needed and then procured the homes at knock-down prices. Imagine hundreds of repossessed homes going to one buyer. Plutarch paints the picture: 'For when Sulla took the city and sold the property of those whom he had put to death, considering it and calling it spoil of war, and wishing to defile with his crime as many and as influential men as he could, Crassus was never tired of accepting or of buying it.'[8]

The money came in thick and fast, but even that wasn't enough for Crassus. He had developed a taste for instant riches. He enjoyed the sport of acquisition more than the fun of spending. He snapped up the homes even of some who had played no role in the Marian regime, but whose property and wealth he coveted. The landlord as bully; the speculator playing on distress; the unscrupulous developer milking rents from countless tenements; the slumlord with no qualms about sending in the bailiffs; the dishonest lender during the sub-prime crisis – the twentieth- and twenty-first-century housing market has had its many villainous characters and practices. Think Peter Rachman, the notorious landlord in west London who intimidated and exploited his tenants in the 1950s and 60s. People like him need look no further than Crassus for the model on which to draw.

Crassus, it seemed, would stop at nothing in his acquisition of property. Land purchases and sales were easy to conduct, the more so as Rome acquired ever more territory through invasions. The Republic of this time provided the first real estate market in history, although it was open to only a lucky few to conduct business.

One of Crassus' more bizarre schemes is mentioned at the start of Plutarch's account. He was accused of 'criminal intimacy' with Licinia, one of Rome's most hallowed vestal virgins. Plutarch suggests that Crassus may have been lusting after something else, something that he seemingly enjoyed more than carnal pleasure:

Now Licinia was the owner of a pleasant villa in the suburbs, which Crassus wished to get at a low price, and it was for this reason that he was forever hovering about the woman and paying his court to her, until he fell under the abominable suspicion. In a way it was his avarice that absolved him from the charge of corrupting the vestal. He was effortlessly acquitted. But he did not let Licinia go until he had acquired her property.

His lust for property, in other words, saved his life.

Sulla denounced Crassus, less out of any moral qualms about his actions (after all, he had set the trend), more to stem his lieutenant's growing power. By this point, however, Crassus could afford not to care. He had smartly invested the wealth he had accrued from the proscriptions, diversifying into commodities and manpower – otherwise known as slaves. His new properties ranged from silver mines in Spain, to large landed estates in the country, to townhouses in the city. His tracts of land were 'as nothing compared with the value of his slaves', Plutarch writes. 'So many and so capable were the slaves he possessed – readers, amanuenses, silversmiths, stewards, table servants; and he himself directed their education, and took part in it himself as a teacher, and, in a word, he thought that the chief duty of the master was to care for his slaves and the living implements of household management.'

It might seem an oxymoron to delicate modern tastes, but Crassus' approach to his slaves had a skilled management touch. He saw training as essential. He set productivity targets for his workforce. They were there to do a job for him, often a skilled job; they would be looked after, as long as they obeyed. He also had a side business in slave rentals to friends and associates. Slaves were attached to a property, sold along with its machinery and animals.

Sulla had inadvertently helped to boost Crassus' portfolio. He created over 450 new senators (one of whom was Crassus himself). He was keen to extend his power base, so he invited into the Senate not just *nobiles* (at the top of the hierarchy), but a new crop of three hundred affluent members of the lower equestrian order.[9] The Senate was ostensibly an assembly of landowners, and those who had been newly promoted needed to own estates to match their status. The price for membership of the Senate for an *eques*, a member of the equestrian order, was 400,000 sesterces (it would rise to one million under Augustus). The cost of land, however, was prohibitively high for many of them, so Crassus leased properties at a discount to specific senators, leaving them indebted to him. This made perfect business sense. The new members of this elite club, who had to be accommodated in an enlarged Curia (Senate House) in the Forum, would ensure influence and leverage for Crassus in the post-civil war political world. He kept the rents manageable for those he needed; other properties he sold at huge margins to people who didn't matter.

This was just the start of Crassus' land grab. Peacetime brought him further opportunities to extend his real estate empire. Having disposed of the dead, it was time to dispossess those still alive.

In the first century BC, Rome was a huge, crowded and growing city of nearly one million people. For the wealthy, with their large homes in the city and their country retreats where they could enjoy better air and escape the intense heat of summer, life was more than tolerable. As most forms of work were regarded as demeaning for the upper classes, and as service in the Senate was unpaid, a good chunk of revenue for the wealthy came from war. The more provinces Rome gained in far-flung places, the more the Republic received in tax revenue – and the more the wealthy benefited from the audacity of their conquering armies (as would later be the case during the European settlement of the New World). The odd proscription of rivals closer to home also produced welcome top-up income.

The two thousand or so members of the elite did not suffer the indignities of the masses. They had assets in gold and silver, while a strong market had developed for art plundered from conquests. Property also provided a useful investment vehicle. In addition, as in other ages, it was a symbol of status and power. The elite's self-standing houses, or *domus*, were located mainly on Rome's seven hills. This was the place to live and network. The Forum, alongside, was where the business of the state was conducted – the site of debate, tribunals, temples, memorials and triumphal processions. From the top of the Palatinate, Capitoline or Esquiline nobles could peer down at the teeming streets below. Like the super-rich of contemporary times in Mayfair, Park Avenue or Palo Alto, they were insulated from the struggles of the rest of society. Their opulent homes lacked for nothing – atriums, stables, fountains, gardens and even running cold water. They tried as often as possible to head off to their mansions outside the city. These were on a different scale – fantasy villas with colonnades and copious gardens, serviced by several hundred slaves.

Crassus' emphasis on urban property, and its potential for wealth creation, was rare. He had his eyes on the *insulae* of ordinary mortals in Rome's crowded warrens. These were buildings of up to eight storeys high, the ground floor of which was usually a shop or other small business. The better off among the lower orders lived on the lower floors. The *insulae* were erected quickly and often shoddily – wooden or mudbrick structures standing on narrow excrement-filled pathways. Lacking water above the ground floor, chamber pots were emptied in the neighbourhood latrine, on the neighbourhood dunghill, or at a nearby fuller's, who used urine to clean or soften wool. Slaves served as water-carriers, porters and sweepers.

These places were firetraps. Fireplaces and chimneys had not been invented; heat came only from an open fire in a brazier. Juvenal wrote in his *Satires*, with only a small amount of exaggeration: 'We live in a city supported mostly by slender props, which is how the bailiff patches cracks in old walls, telling the resident to sleep peacefully under roofs ready to fall down around them.' With virtually no sanitation or management of infrastructure, fires were endemic.

Yet the Republic had no fire brigade. Spotting this gap in the market, Crassus trained his slaves as firefighters and architects. Once he could count on five hundred qualified employees, he put them to work. They would arrive on the scene of a burning house, commiserate briefly with the residents, then offer to buy the building – which was disappearing before their eyes – off them. The owner, fearing that he would be left with nothing, was forced to sell. Crassus' slaves would then extinguish the flames. The buildings were redesigned at ever-greater density and sold at a decent profit. It is a matter of conjecture whether Crassus' eager brigades started some fires or helped others on their way. They may not have needed to, but nor did they rush to intervene until the moment of conflagration was right. 'In this way,' Plutarch recounts somewhat dryly, 'the largest part of Rome came into his possession.'[10]

Just how amoral was Crassus? Like many a skilled politician-cum-businessman, he manipulated the institutions of state and the law to his own benefit. He saw all relations in transactional terms. Everything, everyone, could be bought. The contemporary historian Sallust spoke for many of the Republic's old guard, who saw their social hierarchies undermined by a brash new generation: 'The love of money grew first: the love of power followed. This was, so to speak, the root of evil. Greed undermined loyalty, honesty and the other virtues. In their place it taught arrogance, cruelty, disregard for the gods and the view that everything was for sale.'[11]

Writing in the first century AD, when the Republic was a distant memory, Juvenal similarly denounced the culture of Crassus' time: 'With us the most reverend majesty is that of Riches: even though, Foul Lucre! Thou dwellest in no temple, and we have not reared altars to Coin, as we have for the worship of Peace and Faith, Victory, Virtue and Concord.'

The American historian William Stearns Davis wrote of 'the gilded youth' of the later Roman Republic. His study of political corruption and high finance was published in 1910, in the latter stages of the age of the robber barons, of which he and many liberal intellectuals and politicians were contemptuous (see Chapter 9). His anger towards the inequalities and ruthless acquisition of wealth of his time is reflected in his florid depictions of Crassus, Pompey and Caesar:

> The Roman seemingly was in all his business relations more devoid of sentiment than the most abused Semite. He was in money matters either oppressor or oppressed, either hammer or anvil. In his private life his sympathies extended only to a very narrow circle of associates. His instincts as a moral being were always subordinate to his instincts as a financier, and a financier whose code was that of unmitigated commercialism.

Davis ascribes the venality of this ancient period, which reached a climax in the age of Augustus, shortly after Crassus' death, to the loss of prestige of the old noble families (for that one might read old American money of the mid-nineteenth century). 'Their scions, who had not earned but had inherited riches, were more anxious for spending than for getting. Luxury and squandering rose to ever greater excesses, and culminated under Nero.' It would take some time, he added, for a more frugal and responsible example to be set during the Roman Empire:

The Stoic philosophy and, more slowly, Christianity began to establish other ideals than those of getting and enjoying. The high-born families who had amassed the riches had nearly all died out, thanks to a childlessness caused by luxurious living and to the slaughters of the civil wars and of the tyrants; and property was passing into the hands of ex-slaves and provincials who had a juster knowledge of the use of riches.[12]

Whether these money-obsessed, acquisitive men of the Republic were too busy to father children is, to put it mildly, a moot point. This was an extreme variant of the avaricious-Crassus narrative, but it represents the mainstream view of Davis' time, and of successive generations of historians. The great mid-twentieth-century German historian of Rome, Matthias Gelzer, derides Crassus as a parvenu or spiv: 'Despite his origin from the old nobility, the attributes of the true *grand seigneur* escaped him, and he always remained the calculating bourgeois, who constantly treated even politics as an economic undertaking.'

A surprising characteristic of Crassus is that, despite his vast assets, he lived relatively modestly. He built no house for himself apart from the one in which he lived. The usually critical Plutarch describes Crassus as a generous host 'for his house was open to all'. When he entertained at table, 'his invited guests [were] for the most part plebeians and men of the people, and the simplicity of the repast was combined with a neatness and good cheer which gave more pleasure than lavish expenditure'. As for his demeanour out and about in Rome, he was regarded as a 'careful man, and one who was ready with his help. He pleased people also by the kindly and unaffected manner with which he clasped their hands and addressed them. For he never met a Roman so obscure and lowly that he did not return his greeting and call him by name.'[13] Cosimo de' Medici (see Chapter 4) exhibited similar social skills in early Renaissance Florence. Crassus and Medici were good networkers, assiduous not just at courting those with power and influence, but also managing their reputations among the lower orders. You never knew when you might need someone.

For Crassus, therefore, money was not an end in itself, but a means to an end. He did not need lavish properties on which to emblazon his ego. He needed to amass a large fortune to fulfil his ambition to reach the top, to build up a powerful, independent political position. When it came to financial transactions, he gave no quarter. He would lend money to his friends without interest, 'but he would demand it back from the borrower relentlessly when the time had expired, and so the gratuity of the loan was more burdensome than heavy interest'. He possessed a particular skill for profiting from others' misfortune, be it from fire, war or political intrigue. One time, when briefly captured by pirates in 75 BC, Caesar is said to have lamented: 'How Crassus will rejoice to hear of this.'[14]

If Crassus' ends were clear, his means were flexible. In the 70s BC, while Pompey pursued military honours far away, Crassus consolidated his position closer to home. He worked within the Roman political scene to build a network of patronage and influence, using a mix of wealth, charm and steel. He was keen to offer advice, legal representation and financial support to senators and others who mattered. He rarely committed himself to a political position or alliance. As Plutarch notes, he let his money do the talking. 'He had great influence, both from the favours which he bestowed and the fear which he inspired, but more from the fear.'[15] Indeed it was said among Romans that Crassus had 'hay on his horns', reflecting a Roman practice of tying hay to the horns of dangerous bulls so that those who encountered them knew to be wary. It was through this heady mixture of dependency and fear that Crassus established his power base.

This was a period characterised by unrest: slave uprisings, conspiracies, coups and purges heightened a sense of instability and the scope for corruption. Each generation produced its own laws seeking to ban the purchase of votes. By Crassus' time the penalty for violation was ten years of exile. The laws were more honoured in the breach. The easiest way of getting around impediments was to come to verbal arrangements with go-betweens, known as *divisores*. 'These professional gentlemen would proceed to mark out the Roman tribes into smaller and more wieldy sections, arrange the voters into clubs and fraternities, marshal the faithful henchmen to the electoral *comitia* and duly pay over the stipulated honorarium upon delivery of the election,' writes Stearns Davis, adding that to the America of his time this had 'a painfully familiar aspect'. He adds: 'It is sufficient to remark that under the later Republic almost any man of noble family and deep purse seems to have been able to rise fairly highly in the scale of offices, provided he was willing to spend freely.'

Crassus was an expert in buying influence, but he did so as much through his property portfolio as anything as grubby as a brown envelope. Once a position was secured, it was still important to perform. In 73 BC, as he was holding the praetorship, a high office with the power of military command, Crassus was confronted by a slave rebellion that would threaten the heart of power. In a story made popular by book and film, Spartacus led an escape of his fellow trainee gladiators and precipitated a mass revolt. The Senate's initial response was complacent; it was assumed that the Capuan militia would swiftly put down the uprising. The slaves outfought the soldiers, seizing their weapons and plundering country estates; it was only then that Rome's politicians were galvanised into action. The rebellion threatened the political leadership and the economic fabric of the Republic as the human property of citizens absconded to join Spartacus. Rome was under-resourced to tackle the growing slave army, with most of its forces and leading generals, including Pompey, fighting wars far afield in Spain and the east.

Cue Crassus, offering to equip, train and lead an army, at his own expense, adopting the mantle of national saviour. In keeping with his style, this was not an altruistic gesture of patriotism. It was a calculated risk, but one with a very high prospect of return. Crassus had waited until Rome had no other option but to depend upon him. His underwriting of the Roman forces was an investment, effectively buying stocks in the Republic just when the price was low. Victory against the slave army promised Crassus the chance to outshine his rival Pompey and attain the power afforded by glory. 'No man could be counted rich,' he declared, 'who could not maintain an army from his own resources.'[16]

The Senate gave Crassus absolute power to do whatever he had to do to restore the status quo. In addition to the remnants of the two defeated armies, he raised and financed a further six legions out of his own pocket. He recruited his soldiers mainly from the veterans of Sulla's civil war, who had settled in central Italy with land and slaves. Their possessions were endangered by the revolt and thus they formed loyal and willing soldiers; they also knew that Crassus would guarantee their pay. His initial strategy was to secure central Italy, forcing Spartacus into battle in the south. However, a subordinate legate hoping for glory by the name of Lucius Mummius prematurely attacked Spartacus' army without Crassus' permission and suffered an overwhelming defeat.

In response, Crassus reinstated the ancient Roman punishment of 'decimation' for those who had fled, selecting one man out of every ten at random to be clubbed to death by his fellow soldiers: some fifty legionnaires met their fate in this fashion. 'For disgrace also attaches to this manner of death, and many horrible and repulsive features attend the punishment, which the whole army witnesses.' By deploying such an ostentatious form of discipline, Crassus taught his men 'he was more dangerous to them than the enemy'.[17]

For all the brutality, it still took Crassus six months to break the slave rebellion and save the Roman establishment from the threat of Spartacus. He trapped the rebel armies in the southern toe of Italy, digging fortified trenches across the length of the peninsula. Spartacus' army managed to break through Crassus' line, but was soon defeated in battle. Spartacus stood firm, however, until the last. 'Finally, after his companions had taken to flight, he stood alone, surrounded by a multitude of foes, and was still defending himself when he was cut down.'[18] Crassus and his forces captured and crucified six thousand of Spartacus' slaves on the Appian Way, the road from Capua to Rome. Their bodies were left to rot on the road as a warning against future insurrections.*

---

* The rebellion has entered Hollywood iconography. The 1960 epic *Spartacus*, starring Laurence Olivier as Crassus, included the immortal line 'I am Spartacus', said to have been uttered by each soldier as an offer of self-sacrifice to save his leader. It was a highly political piece of cinema, made in the immediate aftermath of the McCarthy investigations into supposed left-wing sympathisers. Its screenwriter had been blacklisted and anti-communist groups organised vocal protests outside cinemas. President John F. Kennedy famously crossed one of those picket lines to watch a movie that implicitly compared a corrupt, slave-owning Roman Republic to contemporary US society. The movie was the biggest earner for the studio, Universal, for a decade. Its didactic message about the evils of inequality in Roman times struck a chord with American and international audiences.

The older the society, the harder it is to use contemporary indicators to draw conclusions about income distribution and purchasing power. Nevertheless, a number of estimates suggest that the top 1 per cent of Roman society controlled a similar proportion of national wealth to their counterparts in the robber baron period of the late nineteenth century and the present day.[19] The Gini coefficient (the standard measure for inequality) in the Roman Republic of Crassus' time is estimated at 0.42–0.44,[20] a figure that is almost identical to the US calculation for 2013.

For all the notional power wielded by the plebs in ancient Rome, the elite controlled the economic resources and monopolised public office. The nobles paid lip service to the Republic's institutions, such as elections, but these were contested between individuals drawn from the same social class. They viewed the lower classes as morally and intellectually inferior. The automatic equation of penury with moral inferiority was so ingrained that *egens* – the poor or needy – became a common term of abuse. Following the same logic, the term *locuples* – the rich – also took on a broader meaning and was used in aristocratic circles as a term of praise. The basis of wealth as a personal virtue lay in the aristocratic belief that only the rich man had freedom of choice and thus was able to act according to moral principles. As the writer of mimes Publius Syrus stated: 'necessity makes the poor man a liar'. Material necessity forced people to perform tasks considered demeaning for a man of honour. Most obviously it compelled people to sell their labour in return for wages, which in the eyes of the elite effectively reduced them to the level of slavery.[21]

Crassus did not achieve everything that he had hoped to in victory over Spartacus and the slave revolt. Partly this was because he asked for reinforcements for his final assault – a decision he immediately regretted. His rival Pompey, who had been returning to Rome through the north of Italy from his conquest of Asia Minor, saw the benefits that might accrue from intervention. His force overran a group of fleeing slaves with ease. He then sent word to the Senate claiming that although Crassus had overcome the rebel forces at the outset, it was he, Pompey, who had officially ended the campaign. In so doing, Pompey demonstrated that the Romans were just as adept as politicians of modern

times in massaging the message, showing that in war, as in business and
politics, the spin counts for as much as the facts on the ground.

Pompey had stolen a march on his rival. Crassus was furious and
struggled to keep his frustrations to himself. The competition between
the two men posed a grave danger for Rome. According to Plutarch,
it vexed Crassus 'that Pompey was successful in his campaigns and was
called Magnus (that is Great) by his fellow citizens. And once when
someone said: "Pompeius Magnus is coming", Crassus fell to laughing
and asked: "How great is he?"' Crassus' resentment may have had something to do with the rumour at the time that Pompey had demanded
the epithet for himself.

Neither man was prepared to disband his army, each claiming a triumph for his victories and demanding a consulship. Hoping to appease
both men and avoid conflict, the Senate gave way. But one man did
better than the other. Both were elected Consul, even though Pompey
lacked the necessary experience and age, being just thirty-four years old
and never having held political office. Pompey was awarded a triumph
for his earlier victories in the east, while Crassus received the lesser
accolade of an ovation (a triumph could not be awarded for victory in
a war against slaves). As compensation, Crassus gained special dis-
pensation during the parade to wear a laurel crown, a symbol usually
reserved for triumphs, rather than the lesser myrtle crown. In the yearning for status that preoccupied the Roman elite, these symbols
mattered, desperately.

Putting his resentment to one side, Crassus laid on lavish celebrations
for the citizens of Rome out of his own pocket, providing ten thousand tables for the people to feast on pheasant, thrush, raw oysters, wild
boar and peacock. He might have displayed a studied modesty during
his domestic entertaining, but when it came to his role as a benefactor,
he spared no expense – the politician and man of means presiding over
an outdoor banquet for the middle and lower-middle classes who comprised his support.

Reinforcing his image as the public-spirited businessman-cum-states-
man, Crassus sponsored competitive sports and gave other money to
public causes. He granted each family a gift of three months' supply of
corn. While tradition dictated that a military victor dedicate a tenth of

his campaign spoils to a temple, he gave a tenth of his total personal fortune to the temple of Hercules. (Victorious generals had long sought to foster an association with this demi-god in the public mind.) If he could not rival Pompey's achievements on a distant battlefield, he could at least put on a display of munificence back home in Rome.

The two men may have been rivals, but they also had much to gain by working together, combining their popularity, prestige, wealth and connections in order to dominate the Senate. Pompey and Crassus shared power at several points, each always nervously looking over his shoulder at the other. In their first consulship of 71–70 BC, they restored the power of the plebeian tribunate that had fallen into abeyance under Sulla. They also reinvigorated the office of censor. Both of these measures brought them popular support and helped to reconfigure the power structures of Rome to their benefit. Under the census that was held in 70 BC, sixty-four senators suspected of moral or financial corruption were expelled and replaced by loyalists. One assumes that their crime was to have fallen on the wrong side of the two power-brokers of the Republic.

While Pompey spent this period in pursuit of further military glory in the east, Crassus embedded himself at the heart of Roman politics, continuing to weave his web of patronage and indebtedness with consummate skill. He speculated on young politicians' careers by fronting them the necessary money, in the expectation of future returns once they were ensconced in lucrative provincial governorships. The most famous of his protégés was Gaius Julius Caesar, who came under his wing in the mid-60s. In 62 BC, Crassus secured Caesar's election to the praetorship, followed the next year by governorship of one of the Spanish provinces, together with credit up to 830 talents. The young Caesar had run up large debts. 'When men needed help, their necessity was his opportunity.'[22]

Alliances were there to be made – and dropped. Speculation raged that Crassus was behind at least one attempted coup by Lucius Sergius Catiline, one of his young protégés, against the Consul Cicero. The conspiracy was exposed and many of those involved were executed. Crassus kept a careful distance from the senatorial debates around the fate of the rebels. Catiline, who was popular among the plebs, almost succeeded second time around, only to die on the battlefield. While one witness directly implicated Crassus in the conspiracy, the senators brushed over this claim because of their indebtedness to him.

As Plutarch notes, Crassus was 'neither a steadfast friend nor an implacable enemy, but readily abandoned both his favours and his resentments at the dictates of his interests, so that frequently, within a short space of time, the same men and the same measures found in him both an advocate and an opponent'.[23] Plutarch's acute observation could be applied to many a financier over the years. Hug the powerful close, but keep alert to shifts in that power.

It was from Caesar that Crassus would reap the greatest return on his investment. In 60 BC, Crassus and Pompey united once more to throw their collective weight behind Caesar's election to Consul. Pompey wanted his new eastern settlement ratified; Crassus needed to renegotiate a contract with a powerful group of business clients to improve the collection of taxes in Asia. At this point, Caesar did not hold power in his own right, but he was the instrument of these two powerful men: Crassus, his political patron, and Pompey, his father-in-law. Caesar was duly elected, but a number of senators ensured that their ally – Marcus Calpurnius Bibulus – was jointly elected, preventing Pompey and Crassus' total dominance. The Roman elite feared this new and powerful alliance: the writer Varro dubbed Caesar, Pompey and Crassus the *tricaranus* – three-headed monster. Its trepidation was not misplaced. Caesar delivered for his paymasters, using violence and intimidation to reduce Bibulus to virtual house arrest and threatening the Senate until they ratified his measures, while buying off the plebs with populist policies. But he was bored by political machinations. Now that money and power had been consolidated again in the rightful hands of the three rulers, Caesar sought glory in adventure. He set off for Gaul.

No sooner had he gone than the alliance between Pompey and Crassus crumbled; neither was formally in power, but each worked behind the scenes to assert his interests. The streets of Rome convulsed with violence just as money was gushing in as never before. Pompey's victories in Asia had almost doubled national income. Rome occupied most of the civilised world, and yet the explosion of wealth and the greed it gave rise to destabilised the Republic. The populist politician

Publius Clodius used the plebeian tribunate, supported by armed street gangs, to launch attacks on a number of senior statesmen. Caesar's actions were decried as unconstitutional and his campaign in Gaul was called into question – even though it had successfully extended Rome's reach to the Rhine and the English Channel. Pompey was harassed by mobs. Crassus, as ever, remained untouched. Clodius, like most men in Rome, was indebted to him: Crassus had previously defended him from a charge of sacrilege, ensuring his acquittal. While Crassus did not openly endorse Clodius' actions, they were certainly helpful, intimidating his political rivals and limiting their power.

Five years later, with Caesar's first term in Gaul coming to an end, the mutual interests of the three men intersected again. Caesar was now a player in his own right, with prestige and military successes to rival those of the other two. In April 56 BC, the informal triumvirate met at Lucca in northern Italy to revive their alliance, which had served them so well in the past. Caesar wanted an extension of his command in Gaul in order to extend his campaign and consolidate his victories. Crassus and Pompey readily agreed to give him another five years of military command, while ensuring that the rest of Rome's dominions were divided between them. According to their deal, Pompey assumed the right to rule Spain *in absentia*, while Crassus gained jurisdiction over the Near East, seven legions and the right to make war or peace without consulting the Senate or the people of Rome.

Of the three, Crassus potentially gained the most at Lucca. The Parthian Empire, encompassing modern-day Iran and Iraq, had designs further west, towards Armenia. But it was embroiled in civil unrest and deemed to be vulnerable to invasion. Its links to the Silk Route and other trading channels offered opportunities for intervention and profit. Crassus knew that if he succeeded in subjugating that empire, he would fulfil Rome's long-held goal of extending its reach deep into Eurasia. As Plutarch wrote: 'to that ancient infirmity of Crassus, his avarice, there was now added a fresh and ardent passion, in view of the glorious exploits of Caesar, for trophies and triumphs'.[24]

Crassus' ambitions had until this point been accompanied by a certain prudence. By now he was sixty and consumed by a desire for military victories to secure his legacy – a late mid-life crisis, perhaps, or was it more jealousy towards Pompey and Caesar? The Consul and historian Cassius Dio records that Crassus wished 'to accomplish something that involved glory and at the same time profit'.[25] His ambition seemed limitless: 'he would not consider Syria nor even Parthia as the boundaries of his success, but thought to make the campaigns of Lucullus against Tigranes and those of Pompey against Mithridates seem mere child's play, and flew on the wings of his hope as far as Bactria and India and the Outer Sea'.[26]

When Crassus departed for the east in late 55 BC, the Roman elite was lukewarm in its support. A number of key figures had expressed doubts about the military logic for the campaign and the prospects for success. The Parthians had an impressive military machine. Crassus' detractors suspected that his characteristic lust for profit had trumped good sense – and that, no matter how great his ambition, he could not match Pompey for valour or skill on the battlefield. Pompey, keeping his misgivings to himself, accompanied Crassus to the gates of Rome. However, legend has it that as he approached the city limits, the tribune of the plebs, Gaius Ateius Capito, appeared on top of the gates to enact a ritual that would bring misfortune to Crassus for usurping the honour of the Republic. According to Plutarch, he 'invoked curses which were dreadful and terrifying' upon Crassus and his campaign.[27]

Undeterred, Crassus marched his army overland to Syria, via Greece and Asia Minor, arriving in mid-54 BC. His plan was to defeat the Parthians and annex Mesopotamia – which would provide access to the Persian Gulf and overseas trade routes. However, Crassus was not what he had been; he had not fought a military campaign for fifteen years. His seven legions comprised mainly young and inexperienced soldiers, attracted by the promise of rich rewards, although some were veterans of Pompey's campaigns in the east. Plutarch tells the story of Crassus passing through the kingdom of Galatia (much of modern-day Turkey) en route to Syria, where the elderly king was building a new city. Crassus said to him: 'O King, you are beginning to build at the twelfth hour', to which the king replied: 'But you yourself, Imperator, as I see, are not marching very early in the day against the Parthians.'[28]

Once in Syria, Crassus chose to invade via the Euphrates into western Mesopotamia, rather than entering from Armenia with the aid of the local king, Artabazes, who had offered up his forces. This move was initially successful: Crassus secured western and northern Mesopotamia after besieging key strategic towns. He then withdrew to Syria for the winter, to wait for his son Publius to arrive with a thousand Gallic cavalry, veterans of Caesar's recent campaigns in Gaul. Crassus is much criticised in ancient accounts and by modern historians for his decision to withdraw when he had the upper hand. He should, according to Plutarch, have pressed on to Babylon and Seleucia, cities hostile to the Parthians. Instead, he hung around, giving his enemies time to prepare. The reason? Greed: 'Then again fault was found with him because his sojourn in Syria was devoted to mercenary rather than to military purposes. For he made no estimate of the number of his troops, and instituted no athletic contests for them, but reckoned up the revenues of cities, and spent many days weighing exactly the treasures of the goddess in Hierapolis.'[29]

During the campaign, a contingent of Crassus' troops entered the Hasmonean kingdom of Judea and sacked the Great Temple of Jerusalem, replicating Pompey's actions a decade before. Crassus also confiscated the treasures of the Temple of Venus at Hierapolis.[30] Whether the spoils were used to fund the campaign, enrich Crassus personally or found their way into the pockets of individual soldiers is unclear – a combination of all three is likely.

Not only did Crassus' military strategy fall victim to a winter of plunder, but when spring did arrive, he appears to have lost his ability to distinguish those who would bring him profit from those who were exploiting him. As he advanced into Mesopotamia again, an Arab chieftain, Ariamnes, advised Crassus to attack at once, reporting that the Parthian troops were weak and disorganised. Despite evidence to the contrary, Crassus trusted this 'crafty and treacherous man' – who was, in fact, in the pay of the Parthians – and, on his directions, led his troops down onto the desert plain to engage the enemy.[31] Plutarch's account of this part of the campaign presents Crassus as ever more confused, making decisions against sound advice and evidence and disregarding the numerous bad omens that littered his path. The tale is redolent with superstitious warnings. As Crassus was leading his army across the Euphrates:

Many extraordinary peals of thunder crashed about them, and many flashes of lightning also darted in their faces, and a wind, half mist and half hurricane, fell upon their raft, breaking it up and shattering it in many places. The place where he was intending to encamp was also smitten by two thunderbolts. And one of the general's horses, richly caparisoned, violently dragged its groom along with it into the river and disappeared beneath the waves. It is said also that the first eagle which was raised aloft faced about of its own accord.

It was on a desolate plain, near the town of Carrhae, that Crassus faced Surena, the pre-eminent general of the Parthian king Hyrodes, who 'brought Crassus to ruin, who, at first by reason of his boldness and conceit, and then in consequence of his fears and calamities, was an easy victim of deceits'. The Battle of Carrhae was characterised by Crassus' misjudgement, indecision and a refusal to listen to the advice of his generals; he was outmanoeuvred at every turn by the tactics of the Parthians. On the first day, they led Crassus' son Publius and his cavalry into a trap. The brave Publius 'cheered on his cavalry, made a vigorous charge with them, and closed with the enemy. But his struggle was an unequal one both offensively and defensively, for his thrusting was done with small and feeble spears against breastplates of raw hide and steel, whereas the thrusts of the enemy were made with pikes.' Although hit in the arm, Publius refused to leave his men. 'Declaring that no death could have such terrors for him as to make him desert those who were perishing on his account, [he] ordered them to save their own lives, bade them farewell and dismissed them. Then the Parthians cut off the head of Publius, and rode off at once to attack Crassus.'[32]

Parthian troops triumphantly approached the Roman forces, with Publius' head 'fixed high upon a spear, rode close up and displayed it, scornfully asking after his parents and family, for surely, they said, it was not meet that Crassus, most base and cowardly of men, should be the father of a son so noble and of such splendid valour'. Instead of filling the Roman forces with a thirst for revenge, this increased their sense of resignation and foreboding. Crassus was, according to Plutarch, 'prey to many conflicting emotions, and no longer looked at anything with calm judgement'. He saw that 'not many of his men listened with any eagerness' to his orders.

The end came the following day. Surena offered a truce. The enemy leader had sent Crassus a horse with a 'gold studded bridle' to take him across the river for their negotiations. Several of the Roman generals urged him not to accept the offer, convinced that it was a trap. Crassus ignored them and mounted the horse. As he galloped away a scuffle ensued and Crassus was killed. The mythology around his death has produced a number of conflicting stories. Dio's account records that 'the Parthians, as some say, poured molten gold into his mouth in mockery; for though a man of vast wealth, he had set so great store by money as to pity those who could not support an enrolled legion from their own means, regarding them as poor men'.[33] Similar deaths have been visited since on those deemed greedy. In the early thirteenth century, Genghis Khan was said to have executed Inalchuq, a Central Asian ruler who refused him tribute, by pouring molten silver into his eyes and ears.

Plutarch's version has it that after sending the head and right hand of Crassus to Hyrodes, Surena conducted a mock-triumph of his victim, with one of his men dressed up in women's clothing, proclaiming him Imperator, impersonating him and leading a procession bearing the heads of slaughtered Romans. He adds: 'Behind these followed courtesans of Seleucia, musicians who sang many scurrilous and ridiculous songs about the effeminacy and cowardice of Crassus; and these things were for all to see.' He concludes: 'with such a farce as this the expedition of Crassus is said to have closed, just like a tragedy'.[34]

Crassus had speculated his wealth and prestige on the Parthian campaign. The result was one of the most humiliating defeats in the history of Rome. He paid the ultimate price for his greed; his legions lay in disarray, with twenty thousand of his troops dead and a further ten thousand captured.

Crassus shaped the course of the late Roman Republic, an era dominated by wealth and the competition to acquire it. He died just twenty-four years before the fall of a republic that had lasted over half a millennium. The fragile balance of power had been shattered.

Plutarch recounts that 'through fear of him [Crassus,] both Pompey and Caesar had somehow or other continued to treat one another fairly'.[35] Violence, factionalism and corruption gripped Rome in the vacuum left by Crassus' death, culminating in 49 BC in another civil war. Pompey, long jealous of Caesar's military prowess, used his rival's absence in Gaul to take control of the Senate. Caesar was commanded to leave his army and return to Rome as a private citizen. This he refused to do. His crossing of the Rubicon – a river which generals were forbidden by Roman law to cross without disbanding their armies – marked the beginning of the irreversible decline of the Republic. Rome fell under Caesar's autocratic rule. His assassination led to the eventual assumption of power by Augustus, Rome's first emperor. It bears remembering that without Crassus' financial sponsorship, Caesar would almost certainly have languished in the middle ranks of Rome's hierarchy. This was one of his many legacies.

Plutarch identifies in Crassus character traits common to many of the rich and powerful of subsequent eras. Through his early property scams he amassed such a fortune that he is considered the wealthiest man in Roman history, and one of the wealthiest of all time. His annual income (from his real estate and many other investments) at the time of his death was estimated at twelve million sesterces. In a society riven by factionalism, greed and inequality, his total wealth was estimated at 170–200 million sesterces, the equivalent of a year's income for the whole Roman exchequer.

So how does Crassus compare with the super-rich of later periods? It is impossible to give a definitive answer, but some have tried. Given that currencies are hard to translate across eras, and purchasing power differs hugely, one economist suggests a measurement on the basis of human labour. How many people could each member of the super-rich employ in his time? The figure for Crassus is apparently 32,000 Romans – or half the capacity of the Colosseum. This compares with John D. Rockefeller's 116,000 Americans in 1937 and Bill Gates's 75,000 in 2005. The wealthiest of all would be Carlos Slim, who could command some 440,000 Mexicans with his fortune in 2009. Other economists provide their own matrices and results. Whichever is used, Crassus was up there with the wealthiest.[36]

Plutarch's story of Crassus is a morality tale. At the height of the final assault, the soldiers still wanted to hear from their leader, but he was nowhere to be seen: 'He was lying on the ground by himself, enveloped in darkness, to the multitude an illustration of the ways of fortune, but to the wise an example of foolish ambition, which would not let him rest satisfied to be first and greatest among many myriads of men, but made him think, because he was judged inferior to two men only, that he lacked everything.'[37]

Those two men were, of course, Pompey and Caesar. Crassus had not been as gifted as either of them; he had got as far as he had by guile, tenacity and ruthlessness. Having acquired his enormous wealth and consolidated his position, he could have left it at that and history might have been kinder to him.

That is the case for the prosecution. Was Crassus, in the end, more acquisitive than the others, or was he simply less prone to hide his ambition? Some contemporary historians are seeking to reverse what they see as a bias against him, blaming snobbery for the depiction of a man who dirtied his hands with filthy lucre. Not only did he lose at war, but he violated the code of antiquity by amassing a fortune from grubby business rather than the more 'virtuous' route of warfare and the seizure of others' assets. This analysis has some merit in highlighting the perennial resentment by old money of new money. Yet no amount of historical revisionism can hide the extent of Crassus' determination to acquire wealth and status by all means open to him.

Unlike Marius, Sulla, Cicero, Pompey and Caesar, Crassus has had few busts or portraits made in his name. He therefore failed in that all-important test: to secure his legacy. Money might have bought him political power, but it was not a guarantee of military prowess, which in those times was the ultimate determiner of status. Arrogance may have got the better of him, and the battlefield may have been his undoing, but he established a new paradigm for those seeking wealth. Entrepreneur, oligarch and political operator, Crassus is the first and archetypal member of the club of super-rich.

CHAPTER 2

Alain Le Roux – Cleansing the land

Ruthless isn't always that bad.
Stan O'Neal, CEO, Merrill Lynch

He was one of the richest men in English history, yet he holds little place in the popular imagination. Alan Rufus was one of William the Conqueror's henchmen in the late eleventh century. This opportunistic Breton clambered aboard the Norman invasion and was repaid for his loyalty with a swathe of land extending down the spine of the entire country.

The period immediately after 1066 is an early example of regime change and the transfer of wealth and power that accrued in large part from an act of genocide – the Harrying of the North. Estimates suggest up to a hundred thousand people were killed in and around Yorkshire for resisting William's rule. Entire villages were burned and their inhabitants slaughtered, while their farming plots were scorched. Many of those who survived the onslaught died of starvation.

The nobles who served alongside William at the Battle of Hastings, or who subsequently went over to his side, were rewarded with land and property confiscated from the indigenous population. The Domesday Book meticulously documents the impact of this colossal programme of expropriation, revealing that by 1086 only about 5 per cent of land in England south of the River Tees was left in English hands. Locals were purged from high office of Church and state. French became the *lingua franca*. By 1096, not a single bishopric was held by an Englishman. With a new elite in charge, a huge building programme was undertaken. Over the next twenty years more than a thousand castles were built to consolidate the Normans' power and project their prestige.

State-sponsored land extortion and nepotism defined the era. Those who acquired wealth were either known to the King or were related to him, among them his half-brother, Bishop Odo of Bayeux (who became Earl of Kent), and William de Warenne, the first Earl of Surrey. A small coterie became the equivalents of the billionaires of the modern age. One of the richest, and cleverest, was Alain Le Roux. Otherwise known by his adopted English name Alan Rufus, or Alan the Red, or his later title the Earl of Richmond, he was a second cousin of William. His share of the spoils amounted to nearly two hundred manors totalling 250,000 acres. The 'Land of Count Alan' stretched from Yorkshire to London, taking in Norfolk, Suffolk, Cambridgeshire and Northamptonshire, and on into Normandy and Brittany. By the time he died in 1093 at the age of fifty-three, Alan was worth at least £1100, or the equivalent of over £8 billion today, making him one of the richest Englishmen of all time. Except he wasn't English, not until he and his descendants started to identify with a country that he had helped to buy up. Rufus not only enriched himself but paved the way for a new elite to form, cleanse its reputation and become the landowners and establishment of the next millennium.

The Norman invasion of 1066 is still seen, perhaps more than any other event, as being responsible for the birth of modern England. It marked the supplanting of a culture and the wholesale transfer of wealth and power from one elite to another. Guillaume le Bâtard, William the Bastard, illegitimate son of Robert the Magnificent, Duke of Normandy, invaded and expropriated an entire nation's property and land, distributing it to a cluster of loyal lieutenants. It should therefore come as little surprise that a recent rich list of British history puts four knights of the Norman Conquest in the top six of all time.[1]

Duke William of Normandy had been, or so he claimed, designated rightful heir to the English throne by King Edward the Confessor as far back as 1051. His chief obstacle to the crown was the Saxon Godwin family, which held all the important earldoms of England and most of the land. The elder Godwin brother, Harold, was the power behind the throne in the 1060s. In 1064 Harold took a trip across the Channel to Normandy, during which he narrowly avoided being shipwrecked and ended up a semi-prisoner at William's court. Here, willingly or not, he swore an oath upon holy relics to uphold William's claim to the throne: '[William] made Harold stay with him for some time and took him on an expedition against the Bretons. Then after Harold had sworn fealty to him about the kingdom with many oaths he promised him that he would give his daughter Adeliza with half the kingdom of England.'[2]

However, when Edward died just over a year later, Harold, by now back in England, assumed the throne, claiming his oath to William had been made under duress. Harold quickly had himself crowned in his new abbey at Westminster. The Bayeux Tapestry – the embroidered cloth that records the events leading to the Norman Conquest – depicts the members of the congregation looking upwards towards Halley's Comet, a portent of doom to come.

Thus began not just a battle over the immediate crown, but for history. Norman historians used a single contended statement to legitimate their sequestration of land and wealth and their establishment of a new order for a millennium. This was reputation management writ large.

William painstakingly gathered his army and planned his attack. Support from his nobles was not guaranteed, however. He needed to make his case to the Pope, gathering his lieutenants at his new abbey at St Étienne, asking for God's blessing. He received the papal banner to carry into battle, signifying the righteousness of his claim. The cause was based around a narrative of William as upstanding and frugal, juxtaposed against the lecherous and treacherous Harold, who had frittered away his subjects' wealth. William told his assembled troops: 'he spends his wealth uselessly, scattering his gold without consolidating his lands. He will fight for fear of losing the things he has wrongfully seized; we are claiming what we have received as a gift and earned by our favours.'[3] The Pope turned a personal dispute over the English crown into a holy war, legitimising all subsequent actions and benefits that would accrue from success. Suddenly every chancer, soldier and self-styled knight in Western Europe wanted to get in on the act.

One of the adventurers making the Channel crossing to try their luck was Alan, son of Count Eudo of Penthièvre in Brittany and Agnes of La Cornouaille (a region in the south-west of the Breton peninsula settled by Anglo-Saxon princes). Alan was known as 'the Red' thanks to the colour of his beard. The epithet was also to distinguish him from one of his brothers – Alan Niger, or Alan the Black. Because of his father's status as a nobleman, Alan the Red could use the title *comes*, or count, despite not holding any land in his own right in Brittany. Yet in a crowded field of seven brothers, and expecting no inheritance of his own (that was expected to go to the eldest), he needed to make his own way, to seek his own fortune. Joining William's army of invasion seemed the best way of securing wealth and status. This formed a pattern for ambitious younger sons: William de Warenne, who became one of England's richest men, was one; another was Alan's brother Brien. Illegitimate sons, like William the Bastard himself, were even more eager to prove their worth.

William's campaign was an extremely risky venture. England had been invaded and re-invaded several times over the previous two centuries. There was little guarantee that this occupation would be any more permanent. The Bretons had an uneasy relationship with the Normans, as they had been engaged in a war against each other only a few years earlier. William had even taken Harold Godwinson with him on a campaign against the Bretons, to impress upon him his military strength. Alan's cousin was the very same Duke of Brittany whom William had been fighting. This Duke even alleged that William had poisoned his predecessor – Alan's uncle – by dipping his riding gloves in poison.[4] None of this was enough to dissuade Alan from joining forces with the Normans. He was also a kinsman of William: the various intermarriages between the two houses interspersed with bouts of warfare.

A large Breton contingent under the command of Alan and Brien sailed along the north French coast to join William's invasion force. Numbering as many as five thousand men, they made up a sizeable minority of the troops. This was not just a Norman conquest, but a

Breton, Flemish and Lotharingian one, too (Lotharingia stretched as far east as modern-day Cologne and Strasbourg). Young adventurers from across Western Europe gathered under the Pope's banner, lured by the riches of England and the prospect of carving out their own estates.

The story of the invasion is a familiar one. Harold was defending his land on two fronts. He first diverted his army to the north to defeat an invasion by his disgruntled brother and sometime ruler of Northumbria, Tostig Godwinson, aided and abetted by Harald Hardrada, an adventurer seeking to recreate the Viking kingdom in that part of England. Harold saw them off at Stamford Bridge, to the east of York. But he had relied largely on peasant farmers, and on forces cobbled together by two earl brothers, Edwin and Morcar.

On victory, Harold stood down his army, thinking it was too late in the year for William to make the dangerous sea crossing. But as he returned south, he heard news of a fleet sighted off the Channel coast – an armada of seven hundred ships was about to reach the English shore.

As soon as they landed in October 1066, the Normans embarked on a strategy that they would pursue with great efficiency over the next few years – wilful destruction and intimidation. They burned villages and stole food supplies to keep their army going. This forced Harold's hand, and he pressed southwards with his hastily reassembled army to repulse the invaders. The Normans caught him by surprise. The theatre of battle, as every English schoolchild learns, was Hastings.

Alain Le Roux was commanding the sizeable Breton contingent at Hastings, on the left wing of the Norman army, which did not, in the first instance, acquit itself well. William's forces came up against the Saxon defensive shield-wall. Harold's five thousand war-weary men should have been no match for William's fifteen thousand infantry, archers and cavalry. The Normans were forced to fall back, giving every impression of an army in retreat. Historians continue to debate whether this was a ruse, a false flight that tempted the Saxons off the high ground, leading to their inglorious defeat and Harold's death.

William knew that his claim to the throne rested entirely on a spurious promise, made fifteen years previously, and the fact that his great-grandfather was Edward's maternal grandfather. But might was right, and he moved quickly to consolidate his authority. Those who served him well at Hastings were rewarded. Thus began the Norman takeover.

Although decidedly partial, as its name suggests, the *Anglo-Saxon Chronicle* provides one of the most important historical sources from the departure of the Romans to the turn of the twelfth century. It portrays the Battle of Hastings as the beginning of a great national disaster, visited on England by God:

> There were killed King Harold, and Earl Leofwine his brother, and Earl Gyrth his brother, and many good men. And the French had possession of the place of slaughter, just as God granted them because of people's sins. Archbishop Aldred and the garrison in London wanted Prince Edgar for king, just as was his natural right; and Edwin and Morcar promised him that they would fight for him, but always when it should have been furthered, so from day to day the later the worse it got, just as it all did in the end.[5]

Anyone who fought with Harold saw his lands forfeited. Landlords' agents, known as reeves, were dispatched to luckless villages and farms across the south of the country to seize the land. The *Anglo-Saxon Chronicle* describes their actions, using terms not dissimilar to those applied to the Mafia: 'They levied taxes on the villages every so often, and called it "protection money". When the wretched people had no more to give, they robbed and burned the villages. Wretched people died of starvation; some lived by begging for alms, who had once been rich men.'[6] The *Chronicle* records that William 'sold land on very hard terms, as hard as he could. The king gave it into the hands of the man who had offered him most of all, and did not care how sinfully the reeves had got it from poor men'. The King and his close circle 'loved gain much and over-much – gold and silver – and did not care how sinfully it was obtained provided it came to them'.[7] One can assume that Alan, who was one of the first to benefit from forfeited land, was a prime target of the *Chronicle*'s ire.

William's short-term aim was plunder, to pay back those who had helped him to victory. Much of the land confiscated from *thegns* (Saxon landowners) who had died at Hastings was given to his stipendiary knights (the mercenaries who were the staple of armies at the time).[8] These were men motivated more by the prospect of booty than by feudal duty to their lord. They marauded through the countryside until they were paid off with a patch of land to settle down on. Other immediate beneficiaries were churches and abbeys, Saxon and Norman. Norman abbeys had been promised English land by William in exchange for supplying his men and providing their own levies. Saxon churches fell over themselves to offer cash to the new King if he settled local land disputes in their favour. To sweeten the deal, they offered to accept Norman knights as tenants on their land.[9]

William's long-term agenda was to put down roots in his new territory. He emphasised continuity with the years of Edward the Confessor, to foster the idea that he was the natural and legitimate successor. Once the immediate looting was over, he was keen to give Saxon landowners the benefit of the doubt unless they openly rebelled against him. He even gave Harold's corpse back to his widow, Edith the Swan Neck (otherwise known as Edith the Fair), for burial without demanding a ransom, even though she is said to have offered him her dead husband's weight in gold.[10]

Two months after crossing the Channel, on Christmas Day 1066, William was crowned at Westminster, the same venue as Harold's coronation only a few months earlier. The service was conducted according to English custom. Eager not to inflame tensions, William even asked the Anglo-Saxon Archbishop of Canterbury, Stigand, who had crowned Harold, to be in attendance. He was accompanied by a strange array of Normans and Bretons. The carefully cultivated sense of triumph, majesty and continuity was shattered when a detachment of William's own men, believing the chants of affirmation to the throne to be cries of dissent, set fire to the buildings around the abbey. As the congregation fled in terror, the remaining bishops completed the ceremony. This was a harbinger of the tension and violence to come.

William might have controlled Canterbury, the religious centre, and Winchester, the ceremonial seat of kings, but his position overall remained precarious in a country that was both hostile and alien to him. The newly crowned King needed a group around him that he could trust. Throughout the initial period of occupation, William could rely on fewer men than he dared to admit. Many of the knights who had come over with him would eventually choose to return to their French estates, despite the rewards on offer in England. Some left for their own safety. They had little reason to assume that Norman rule would last in a land prone to frequent invasion. Some knights, possibly displaying the occasional ethical instinct, even refused to take part in the land seizures. Gilbert d'Auffray, a Norman nobleman, 'declined to have any part in plunder. Content with his own, he rejected other men's goods.'[11] Alain Le Roux, however, was in it for the long haul.

When William returned briefly to Normandy in 1067, he took with him as hostages several important members of the Anglo-Saxon nobility. Stigand and the northern earls Edwin and Morcar were spirited over the sea to where the Conqueror could keep an eye on them.[12] There, he paraded them through the city of Rouen along with many of his looted treasures from English abbeys.[13] Alan, Odo, William Fitz Osbern, first Earl of Hereford, and Robert of Mortain – his most loyal lieutenants – were left behind as William's chief regents in England. They also meticulously set about enriching themselves.

It did not take long for the restive English to move against their conquerors. The city of Exeter, which had been harbouring Harold's wife, was the first to rebel. The pretext was the high taxes, or gelds, demanded of the locals. Anyone who could not pay found their lands forfeited as if they had rebelled. Harold's sons landed in the West Country with an army from Ireland, but Brien, Alan's brother, defeated them in a bloody battle.[14] In spite of his victory and successful subjugation of Exeter, the experience of continual warfare may have been enough to persuade Brien that the sojourn to England was not worth the bother. He returned home soon after.

The main rebellion had been brewing in the lawless north. The stretch of English land between the Humber and the Scottish border was fiercely Danish in character, with its own aristocracy resistant to outside pressure. Months after the invasion down south, William appointed Copsig, a Saxon, as the new Earl of Northumbria. Copsig had been the deputy of Tostig Godwinson, Harold's brother, who had been deeply unpopular during his own lordship over the north. Copsig fared no better. While collecting a heavy levy to pay for the upkeep of the Norman army, he was chased by a group of Northumbrians and hid in a church. They set alight to it until he ran out, then killed him and cut his head off.[15] In York, according to one account, the Saxon Earl Waltheof 'alone killed many of the Normans, cutting off their heads one by one as they escaped through the gate'. William responded by appointing the first Norman earl, Robert of Comines, to replace Copsig. He suffered a similar fate.

In the summer of 1069 the northern earls planned a full-scale uprising against Norman authority. Edwin and Morcar, who were back in the country, enlisted Edgar the Aetheling, a scion of the English royal line who, in hereditary terms, had a better claim to the throne than either William or, indeed, Harold. Soon, almost all the wealthy and notable members of northern English society had turned against the King. The exception was the Archbishop of York, who warned the rebels not to fight an impossible battle against the Norman war machine.

They pinned their hopes on outside help. In September a large Danish military contingent sailed up the Humber and marched on York. The Normans were so terrified that the Danes would attack their castle they began burning houses to prevent their materials being used in the siege. The chronicler John of Worcester reported: 'The fire spread too far, encroached on the whole city and burned it together with the monastery of St Peter.' The tactic failed to halt the Danes, who entered the city, massacred up to three thousand Normans and 'made off with an immense plunder'.[16] But the Danes were not fighting for a claim to the throne, only for loot. They had an enormous army to feed, and were only too happy to oblige when William bribed them to go back home, leaving the local rebels to fend for themselves.

While the rebel earls were summoning their motley army, with a ragtag of villagers enlisting either under duress or on the promise of livestock or more crops, William – who had heard about the rebellion while in Nottingham – amassed forces on an entirely different scale. He brought in reinforcements from northern France for a battle he was determined to win: he needed to establish his hegemony, once and for all. Edwin and Morcar went on the run. William's march was swift, as the *Anglo-Saxon Chronicle* notes: 'King William came on them by surprise from the south with an overwhelming army and routed them, killing those who could not escape – which was many hundreds of men – and he ravaged the city.'

The Harrying of the North was one of the most brutal chapters in British history – a combination of genocide and ethnic cleansing. Most of all it was about the transfer of assets: hundreds of square miles of land that would lie desolate, to be built upon afresh.[17]

Across Yorkshire, Northumbria and Durham, the onrushing Norman forces destroyed everything in sight. The plan from the outset was to wipe out all resistance, and to starve any survivors into submission. It made little difference for the inhabitants whether they had taken up arms against the occupiers or not; guilt had been established by association. Seeds were confiscated and burned, ploughs were broken and livestock slaughtered.[18] Land was laid waste, made useless for years to come – partly as punishment, partly to choke off supplies of food to any invading army. John of Worcester described conditions so unbearable and 'famine so prevailed that men ate the flesh of horses, dogs, cats and human beings'.[19] Some peasants sold themselves into slavery so that they would at least receive food from their masters. Another historian, Simeon of Durham, noted that starved corpses along the roadside were so common that they spread disease among the living; wolves came down into the villages to feast on the bodies.[20] The Evesham Chronicler wrote that groups of destitute victims flocked to his monastery seeking alms for years afterwards.[21]

There was to be no pardon. According to Orderic Vitalis, a Benedictine monk and one of the great chroniclers of his age, William 'continued to comb forests and remote mountainous places, stopping at nothing to hunt out the enemy hidden there'.[22] For the few who remained alive, punishment varied: some rebels were allowed to go into exile, some were imprisoned, others were allowed their 'freedom' only after their hands had been cut off, or their eyes gouged out.

Furious at the cycle of rebellion against his authority, William abandoned his earlier efforts to come to an accommodation with aristocratic Saxon society, settling instead on the complete removal of the old elite. The Harrying of the North was a conscious scorched-earth policy, rather than the excessive exuberance of a victorious army. The historian

William of Malmesbury tells of how the orders, which came directly from William, were carried out to the letter:

> He then ordered both the town and fields of the whole district [of York] to be laid waste; the fruits and grain to be destroyed by fire or by water, more especially on the coast, as well as on account of his recent displeasure, as because a rumour had gone abroad that Cnut, king of Denmark, was approaching with his forces. The reason of such a command was, that the plundering pirate should find no booty on the coast to carry off with him.[23]

Even in the early to mid-twelfth century, when William of Malmesbury was writing, the area was still suffering the after-effects of the slaughter:

> Thus the resources of a province, once flourishing, and the nurse of tyrants, were cut off by fire, slaughter and devastation; the ground, for more than sixty miles, totally uncultivated and unproductive, remains bare even to the present day ... Should any stranger now see it, he laments over the once magnificent cities, the towers threatening heaven itself with their loftiness; the fields abundant in pasturage and watered with rivers: and, if any ancient inhabitant remains, he knows it no longer.[24]

There had never been such lofty towers in Saxon Yorkshire, but the contemporary historians had no other vocabulary to describe such destruction than to rephrase depictions of biblical horrors such as the siege of Jericho. So wasted was the area that it became a natural place of migration for the Cistercian order of monks from eastern France, who took a vow of poverty, living as close to nature as possible. They founded some of Yorkshire's great abbeys, such as Jervaux and Rievaulx, in the twelfth century, but so bad were conditions for them that some starved in the early days.

After months of systematic barbarism, William celebrated Christmas in 1070 from inside the burned-out shell of York Minster. Surrounded by the remains of a charred city, its streets deserted but for baying stray dogs and the odd starving, disorientated elderly woman or child in rags, the Conqueror grasped his sceptre and donned his finest robes for a ceremony celebrating his rule.

Having laid waste to the land, William went after the money. In a world before banks, this meant ransacking the monasteries where landowning families kept their gold, entrusting to God the security of their assets. Apparently forgetting the papal blessing of their invasion, the Normans despoiled churches and abbeys, making off with riches. The motive might have been to confiscate the wealth of the Saxon nobility rather than punish the English Church *per se*, but evidence suggests Norman soldiers could not resist helping themselves to the odd trinket from the altar. Forgetting his earlier piety, William 'ordered that all the monasteries all over England be searched and that the wealth which the richer English had deposited in them, because of his ravaging and violence, be seized and taken to his treasury'. He then held a special council to remove English abbots and appoint 'men of his own race' instead.[25] Nor were bishops immune. Aethelwine, Bishop of Durham, was imprisoned and began a hunger strike from which he died.[26] Stigand's wealth, despite being sent to Ely Abbey for safekeeping, was taken by William.[27]

England was a valued prize; thanks to a solid system of tax collection and unified coinage, it was relatively wealthy. But for William and his entourage it remained an outpost, territory of second order (and culture) to Normandy itself. His army of opportunistic adventurers wore their loyalties lightly. William of Malmesbury describes the shifting attitudes of the Norman strongmen and would-be aristocrats. They were, he said:

Exceedingly particular in their dress and delicate in their food, though not to excess. They are a race inured to war, indeed they can hardly live without it, fierce in rushing against the enemy, and, where force fails of success, ready to use stratagem, or corrupt by bribery. They live in large edifices with economy, envy their equals, wish to excel their superiors, and plunder their subjects, though they defend them from others; they are faithful to their lords, though a slight offence renders them perfidious. They weigh treachery by its chance of success, and change their sentiments with money.[28]

Even after the Harrying of the North, insurgencies continued, particularly during William's periods of absence. A revolt in 1075 involved two Saxon earls, Siward and Waltheof, along with a Norman, Roger de Breteuil. The key figure was the Earl of East Anglia, Ralph de Gael, a Breton who had held lands on both sides of the Channel since before the conquest. The pretext was the King's refusal to sanction Ralph's marriage – the rebellion was more a jockeying for influence than a concerted attempt to restore the Saxon monarchy. The revolt was destined to fail: the protagonists were disorganised and disheartened from the outset. Waltheof confessed the conspiracy to the new Archbishop of Canterbury, Lanfranc, an abbot from Caen, an Italian by birth and one of the figures upon whom William relied.

The King's forces assembled in far greater number under Odo and crushed the rebels. The victors ordered that the right foot of all rebel soldiers be cut off. Waltheof, the last of the great Saxon earls to fall, was led out of the city of Winchester, beheaded with an axe, and thrown into an unmarked grave – even though his betrayal of his colleagues had helped the crown. Only later did sympathetic locals recover his body and give it due burial.[29] Ralph and his countess, who had held out in Norwich while he had sailed to Denmark for help, were given forty days to leave the country, as long as they handed over all their lands first.

When William returned, he held a court at Westminster at which the rebels were punished:

> And the king was at Westminster that midwinter; there all the Bretons who were at the bride-feast [of Ralph] at Norwich were condemned:
>> Some were blinded and some exiled from the land, and some were reduced to ignominy.
> Thus were traitors to the king laid low.[30]

The term 'reduced to ignominy' denoted forfeiture.

Who better to reward with Ralph's lands than Alain Le Roux? He had declined to take part in the revolt led by his Breton countryman, and William was keen to reward him. There was no shortage of vacated land to choose from. Alan was given Ralph's lands, along with those of Eadgyfu the Fair, a wealthy Saxon noblewoman who, as Ralph's step-mother, had sided with the rebels. Alan took her £366 worth of estates across East Anglia without having to lift a finger.[31] The coat of arms of the University of Cambridge incorporates a cross ermine, a symbol of Brittany that dates back to the influx of Bretons allied to Alan.

By the mid-1070s, William had so comprehensively destroyed or exiled the Saxon nobility that he could not find a friendly local to take the role of Earl of Northumbria, so he kept the title for himself. Elsewhere, a small number of Norman grandees were awarded huge, geographically contiguous estates. This marked a change in William's earlier policy of doling out land piecemeal to prevent any of his lieu-tenants from building up an alternative power base. In an area as restless as the north, he needed one undisputed lord in each locality, and they needed to be people he could trust. He turned, first and foremost, to the loyal Alain Le Roux.

As he travelled back south after the Harrying of the North, William distributed the land as he went, but only to those he trusted. He gave Alan the 'honour' (a term for lordship over an area) of Richmond in north Yorkshire.

> I, William, called the Bastard King of England, do hereby grant and concede to you, my nephew Alan, Count of Brittany, and to your heirs in perpetuity all the manors and lands which late belonged to Earl Edwin in Yorkshire, with the king's fees and other liberties and customs, as freely and in as honourable way as the said Edwin held the same.

So reads the royal proclamation in the Register of Richmond. The land handed on a plate to Alan stretched for thirty miles down the Great North Road, and covered several strategically important crossings over the Pennines which could be used by Scots or rebellious Northum-brians. The honour comprised no fewer than 199 fiefs, or manors, each occupied by a tenant who owed fealty to Alan or kept by Alan him-self.[32] Edwin was now dead, killed by his own followers while fleeing to Scotland from the unstoppable Norman army. Alan maintained most of Edwin's Yorkshire land more or less as it had been, even using Saxon stewards to look after it.[33]

Over thirty years of Norman rule more than one hundred castles were built, the likes of which the English had not seen before. Anglo-Saxon nobles had lived in far less imposing castles, built within walled towns, or boroughs, rather than outside them. The new, impregnable stone structures were designed to terrorise the inhabitants of the surrounding countryside into submission. The message was clear: resistance is futile. Such was their domination of the landscape that it was said no castle was more than a day's ride from the next. This militarisation of the land was part a projection of wealth and power, part an exercise in self-preservation. These compact military bases allowed relatively small bodies of armed men, the permanent garrisons, to exercise strategic control over large areas. The *Anglo-Saxon Chronicle* saw the string of castles ordered by Odo as the root of all the evils visited on the local population. Odo, it said, 'built castles widely throughout this nation, and oppressed the wretched people; and afterwards it always grew very much worse'.[34]

Alan remained a staunch supporter of the new monarchy. At one point he was betrothed to Matilda (or Edith, as she was originally known), daughter of King Malcolm III of Scotland. What happened to their nuptials is a source of historical conjecture. One version is that he rejected the proposal, seeing it as a ruse by the Scottish monarch to increase his influence in England.[35] Another has it that the educated and glamorous Matilda saw off a number of suitors, one of whom was Alan. A third account suggests that the marriage plans collapsed after Malcolm got into a dispute with William Rufus (the Conqueror's third son who succeeded him as William II), tried to seize his lands, and died in battle. Matilda didn't do too badly in the end, marrying Henry I and becoming Queen of England. In any case, Alan's interests seemed to lie elsewhere. Some accounts say he had a long-standing relationship with Gunnhild, the daughter of Harold Godwinson; others claim that they might even have married. A somewhat different version has it that he abducted Gunnhild, who was supposed to be a nun. Either way, Anselm, the Archbishop of Canterbury, was not amused. On Alan's death, he suggested that she lie with his corpse and 'kiss his naked teeth, for the lips have now rotted away'. She rejected Anselm's advice and reportedly lived with, and possibly married, Alan's brother and successor, Alan the Black.[36]

The centre of Alan Rufus's power was Richmond Castle. Construction of this giant edifice began immediately after he received the honour from William. He chose a site at the northernmost tip of his territory, near the old Roman stronghold of Cataractonium, later known as Catterick, and several miles away from Edwin's previous base of Gilling. This was barren, desolate land but the topography was perfect. On one side was a sheer cliff dropping to the River Swale. This provided excellent defence, giving rise to the Riche Monte, or strong hill.

The castle was built to the most modern specifications. It was a triangular structure that overlooked a strategic pass through the mountains, with a stone hall as residence for the lord.[37] These squat, two-storey buildings, with stone walls up to eleven feet thick and the keep tower one hundred feet high, were the status-symbol properties of their day. Initially, at least, the Norman fortresses were not opulent, but they were built on a new scale. The construction plans for Richmond Castle were so complicated that stonemasons were brought in from Normandy and Brittany. The place names French Gate and Lombards Wynd in Richmond suggest the concentration of foreign workers in the area at the time.[38] The costs of bringing them over the Channel and so far north would have been extremely high, but in their quest for not just military but cultural domination of the locals, the Normans were happy to spend – and to be seen spending.[39]

This was the architecture and politics of dominance, imposing itself on the bleak landscape beyond. The design had one purpose: to over-awe the Saxons and serve as a stronghold against any future attempts at rebellion from them, or incursions from the Scots or Danes. It is not clear how often Alan stayed at the castle (its great hall is likely to have been completed only after his death), but he may well have presided over jousting competitions in the Earls' Orchard on the grounds below. In subsequent centuries, Richmond saw virtually no 'action', suggesting either that the mere presence of the castle was enough to persuade aggressors to think again, or that the danger was exaggerated from the outset, in order to reinforce a sense of fear.

Local villages catered to the needs of the soldiers garrisoned inside all Norman castles. If food was not handed over, it was simply seized. Local reeves, the middlemen, were in charge of taking the lord's cut of local produce and keeping it safe inside the castle. The medieval writer Henry of Huntingdon described these men as 'more frightful than thieves and robbers'.[40]

Over time a town grew up around Richmond Castle. The decimated population was gradually replenished with incomers; it took time for the charred land to return to cultivation. The castle stayed in the hands of Breton dukes for most of the next three hundred years. It was only in the fourteenth century that the French connections were broken; by then, the frequent absences of the Breton nobility from their English estates meant that the honour system was in an alarming state of decay. In the Georgian era, thanks to wool and lead, Richmond flourished. But the castle gradually lost its purpose and fell into ruin (although some rooms in the tower were controversially used to imprison conscientious objectors in the First World War).

Alan's property empire grew fast, extending across eight counties and up the entire length of Earningas (later Ermine) Street, the old Roman road from London to Lincoln and York. Most of it was acquired through forfeiture and violence, but sometimes the conquering class used other means to apply pressure on the Saxons. The Normans would also take to the courts to claim their rights; they would win as a matter of course. Alan was concerned enough about his estates to take one Saxon priest to court in a dispute over a single hide of land in Cambridgeshire – the smallest possible measurement of ownership.[41]

Keen to build not just military fortifications, he patronised the Church too, founding priories in East Anglia, notably the abbeys in Bury St Edmund's and York, both of which in later years would rank among the wealthiest ecclesiastical institutions in England.[42] These were not just acts of piety. The presence of a church allowed the owner to make a claim on the outlying land. Churches were an integral part of the feudal system, supplying armed men when the need arose. Norman abbots fought at Hastings because William had promised them English land. Hierarchies were observed and entrenched in every church: the priest would wait for the lord before beginning every service, and the lord and his family would occupy their own pew, helping to foster a sense of deference in the local community.[43] The place of worship, no less than the castle or great hall, was a status symbol. The foundation or endowment of a church or monastery was one of the acts expected of someone of Alan's status. That put them in a position of social prestige and ensured that monks would pray for their souls in the world to come and might provide insurance against misdeeds committed on earth. Was the construction of St Mary's Abbey in York at least partly to atone for Alan's role in the Harrying of the North?

It is thanks to one book that historians have been able to track the vast shifts in population and holdings during the second half of the eleventh century: Domesday. This extraordinary document, or set of documents, not only provides a comprehensive guide to assets, wealth and status; it also shines a light on William the Conqueror's obsessive determination to control an unruly nation. In 1085 William told his council in Gloucester that he wanted to know exactly what had happened to every piece of land in his kingdom. The *Anglo-Saxon Chronicle* takes up the story:

After this had the king a large meeting, and very deep consultation with his council, about this land; how it was occupied, and by what sort of men. Then sent he his men over all England into each shire; commissioning them to find out 'How many hundreds of hides were in the shire, what land the king himself had, and what stock upon the land; or, what dues he ought to have by the year from the shire.' Also he commissioned them to record in writing, 'How much land his archbishops had, and his diocesan bishops, and his abbots, and his earls'; and though I may be prolix and tedious, 'What, or how much, each man had, who was an occupier of land in England, either in land or in stock, and how much money it were worth.' So very narrowly, indeed, did he commission them to trace it out, that there was not one single hide, nor a yard of land, nay, moreover (it is shameful to tell, though he thought it no shame to do it), not even an ox, nor a cow, nor a swine was there left, that was not set down in his writ. And all the recorded particulars were afterwards brought to him.

Everybody was counted. Nobody could conceal assets, no matter how small, from the tax collector. The fear it instilled led to its Anglo-Saxon title of Domesday, denoting the Day of Judgement. The King's agents scoured every corner of the land, conducting a survey of unparalleled precision. Some 45,000 landholdings in more than 13,000 locations were recorded and assessed, according to their pre-conquest and present-day valuations. The findings were written up in Latin in two huge volumes, comprising two million words over 913 pages, that were housed in the royal treasury at Winchester. Strangely, however, data from that city and from London was not collected. There may have been gaps, but this was statistical, social and economic information with no parallel in Europe.[44]

Produced with astonishing speed in a matter of months, the Domesday Book allows historians to assess the extent to which William really did change the economic and social make-up of England by supplanting one elite with another. The figures are stark. Of the nine hundred tenants-in-chief – those who held their land as a direct grant from the King – a desultory thirteen were English. The old Saxon royal family, the line of Edward the Confessor, owned just £65 worth of land by 1086. Edgar the Aetheling, after his dalliance with the northern rebels, accounted for just £10 of this, his humiliation complete.[45] Among the subtenants, the English fared better, but they still made up only around one-fifth of the total; those who did cling on held much less land than their Norman peers.[46] In the re-mapped England, the King and Queen personally owned up to a fifth of all the land. The Church accounted for just over a quarter of the total. William's invading kinsmen held half of all the private land, leaving pre-conquest chief tenants with a fraction over 5 per cent.[47] It was not only rural society that underwent radical demographic change. In the ancient royal city of Winchester the proportion of the population with Saxon names fell from over 70 per cent at the time of the Domesday Book to under 40 per cent by 1110.[48]

From the 1070s onwards, Alan was at the forefront of the policy of settlement embodied in the practice of 'enfeoffment', whereby new tenants would be granted land in exchange for owing feudal duties of labour – of both peacetime and wartime varieties – to the lord. Alan moved in a number of enfeoffed tenants who acted as middlemen between himself and the Saxon peasants who worked on his land. According to one count, thirty-eight of the forty minor landholders enfeoffed by him were Bretons. It appears that Alan also used the opportunity to bring over three of his illegitimate brothers – Ribald, Bodin and Bardulf – who were not in line to inherit any family lands in Brittany, in order to give them a share of the spoils.[49] This marked a departure from Alan's policy in his East Anglian estates, where he allowed a large number of Saxons to remain in place.[50] The extent of the destruction wrought in the north left him no choice but to find new tenants from elsewhere if he wanted the land to be worked at all.

By 1086, a fifth of England was in Breton hands. The conquest was no longer confined to the replacement of one elite with another. The middle stratum of society was also being dismembered. Ilbert and Drogo, Yorkshire's other big landowners, brought in large numbers of Norman, Breton and Flemish tenants to secure their takeovers.[51] Such was the extent of the migration and colonisation that by the 1140s a local chronicler of the north-east of England listed the Flemish as one of the six main population groups.[52] Whole estates were transferred, overnight in some cases, into new hands. Brihtric, possibly the wealthiest Saxon *thegn* in 1066, saw all of his £560 worth of land go to William Fitz Osbern.[53] Yet such examples illustrate a transfer between elites, not the creation of anything particularly new. A small stratum of extremely wealthy people had dominated English society long before the Normans. Harold's father, Earl Godwin, was undisputed top dog and chief landowner in his day, perhaps more powerful than the King himself. William learned the lessons from this. He created a caste of mighty – but not over-mighty – subjects, each with his own fiefdom, but each beholden to the King.

The new Norman aristocracy was more finely balanced in terms of wealth and power than the Saxons had been. Alan Rufus, William de Warenne, Odo, William Fitz Osbern and Robert of Mortain enjoyed similar status to one another. There was, after all, plenty of land to go round. The most politically connected and perhaps most feared (after the Conqueror himself) was Odo. He was extremely conscious of his reputation and is likely to have been the patron behind the famous tapestry that bears the name of his Norman diocese. It depicts him in a heroic role, 'encouraging the boys', as the inscription puts it, at the Battle of Hastings. As Earl of Kent, Odo added much of south-east England to his French holdings, and for several years he was a loyal servant of the King, leading troops against a number of rebellions. The King's other half-brother, Mortain, was rewarded for his loyalty, to the tune of eight hundred separate manors by the time of Domesday, mostly concentrated in the south and south-west of England.

Alan was rare in that, as a non-Norman, he had successfully infiltrated an elite that was founded on Norman royal blood-ties. Most of those who formed the new super-rich after the Battle of Hastings were already top magnates in the Duchy of Normandy with close links to the ducal family.[54] Some, like the Warenne family, were relatively minor nobles at home who were catapulted to greater wealth and status because of the lands they seized after the conquest.

Such was Alan's dominance of north Yorkshire that this part of England is described in Domesday as the 'land of Count Alan'. He was truly the lord of all he surveyed. Yet while the scale of his land was unmatched, paradoxically its asset value was quite different. The north still had not recovered from its vicious treatment at the hands of the Norman armies. Where land elsewhere in the country had increased in value, in Yorkshire it had plummeted. Richmond had a high number of manors listed as 'waste', meaning they produced nothing. One reading of Domesday suggests that Alan's Yorkshire estates may have declined in value by over a half since 1066. Drogo suffered even worse: his estates' pre-conquest worth was £553; by 1086, this had fallen to £93.[55] Herein lies a paradox of the conquest of the north – in order to achieve ultimate economic power over the area, the Normans felt they had first to destroy the local economy. In the circumstances Alan did well to keep Richmond itself at 80 per cent of its pre-conquest value, suggesting that the manors that did work were profitable.[56]

The immediate decline in land value brought about by the Harrying of the North suggests that Alan looked elsewhere in England to increase his wealth. Outside Richmond, he had another forty-three manors at the time of Domesday, spread mainly across the eastern counties. Apart from the few that he had been rewarded with in the immediate aftermath of Hastings, they fell into his hands after the Saxon earls were defeated and exiled in the early 1070s. As Orderic Vitalis chronicled in his *Historia Ecclesiastica*, William 'divided up the chief provinces of England amongst his followers'.[57] Alan had holdings in twelve counties altogether, and in Lincolnshire and Cambridgeshire he held more than twice as much land as any other noble.[58]

Along with the super-rich came the merely rich. Ilbert of Lacy received over 150 manors in the west of Yorkshire, 10 in Nottinghamshire and 4 in Lincolnshire. He built a castle at Pontefract. His brother Walter ended up in the west of England with lands in Herefordshire and Gloucestershire. Roger de Busli – or Roger of Bully, as he came to be known – ran 86 manors in Nottinghamshire, 46 in Yorkshire, others in Derbyshire, Lincolnshire and Leicestershire, and one in Devon. He built a number of castles, such as Tickhill in the West Riding, which became an important fortification during the reign of King John. Drogo de la Beuvrière was given the peninsula of Holderness, previously the domain of William Malet (once an ally of William the Conqueror but apparently a hapless first High Sheriff of Yorkshire) and the rebel Earl Morcar. In Totnes, Devon, the Breton lord Judhael took ownership of the estates of no fewer than thirty-nine Saxon landholders.[59]

Many of the great magnates of William's reign did not last long. Their propensity to conspire, or concentrate too much power into their own hands, often led to a fall from grace. Ralph de Gael fell in 1075. The fervidly ambitious Odo also threw it all away when he too decided to rebel. He was arrested in 1082 and jailed for five years. As was the custom, his lands were declared forfeit. He was allowed to retire to France. After William's death he tried his luck at getting his lands back. He sided with Robert, another of the Conqueror's sons, in an unsuccessful attempt to unseat William II from the throne of England. Captured at Pevensey Castle, Odo was banished from the country with nothing but the clothes on his back. He died on his way to the First Crusade, perhaps trying to rebuild his fortune from scratch, in 1097.

His fate did not dissuade others, though, and the rebellions continued against the new monarch.[60] Alan Rufus would have no part in them. He died in 1093, still holding on to the fortune, land and titles that he had amassed under William II's father. He remained loyal to the last. Unlike other members of the super-rich club down the years, he appears not to have had a super-sized ego. Even right at the end, he was happy to do the dirty work for his kings, pillaging the city of Durham to punish its bishop for contradicting the King.[61] In a final act of fealty, on his deathbed, he bequeathed the abbey of St Mary's in York to William Rufus.[62] In his later years, apparently encouraged by Gunnhild, he had grown more attached to East Anglia. Given that his power base and religious foundation were in Yorkshire, it was a surprise that he expressed the wish to be buried inside the abbey at Bury St Edmund's. More than forty years later, at the request of the Breton elite, his body was removed from there and reinterred at St Mary's.

Alan had no recognised sons, so his Yorkshire land passed first to his brother, Alan the Black, and then to a much younger brother, Stephen, Count of Tréguier. By the 1140s, Stephen's son Alan was styling himself as the first Earl of Richmond (it seems the first Alan was uninterested in such titles – the more modest French 'count' sufficed for him).[63] The family would hold the earldom only until 1171, when the male line died out and the lands reverted to the crown. By then, the demographics of England had changed for ever, with the invading Normans and Bretons assimilating into, and dominating, the culture of their new land.

William the Conqueror's death in 1087 was anything but peaceful. He was fifty-nine years old and had ruled England for twenty-one years and Normandy for a further thirty-one. There are two accounts of his death: one from an anonymous monk in Caen; the other a later but more reliable account from Orderic Vitalis. It is a gruesome tale laden with much moralising about greed and violence, and pleas from the King for divine forgiveness.

According to the tale, the portly King was out on a mission to subdue the town of Mantes, on the southern fringe of Normandy, when he was thrown against the pommel of his horse and his internal organs ruptured. He was taken to Rouen, where his condition worsened. Mindful of the afterlife to come, he 'gave way to repeated sighs and groans'. Fearing that the end was nigh, he confessed his sins and ordered that his treasure be distributed among the churches and the poor, 'so that what I amassed through evil deeds may be assigned to the holy uses of good men'. Orderic Vitalis says he then sought to atone for the Harrying of the North:

> I treated the native inhabitants of the kingdom with unreasonable severity, cruelly oppressed high and low, unjustly disinherited many, and caused the death of thousands by starvation and war, especially in Yorkshire. In mad fury I descended on the English of the north like a raging lion, and ordered that their homes and crops with all their equipment and furnishings should be burnt at once and their great flocks and herds of sheep and cattle slaughtered everywhere. So I chastised a great multitude of men and women with the lash of starvation and, alas, was the cruel murderer of many thousands, both young and old, of this fair people.

As soon as he died, the various nobles and other hangers-on who had attended the vigil ran off, desperate to protect their property from forfeiture. Those who stayed behind, says Orderic, 'seized the arms, vessels, clothing, linen, and all the royal furnishings, and hurried away leaving the king's body almost naked on the floor of the house'. Further ignominy was to befall William. First came a fire that nearly destroyed Rouen. Then, says the monk of Caen, when it was time to bury the heavy body, it was discovered that the stone sarcophagus was too small. As the assembled clergy tried to squeeze in the bloated corpse, 'the swollen bowels burst, and an intolerable stench assailed the nostrils of the bystanders and the whole crowd'.

This gory scene is reminiscent of the tale (likewise possibly apocryphal) of Crassus' demise and the molten gold. The contemporary historical record is filled with recrimination. The *Anglo-Saxon Chronicle* was quick to pass judgement:

> *He had castles built*
> *and wretched men oppressed.*
> *The king was so very stark*
> *and seized from his subject men many a mark*
> *of gold, and more hundreds of pounds of silver*

that he took by weight, and with great injustice
from his land's nation with little need.
He was fallen into avarice,
and he loved greediness above all.[64]

So began the second battle, for legacy.

Having taken the land and wealth of the country, the Normans sought to create a narrative that would place them on the right side of history. The first revisionist version came from the Conqueror's chaplain, William of Poitiers. In his chronicle, *The Deeds of William, Duke of Normandy and King of England*, he describes the wickedness of Saxon England and the piety and honour of William and his men. The Normans are portrayed as more civilised, more Christian, than the landowners they displaced. A later historian ascribes to this an ethnic or genetic sense of superiority: 'the Normans had a clear conception of themselves as a *gens*, an all-conquering, expansionist race who lorded it over other peoples by their military prowess and cunning'.[65]

It was not as straightforward, however, as one group of people displacing another. Intermarriage between noble families had been customary long before the conquest. Although the Norman court might have separated itself off from the rest of the country by conducting its affairs in French, a new common identity – called 'Anglo-Norman' by some historians, although not by any contemporaries – began to emerge among the elite. Before a battle in the 1130s, the Bishop of Orkney gave a speech to the assembled aristocracy during which he referred to them as 'great nobles of England, Norman by birth'.[66] By then, the Norman victory had come to be seen as the birth of a nation, an act of historical progress.

In the twelfth century, when surnames in their modern form started to emerge, many nobles of mixed heritage chose Norman names over Saxon ones, sometimes from their mother's line. For instance, Geoffrey of Raby took the name Neville, founding a house that, as the earls of Warwick, would become England's most powerful family during the Wars of the Roses.[67]

With the great family names came the development of heraldry. Coats of arms were used to allude to the lands nobles owned and the deeds they had performed. Anglo-Norman families like the Hertfords and Pembrokes added chevrons to their heraldic designs to highlight the grandeur of their great halls.[68] The Beaumonts, another family who enriched themselves from the conquest, were particularly fond of stressing their supposed lineage from Charlemagne, whether real or imagined, as the Frankish Holy Roman Emperor came to be seen as the embodiment of the spirit of chivalry that was becoming fashionable among Europe's feudal elite.[69] Despite this cultural fusion, that elite became harder to break into than before. Before the conquest, inheritance had been a negotiated process. It was not confined to the eldest son: estates and wealth were commonly split between several offspring. The Normans brought with them the notion of primogeniture, a single male successor, which over time created a more rigid landowning elite. This system would form the basis not only of property law but of an aristocracy and gentry from which the political class would be largely drawn well into the twentieth century.

Among radical circles for centuries afterwards, 1066 came to be seen as the date when everything started to go wrong, when a small group of thieves stole the national wealth and deprived the majority of the population of their natural rights. By contrast, Saxon England was idolised as a pre-feudal, more egalitarian and democratic society, where peasants and women enjoyed more rights. This is mostly untrue – Saxon *thegns* were already centralising their estates and placing restrictions on the freedom of peasants to work and move long before the conquest. They insisted that those who worked their lands lived within sight of the great hall so they could not run away.[70] Aelfric put these words into the mouth of a Saxon ploughman: 'Because I fear my lord, there is no winter so severe that I dare hide at home. Each day I must yoke the oxen and fasten the ploughshare to the plough. Then I must plough a full acre or more every day.' At the other end of society, St Wulfstan wrote of Saxon *thegns* who spent their time 'dicing and feasting' in the shade of their trees whilst their peasants undertook back-breaking labour in the fields.[71] Seen in this context, the Norman practice of building a castle to control a particular area does not seem particularly innovative.

So strong was the conventional wisdom of the Norman Conquest as an exploitative, parasitic 'foreign' aristocracy that some medieval noble families took it upon themselves to pay for some reputation management. They commissioned chroniclers to try to prove that their claims to their lands and heraldry pre-dated 1066. For example, around 1200, the Earl of Warwick commissioned a historian to write a romance retrospectively linking his family's local roots to the era of the Saxon King Aethelstan.[72]

Radical movements during the English Civil War in the 1640s saw the conquest as the beginning of the nation's degeneration into absolutism and tyranny. Leveller pamphleteers intoned that the fight against King Charles I was a historic struggle to rid England of the 'Norman yoke'. These radicals saw Charles's execution and the declaration of the Commonwealth as returning England to a time when the 'Anglo-Saxon freeman' could enjoy his liberties. Even the eighteenth-century Tory theorist William Blackstone saw 'feudalism' as a foreign imposition, a system based on a tyrannical model of kingship.[73]

Modern estimates of the worth of fortunes made a millennium ago are, by definition, imprecise. They depend on estimates of inflation, plus purchasing power (at a time when, apart from land and heraldry, there was little to purchase) and a number of other factors. But there is no doubt that, in the post-conquest England of 1086, a small number of grandees owned enormous slices of the national pie. Some modern-day accounts list Alan Rufus as the richest of them all; his fortune of £1100 amounted to about 1.5 per cent of the total national income at the time. Compare that with the £11.3 billion owned by Alisher Usmanov – the Uzbek-born tycoon listed in the *Sunday Times*' Rich List for 2013 as Britain's wealthiest man (see Chapter 12) – which is a 'mere' 0.5 per cent of the national income today.[74] (Now, just as then, it is intriguing to note the preponderance of foreigners at England's top table.) As the *Sunday Times* put it in a headline in 2007: 'Alan the Red, the Brit who makes Bill Gates a pauper'.

Alain Le Roux was perhaps the richest noble who was not a direct relative of the King or a clergyman; only two, William de Warenne and Roger de Montgomery (the 1st Earl of Shrewsbury), had comparable fortunes. Odo and Robert of Mortain were the other high-flyers, alongside Lanfranc, the Italian Archbishop of Canterbury, most of whose fortune may have come from pre-conquest church land. Each of these magnates was richer than the current Duke of Westminster, the highest-placed aristocrat on Britain's current rich list with an estimated wealth of £7 billion.

Given his role in the Harrying of the North and other assorted acts of expropriation and greed, how has Alan Rufus escaped opprobrium? The answer may be somewhat prosaic. In spite of his vast wealth, so little is known of him that history has largely passed him by. His lack of appetite for rebellion or intrigue against the established order kept him out of the limelight, and out of harm's way. He was more 'yes man' than leader, focusing on what he liked best – the expansion of his land-holdings. Many of the world's super-rich have followed his example, doing whatever it takes to keep on the right side of political power. The second generation of Russian oligarchs are a case in point, abiding by Vladimir Putin's warning that they could expand their fortunes as long as they did not mess with him (see Chapter 12). The smart ones – those who have stayed out of trouble and maintained a style to which they have grown accustomed – have followed his strictures to the letter.

Alan Rufus had one big chance in his lifetime to amass a fortune and he took full advantage of it. In so doing he and the other Norman invaders procured huge wealth for themselves, their families and their acolytes. But they did far more than that: through their land grabs, they established a new political and financial order and a social hierarchy that would become the bedrock of English society for centuries to come.

CHAPTER 3

Mansa Musa – Travelling show

Run for your life from any man who tells you
that money is evil. That sentence is the leper's
bell of an approaching looter.

Ayn Rand

Not many people in history can claim to have dished out so much gold
that they sent its price plummeting across the world for a decade. But
Mansa Musa was no ordinary statesman or member of the super-rich
club. The leader of the Malian Empire in the fourteenth century – the
tenth Musa, the King of Kings, the Ruler Moses, as he was variously
titled – presided over one of the wealthiest courts that ever existed. Yet,
such has been historians' inability to cope with the idea of a super-rich
African monarch from the Middle Ages, and such has been the wanton
destruction of the heritage of his once-mighty land, that few people
today have even heard of Mansa Musa.

He probably has a better claim than anyone else to the title richest
man in history – at least that is what a plethora of rich list websites
claim. One calculates the contemporary value of his wealth at $400 bil-
lion, although its inflation-busting tables should be treated with caution.
Musa was the ultimate example of the monopolistic commodities
owner. But unlike his Russian oligarchic equivalents of the present day,
he didn't have to seize anything. There was nothing self-made about

him. Instead, he was blessed with the good fortune of inheriting a kingdom with an abundance of a metal craved by traders around the world. By royal proclamation, it was decreed that all the gold was his by right, providing him with a never-ceasing torrent of wealth.

One event has enshrined Musa's place in history – his epic journey in 1324 to Mecca for the Hajj. The caravan beguiled all who saw it pass, with thousands of lavishly dressed slaves and merchants stretching as far as the eye could see, and one man resplendent on his horse. Everywhere Musa went on his year-long trek he showered those he passed with gold. The closer he came to his destination, the more his religiosity grew; it is said that on each Friday he paid for a mosque to be built on a chosen spot. He dispensed so much that he even ran short and had to borrow money to tide him over. On leaving Mecca, he offered money to those who claimed lineage from the Prophet to return with him, to spread Islam. He returned to his homeland via Timbuktu, the oasis city that – thanks to his investment in it – would become one of the world's fabled seats of learning.

By the end of his twenty-five-year rule, his kingdom was one of the most powerful and prosperous in the world. It stretched from the Atlantic coast in the west to Songhay, far down the Niger, in the east; and from the salt mines of Taghaza in the north to the legendary gold mines of Wangara in the south. The four hundred cities under his rule were synonymous with prosperity, culture and Islamic scholarship. His reign was one of the most ostentatious demonstrations of wealth and piety. To Mansa Musa, there was no contradiction in this. Both were his duty.

In 1324, like millions before and since, a devout Muslim prepared to make the Hajj, the pilgrimage to Islam's holiest sites. Before setting off from West Africa for the 2500-mile overland trip to Mecca and Medina, Mansa Musa left little to chance. In a curious mix of Islamic and pre-Islamic beliefs, he consulted his occult diviners to find out the most auspicious day to depart. Twenty-five years earlier, one of his predecessors, Sultan Sakura, had been assassinated on his way back from Hajj. Sakura was a freed slave who had captured the throne of Mali, and his premature death ensured that the kingdom fell back into the hands of Musa's family. He had been travelling along the dangerous Red Sea route, through Eritrea and Sudan.

Musa vowed not to repeat that mistake. He would stick to the land route – through Egypt and across the vast desert that separated most of Africa from the Mediterranean world. It would take him through the eastern fringes of his vast Malian Empire, through what now constitutes Niger, Chad and Libya, before stopping for three months and replenishing stocks in Cairo, the city where Africa meets the Middle East. As well as being safer, this route would allow him to show off his extraordinary wealth, and therefore the potential power of his kingdom, to all comers. He was particularly interested in a demonstration of one-upmanship towards the Sultan of Egypt, a man whose reputation and authority across the region had previously exceeded his.

The pilgrimage would allow the Malian King to build his profile in parts of the world where his land, if it was known at all, was regarded as mysterious and exotic. He wanted to establish himself on the world stage.

Rulers of Mali had been doing the Hajj since the start of the thirteenth century. But Musa's trip would be on a scale different from any that went before – or would come after. His entourage totalled sixty thousand men and twelve thousand slaves, all lavishly dressed in brocade and Persian silk. Several would attend to his wife, Inari-Kunate, and other members of the court. Merchants and clerics – men of money and devoutness – were integral to the journey. Each slave carried a gold bar weighing six pounds on his back for the entire route. The camel train bore as many as one hundred loads of gold dust and nuggets, each weighing three hundred pounds. But the vast majority of the personnel and the goods they were carrying were devoted to one man, sitting tall on his horse in the middle of the vast caravan – the King himself.

The founding of the Malian Empire is widely attributed to the magician Sundiata Keita, who ruled from 1230 to 1255. Sundiata was a royal slave among the Susu, a people who had inherited the Ghanian Empire in the eighth century, a time when Europe was mired in the Dark Ages. According to legend, Sundiata seized the major territories through which gold was traded, raising armies of spirit fighters to vanquish his foes. The story is recounted in a poem entitled the *Epic of Sundiata*, which has been handed down through the generations by *griots*, singers-cum-oral historians. Sundiata had been expelled from court as a child by one of his father's wives, and lived in exile at the courts of other rulers. As a young man, he managed to rally an army to unite various towns and defeat the Susu. One *griot*, Djeli Mamadou Koyate, describes Sundiata as 'a lad full of strength; his arms had the strength of ten and his biceps inspired fear in his companions. He had already that authoritative way of speaking which belongs to those who are destined to command.' The epic describes three sources of enrichment:

> *Those who would farm*
> *Let them farm!*
> *Those who would trade*
> *Let them trade!*
> *Those who would do battle*
> *Let them battle!*
> *It was battling that Sundiata did!*[1]

Musa, who could trace his lineage back to the grandson of Sundiata's half-brother, acceded to the throne in 1312. By that time, the Malian Empire was already considerable. It consisted of lands belonging to the Ghanian Kingdom and the territory that was called Melle; but few travellers had ventured that far. By the end of his life, his kingdom would be one of the most powerful in the world, having overrun the rival Songhay Kingdom, adding the famous cities of Gao and Timbuktu.

Gold dominated every aspect of life in Mali. It was a measure of the power of the leader and the prestige of his land. Lavish displays of material wealth had long been a duty for the kings of Mali; Musa took these to a new level. Yet, for all its wealth, Mali was still seen as a backwater, far removed from the Mediterranean or other centres of education and trade. So keen was he to be taken seriously whenever an outside dignitary came into town, he was required to conform to strict ritual. Audiences would be held under an ornate cupola in Musa's palace in Niani, the now lost capital of the empire. There he would sit on an ivory throne, under a silk sunshade with a golden eagle atop it. He would carry gold weapons, including a bow and arrow.

Everything was about show, designed to impress his countrymen and outsiders. According to the writer Ibn Khaldun, Musa's prize possession at court was a gold stone weighing twenty *qintars* – an extraordinary seven hundred kilograms. His throne, crafted from hard black ebony, sat on a platform at the centre of the imperial courtyard. Musa never spoke in public, but whispered words to his *jeli*, a herald, who spoke aloud the ruler's words. Anyone who invoked his ire could meet a violent death. His writ demanded absolute obedience. Among the many crimes that would lead to execution was sneezing in his presence. The historical record does not give any clues as to how many unfortunate courtiers suffered this fate. If Musa himself needed to sneeze, all those present beat their chests to drown out the sound. Nobody was allowed to see him eat – he always took care to eat in private, even when travelling. The aura of a semi-divine king had to be preserved at all times.

One law, dating back to the previous Ghanian rule, established the Malian kings' wealth in perpetuity. This dictated that all larger pieces of gold were rightfully the property of the Mansa. 'Larger' meant anything weighing more than a few grams – in other words pretty much everything of value. The miners were allowed to keep gold dust and flakes. The empire taxed every ounce that crossed its borders, while private buying and selling of gold within the empire was banned and, inevitably, punishable by death. All gold excavated or found had to be weighed, bagged and immediately handed over to the treasury, thus guaranteeing the king a steady and inexhaustible supply of wealth. It probably didn't cross Musa's mind that any of these practices might constitute extortion. After all everything belonged to him to begin with.

The King was possessed of a restless ambition. No matter how rich he was (a figure that was not calculated), he suspected his subjects could be doing better. He concluded that the best way to increase productivity, and therefore his own income, was to grant the operators of the lucrative gold mines a certain degree of autonomy. In an early example of profit sharing as a form of incentive, he decreed that they could keep more of the small amounts, as long as the rest went to him. He had learned from experience that when direct rule was too strictly imposed, the workers engaged in go-slows and production declined dramatically. Musa would not make that mistake. His tactic worked spectacularly. He sat back, relying on copious amounts of tribute from the mines, which duly arrived. His treasure chest for his trip to Mecca grew steadily.

The story of the Mansa's extraordinary Hajj has been passed down over the centuries through oral histories and journals. Arab writers and travellers have filled in some of the gaps, providing a broader overview of the people and places of the times. Some of the writings have lain hidden for years. Thousands of manuscripts are still to be deciphered from private collections that have been handed down by Malian families over the ages and have only recently come to light.

One of the most important accounts comes from the late fifteenth-century man of letters and diplomat Mahmud Kati. His work, *Tarikh Al-Fetach*, was translated first into French in 1913 and then into English as *The Chronicle of the Seeker of Knowledge*. It is not known whether he finished the book or left that task to his descendants. Referring to Mansa Musa as the 'Mali-koy Kankan Musa', Mahmud Kati describes him as 'an upright, godly and devout sultan'. He adds: 'His dominion stretched from the limits of Mali as far as Sibiridugu [now Sierra Leone], and all the peoples in these lands, Songhay and others, obeyed him. Among the signs of his virtue are that he used to emancipate a slave every day, that he made the pilgrimage to the sacred house of God, and that in the course of his pilgrimage he built the great mosque of Timbuktu.'

While corroborating much of the oral history, Kati produces a novel explanation for Musa's Hajj:

His mother Kankan was a native woman, though some say she was of Arab origin. The cause of his pilgrimage was related to me as follows by the scholar Muhammad Quma, may God have mercy on him, who had memorized the traditions of the ancients. He said that the Mali-koy Kankan Musa had killed his mother, Nana Kankan, by mistake. For this he felt deep regret and remorse and feared retribution. In expiation he gave great sums of money in alms and resolved on a life-long fast. He asked one of the ulama [wise men] of his time what he could do to expiate this terrible crime, and he replied, 'You should seek refuge with the Prophet of God, may God bless and save him. Flee to him, place yourself under his protection, and ask him to intercede for you with God, and God will accept his intercession. That is my view.' Kankan Musa made up his mind that very day and began to collect the money and equipment needed for the journey. He sent proclamations to all parts of his realm.

Musa, it is written, 'set out in force, with much money and a numerous army'. The social structure for his entourage was rigid. Everyone knew their place and their role. First came specially selected soldiers, up to eight thousand in all. Following them was the Mansa's special unit of five hundred, marching in front of him, each bearing an ornamental staff made of gold. Then came Musa himself, on his horse, then his wife, in a carriage. Surrounding them were the nobles, then the merchants — all with slaves to be bought and sold as required along the journey. 'The members of his entourage proceeded to buy Turkish and Ethiopian slave girls, singing girls and garments,' wrote the fifteenth-century Egyptian historian al-Maqrizi, 'so that the rate of the gold dinar fell by six dirhams. Having presented his gift he set off with the caravan.'

Another famous chronicler was the Moroccan adventurer Ibn Battuta, who traced Musa's route only months after he had completed it. This is one account he wrote of a later journey, undertaken by a wealthy Iraqi pilgrim in 1326:

Included in this caravan were many water-carrying camels for the poorer pilgrims, who could obtain drinking water from them, and other camels to carry provisions for distribution as alms and to carry medicines, potions and sugar for those who should be attacked by illness. Whenever the caravan halted, food was cooked in great brass cauldrons, called dasts, and supplied from them to the poorer pilgrims and those who had no provisions.

Social convention required the wealthy to provide goods to the poor whenever they travelled. This form of charity was the closest society came to the provision of even the most basic income. The more a man was worth, the more generosity was expected of him (a stricture that would be adopted centuries later by the likes of Andrew Carnegie and Warren Buffett). Musa took philanthropy, or at least his interpretation of it, extremely seriously. Wherever his caravan stopped, he ordered his men to distribute large amounts of gold. His instructions were flamboyant, but usually vague. How much should be given away and to whom? With a dismissive wave of the hand, Musa would leave the business side to the merchants travelling with him.

The further they travelled eastwards across Africa, the more the news spread. Mansa Musa was a sensation. When the caravan arrived in the smallest village or the largest town, the local folk stopped what they were doing to gawp at this exotic king from a strange land. The mid-twentieth-century historian E.W. Bovill suggests that Musa 'was, in fact, the first to penetrate the iron curtain of colour prejudice which shut off the Negro from the civilised world'.[2] Residents of fourteenth-century Mali might well have made the claim that theirs was the civilised world, compared to the poorer nations north of the Mediterranean.

As his caravan emerged from its arduous trek through the Sahara Desert it finally reached Cairo. Musa decreed that it should stop in the shadows of the pyramids, to take stock. Cairo was one of the world's great cities and also the world's largest gold market. He needed to make the right impression. They camped on the edge of town for several days, before entering through the western gate to a tumultuous welcome. Historians have questioned the reasons for the delay. It is possible that Musa was showing respect to his hosts by avoiding a display of triumphalism, ensuring that he was not treading on the toes of the Egyptian Sultan and his court. More likely is that he was competing for reputation. Musa wanted to be seen as the more pious of the two leaders, the more prestigious, even. Protocol required that on meeting the Sultan, Musa would be the one who would have to bow down before him. For Musa, that would be a humiliation.

One of the Sultan's officials, Al-Abbas Ahmad, related the story to the scholar and historian Chihab al-Umari a few years later: 'When I went out to meet him, on the orders of the great Sultan, al-Malik al-Nasir, he treated me generously and attended to me most respectfully.

But he would not speak to me except through an interpreter, although he mastered Arabic. Then he sent to the royal treasury a great amount of gold nuggets.' This gift is estimated to have been worth as much as fifty thousand dinars, the equivalent of £6 million today: not ungenerous, it would seem, as a token gesture of respect. Musa's agenda was clear: he wanted to show the Sultan the extent of his wealth. Status was everything. But he didn't reckon on the effect his largesse would have on the market. This sum, added to other gifts he had already bestowed during his journey, sent the price of gold plummeting. Al-Umari, writing ten years after the event, estimated that the gold price in Egypt was still at least 10 per cent below its previous level. No single act of generosity (or cavalier disregard) has had such a long-lasting effect.

As to the meeting with the Sultan, an artful compromise was agreed, just in time. 'When we stood in the presence of the Sultan we asked [the Malian King] to prostrate and kiss the floor,' Al-Abbas Ahmad reported. Musa 'hesitated and seemed to be ready to refuse stubbornly. One of his companions whispered something into his ear, after which the guest said "I prostrate to Allah who has created me." Then he prostrated.' The formula allowed both sides to save face. Musa was more willing to throw a vast fortune of gold at the Sultan than to bow before him – he had all the wealth that earthly life could bring. What mattered were reputation and status.

After leaving Cairo for the final leg to Mecca, Mansa Musa stumbled upon another tense question – who was responsible for the upkeep of the holy sites? Cairo had previously been ruled by the Shi'ite Fatimid dynasty, which had courted controversy by making money out of pilgrims. Islamic legal scholars had decreed that a tax on pilgrims was illegal under *sharia* law, but the Fatimids, as other rulers over the centuries have done, got away with it anyway. When Saladin overthrew them in 1169, one of his first acts was to abolish the taxes, a decision that brought him considerable popularity. Ibn Jubayr wrote of the money-making schemes run by the Fatimids and their allies in the cities of the Hejaz: 'They [the pilgrims] were constrained to pay seven and a half dinars per head, even though they were incapable of doing so. One type of punishment they had invented was to hang them by their testicles, or some other frightful thing. At Jidda equal or worse tortures awaited those who had not paid the tax at Aydhab and whose names were not accompanied by a notice of payment.'

Musa saw a business opportunity – taking advantage of the alienation felt by some worshippers towards their earthly rulers. He stepped up his distribution of gold, specifically to those travelling to Mecca, to fund their journeys and accommodation there. He particularly wanted to make a show of his piety and munificence on a Friday, the Muslim day of prayer. It was on that day, and only that day, each week that he ordered the construction of a mosque wherever his entourage had reached: philanthropy with a purpose, a familiar formula.

In a matter of months an obscure king from a faraway land had become a key player in the political and religious firmament. Spurred on by the tumultuous receptions he encountered, Musa ordered his merchants to hand out ever more gold dust, in increasing quantities and speed. Such was his steady supply of income from the goldfields back home that he was quite prepared to spend everything he had brought with him – or perhaps he had no interest in counting. Just as the caravan was reaching the holiest of cities, his courtiers had the tricky task of informing the King that he was running low. To their surprise and evident relief, he was not unduly perturbed. The investment had brought dividends. Across North and West Africa and into the heart of the Islamic world, Musa's Hajj had brought him huge attention.

For his journey back to Mali, Musa found himself in the curious position of having to borrow money. His business skills were not always as acute as might have been assumed for a man of his means. Moneylenders in Cairo and other places en route knew that Musa would have no problem repaying the loans once he was home, so they demanded whatever rates of interest they fancied. They had seen what had happened on Musa's outward journey, when local merchants had taken advantage of the gold rush to sell their wares at artificially inflated prices. The items that had most attracted Musa's retinue were fine clothes and female slaves, which Egyptians had sold at up to five times their market values. Musa saw another opportunity to boost his prestige. He offered to pay back any loan at the startlingly high interest rate of 150 per cent. He could have negotiated a lower rate, but he was keen to confirm his generosity, to show that people like him did not have to try too hard.

Fourteenth-century Mali produced two-thirds of the world's gold. The most valuable and prestigious of all rare metals – of all commodities – was to be found in a single kingdom of half a million square miles. One man, and one man alone, had access to it. Such a concentration of ownership in one country of this most alluring of commodities has never again been repeated. This monopoly brought untold riches to Mali, but its value was greater than that. It was the ultimate demonstration of prestige, in a way that a similar wealth of, say, oil or aluminium could never be.

To understand the legend of Mansa Musa, it is important to consider for a moment the psychological value of gold. Humans have long had a love affair with it that is part monetary, part aesthetic, part emotional. Its rarity is central to each of these considerations. Even today, after centuries of ever-advancing mining technology, the world's total reserves of gold would fit into one oil tanker.[3] Gold has always been about more than money, which is a more prosaic and transactional concept. Unlike other metals in the pre-modern age, it had no use but for its public display or for its private keeping in life and burial in death.

Ancient kings would speak of their gold *treasure* rather than their gold *treasury*; its iridescence gave it an ethereal quality. Some indigenous peoples have believed the metal to come from the sun and the gods. For the Ashanti kings, possession of gold elevated them to a superior status, allowing them to communicate with gods and ancestors. Likewise, in death, it has been common in both West Africa and other cultures around the world for the rich to be buried with their gold ornaments, or for their bodies to be sprinkled with gold. Gold was something to be hoarded, kept locked away and coveted by jealous neighbours. Croesus, the Anatolian king whose name became synonymous with material wealth, was certainly a hoarder. Like many ancient rulers, his vast gold reserves were not for circulation, except when he would ostentatiously bear gifts. On one occasion, he gave an oracle 117 ingots of pure gold each weighing 150 pounds, plus a golden lion weighing 600 pounds.[4]

Gradually, people came to realise that gold was much more useful as a means of exchange than as an object to own. By the Middle Ages, it had become the world's primary currency for trade. But unlike wealthy kingdoms such as Mali, cash-poor Europe still had extremely small amounts of it. Hence the demonic zeal to acquire as much of this magical substance as possible among the early colonialists in the Americas and Africa: the gold rush.

Mali's kings controlled three significant goldfields – at Bambuk, Bouré and Galam. Most of the gold was easy to excavate, from panning and shallow digging. Bouré became the region's principal goldfield in the twelfth century, shifting the centre of power southwards from Ghana to Mali. The mansas controlled access to Timbuktu and the cross-Sahara camel routes. There the bullion traders paid a heavy tribute to local middlemen and, from them, to the ruler. A generation after Musa's pilgrimage, it was said that gold was being used in Mali to manufacture not only jewellery but musical instruments and, rather impractically, weapons of war.[5] The preponderance of gold in Malian society gave its inhabitants a reputation in North Africa as people who would pay over the odds for traded goods – just as Musa had on his Hajj. Cairo's merchants told al-Umari: 'one of them might buy a shirt or cloak or robe or other garment for five dinars when it was not worth one'.[6] While most of the population in Musa's kingdom were poor, families would own perhaps one prized possession or item of jewellery made from gold, which would be used on special occasions like marriages. If they could not afford that, painted clay jewellery served as a suitable alternative, and was regarded as aesthetically acceptable.

After gold, the second most important symbol of power was horses. The difficulty and expense involved in bringing them to the desert kingdom, and keeping them, added to their symbolic and financial value. The animals would be taken across the Sahara, and once in Mali those that survived would be assiduously attended by up to six slaves. The ultimate status symbol was achieved when one of the kings of the Soninke Empire, another gold-rich country to the west of Mali, was able to 'tether his horse with a gold nugget as large as a big stone'.[7]

Yet, if the legend is to be believed, Musa was not overwhelmed by the allure of gold or other demonstrations of ostentation. He had been born into wealth. One might even say he was bored with it. He needed a new challenge and found it in religion.

Overcome by the piety of the Hajj, he resolved to give up all his other obligations and to devote himself to worship. Al-Umari claimed that the Mansa was so deeply affected by the pilgrimage that he intended to return to Niani only briefly, in order to sort out his affairs of state, 'with the intention of abdicating in favour of his son and leaving all power in his hands, so that he might return to the Venerable Mecca to live in the neighbourhood of its sanctuary'.

It is impossible to know how much of Musa's journey was driven by the need for status and recognition, and how much was motivated by real religious feeling. It is likely to have been inspired by both. Money, power and religion were inextricably linked. After the conversion of the ruling class to Islam in the thirteenth century, religious credibility contributed to the political legitimacy of the rulers of Mali. The Keita clan, to which Musa and most other mansas belonged, claimed to be descended from Bilal ibn Rabah, the first muezzin – or prayer caller – in the Islamic religion. This claim may well have been invented, although it is known that Bilal was black.

While Musa was in Mecca, emissaries from Mali had travelled all the way to keep him abreast of developments back home. The news was not good: the people were discontented. His son, Mansa Maghan, who had been left in charge (just as Musa himself had been when his own father went on his travels), had by all accounts performed poorly – an occupational hazard, perhaps, of the second-generation wealthy. Maghan had allowed the city of Gao to fall into rebel Songhay hands, and his subjects were restive.

Musa was despondent, realising he would not be able to realise his goal of passing on his wealth and relinquishing power to his son. He settled on a compromise. He would return to his kingdom, but instead of projecting its worth through its gold, he dedicated the remaining years of his rule to spreading Islam throughout his territory. He began straight away. Before leaving the holy city to start his return, he offered a large payment of gold coins to any scholar who could claim lineage from the Prophet Mohammed and who would settle in Mali with their family. Mahmud Kati takes up the story: 'The Mali-koy then sent a crier to the mosques to say, "Whoever wishes to have a thousand *mithqals* of gold, let him follow me to my country, and the thousand is ready for him.'" Four took the King up on his offer. He also attracted the poet and architect Abu Ishaq Ibrahim al-Sahili from Granada in Muslim Spain. Before he could put his new spiritual plans for Mali into action, he needed to restore order. He took a detour to Gao on his journey back home. Spurred on by the Musa's decision to stay on the throne, one of his generals, Sagmandir, re-established the authority of the Malian Empire in the city, driving out the rebels. Musa entered Gao in a lavish procession. He reminded his subjects of his power by taking the two sons of his new vassal hostage.

Mansa Musa should be remembered not merely for his gold or his journey to Mecca, remarkable though the story is. He was also responsible for bringing to life one of civilisation's great cities, Timbuktu, where he embarked on a mosque-building programme of breathtaking speed.

The city has long evoked a sense of remoteness and danger. As the *Oxford English Dictionary* puts it, it is 'the most distant place imaginable'. Founded by Tuareg nomads in the twelfth century, it was only in Mansa Musa's time that it became a global centre of culture and learning. Known as the City of Gold, it grew to be the most prominent of the four hundred towns and cities in his realm. One scholar wrote: 'It covers a wide area, favourable to cultivation, densely populated, with flourishing markets. It is now the terminus for caravans from the Maghrib, Ifriqiyya and Egypt, and goods are brought there from every quarter.'[8]

The Malian Empire sat between the lucrative gold mines of West Africa and the fertile Niger River, the vital transportation hub for the landlocked country. The location provided perfect trading opportunities in commodities ranging from gold and silver to textiles and leather, from rice and figs to nuts and wine. Gold and silver were traded from Tunis to the particularly valuable European markets of Valencia, Naples and Florence. Cities on these trading routes, including Timbuktu and Gao, attracted skilled metalworkers and goldsmiths, known as *sanu fagala*, or 'killers of gold'.[9]

Europeans, from Granada to Genoa, wanted gold. The miners of sub-Saharan Africa wanted salt. The sources of the two commodities were far from each other, so middlemen would cut the deals in Timbuktu, Walata and Gao. They engaged in the practice of 'silent trade'. Merchants would lay their wares out on the floor of the market and depart. Buyers would enter and place the amount of gold they were willing to pay next to the goods – then leave themselves. The merchants would return and, if they deemed that the gold equalled the value of the product, the trade would be done. The Sudanese slave trade was also conducted through these towns, where the enslaved souls had no prospect of escape save for running into the endless Sahara.

Musa's job was to provide safety for the traders to conduct their business, and reap the rewards in tolls and taxes. Ibn Battuta wrote that the King's large standing army made the country safer than most from bandits.[10] Fear of the Mansa's wrath made the trade routes of Africa relatively secure at a time when many of the highways of Europe were lawless and dangerous.

In Timbuktu, the architect al-Sahili built Sankore Madrasah, an ancient centre of learning that would promote scholarship among thousands of astronomers, mathematicians and Islamic jurists each year. Another grand building was the Jingereber Mosque, dating to around 1327, immediately after Musa's return from the Hajj. Together with Sankore and the Sidi Yahya Mosque, the Jingereber may have constituted the world's first university – not that Western historians would have known or given credit.* Such was the unrivalled beauty and grandeur of the city in the fourteenth century that it gave rise to the West African proverb: 'Salt comes from the north, gold from the south and silver from the country of the white men, but the word of God and the treasures of wisdom are only to be found in Timbuktu.'[11]

Under Musa, the Malian Empire was not only wealthy but of a staggering size, second only to the Mongol Empire. Unlike Genghis Khan, who had ruled with such brutality a century earlier, Musa was less prone to using violence to subjugate the many peoples under his rule. He controlled all facets of life in his lands, but he did so with dexterity.

---

* It was designated a World Heritage site by UNESCO in 1988, along with the Great Mosque of Djenne. It still stands today, although it was badly damaged by Islamist fighters in 2012.

He appointed all the provincial governors (*ferbas*) and mayors (*mochrifs*), but he granted the provinces and cities, particularly rich ones like Timbuktu, considerable autonomy to run their own affairs – so long as they pledged allegiance to him and handed over all the riches they produced. Musa had at various times during his reign between thirteen and twenty-four vassal rulers paying tribute to him.

The man of letters, Kati, concludes his chronicle with the following observation: 'As for Mali, it is a vast region and an immense country, containing many towns and villages. The authority of the Sultan of Mali extends over all with force and might. We have heard the common people of our time say that there are four sultans in the world, not counting the supreme sultan, and they are the Sultan of Baghdad, the Sultan of Egypt, the Sultan of Bornu, and the Sultan of Mali.'

After Musa's death his empire began to wane. Ibn Battuta eventually made it back to Mali from his Hajj, only to find a new ruler on the throne. It wasn't Mansa Musa's son, Mansa Maghan. As feared, he proved a useless leader and was ousted after only four years by his uncle, Mansa Sulayman. According to Battuta, Sulayman was also a great disappointment, but such was Mansa Musa's prestige that it probably would have been impossible for anyone to emulate him. The 'generous and virtuous' Musa had passed on his own and his nation's wealth to Sulayman, 'a miserly king from whom no great donation is to be expected', the chronicler wrote.

Much of the Musa story is conjecture, dependent as it is on the writings of a small number of Arab scholars and oral histories. Even his death is a matter of guesswork: estimates of the year range from 1332 to 1337. But while some details of his life might be vague or disputed, his significance is not. He not only controlled markets – he was the only man to have directly controlled the price of gold to Mediterranean consumers – but established a model for philanthropy, albeit a crude one that would be refined by later generations of the global super-rich.

He set an example that for centuries many others followed, particularly in the Muslim world. Hajj pilgrims in subsequent centuries were merchants hoping to make new contacts and expand their businesses. Islamic theorists saw trade as an admirable vocation, not incompatible with piety. The sixteenth-century Ottoman scholar Hasan Celebi Kinalizade later advised sovereigns: 'According to the Imam Shafi'i, commerce was the best [way of acquiring wealth] because it was the Prophet Mohammed's noble profession.' He added: 'In the acquisition of wealth, one should refrain first from oppression and injustice; secondly from shameful activities, and thirdly from disgraceful or dirty occupations.'

Musa's Hajj galvanised traders around the world, who heard of the potential riches in his kingdom. Almost none of them, however, knew how to get there, which led to a sudden demand for reliable routes. In 1339, Mali appeared for the first time on a European *mappa mundi* – map of the world. The man depicted on it was named 'Rex Melly' (King of Mali).[12] The navigational chart drawn up by Angelino Dulcert of Majorca was completed shortly after Musa's death. They were not to know then that with the demise of Musa the allure, and wealth, of Mali would steadily diminish.

In 1367, another map showed a road leading from North Africa through the Atlas Mountains into western Sudan. In 1375 a third map, the Catalan Atlas, showed a richly attired monarch holding a large gold nugget in the area south of the Sahara. It was drawn up for Charles V of France by an Aragonese Jew called Abraham Cresques, presumably on the basis of information passed on by traders who had made the journey across the Sahara. Musa appears seated, dressed in royal robes and a crown, with a golden sceptre in one hand and a large gold nugget in the other. Approaching him is a trader riding a camel, representing the caravans that gave Mali its enormous wealth. The accompanying Latin inscription reads: 'This Negro lord is called Musa Mali, Lord of the Negroes of Guinea. So abundant is the gold which is found in the country that he is the richest and most noble king in all the land.'[13] The cartographers and illustrators who produced the fourteenth-century maps may not have known details of Musa's physical appearance. They dressed him in ways they found familiar, making him look like a European or North African king.

Cartographers, just as historians, reflect their times, and by the mid-fifteenth century, when Portuguese explorers first reached Mali, the kingdom was a shadow of its former greatness. As a result, the Mansa

Musa depicted on the maps of the 1480s was a parody of imperial preju-
dices – a naked savage with a crown.

By then, the Malian Empire was withering away, weakened by palace
intrigue that prevented an orderly succession of imperial power and by
the desire of smaller states to break free of its rule to reap the benefits
of the salt and gold trade. Its trade routes had lost their attraction for a
new generation of Europeans who had taken to the sea, rather than
trekking across the desert. Most important of all, by the end of the fourteenth century the price of gold had slumped. The Songhay Empire
captured Timbuktu in 1468. The loss of the City of Gold was a major
blow in revenue and prestige for Mali, which was succeeded by neighbouring Songhay as the regional superpower. The foundations laid by
Musa on his return from the Hajj had been squandered.

Even under the Songhay rulers, Timbuktu continued to thrive for
a while. Such was the city's power and wealth that the new kings kept
a large military presence there, in case Timbuktu decided to go it alone
and break from the rest of their empire. They did, however, give it a
certain amount of autonomy on matters of learning. Some 180 Koranic
schools were operating at that time, enrolling 5000 students.[14]
Possession of the written word – in the form of books – came to be an
important new symbol of wealth and power in a society where gold had
long been relatively common. Wealthy citizens spent their time amassing libraries, debating sacred texts, trying to outdo each other with their
knowledge of Islamic law and jurisprudence. Only so many mosques
could be refurbished, but, if one was wealthy enough, the number of
books that could be commissioned, produced and collected was almost
infinite. The Andalusian chronicler Leo Africanus noted: 'Here are
great stores of doctors, judges, priests, and other learned men, that are
bountifully maintained at the King's cost and charges. And hither are
brought diverse manuscripts and written books out of Barbary, which
are sold for more money than any other merchandise.'[15]

This was a rare age when reputations were made not through war or
conquest, but through education. Timbuktu's scholars would travel
widely and study in the rest of the Muslim world, such as at the al-
Azhar Mosque in Cairo and the Qarawiyyin Mosque in Fez, Morocco.
Timbuktu may have been a place of knowledge, but that knowledge

was carefully curated and kept out of the hands of the poor. Public libraries did not exist. To be inducted into the literate, intellectual elite, one had to be of the right stock, educated at one of the city's schools, personally connected with the scholars themselves. The clerical elite was unlikely to have numbered more than three hundred men.

The city became increasingly vulnerable to outside powers. Initially, a group of Tuaregs held sway. The nominal ruler, Akil, lived outside the city and appointed an agent, Ammar, to collect his taxes. Ammar would do so on the promise that he received one-third of the income, but every time he did his job Akil would ride into town with his men and make off with all the money.[16] Understandably riled, Ammar wrote to the Songhay offering to betray his ruler and turn the city back to them. The Songhay army gladly obliged and pillaged the city for their trouble.

The empire came suddenly to a juddering halt. Some 250 years after Mansa Musa had used his vast gold reserves to turn Timbuktu into one of the world's great cities, an onslaught from the north put an end to that dream. In 1591, the ruler of Morocco, Sultan Ahmad al-Mansur, sent an expeditionary force of mercenaries, led by Judar Pasha, to overcome the Songhay. They besieged Timbuktu, killing or jailing most of its scholars. The pretext for the attack was the same old quest for control of resources – domination of the salt and gold trade across the Sahara.[17] The Sultan's excuse for the carnage was the failure of the Songhay to pay one particular tariff. Ahmad had a further reason for invading: control of such a prestigious Islamic city would help his claim to be Caliph – nominal head of the Muslim world – which he was pressing against rival Ottoman sultans.

The assault on Malian culture was on an epic scale. By way of example, the writer and scholar Ahmad Baba al-Massufi, who was deported to Morocco, had sixteen hundred volumes from his personal collection stolen or destroyed by the invaders. He claimed that his was the smallest library of any of his peers. Tens of thousands of irreplaceable documents must have been lost to history as a result of the invasion. All Timbuktu's money could not buy back the city's lost culture. It would never retrieve its position as a centre of learning and the written word. One of Musa's most important legacies was destroyed.

By this point, the Europeans had begun their slave trade on the west coast of Africa. Many inhabitants from the Malian and Songhay empires were summarily shipped off. Europe's imperial entanglement with the continent lasted a further five hundred years. Africa became in the popular imagination a primitive area that required civilising. To Victorians, the idea that there could have been an African society comparable to the British Empire in terms of wealth and cultural influence would have been laughable. As the centre of global wealth shifted to Europe, the former riches of African and Asian societies were forgotten or ignored. Mali, after its disintegration, was a failed state. Timbuktu was an impoverished and forgotten town of mud-walled buildings, synonymous with the ends of the earth. Almost all traces of Mali's greatness had disappeared. Poverty and greed, coupled with shifting fashions in the West for 'exotic' art from far away, led to systematic looting of archaeological sites. The history of Mansa Musa was erased.

The contrast with the fame he had acquired during his life could not be more stark. In both extremes, ethnicity may have a role to play. His looks certainly made an impression en route to Mecca. Musa played up the exoticism and novelty of the wealthy black African Muslim ruler on the Hajj. Ever conscious of his image, ever eager to prove himself, he became his own spin-doctor during his travels, telling extravagant stories of Mali as a land of unimaginable wealth. According to al-Umari, Musa told North Africans of a 'gold plant that blossoms after the rains' which sported 'leaves like grass and roots of gold'. Malians and other sub-Saharan Africans referred to lighter-skinned Arabs, such as the traveller Ibn Battuta, as 'white men'. There was clearly a sense of different ethnic identities, but not of one being superior to the other. Ibn Battuta was impressed with the wealth and scholarship he found in Mali, and Mansa Musa had paid due homage to the Arab rulers he met on his pilgrimage. It was only the arrival of European imperialism that brought ideas of racial superiority and relegated African wealth to the footnotes of history.

Mali was 'rediscovered' in the early years of European colonisation of Africa in the first half of the nineteenth century. In 1829, Alfred Lord Tennyson described it as mysterious and unfathomable in his poem

'Timbuctoo'. Such was the town's allure that he compared it to the great lost city of gold, El Dorado, and the mythical island of Atlantis. In the carve-up of the continent, France seized the land that had comprised much of the Malian Empire, subsuming it into their greater French Sudan. Throughout this period, it was seen as a cultural backwater, a staging post initially for slaves and then for other commodities. From the 1890s onwards, the French West African economy was based on plantations for goods like cotton. To save shipping costs, workers were brought to work on the coast; the interior of the continent remained underdeveloped. Once again, Mali had fallen victim to a commodity-driven economy, this time one which left the vast majority of the population impoverished.

The notion of an African cultural heritage was deemed absurd. One traveller exclaimed: 'I have not described the country of the African blacks, because naturally loving wisdom, ingenuity, religion, justice and regular government, how could I notice such people as these.'[18] French imperial politician Jules Ferry said in the 1880s: 'The higher races have a right over the lower races, they have a duty to civilise the inferior races.' Mali's inhabitants would be classed as subjects, not citizens of the French Republic. The French found themselves unable to imagine a chapter of history in which an African kingdom held sway over such vast lands and commanded respect so far away.

Yet, thanks to the ingenuity and dedication of many Malians, thousands of manuscripts were stashed away in private 'libraries' – hidden from Moroccan and then European invaders in wooden trunks or buried in boxes under the sand or in caves. The first concerted attempt to uncover and better preserve Mali's ancient scrolls got under way in 1970, when UNESCO helped establish the Ahmed Baba Institute for Documentation and Research in Timbuktu (named after the great sixteenth-century scholar). Gradually it collected and documented some twenty thousand irreplaceable manuscripts dating back to 1204 – that is, before even Mansa Musa's time. Many were unbound and in very poor condition. Termites had eaten into some. But the painstaking work produced remarkable historical gems. The vast majority of the documents were written in Arabic. A few were in African languages, such as Songhai and Tamashek. One was in Hebrew. They covered subjects ranging from astronomy to music, medicine, poetry and even women's rights.

In 1993 UNESCO stepped in again, this time to try to stop the removal from the country of valuable cultural artefacts, notably clay statues from Musa's time.[19] A 2003 report by the US philanthropic body the Ford Foundation detailed the richness of the work that had been discovered, noting: 'Upon closer inspection, they may compel scholars to rewrite the history of Islam and of Africa and to abolish once and for all the persistent Western stereotype of black Africans as primitive and lacking in intellectual traditions.'

In 2012, one of the modern world's greatest acts of cultural vandalism took place. Tuareg rebels – some of whom had fled Libya after the Western-led overthrow of Muammar Gaddafi – seized the north of the country, removed the President and declared a fundamentalist Islamic state. They seized Timbuktu in April of that year and began imposing a strict version of *sharia* law, carrying out amputations and public executions. Women could be whipped for going out in public without a veil, while men could be lashed for smoking cigarettes. At the same time the rebels systematically destroyed cultural sites, including the ancient tombs of Sufi saints, which they denounced as contrary to Islam, because they encouraged Muslims to venerate saints instead of Allah. French forces eventually drove them out and restored a semblance of order, but as they retreated, the Islamist forces set fire to the Ahmed Baba Institute and Timbuktu's library. By the time of the destruction only a fraction of the documents had been digitised. Much of the collection was lost just when hope had been growing that the world would be given the opportunity to appreciate the great culture of the Malian Empire.

The rebels are gone, for the moment, but Mali remains extremely fragile. It is now one of the ten poorest nations in the world, even though it is the third-largest producer of gold in Africa (after South Africa and Ghana). There is no more miserable example of a country under the curse of a single commodity. A recent report by Human Rights Watch described villagers working in primitive and dangerous conditions, digging holes with picks to excavate gold. They burrow shafts up to sixty metres deep, often lowering down children to dig out whatever they can find. Uranium is often used to separate the various metals in the ore, without any protection. These so-called artisanal mines produce an income of a couple of dollars a day for adults and about fifty cents a day for children as young as six. Whatever gold dust or nuggets are found are handed over to middlemen, ending up in designer jewellery stores in Manhattan or Zurich. Half the entire population lives below the UN-recognised poverty line of $1.25 a day. Yet that same commodity gold was, eight centuries before, at the heart of that same country's wealth and imperial power. Many African societies have fallen victim to the commodity curse, from the subjugation of ancient Egypt to Rome thanks to its grain, to the Congo of Mobutu and the kleptocrats in the twentieth century (see Chapter 10).

Eight centuries after his death, Mansa Musa is now recognised for his ostentatious wealth, alongside his power and patronage of great culture. He routinely makes it to the top of lists of the richest people of all time. The name Mansa Musa might have been remembered in the same way as Cosimo de' Medici is synonymous with great learning and art in Renaissance Florence (see Chapter 4). Yet his story is little known and little told. His legacy is still in the early stages of being uncovered and appreciated. He was the ultimate man of inherited and unearned wealth, who had to do nothing to earn his riches, but watch and wait as the gold revenues poured in. Yet he was a man of piety and learning, creating universities and promoting the development of his vast domain. His patronage would match, perhaps exceed, that of any of the super-rich throughout history.

CHAPTER 4

Cosimo de' Medici – Art, money and conscience

What good is wealth sitting in the bank? It's a
pretty pathetic thing to do with your money.
Ted Turner

He was passionate about his profession: 'Even if money could be made
by waving a wand, I would still be a banker.'[1] So declared Cosimo de'
Medici, uncrowned king of the Florentine Republic, creditor to the
Pope.

In 1397, Giovanni di Bicci de' Medici founded the Medici Bank in
Florence. Almost a century later, in 1494, the bank collapsed, but a
dynasty had been established, providing a succession of pontiffs and
royals. The moneymen had achieved the pinnacle of respectability.
Cosimo, the most successful financier of the family, knew every rule . . .
and how to get around them. A man who made his money through
monopolies, cartels and illicit deals was at the centre of a network that
stretched across Europe.

He is now remembered not for that, but as one of the great figures
of art history, a sponsor of the Renaissance. For almost half of the fifteenth century he ruled Florence, even though he held few official
titles. Bribery was his chosen method for building his business and
preserving his market monopoly. Even when imprisoned early in his

career, as rival factions sought to eliminate his threat, he ensured he had friends in the right places to save him.

The story of Cosimo de' Medici – or Cosimo the Elder, as he is now remembered – is about money and conscience. He built up his father's business, turning it into a banking empire through usury, a sin before God. And which organisation was the chief beneficiary of his loans? The papacy. In a classic auditing sleight of hand that would do the modern super-rich proud, the books were drawn up differently, exploiting loopholes to get around usury accusations. Yet, as he neared the end of his life, Cosimo was troubled by his actions. God, he feared, would see through his dealings but perhaps would pardon him if he dedicated his wealth to higher causes.

Cosimo devoted much of the family fortune to creating a new Florence. He built palaces and churches and amassed one of the largest libraries in Europe, commissioning the translation of Plato's entire works into Latin. He supported artists from Donatello to Fra Angelico. He was one of the founding fathers of the humanist movement that became the bedrock of Italian life. On his death, he earned the title *pater patriae*, father of the fatherland.

He set an example for future generations, from the American robber barons who gave their names to museums and charitable endowments, to the giants of finance and technology in the twenty-first century. It mattered less how the money was earned, so long as some of it would later be put to good use. Medici's patronage – born largely of the fear of divine retribution – helped to cleanse his reputation for posterity.

The Italy of the fourteenth century was a fractured mass of principalities and republics, beset by war and pestilence. Each of the major cities had its own government and constitution, joining and breaking alliances with the others at will. At the heart of the turbulence was the rivalry between the Holy Roman Empire in the north and the Papal States of the south, both claiming to be the moral leader of the Christian world. In rural areas, the feudal rights of the old-school nobles depended on recognition from the Empire, whereas in the cities the newly emerging urban classes backed the Pope. The politics of the Italian states were in constant flux, as factions multiplied, cities declared independence, and coups were plotted.

At the heart of this internecine swamp was the Florentine Republic. More than half of its people had been killed by the bubonic plague of 1348. In all, a third of Europe's population was wiped out. Politics in the city were in turmoil. The mercantile class, which had gradually been usurping the power of the nobles, found themselves at the wrong end of a rebellion. In June 1378 the city's wool workers attacked official buildings, briefly taking over the government and demanding greater rights on behalf of poor workers not represented by any of the city's guilds. This *Ciompi* Rebellion – the name deriving from the clogs the rioters wore in the wash houses – was repulsed in a couple of months after the guilds, led by the butchers, closed ranks. But the insurrection traumatised the established order. It influenced the thinking of Niccolò Machiavelli.

The Medicis were in a mess. They had made the wrong call in supporting the revolt. As punishment, all branches of the family were exiled, with one exception – Averardo de' Medici. It was his son, Giovanni di Bicci de' Medici, who founded the bank that bore the name; his grandson was Cosimo de' Medici. The family tree can be traced back to the early part of the thirteenth century, gradually making its way up the social ladder through the wool trade. Over the next five centuries the Medicis would become one of the great families in Europe, producing four popes and a dynasty that would be enshrined as a hereditary dukedom.

The first Medici of any prominence was Giovanni. His rise was slow and cautious. He had concluded from the *Ciompi* episode, from wars and civil strife, and from the precariousness of wealth that the best – perhaps the only – way to succeed was to keep your head down. Rich merchants were required to participate in government from time to time, but whenever his name was put forward Giovanni would rather accept fines than serve. On his deathbed, he warned his sons: 'With regard to state affairs, if you would live in security, take just such a share as the laws and your countrymen think proper to bestow, thus you will escape both danger and envy; for it is not what is given to any individual, but what he has determined to possess, that occasions odium.'

He added: 'Do not appear to give advice, but put your views forward discreetly in conversation. Be wary of going to the Palazzo della Signoria; wait to be summoned, and when you are summoned, do what you are asked to do and never display any pride should you receive a lot of votes.'

He concluded with his most important instruction: 'avoid litigation and political controversy, and always keep out of the public eye'.[2]

Giovanni's was not a rags-to-riches story, but neither was he wealthy; he and his brothers shared a small inheritance of eight hundred florins on their mother's death.[3] The Medici family had been involved in commerce and banking, but it was not a market leader. The Bardi and Peruzzi banks had built vast fortunes, only to fail spectacularly in the 1340s thanks in no small part to King Edward III of England reneging on his debts. These collapses provided an opening into which the Medicis marched. Giovanni's wealthier cousin employed him and his brother at his bank. Giovanni used the money from his wife's dowry in 1385 to establish himself as the head of the bank in Rome. When the cousin retired in 1393, Giovanni bought out the bank; he had identified one client that would provide an endless source of income and, if played correctly, political cover − the Church.

Giovanni's son, Cosimo di Giovanni de' Medici, was born on 27 September 1389, the day upon which are commemorated the early Christian martyrs, Cosmas and Damian, the patron saints of physicians (Cosimo later had them depicted in paintings he commissioned.)[4] He and his twin brother were named after the saints, but Damiano died at birth. Death meant eternal judgement and Cosimo was always troubled by the circumstances of his beginning. He and his younger brother Lorenzo received their first education at the monastery of Santa Maria degli Angeli. This was unlike other schools; its focus was on the study of rediscovered texts of the classical world. He also learned German, French and Latin and received a grounding in Hebrew, Greek and Arabic. The two boys were put under the supervision of Roberto de' Rossi, who introduced them to humanist scholars such as Poggio Bracciolini, Leonardo Bruni and Niccolò de' Niccoli. They instilled in Cosimo a passion for the pre-Christian classical world, for the revival of the language, learning and art of the ancient Greeks and Romans. His father had other priorities, sending him into apprenticeship in the family firm, where he displayed an instinctive aptitude for business.

These two facets of Cosimo's education shaped the man he became. A generation later, in his *History of Florence*, an admiring Machiavelli wrote: 'He was of middle stature, olive complexion, and venerable aspect; not learned but exceedingly eloquent, endowed with great natural capacity, generous to his friends, kind to the poor, comprehensive in discourse, cautious in advising, and in his speeches and replies, grave and witty.'[5]

Cosimo was eight years old when the Medici Bank was established. As the eldest son, he was already being groomed by his father to take over. Even in his family's personal affairs, Giovanni was astute in identifying business opportunities. In early 1416, the twenty-seven-year-old Cosimo was required to marry the niece of his father's banking partner, Contessina de' Bardi. For the Bardis, whose finances and standing had taken a battering, it was a good deal. For the Medicis, it was a step up. Cosimo did not complain; he took the same transactional approach to his nuptials as the two families. This was an arranged, or rather a strategic, marriage. Such contracts were normal for the time. She was a Bardi, he a Medici. They made sure it worked, just.

The dowry Contessina brought with her was not a large one, although it did include the Palazzo Bardi, the family palace. She was tubby, fond of cheese, fussy and cheerful. She was denied access to her husband's study, which was not uncommon in those days, and bore his long partings without fuss. As for Cosimo, he was polite to her, but rarely bothered to write when he was away. Contessina bore him two sons, Piero *'il Gotoso'* (the Gouty) and Giovanni. Cosimo had a third son by a slave girl, conceived during a business trip to Rome. His agent in the city had been given the task of procuring a slave and proudly produced one who was a 'sound virgin, free from disease and aged about 21'. Their child, Carlo, had marked Circassian features. He was brought up just like the other boys in the family household. Cosimo educated his three sons for different careers. Piero, the eldest, would be groomed for government; Giovanni, the favourite, was destined for the bank; Carlo, the illegitimate one, would be admitted to the Church as a prelate as soon as he came of age.

One of the many ethical curiosities of this era was that the ownership and impregnation of slaves were entirely respectable, whereas the day-to-day activity of banking was not. Cosimo didn't bother himself with such issues – not then anyway – and the process of building up the bank continued apace. His father had appointed him as permanent manager of the Rome branch – the one with direct access to the Church and the major source of profit for the entire business.

The Medicis were merchants as well as bankers. Using a growing network of agents around Europe they bought and sold goods for rich clients: tapestries, wall hangings, painted panels, chandeliers, manuscript books, silverware, jewels, slaves. They would speculate, buying shiploads of alum (for the textile business), wool, spices, almonds or silks, moving them between southern and northern Europe, and selling them at a margin.

They employed the same rules of arbitrage in banking, playing different exchange rates against each other, exploiting the time it took to travel from one financial centre to another. The methods that underpinned international finance were well established: double-entry book-keeping (an accountancy procedure that records both debits and credits), the bill of exchange (a written order committing parties to a fixed transaction at a specific point in the future), the letter of credit, the deposit account. By the time Giovanni retired in 1420, his bank had branches in Venice and Geneva as well as Florence and Rome. Under his leadership, it had enjoyed steady growth. His initial investment had amounted to 5500 gold florins; his two business partners put in 4500. Over the next twenty-three years, the bank would make total profits of more than 150,000 florins, of which Giovanni took three-quarters – a return of over twenty times his initial investment.[6]

On Giovanni's death in 1429 there was only one possible successor. Cosimo was forty years old and a well-known figure in the public life of Florence and beyond. Although careful to keep in with the right people, he was far less circumspect than his father had been. Machiavelli observed the following:

Cosimo de' Medici, after the death of Giovanni, engaged more earnestly in public affairs, and conducted himself with more zeal and boldness in regard to his friends than his father had done, so that those who rejoiced at Giovanni's death, finding what the son was likely to become, perceived they had no cause for exultation. Cosimo was one of the most prudent of men; of grave and courteous demeanour, extremely liberal and humane. He never attempted anything against parties, or against rulers, but was bountiful to all; and by the unwearied generosity of his disposition, made himself partisans of all ranks of the citizens. This mode of proceeding increased the difficulties of those who were in the government.[7]

If Giovanni had laid a stable foundation, it was Cosimo who constructed the dazzling edifice of Medici power and legacy. He inherited his father's keen sense of the precariousness of their profession. He injected ruthlessness, fuelled by a vicious power struggle. Using his money and influence, he manipulated Florentine politics without assuming a formal title. This seeming self-deprecation was a tactic; behind the scenes, he pulled the strings.

Even before he had taken over the bank, Cosimo's ambition had caught the attention of rival families. Ranged against the growing power of the Medicis' 'new money' were the old families, led by Rinaldo de' Albizzi. These families saw Cosimo as a threat to their ruling power, and resented a new tax system established in 1427, for which they blamed Cosimo's father. Cosimo was careful to observe proprieties, but as the humanist writer Vespasiano da Bisticci suggests, his diplomatic demeanour was only on the surface. 'He was a man in a hurry: He was grave in temperament, prone to associate with men of high station who disliked frivolity, and averse from all buffoons and actors and those who spent time unprofitably.' He adds: 'By his twenty fifth year he had gained a great reputation in the city and, as it was recognised that he was aiming at a high position, feeling ran strong against him.'[8]

Florence was one of the five biggest cities in Europe, with a population of almost a hundred thousand. Its prestige and ambition were not always matched by its economic rigour. Cash was frequently in short supply, due largely to the number of wars the city-states indulged in. The latest skirmish had been with Milan. Albizzi and his allies attempted to win back popular support by declaring war on the city of Lucca, for having the temerity to support Milan. Cosimo had misgivings about the decision, but fearful of being outmanoeuvred, he kept his concerns to himself and joined the Committee of Ten that was responsible for directing the war. The campaign was a disaster: Milan paid the formidable *condottiero*, or mercenary leader, Francesco Sforza to protect Lucca. After pounding the city for days and getting nowhere, Florence had to pay Sforza, too – a huge bribe of fifty thousand florins to leave the city. Cosimo was shocked by the needless expense.[9] Even with Sforza out of the picture, the Florentine army, led by Albizzi, failed in its siege. Cosimo resigned from the Committee of Ten and left for Verona, allowing Albizzi to stir up discontent against him for his lack of patriotism.

By 1433, tension between the ruling factions had reached a peak. In May, the door of Cosimo's palace was daubed with blood. He understood the intended message and began to safeguard his assets. He retired to a small converted medieval fort, the Villa il Trebbio, outside the city, and secretly transferred vast sums of money out of Florence to the bank's branches in Rome and Venice, as well as to various monasteries that had volunteered themselves as safe-houses.

Albizzi moved against him quickly, using the intricate political system to engineer a coup. Though bribery, corruption, intimidation and violence were used to secure power, Florentines were inordinately proud of their republican system of elections, seeing it as a guarantor of freedom and a contrast to the various tyrannies in outlying states. This is how it worked: eight members of the great and the good representing different quarters of the city and different guilds were picked out (from eight leather bags called *borse* that were kept in the sacristy of the church of Santa Croce) to become priors, or *priori*. They were required to move out of their homes and were locked in the Palazzo dei Priori (now the Palazzo Vecchio), a grand edifice with a watchtower. They were paid a modest salary to cover their expenses and had at their beck and call a large staff of green-liveried servants as well as a *buffone*, who told them funny stories and sang for them when they were eating their meals.[10] They were joined by one more man, from a higher guild, who became the *gonfaloniere della giustizia*, the head of government. These nine formed the *signoria*, or local council. In theory this was collective administration, with a system of checks and balances and accountability that stood up to any constitutional test. If they couldn't come to a decision, or if they wanted broader endorsement, they would call a bigger *parlamento* outside on the Piazza Signoria.

The reality was far murkier. Whoever was running the show had control over not just the political but the business interests of Florence. It was vital to get your own people on to the *signoria*. Albizzi made sure he did just that; seven of the nine members of the government were his supporters.

In September 1433, Albizzi and the Florentine government called Cosimo to return to Florence to appear before the *signoria*. Against the advice of his friends, he agreed. On arrival at the Palazzo dei Priori he was promptly imprisoned in a small, damp room halfway up the tower with only a crack of a window looking away from the town and on to the Arno River. He was charged with 'attempting to elevate himself above the rank of an ordinary citizen'.[11] This was one of the most serious accusations that could be levelled within the city. Yet the outrage was manufactured, as the city's top financiers were all doing that. Once in a while, however, resentment of the rich among the populace could be whipped up for a specific purpose. Every possible shred of evidence was used against Medici. The *palazzo* he was building for himself up the road on the Via Largo was cited as evidence of his hypercharged ambitions. It was seen as too ostentatious, a sign of dangerous self-aggrandisement.

Cosimo's rise to prominence had unsettled more than just one or two families. He was disturbing the established order. Machiavelli reported Albizzi as complaining that Cosimo 'alone, by the popularity acquired with his enormous wealth, kept them depressed; that he was already so powerful, that if not hindered, he would soon become prince'.[12] The businessmen were forced to take sides. Niccolò da Uzzano, an elderly and influential statesman, lavished praise on him:

Those actions of Cosimo which lead us to suspect him are, that he lends money indiscriminately, and not to private persons only, but to the public; and not to Florentines only, but to the *condottieri*, the soldiers of fortune. Besides, he assists any citizen who requires magisterial aid; and, by the universal interest he possesses in the city, raises first one friend and then another to higher grades of honour. Therefore, to adduce our reasons for expelling him would be to say that he is kind, generous, liberal, and beloved by all.[13]

Albizzi pushed hard for the death sentence, but the usually pliant members of the *signoria* were reluctant to go so far. They wanted to keep their options open; many were indebted to Cosimo. Surely banishment would suffice? The decision was debated for days, with an increasingly frustrated Albizzi calling a *parlamento* of the citizens of Florence, and making sure that Medici's supporters were excluded. From inside his cramped cell, known ironically as the *Alberghetto*, or Little Inn, Cosimo tried to discern his fate. He refused to eat or drink, fearing that his food was poisoned, until his jailer, Federigo Malavolti, sought to reassure him:

Cosimo, you are afraid of being poisoned, and are evidently hastening your end with hunger. You wrong me if you think I would be a party to such an atrocious act. I do not imagine your life to be in much danger, since you have so many friends both within the palace and without; but if you should eventually lose it, be assured they will use some other medium than myself for that purpose, for I will never imbue my hands in the blood of any, still less in yours, who never injured me; therefore cheer up, take some food, and preserve your life for your friends and your country. And that you may do so with greater assurance, I will partake of your meals with you.[14]

Malavolti brought in an entertainer called Il Farnagaccio to calm the prisoner's nerves; the joker was familiar to Cosimo and also a friend of the *gonfaloniere*. With his jailer tactfully absent, Cosimo passed the joker a piece of paper directing him to the Santa Maria Nuova Hospital, where the director would give him eleven hundred Venetian ducats, of which he could take a hundred as payment, and the rest should be passed to the *gonfaloniere* as a bribe.

As the *parlamento* debated, Cosimo received news that his allies were rallying to his support. Niccolò da Tolentino, captain of the Commune, marched with his army of mercenaries to six miles outside the city walls, while local peasants took arms to support Cosimo's brother Lorenzo. The Venetian Republic, which depended on the local branch of the Medici Bank to finance its extensive trading interests, dispatched a delegation of ambassadors to secure Cosimo's release. Pope Eugenius IV sent word ordering intervention on his behalf.

Time was running out. Determined to secure a death sentence, Albizzi arrested Cosimo's allies and had two of them tortured by the city's rack master. Eventually, the humanist poet Niccolò Tinucci signed a confession, stating that Cosimo had intended to foment a revolution with the aid of foreign troops. This was the incontrovertible evidence that Albizzi needed; but by now members of the *signoria*, as well as the *gonfaloniere*, had been successfully bribed.

Cosimo and the rest of the Medici family were banished to Padua for ten years, and prevented from holding public office in Florence for ever. On 5 October 1433, he was escorted under armed guard across a high mountain pass on the north-east border of the republic's territory and into exile. Through back-handers and his extensive network of influential contacts, Cosimo de' Medici had escaped death.

From exile, briefly in Padua and then in Venice, Cosimo carefully watched events unfold in Florence, which was struggling to pay off huge debts without the assistance of Medici money. He was told that no other banker could be found to supply the government 'with so much as a pistachio nut'.[15] This was, as Vespasiano records, a golden opportunity: 'His wealth was so great that he was able to send to Rome enough money to re-establish his position. In fact, his credit increased vastly everywhere, and in Rome many who had withdrawn their money brought it back to his bank.'[16] Six months into his exile, with an empty city treasury and after the defeat of the Florentine army by

Milanese mercenaries, Medici supporters occupied each of the *signoria* seats as well as the position of *gonfaloniere*. Within a month, while Albizzi was absent from Florence on business, the *signoria* sent word to Venice, urging Cosimo to return.

Albizzi was summoned to appear at the Palazzo dei Priori. He ignored them, fleeing to the outskirts of the city and preparing to do battle. Bloodshed was averted only with the intervention of Pope Eugenius, who convinced Albizzi to give up his resistance in return for comfortable exile. The next day a *parlamento* voted to overturn the banishment of the city's paymaster. Machiavelli describes Medici's triumphal entrance into the city in gushing tones: 'it has seldom occurred that any citizen, coming home triumphant from victory, was received by so vast a concourse of people, or such unqualified demonstrations of regard as he was upon his return from banishment; for by universal consent he was hailed as the benefactor of the people, and the FATHER OF HIS COUNTRY'.[17] As Cosimo made his way to his home at the Palazzo Bardi, less than a year after being on the verge of execution, crowds lined the streets to cheer him 'in such a manner that one would imagine him to be their prince'.[18]

The republic's finances were in tatters. Cosimo instructed his bank to bail out the exchequer, even though he suspected that none of the capital, let alone interest, would be repaid. He rewarded those who had helped bring him back and made sure that second time around in Florence he would not leave himself prone to future threats. He learned from the experience that if he 'were to rule successfully, he must appear scarcely to rule at all'.[19]

Yet this public reluctance to step into the fray was a ruse. From behind the scenes, Medici ruled ruthlessly. He ensured that Albizzi and his acolytes would never again pose a challenge. To that end, he could count on the indebted – in both senses of the word – *signoria* to do his bidding. Anyone who had been close to Albizzi was exiled; the standard ten-year sentence would be repeatedly extended to keep them out of the way. Paid informers monitored the actions of enemies in exile. Families were split up. One law made it illegal to write letters to or receive them from Albizzi's exiles. Machiavelli noted:

Every word, sign, or action that gave offence to the ruling party was punished with the utmost rigour; and if there was still in Florence any suspected person whom these regulations did not reach, he was oppressed with taxes imposed for the occasion. Thus in a short time, having expelled or impoverished the whole of the adverse party, they established themselves firmly in the government. Not to be destitute of external assistance, and to deprive others of it, who might use it against themselves, they entered into a league, offensive and defensive, with the pope, the Venetians, and the duke of Milan.[20]

Tax was an important political tool. A new property levy, the *catasto*, had been introduced in 1427. Part Domesday Book, part Council Tax, it was the first effective method of compiling data and collecting revenues. As a result (as is the case in modern Italy with all taxes), it was deeply unpopular. Cosimo decided to set an example by endorsing the tax, even though he disliked it, letting it be known for patriotic purposes that he had become the highest taxpayer in Florence. The amount he actually paid, however, was far lower than the amount he should have paid. Using a time-honoured device, he kept special accounts that exaggerated his bad debts. His liability was calculated from a much-diminished declaration of his income: tax efficiency, or tax minimisation – two much-loved methods of the contemporary rich.

Cosimo used his influence over the administrative apparatus to ruin anyone who opposed him by ensuring that the value of their property was vastly overestimated. Tax officers were not noted for their impartiality when assessing the payments due from the regime's critics.[21] They also bought up the estates of men banished from the republic at bargain prices. Shades of ancient and modern. Governments throughout the twentieth and twenty-first centuries have used tax authorities to target political opponents, an accusation levelled at regimes from Chile's military dictatorship under Augusto Pinochet to Cristina Fernández de Kirchner's left-leaning government in Argentina. Nobody has been more adept at using the system to break his enemies than Vladimir Putin in contemporary Russia. Nobody used property as an instrument of extortion and self-aggrandisement more ruthlessly than Crassus.

Financial manipulation was a more effective tool of control than crude political or military power. For good measure, Medici cut all the Bardi family out of his extensive operations. There is no word as to whether his wife objected; one assumes she thought better of it. Cosimo thrived on the ambiguity and creative tension of his position. Anyone who wanted to get on in Florence knew where to turn. It became customary for parents to implore him to become the godfather of their first-born male children.

As Vespasiano remarked, 'whenever he wished to achieve something, he saw to it, in order to escape envy as much as possible, that the initiative appeared to come from others and not from him'.[22] Machiavelli supports this contention:

> Although his habitations, like all his other works and actions, were quite of a regal character, and he alone was prince in Florence, still everything was so tempered with his prudence, that he never transgressed the decent moderation of civil life; in his conversation, his servants, his travelling, his mode of living, and the relationships he formed, the modest demeanour of the citizen was always evident; for he was aware that a constant exhibition of pomp brings more envy upon its possessor than greater realities borne without ostentation.[23]

Therein lay one of the secrets of his enduring success. Another was the business model. The bank's *modus operandi* was little different from the methods of today. Indeed, it could be seen as a precursor. Bankers took positions on currencies; they made long bets on riskier ventures, hedging them against more stable transactions. They made sure that even if they broke the law, in either letter or spirit, friends in high places would provide them with legal and political cover.

Until the mid-seventeenth century, the terms 'banker' and 'exchanger' were interchangeable. Bills of exchange enabled short-term loans by lending money to clients in one country, to be repaid after a certain time in another. For example, the Medici Bank in Florence would agree a loan to a merchant and ninety days later that trader, or his agent, would be required to repay the sum to the Medici Bank in, say, London. The time frame would reflect the average time it would take to make the journey. The bank would then speculate on the exchange rate. The Medicis stayed abreast of currency fluctuations via updates from their correspondents in the various European cities. The difference between rates tended to be largest in spring, just before merchant ships set off abroad and when the demand for credit to finance trading was highest. If the winds of fate and exchange blew in your direction, it was easy to make a fortune. This proved spectacularly lucrative. Only one of all Cosimo's exchanges resulted in a loss.[24]

Merchant trade accounted for only a modest proportion of the bank's profits, but it represented an important way of balancing cash flow around Europe. Sale of goods was normally agreed only after the buyer had seen them, thus a cargo travelling from Florence to Bruges did not have a certain buyer at the end of the journey. The journey itself could be risky – ships could sink, pirates could seize cargoes. The Medicis spread their risk over a wide variety of goods and customers, trading in raw silk, olive oil, wool, citrus fruits and other items for which there was a steady demand.

In the Florence of the day there were two parallel economies and two parallel currencies. The poor existed to produce the raw materials and to service the wealthy; beyond that, they were not economic players, although the *Ciompi* Revolt had provided a salutary lesson that it was wise to keep the artisans on side. The gold florin existed for the wealthy and the middle class; it was the currency of consumer durables and luxury items, from tapestries to silverware, from manuscript books to jewels, and for the purchase of slaves. It was the basis of bookkeeping and internal and external trade. The rest, the cobblers and saddlers, the barbers and wool workers, had to make do with the *picciolo*. This coin, made of low-grade silver, frequently lost value. Over two centuries its purchasing power against the florin depreciated sevenfold. Naturally, this was the currency that the Medici Bank chose to pay its workers on piece rates in its wool business. When profits were low, manufacturers would encourage the mint to reduce the silver content in the *picciolo*, meaning that while wages were notionally left

unchanged, the actual value for the workers fell.[25] While the very
poorest workers did not face income tax, they were charged daily for
basic transactions. Every time they crossed through the city gates a tax
collector was there to greet them, charging them for their buckets of
fish or grain from the mill. Those earning the least faced the biggest
tax burden. Just in case they might acquire the cash to succumb to
temptation, laws were in place to prevent the lower class from buying
luxury goods. Sumptuary laws had been in place since ancient Greece,
governing, among other things, the clothing of women, prostitutes,
Jews, Muslims and other assorted heretics.

The Medicis' most important business relationship was with the
Church. Each rule was tailored to maximise the bottom line while pro-
tecting the bank from accusations of contravening God's will. Cosimo
had learned the practice from his father. Giovanni had befriended the
Neapolitan priest Baldassarre Cossa after he became a cardinal in 1402.
In May 1410, with help from the bank, Cossa was consecrated Pope
John XXIII – except that he wasn't the pontiff. Three men were vying
for the title. Cossa was recognised by France, England, Prussia and parts
of the Holy Roman Empire, plus Venice and Florence. But Rome
regarded him as an 'anti-pope'. The Avignon Pope, Benedict XIII, was
the nominee of the kingdoms of Aragon, Castile and Sicily, while
Gregory XII was favoured in some German-speaking areas. The normally cautious and reserved Florentine banker threw in his lot behind
Cossa, a former pirate with a colourful past. It was an unlikely friendship and a risky punt.

The Council of Constance was convened in 1413 by the Holy
Roman Emperor to call an end to this division in papal power; all three
contenders were invited. John XXIII, who was sheltering in Florence,
set off with his entourage. The twenty-five-year-old Cosimo and the
Rome branch of the Medici Bank went with him. That a young banker
was part of the entourage of a man vying for the papacy seemed to
strike neither party as strange.

For three weeks, the sleepy town of Constance (in what is now the
southern tip of Germany) was filled with three popes, assorted priests,
bishops, theologians, lawyers, bankers and more than a thousand

prostitutes – up to a hundred thousand visitors in all.[26] When the council resolved that all three popes should abdicate and an election be held, John XXIII fled in disguise to Freiburg, seeking refuge and demanding to be appointed Legate of Italy, with a pension of thirty thousand florins. He was refused refuge. Later he would be arrested and accused of heresy, incest, sodomy and fornication with two hundred ladies of Bologna. He was described as 'addicted to the flesh, the dregs of vice, a mirror of infamy', and imprisoned.[27]

The Rome branch of the Medici Bank immediately attached itself to the new Pope, Martin V; they went where the power resided. Yet, on the quiet, they remained loyal to Cossa, paying a ransom (via proxies) of 3500 florins for his release from prison in the Castle of Heidelberg. The bank was ensuring that both sides of the dispute would be beholden to it. As an expression of thanks, Cossa endowed the sacred finger of John the Baptist and his collection of rare jewels to the Medicis, who in return persuaded Martin V to pardon Cossa of his sins. Thus the Medicis were profitably loyal to one of their friends, while successfully navigating the twists and turns of papal succession.

Much of the bank's activity was now in one city: the Rome branch held the papal account for most of the fifteenth century, managing the Church's accounts and its trade with foreign lands, and handling its savings and borrowing. For most of the bank's history, such dealings accounted for over 50 per cent of its profits.[28]

Yet usury – the practice of making a profit from loans – was a sin. It contravened the admonition of St Luke to 'give, without hoping for gain'. As one writer notes: 'In Dante's hell, sodomites and usurers are punished in the third ditch of the seventh circle where flakes of burning ash sift for all eternity on an unnatural landscape of scorching sand.'[29] He adds: 'In the opening story of Boccaccio's *Decameron*, two usurers are terrified that their dying guest, a great and unrepentant sinner, will be refused burial and that because of their profession the local people will chase them out of town or even lynch them, in which case they will be left unburied.'[30] The Lateran Church Council of 1179 had decreed that usurers should be denied a Christian burial; the General Church Council of Lyon had confirmed the ruling as recently as 1274. Usury could be expiated only through full restitution of what had been sinfully gained. For the avoidance of doubt, 'Their bodies should be buried in ditches, together with dogs and cattle,' wrote Fra Filippo degli Agazzari, a prior from Siena.[31]

So how did both sides get around this inconvenience? Through ingenuity and ethical flexibility, they came to an arrangement that satisfied the needs of all.

While usury was banned, 'discretionary deposits' were not. When the Pope or a bishop put money in a bank, they needed a return on their investment; however, a fixed interest rate was prohibited. Instead the bank, at its discretion, gave the deposit holder a 'gift', which normally amounted to around 8–12 per cent of the deposit per year; there was no contractual obligation upon the bank to do so, and thus the investor was not giving in the hope of gaining. The other advantage of this arrangement was that the name of the depositor would remain secret, ensuring privacy over financial affairs – a precursor to the Swiss bank or the offshore haven of contemporary times. These murky accounts would protect assets from the sudden vagaries of papal succession, unlike investments in real estate.[32] On the other hand, when the Church asked for a loan, the bank could not ask for interest. Instead, it overcharged the Church for goods such as jewels and silks in order to reclaim the money owed. Everyone was content. Everyone turned a blind eye. Some in the Church were uncomfortable with the practice – Archbishop Antonino of Florence labelled it 'mental usury' – but the fear of public excommunication usually bought silence of churchmen like him. Most were happy to use the deliberate ambiguity of language to mask the practice. The holders of these accounts included high-ranking cardinals such as Pope Martin V's nephew.

The mechanics of papal banking were complex. Local collectors recovered payments for indulgences (a certificate you could buy, presigned by the Pope, that would exonerate you from your sins and grant you access to heaven) and other assorted taxes due to the Church. They then handed the receipts to the nearest Medici branch or subsidiary. The branch would transmit the money to Rome by writing the sum received from papal collectors to the credit of the Medici bank. This created cash-flow problems as Rome raked in its revenue;

many of the branches across Europe owed Rome a significant amount.[33] The transportation of cash across Europe was a dangerous business, risking robbery on the road. A number of complicated techniques were used to circumvent this problem. Expenditure on luxury goods such as silk, art and silverware from northern Europe, as well as English wool, was a popular alternative. Almost all banks ran such parallel trade operations.

The papal account held other advantages for the Medicis. Cosimo had the power to determine who was in favour and who was not, in the Church as in the rest of public life. His officials were responsible for collecting payments from new bishops in return for bills of nomination; if the money was not paid, the Medicis could complain to the Pope and the bishop would be struck off. Spiritual sanction was another of his many tools for collecting revenues and exercising his authority.

In 1438, the Church presented Cosimo with his greatest opportunity so far. The split between the two halves of the ancient Roman Empire – Byzantium and Rome – had reached a peak in the thirteenth century during the Fourth Crusade when Western troops had desecrated and destroyed Constantinople, raping and murdering as they went. With this act, the Great Schism between the Eastern and Western churches was cemented. Two centuries later, a common enemy, Islam, forced both branches of the Church to seek a reconciliation, of sorts. John VIII Paleologus, the Byzantine Emperor and head of the Orthodox Church of Constantinople, appealed to Pope Eugenius IV to protect Christendom from the advance of the Muslim army of the Ottomans across Turkey. The two churches agreed to meet in Ferrara to seek an alliance. In April 1438, John arrived with a seven-hundred-strong delegation. The cost of hosting all these people quickly overwhelmed Eugenius. The Pope was broke; he turned to one man for loans – of ten thousand gold florins at a time. Cosimo was happy to oblige. He sat back and watched the situation carefully from Florence.

A terrible misfortune played perfectly into his hands. Plague, an occupational hazard in this period, broke out in Ferrara. Cosimo dispatched his brother Lorenzo to suggest that the Ecumenical Council relocate to Florence. He said his city would pay fifteen hundred florins per month to cover the costs for as long as the guests needed it. The prestige and political benefits were stunning. Cosimo calculated his generosity down to the last penny. That meeting in Florence in 1439 marked the peak of the bank's profits: some 14,400 cameral florins were made, more than double the average annual profits of the Rome branch over the next twelve years.[34]

Cosimo abandoned his self-imposed life in the shadows; the grand show proved too much for his ego to resist. Ahead of the arrival of the council he ensured his own election as *gonfaloniere* so that he would be standing at the head of the city republic to greet the Pope and the Emperor. This was celebrity politics. Yet his best-laid plans went awry. On the ceremonial entry of the two delegations, the heavens opened, emptying the streets of the welcoming crowds and forcing the processions to shelter in a nearby palazzo.

For six months during this giant conclave, East cohabited with West in Florence. The city was filled with people from exotic lands: Russians, Armenians, Ethiopians. One of the most important members of John VIII's entourage was the eighty-year-old Greek scholar Gemistos Plethon. During his sojourn in Florence, Plethon gave lectures on Plato, who was little known in Italy at the time, which Cosimo ensured he attended. The ideas espoused by Plethon inspired Medici to foster a circle of humanist collectors, translators and scholars who became known as the Platonic Academy. In coming years, scholars fleeing Constantinople would take with them rare Greek manuscripts on subjects ranging from philosophy to alchemy and astrology, adding to Florence's status as the centre of learning and culture.

Cosimo's financial backing for the council was not just the move of a smart banker or a consummate player on the political scene; it represented the start of his role as one of the great patrons of art and culture. He understood the power of patronage, the allure of art and architecture, and their ability to secure for him a place in posterity and possibly absolve him of his sins. Vespasiano chronicles him as saying: 'I know the ways of Florence, within fifty years we Medici will have been exiled, but my buildings will remain.'[35] The intellectual and cultural exchange that Cosimo sponsored during the council fertilised the early flowering of the rebirth — or *rinascimento* — of ancient learning that took place over the remainder of the fifteenth century. Poets and scholars such as Dante, Petrarch and Boccaccio had already laid the groundwork. But it was only thanks to the Medicis' money that concerted work was done to locate manuscripts that had been neglected in monasteries across Europe and bring them to Florence.

A century after the Great Plague and with the city no longer fighting wars on every front, Florence was thriving again. A building boom was in full swing. After 140 years of construction, the basilica of Santa Maria del Fiore – the Duomo – was consecrated in 1436. The nearby basilica of San Lorenzo, which became the family church of the Medicis, was reconstructed, although work was hampered for years by architectural disagreements. Other smaller churches were springing up, sponsored by the Medicis and other wealthy families.

The compulsive competitiveness of the super-rich was evident across the city; they needed their status symbols. Up to a hundred lavish private palaces were constructed. The wool-trading magnate Giovanni Paolo de Rucellai built his impressive townhouse in the middle of the city. Close by was the Palazzo Strozzi, home of the one family that could count itself as a serious rival to the Medicis. Palla Strozzi had been one of the leading figures behind Cosimo's brief exile and was duly banished. His son, Filippo Strozzi the younger, after making his fortune as a banker in Naples, sought to reconcile with the Medicis and was allowed to return to Florence in 1462. He did what families like his did: began to build a residence that would signal the return of his dynasty. He didn't live to see it open, and after another dispute the Medicis confiscated it. On the other side of the Arno River was a palace built by Luca Pitti, a banker who aligned himself completely with Cosimo de' Medici. The Pitti Palace became home to some of Florence's grand dukes (including Medicis) and to the first king of the united Italy in the nineteenth century.

Cosimo wanted his mansion to inspire awe and trepidation in equal measure. Having already flirted with death, he did not want to be accused of ostentation. 'He used to say that in most gardens there grew a weed which should never be watered but left to dry up,' wrote Vespasiano. 'Most men, however, watered instead of letting it die of drought. This weed was that worst of all weeds, Envy, and there were few except the truly wise who did not make shipwreck through it.'[36] Medici rejected the first plans of Filippo Brunelleschi – a decision that caused consternation. Brunelleschi was the city's foremost architect: the cathedral's dome, which inspires awe to this day, had his copyright. Instead, Medici turned to his trusted friend Michelozzo di Bartolomeo Michelozzi. He, along with the sculptor Donatello, had accompanied Medici into political exile.

Construction eventually began in 1444 of a building that would be part home, part embassy and part business centre. With its stern stonework, the outside of Palazzo Medici has the forbidding feel of an urban fortress. It was also open to the public – on the master's terms. Two arches allowed Florentines to wander into the courtyard, where they could discuss their business or civic concerns, or apply to waiting officials for a bank loan. The message was deliberate: power had now shifted from the Palazzo dei Priori, where the *signoria* still met, up the road to the Medicis' palace. Foreign delegations went straight to see Cosimo. During the council of the churches in the late 1430s, he felt he needed the official title of *gonfaloniere* to confer authority. By this point he didn't; the name was enough. Medici was the person who got things done. Aeneas Silvius de' Piccolomini, Bishop of Siena and later Pope Pius II, remarked: 'Political questions are settled in [Cosimo's] house. The man he chooses holds office. He it is who decides peace and war. He is king in all but name.'[37]

In April 1459, Cosimo pulled out the stops to entertain Galeazzo Maria Sforza, the teenage son of his now friend and ally Francesco Sforza, the mercenary Milanese. It was important to enshrine the reconciliation of the two families. Young Sforza returned the compliment, lavishing praise on the new palazzo, a house whose value was:

> As much in the handsomeness of the ceilings, the height of the walls, smooth finish of the entrances and windows, number of chambers and salons, elegance of the studies, worth of the books, neatness and gracefulness of the gardens as it is in the tapestry decorations, cassoni of inestimable workmanship and value, noble sculptures, designs of infinite kinds as well of price silver, the best I may ever have seen.

Everything was done to affect. Cosimo wanted to be seen as avant-garde, but not too much. For the inner courtyard, he commissioned Donatello to produce a bronze sculpture of the biblical David. This would be the first freestanding nude created since the classical era, a radical Renaissance expression of human beauty. Beneath the statue was inscribed the legend: 'The victor is whoever defends the fatherland. God crushes the wrath of an enormous foe. Behold! A boy overcame a great tyrant. Conquer, o citizens!'[38] Some would denounce it as an endorsement of homosexuality. More on Medici's mind was the republican message he was sending: David versus Goliath. The republic was the powerbroker, representing the triumph of justice over tyranny, standing up for the downtrodden against an over-mighty elite.

While anyone could show up downstairs, access to one particular room on the first floor was a sign of social and political success. Cosimo may have had an ambivalent view of religion, but he knew its worth. Access to his private chapel, his tiny place of worship with barely ten seats available for a private mass, was an honour afforded a select few. Guests would marvel at the ceiling carved from wood and adorned with gold leaf, and the floor covered in marble mosaic. The altar panel representing the Madonna in adoration of the Christ Child was the work of the eminent artist Fra Filippo Lippi.

The *pièce de résistance* was the fresco encircling the chapel – a series of wall paintings that imagined the Medicis and their friends in biblical scenes. Cosimo can be seen in plain merchant clothes on top of a brown mule. His sons Piero and Giovanni and his grandsons Lorenzo and Giuliano are close by. The illegitimate Carlo plays a cameo role. Men with bears, presumably representing the Byzantine Empire, are depicted, as are a leopard, a lynx and a monkey, denoting the exotic Eastern menagerie that Emperor John had brought with him to the council. The Medici coat of arms of five red balls, or *palle*, makes an appearance, as it did on other great works in the city. Fra Angelico's *Coronation of the Virgin*, one of the many paintings commissioned by Cosimo when he undertook the restoration of the monastery of San Marco, just up the road from the Palazzo Medici, could be seen as a similar bank branding exercise. Around the edge of the luxurious carpet depicted in the picture run the Medici red balls on a golden field.

Elsewhere, Cosimo's public works – his churches, hospitals, monasteries and orphanages – became the arenas in which he declared his family's power under the guise of munificence. He was the chief funder of a statue to St Matthew in the grounds of the church of Orsanmichele. After that came the novices' dormitory and chapel at Santa Croce, the choir of Santissima Annunziata, the library of the church of San Bartolomeo and more. He was behind the formation of a religious co-fraternity, the Good Men of San Martino. His largesse extended to a college for Florentine students in Paris, renovation of the church of Santo Spirito in Jerusalem and additions to the Franciscan monastery at Assisi.[39] On the advice of Pope Eugenius, he embarked on one of his most passionate projects, the rebuilding of the San Marco. He paid for the living expenses of the Dominican monks there and for the transfer of books to the library. He poured so much money into it that the friars felt obliged to protest, but to no avail. 'Never shall I be able to give God enough to set him down in my book as a debtor,' Cosimo replied. God's credit ratings sufficed for the banker.

The deathbed advice of his father, Giovanni, had been well and truly forgotten. Cosimo tacitly encouraged a cult of personality. Some of the church projects were studies in self-glorification. Poems were commissioned to sing his praises. One was from Anselmo Calderoni, the official herald to the *signoria*:

> *Oh light of all earthly folk*
> *Bright mirror of every merchant,*
> *True friend to all good works,*
> *Honour of famous Florentines,*
> *Kind help to all in need,*
> *Succour of orphans and widows,*
> *Strong shield of Tuscan borders!*[40]

As he grew older, two competing impulses dominated Medici's life. His yearning to control, from behind the scenes, every aspect of Florentine life grew ever stronger. At the same time, he became possessed of a fear of death and divine retribution. Plagues, earthquakes and wars continued to afflict Florence – with the poor suffering most. It was not easy to criticise him in public – it certainly was not a path to success in Florentine life – but resentment was growing, particularly at the conduct of foreign policy. Cosimo had dictated that Florence switch allegiances from its old ally, Venice, to Milan. The reason? Sforza, now Duke of Milan and nicknamed the 'bastard upstart official' (he was one of seven illegitimate brothers), was one of the largest clients of the Medici bank. In a classic piece of insider trading, the bank had pulled money out of Venice before the political decision was taken. Venice tried to foment against Florence, joining forces with Naples to attack. With no other choice, the population rallied round. It was the intervention of a greater enemy, the Ottoman Sultan Mehmet II, which proved decisive. The Ottomans' capture of Constantinople forced the Christian city-states to put aside their differences. In 1454 the Peace of Lodi was signed and a 'most Holy League' was declared uniting Rome, Milan, Venice, Florence and Naples against the Turks.

Alongside the grand architectural projects and the iconography, Medici spent much of his time and money in his later years as a patron of humanist scholarship. Machiavelli chronicles:

> Cosimo was a friend and patron of learned men. He brought Argiripolo, a Greek by birth, and one of the most erudite of his time, to Florence, to instruct the youth in Hellenic literature. He entertained Marsilio Ficino, the reviver of the Platonic philosophy, in his own house; and being much attached to him, gave him a residence near his palace at Careggi, that he might pursue the study of letters with greater convenience, and himself have an opportunity of enjoying his company.[41]

Cosimo installed Ficino, the son of the family's doctor, in a cottage on his estate in the Mugello countryside to the north-east of Florence. There he translated Plato's works into Latin, and read and discussed them with Cosimo. It was the first time all Plato's dialogues had appeared in a form Western Christendom could read. Niccoli, an influential humanist and friend of Cosimo, was an avid collector of rare ancient manuscripts, paying agents to search for them across Europe and almost bankrupting himself in the process. Cosimo bailed him out, and by the time Niccoli died in 1437 he had bequeathed him his collection of eight hundred manuscripts. Half of these became the heart of the Medici Library, founded in 1444; the rest were split between Cosimo's private collection and the library that he founded at San Giorgio Maggiore in Venice in gratitude for its hospitality during his exile. At one point Cosimo employed over forty-five copyists, who produced over two hundred manuscripts in two years. He also patronised collectors such as Poggio Bracciolini, whom he had met at the Council of Constance. Bracciolini searched out ancient texts throughout Europe, often using covert methods such as bribing reluctant abbots and copying manuscripts when forbidden to do so.

Towards the end of his life, Cosimo spent more time in his mountain estates. He had become increasingly immobile, inflicted by gout, a hereditary form of arthritis involving painful and ultimately chronic inflammation of the joints. The sight of Cosimo and his two sons, never the most prepossessing in appearance, having to be carried in chairs up the steps at the Palazzo Medici was a humiliation he could not bear. He was increasingly vexed by the question of reputation and legacy. In a moving passage, Vespasiano sheds light:

> Now Cosimo, having applied himself to the temporal affairs of the state, the conduct of which was bound to leave him with certain matters on his conscience – as is the case with all those who are fain to govern states and take the leading place – awoke to a sense of his condition, and was anxious that God might pardon him, and secure to him the possession of his earthly goods. Wherefore he felt he must needs turn to pious ways, otherwise his riches would be lost to him. He had prickings of conscience that certain portions of his wealth – where it came from I cannot say – had not been righteously gained.[42]

He worried that the dynasty he and his father had so fastidiously built would wither away. 'I know that at my death my sons will be involved in more trouble than the sons of any citizen of Florence who has died for many years,'[43] he is said to have remarked. His misanthropy was not helped by his health. Death, he suspected, was always round the corner. 'He was always in a hurry to have his commissions finished because with his gout he feared he would die young,' noted Vespasiano.

Increasingly ill, he withdrew from public office. On his estate at Il Trebbio or at his Villa Careggi he would prune his vines and tend his olives (in the brief periods when he could walk) or chat to country folk. He would sit for hours, lost in thought, doing most of his business in his windowless, candlelit chapel. In the search for intellectual and spiritual justification for his actions, he had Ficino read Plato aloud to him. He was particularly interested in the philosopher's ideas about the immortality of the soul; he pondered the idea of a republic ruled by a philosopher king and whether that applied to him. He commissioned Bartolomeo da Colle, the chancellor of the palace, to read Aristotle's *Ethics* to him. He heard mass regularly.

When his wife, Contessina, asked him why he spent so long sitting with his eyes shut, he would say: 'to get them used to it'. When she urged him to try to get up from his chair, he is said to have replied: 'When we are going to the country, you spend weeks preparing for the move. Allow me a little time preparing my own move to the country from which I will not return.'[44] Gloom took hold of the family. One of his grandsons, Cosimino, died just before his sixth birthday. Two years later, his favourite son, the hugely overweight Giovanni, died of a heart attack.

In 1464, aged seventy-five, Cosimo died while listening to Ficino reading Plato. He had made his funeral arrangements long in advance. Most important was reconciliation with God. He was desperate for a Christian burial. He knew that this was denied to usurers and, in the fashion typical of the Medicis and the papacy, in his dying days he struck a deal with Pope Eugenius that worked for both sides. He would be absolved of his sins if he poured more money into church restoration. This he readily agreed to do. He paid for mass to be said for his soul for 365 days.

His funeral, noted Machiavelli, 'was conducted with the utmost pomp and solemnity, the whole city following his corpse to the tomb in the church of St Lorenzo, on which, by public decree, was inscribed, "Father Of His Country"'.[45] Cosimo the Elder lies beneath the very centre of the nave of the church of San Lorenzo, in a mausoleum that was built later for other members of the Medici dynasty. His friend, the sculptor Donatello, is also buried there.

The business quickly deteriorated. Cosimo had left the bank under-capitalised and overstretched, with a number of large debts to call in. His son Piero the Gouty took charge at the age of almost fifty, but spent most of the next five years bedridden. It was Cosimo's grandson, Lorenzo, who took the dynasty to new heights, albeit not through its banking activities. Illustriously titled '*Il Magnifico*', he survived attempted assassination in 1478 to become the unofficial king of Florence for a total of twenty-three years. His era marked the high point of the Renaissance; his court fostered a flowering of art, music and poetry, turning Florence into Italy's cultural capital. He had Michelangelo live at his home for five years, at the height of his cre-ativity. He sponsored and befriended Botticelli and Leonardo da Vinci. This was Florence's Golden Age.

Yet Lorenzo had no appetite for business and shortly before his death, aged forty-three, the Medici Bank failed and the family was driven out of the city. Florence fell under the control of Girolamo Savonarola, a Dominican monk who led a puritanical republic against the heresy and 'paganism' of the humanists. Manuscripts, artworks and musical instruments, alongside gambling tables, cosmetics and women's hats, were hurled on to his 'bonfire of the vanities' – a fire up to sixty feet high and forty feet wide created on the Piazza della Signoria. Savonarola successfully played on popular discontent, particularly among the poor, against the gilded wealth of the new Florence. He was eventually denounced as a heretic, imprisoned in the Alberghetto (where Cosimo had been detained) and burned at the stake.

The Medicis returned to Florence; but this time, and unlike Cosimo the Elder, there was no need to operate in the shadows. They assumed public office, reaching the papacy with Leo X and Clement VII and the throne of France with Henry II's bride, Catherine, and Maria, who married Henry IV.

A family that in 1378 had supported an insurrection of the urban poor was transformed into one of Europe's enduring aristocratic houses. Cosimo de' Medici succeeded in bringing first wealth, then status.

Some eighty years after his death, the Florentine historian Francesco Guicciardini said of him: 'He had a reputation such as probably no private citizen has ever enjoyed from the fall of Rome to our own day.'[46] The Medici model – self-enrichment, reappraisal and philanthropy – was to be replicated by others in history, not least the robber baron Andrew Carnegie (see Chapter 9). Machiavelli summed up Medici's ethical contortions: 'Though he was constantly expending money in building churches, and in charitable purposes, he sometimes complained to his friends that he had never been able to lay out so much in the service of God as to find the balance in his own favour, intimating that all he had done, or could do, was still unequal to what the Almighty had done for him.'[47]

According to the *Zibaldone*, the 'notebook' (or chronicle) written by the entrepreneur Rucellai, Cosimo told him: 'All those things have given me the greatest satisfaction and contentment because they are not only for the honour of God but are likewise for my own remembrance. For fifty years, I have done nothing else but earn money and spend money; and it became clear that spending money gives me greater pleasure than earning it.'

CHAPTER 5

Francisco Pizarro – Conquest and plunder

Everybody has equal opportunity, and I think
that is true for everything.

Mukesh Ambani

The most basic form of wealth acquisition is plunder, or to give it a more modern term, commodity exploitation. In the early sixteenth century, the Spanish and Portuguese embarked on a global race to extract natural resources from lands in the New World that young adventurers were discovering at a frenetic pace. Francisco Pizarro and his fellow conquistadores brought back untold wealth to their king. Yet many of them died along the way or had their assets taken away from them. They failed the first essential test of those who acquire wealth – to provide for themselves and their descendants, and so establish an enduring legacy.

For years these men ventured into unknown territory in search of gold and silver. Their determination eventually paid off when the leader of the Incas offered all his empire's riches in return for his freedom. They were presented with so much gold that they struggled to melt it down quickly enough. Once the Inca emperor had served his purpose, he was unceremoniously garrotted. As the gold made its way home, and as stories emerged of untold riches to be stolen, Spaniards made their way across the rough seas, leading to warfare between rival groups. The speed with which an entire continent was explored, subdued and settled amazed even the conquistadores themselves. By 1550, nine years after Pizarro's death, tens of thousands of colonists had spread across these vast lands.

So strict were the social norms back home in Castile that many invaders decided to stay in the new territories, where they could enjoy their wealth unencumbered by questions of class. Yet, while they enjoyed freedoms and better lifestyles in their adopted homes – procuring land, wives, mistresses and slaves – few managed to hang on to their gains as the Spanish state moved in to consolidate its power. Politically and economically, the most important beneficiary was the crown. It signed off on the contracts, ensuring that it received a minimum stake of 20 per cent on everything that was seized. This was known as the Royal Fifth.

The early conquistadores provided a source of capital and wealth for the Old World that would ensure its hegemony for five centuries. They produced a business model that proved remarkably durable. Extractive colonisation continued unabated well into the twentieth century, courtesy of Western multinationals in what was then termed the Third World. In more recent times a small slew of Russians have divided up their country's commodities with the connivance of the state and its leaders. While the manner of conquest may have become more sophisticated over time, the race for ownership of resources has not.

The first to set sail across the Atlantic was Christopher Columbus – or Cristoforo Colombo, as he was known in his native Genoa, or Cristóbal Colón, in his adopted Spain. For over a decade, between 1492 and 1503, he made four trips in search of what he hoped were the Indies, only to discover the American continent. Before that, he had spent years lobbying royalty for the resources to make his journeys; each of his speculative proposals was rebuffed. After rejections from King John II of Portugal and Henry VII of England, he finally received the reluctant acquiescence of Queen Isabella I of Castile, who persuaded her husband and fellow monarch Ferdinand II of Aragon to join. Receiving Columbus in the Alcázar in Córdoba (seat of the newly acquired land of Granada), the two monarchs granted him an annual allowance of twelve thousand *maravedis* (the gold and silver coinage in use in Spain at the time) and the right to become governor of all lands where he set foot. He was also given the rights to 10 per cent of any gold or silver he found. Just as importantly, he was made a hereditary noble, awarded the status that he and many of his fellow adventurers craved. The deal was entitled the *Capitulación de Santa Fe*, and it would set the terms for a generation of discovery.

Columbus's first expedition cost a mere two million *maravedis*, roughly the annual income of a minor Spanish noble.[1] Out of this modest investment would grow one of the world's richest empires, and the fortunes of many a European in the New World. Yet Columbus's story ends in acrimony, as so many of them did. When the Spanish established their first colony on Hispaniola (the island that comprises modern-day Haiti and the Dominican Republic), they met with stiff resistance. It took some time for authority to be restored and the colony to be refounded, much to the King's displeasure back home. By 1495, the crown had broken its monopoly deal with Columbus, and begun handing out licences to other adventurers. Competition was becoming intense.

In these early years, no explorer was sure of what to expect or how much he could get away with. They sometimes didn't even know where they were; Columbus went to his death still claiming to have landed in Asia. He was sent home in chains by a new, royally appointed governor, because Hispaniola had become so unruly. He stood accused of torture, mutilation and other assorted abuses of authority. Given that such behaviour was standard practice, his detractors were probably motivated largely by rivalry. Returning to Spain, Columbus and his brothers were briefly jailed. On his release he was refused the governorship of the West Indies and had his 10 per cent share of income from the new lands revoked, even though it had been agreed under the *Capitulación*. Increasingly ill and embittered, he died aged fifty-four, long before his achievement was properly commemorated.

Battles such as this set the tone for the relationship between the crown and the conquerors, and the conflicts that would entangle the

Pizarro brothers in Peru more than four decades later. Increasing quantities of gold, emeralds, and pearls were now being discovered. This was
the lawless and highly lucrative world into which Francisco Pizarro was
drawn.

Trujillo is a picturesque walled town in a largely forgotten part of Spain
in the south-western province of Extremadura some distance from sea.
It is from this one small pocket of the country that a succession of conquistadores has come. This was the home of the four Pizarro boys, three
of whom, including Francisco, were illegitimate.

Born probably in 1471 (the exact year is unknown), Francisco was
the son of an infantry colonel, Gonzalo Pizarro Rodrigues de Aguilar,
who had served in Navarre and in the Italian campaigns under
Gonzalo Fernández de Córdoba. His mother, Francisca Gonzalez
Mateos, was the young handmaiden of Aguilar's aunt, who lived in a
nunnery. As it was deemed inappropriate for the bastard son of a noble
of the second order to live in the family home on the main square, the
Plaza Mayor, Francisco had to live with his mother just out of town. So
desperate was he to prove his status and emulate his father that young
Francisco called himself 'the son of Captain Gonzalo Pizarro'. He had
another role model (and rival) whom he was eager to outshine: his
second cousin on his father's side was none other than Hernán Cortés,
whose conquest of the Aztec Empire of Mexico was becoming the stuff
of legend.

Pizarro's status is a matter of historical dispute. His parents paid little
attention to his education and he grew up illiterate – something that
was not uncommon at the time, even for nobles.[2] Some historians
describe him as a swineherd. While his home was in rural surroundings and animals would naturally have been part of his upbringing, this
seems an unfairly pejorative depiction of his standing.[3] The rivalry of
the time has transferred itself to the present day, with defenders of
Pizarro accusing historians partial to Cortés of being behind such
stories.

The 'Trujillo effect' would have a significant bearing on the conquests.
This one small town provided a considerable number of conquistadores.
The kinship element was important. Cortés's example spurred on the

young men of the region, not least the Pizarros, to try their luck. Francisco first travelled to the Americas in 1502, as part of the largest fleet ever to set sail for the new lands. The thirty ships, led by the new governor of Hispaniola, Nicolás de Oviando, took 2500 men from Spain to pacify the unruly island. Seven years later, Pizarro was part of an expedition to the Gulf of Uraba, on the coast of modern Colombia, led by Alonso de Ojeda, another exuberant adventurer who had flirted with death while finding great riches in the land that came to be known as Venezuela.

Pizarro's progress was slow by the standards of the time. He had to wait another four years for his next adventure. By then he was over forty years old, but this was his breakthrough. In September 1513, a small group of Spaniards led by Vasco Nuñéz de Balboa reached the top of a mountain range overlooking the Chucunaque River in the isthmus of Panama. Balboa's men had been drawn south from the Spanish settlements in the Caribbean by rumours of 'rivers of gold'. Below them the waters of what they called the *Mar del Sur*, the South Sea, came into view. They had become the first Europeans to see the Pacific Ocean. Giving thanks to God, they scratched crosses and the name of Ferdinand, the King of Aragon, with their swords into the bark of the trees there.[4]

Pizarro was by now seen as one of the more experienced and reliable adventurers. One of his uncles, Juan, had amassed land on Hispaniola, giving Francisco a ready-made base for his chosen career. Vincente de Valverde, a Franciscan friar and distant relative of both Pizarro and Cortés, accompanied him on several of his expeditions. He described him as a natural, as having been 'bred in the Indies'.[5]

The common practice among this first generation of conquistadores was to enter into 'companies' – usually temporary partnerships – with others in order to protect and extend their business interests. The early conquerors preferred to call each other *compañero*, partner – a term with business connotations – rather than to use military language.[6] They saw themselves as entrepreneurs. Once they had identified their expedition, the companies would first need to raise private capital for ships, supplies and men. This could come from the Castilian nobility and backers at court, but it often came from banks in Italy, particularly Genoa. The companies had to secure royal permission for their expeditions by convincing the crown that they were worth the effort. As a result, successful expeditions tended to include men from all social stations – they needed soldiers and sailors; they attracted poor men seeking their fortune; but they also needed accountants and clergymen for the conversion of the local population. Most of all, they needed influential men with contacts at court.

Class played an important part in the balance of risk and rewards. As an illegitimate son, Pizarro had seen from birth certain avenues closed off to him in Spain. The New World was different. He had more freedom to make his own way in a nascent colonial society, unencumbered by the tight social norms of the old country. Many of the men who made up the sailors and foot-soldiers of each expedition, who came from the lower rungs of Spanish society, decided to stay in their adopted lands, instead of returning to a country where they would be looked down on, no matter how much money they had made. Some of the men on Columbus's first voyage, before they even left, sold the guns and horses they had been given, bought cheaper, inferior replacements, and pocketed the difference.[7] They wanted to stay in the New World, and the desire to live like a landed gentleman there was strong and enduring.

Pizarro rose rapidly through the ranks of the new society, making a name for himself as a strong commander, loyal to whoever happened to be his boss. He was prepared to show his ruthless side and was intensely political, turning on old allies when it was expedient. He ingratiated himself with the governor of the new colonies, Pedrarias Dávila. In 1518 on the orders of his boss, he arrested his old captain, Balboa, on charges of treason. Balboa was a far more popular figure than his successor, Dávila, and was therefore seen as a threat. The story has it that when a startled Balboa saw Pizarro approaching him with a contingent of heavily armed men, he exclaimed: 'But you are Pizarro. You used not to come out and greet me in this way.'[8] The following year, Balboa was rushed through a hasty trial and beheaded.

After disposing of Balboa, Pizarro was rewarded with the titles of mayor and magistrate of the recently founded Panama City. During his four-year tenure, news reached the Spanish colony of a gold-rich territory they called Viru. The name derived from the river on which it stood, Piru.

The man in charge of the expedition, Pascual de Andagoya, had fallen ill and had to abort his journey south. Pizarro seized the opportunity, forming a company to exploit the possible riches of the unknown land. In 1524, he came to a deal with Diego Almagro, a soldier, and Hernando de Luque, a priest, to explore the Pacific coast south of Panama. De Luque provided ships and money. Almagro, another illegitimate son, was a runaway servant who had stabbed a rival in a fight back in Spain and subsequently fled to the Indies to start anew. Also known as *El Adelantado* and *El Viejo*, he had been a friend and ally of Balboa. But such concerns were brushed aside. Pizarro's offer was too good to resist. Almagro and Pizarro were both men of the New World; there was little for them to return to back home. Under the deal, which they dubbed the *Empresa del Levante*, Pizarro was to be the boss. The trouble was it was oral, a gentlemen's agreement, and these were no gentlemen.

The first expedition to Peru set off in September 1524 with around eighty men and forty horses. They got only as far as the Colombian coast before being turned back by bad weather, lack of food and skirmishes with natives. Two years later they were off again, even though Dávila had been unimpressed by their first venture and was reluctant to give them permission. In the end, the governor acquiesced, partly because his focus was elsewhere. He too was embarking on a venture – to unearth the riches of Nicaragua. Second time around, in 1526, Pizarro and his merry band made it to the mouth of the Colombian river of San Juan. Pizarro stayed in the area, commanding his experienced New World captain Bartolomé Ruiz to explore further down the coast. Having crossed the equator, Ruiz encountered a raft containing native Incas and a booty of textiles, ceramic objects and some gold, silver and emeralds. He kept three of the raft's crew, to be trained as interpreters, before letting the rest go.

The men's stories, and the objects they had seen, whetted the appetites of the other explorers. It was decided that Almagro and de Luque would sail back to Panama to seek reinforcements. Even though they took some gold with them, the new governor, Pedro de los Ríos, ordered the entire operation to return, sending two ships down the coast to bring Pizarro back. A furious Pizarro refused to obey, drawing a line in the sand and writing:

There lies Peru with its riches;
Here, Panama and its poverty.
Choose, each man, what becomes a brave Castilian.

Thirteen men chose to stay with him – later to be known as the Famous Thirteen. They constructed a small boat and sailed to the nearby Isla Gorgona, where they remained for seven months before new provisions arrived. Almagro and de Luque rejoined them and by April 1528 they had made it to the north-western region of Tumbes, just inside Peru. There they received a warm welcome from the natives, who called them 'Children of the Sun', because of their gleaming armour. After exploring further down the coast, they decided to return to Panama to prepare for what they hoped would be the decisive expedition to discover the gold-rich new lands of the south.

Back in Panama, an increasingly jealous Ríos refused permission for the third expedition. Pizarro immediately headed back to Spain, to seek an audience with King Charles I. In Toledo, he described to the monarch the territory he had explored 'to extend the empire of Castile'. The King was impressed, but as he was about to set off for Italy, he left it to his queen, Isabella of Portugal, to sign the *Capitulación de Toledo* – a licence to Pizarro to conquer Peru. He was officially named governor of the still-to-be-conquered land, and invested with all authority and prerogatives. This formalisation of Pizarro's status would later sow the seeds of discord with Almagro. Pizarro set off from Toledo back to his hometown of Trujillo to convince friends and family to join him. Among them were his three brothers, Gonzalo, Juan and Hernando. The last of these was the only one who was legitimate and the only one who would survive their adventures.

By 1530, Pizarro and Almagro were in their fifties. One might have thought that the wealth they had acquired from the conquest and settlement of Panama would have knocked some of the edge off their ambitions. The reverse was the case. His entourage reinforced, Pizarro assembled a force of 180 men, 27 horses and 3 ships. When they arrived back in Tumbes in July 1532, they found it deserted and destroyed. They advanced inland, startling local populations as they fired their guns in the air and rode their horses with a swagger.

The supreme Inca leader, Atahualpa, watched them carefully but let them travel unimpeded. He could not possibly have seen how such a small force could pose a threat – by then, Pizarro's small battalion had been depleted yet further through disease. The Inca Empire stretched over the Andes from Ecuador to Argentina, from the coast of Peru to the slopes of the Amazon basin. Atahualpa had tens of thousands of men at his disposal. His confidence was already high. For two years he had been fighting his older brother, Huascar, over the title and inheritance that their father, Huayna Capac, had divided between them. Atahualpa had finally defeated and captured Huascar in a battle at Quito (capital of present-day Ecuador). On his victorious march back to Cuzco, his seat of power, Atahualpa ordered his men to rest and to wait near the town of Cajamarca for the arrival of the strange men from afar.

This was one of the defining moments in the conquest of the New World; one of the most transparent examples of European brutality and greed for gold cloaked in religiosity. It was also a testament to Pizarro's cunning, determination and extraordinary courage.

In Cajamarca, Atahualpa didn't think for one moment that he was in any danger. Indeed, he was looking forward to greeting the visitors, on his own terms. He had brought them into one of the most mountainous and impenetrable parts of his empire. He ordered his procession of eighty thousand armed men, sturdy veterans and nobles among them, to set up camp just outside the town.

As they waited, the Spaniards feared that the Incas' huge army might descend on them and slaughter them at any time. Their nearest reinforcements were a thousand kilometres away in Panama. Fear in their camp proved to be a great leveller between the high- and low-born men, according to the chronicler Cristóbal de Mena: 'There was no distinction between great and small, or between foot-soldiers and horsemen. Everyone performed sentry rounds fully armed that night. So did the good old Governor [Francisco Pizarro], who went about encouraging the men. On that day all were knights.'[9]

Eventually Atahualpa approached the town, accompanied by seven thousand men dressed in ceremonial garments and armed only with small axes. Unbeknown to him, the Spaniards had mounted their four cannons on rooftops in the centre of the town. Horsemen were concealed in surrounding streets. The expedition's priest, and later Archbishop of Peru, Vicente Valverde, went to meet the Inca King in Cajamarca's main square. Bible and breviary in hand, he delivered a sermon to the Inca leader, via an interpreter, that started with Adam and Eve, moving on to Jesus's death on the cross and his ascent to heaven. In his sonorous voice, Valverde declared that all should bow down before God, Christ and the King of Spain, 'the monarch of the world'. He concluded his proclamation with the words: 'The Lord our God, Living and Eternal, created Heaven and Earth, and one man and one woman, of whom you and I, and all the men of the world, were and are descendants.'[10] This was the *Requirimento*, a document read out to groups of indigenous people requiring them to submit to the authority of the Pope and the Spanish crown, and convert to Christianity.[11] When it generated no response, as was often the case, the Spanish were able to engage the natives in a 'just war' against heretics.

At this point, the narratives vary. One story has it that Atahualpa was offered the Bible but didn't know what to do with it. Valverde, trying to help, took it back but touched the King in doing so. Atahualpa then gave him a blow to the arm. A simpler version says that the Inca leader took the gospel and threw it on the ground, declaring he would be 'no man's tributary'. Either way, Pizarro took his reaction as a cue to teach the locals a lesson. It is also possible that some Indians in the town who were loyal to Huascar may have provided intelligence to the Spaniards in an act of revenge against Atahualpa. Valverde absolved the troops of the blood they were about to spill. Thus began a slaughter that was extravagant even by the standards of the conquistadores. Pizarro's cavalrymen raced around the town, hacking to death everyone in sight. None of the Incas had seen horses before; terrified and effectively defenceless, few of the seven thousand survived. If that figure is correct (Spanish historians argue about the death toll), each conquistador must have killed one native roughly every twenty seconds.[12] Atahualpa's retinue was loyal to the end, refusing to drop his litter, even after their arms and legs had been hacked off, supporting it even with their stumps. The streets, according to the chronicles, flowed with blood – not that one would have known that from the picture painted by Hernando Pizarro. In a letter to the Royal Audience of Santo Domingo, the capital of Hispaniola, he describes in considerable detail the events leading up to Cajamarca. As for the actual killing, he states:

> The friar [Valverde] went to the Governor and reported what was being done and that no time was to be lost. The Governor sent to me, and I had arranged with the captain of the artillery that, when a sign was given, he should discharge his pieces, and that, on hearing the reports, all the troops should come forth at once. This was done, and as the Indians were unarmed they were defeated without danger to any Christian.

The one person Pizarro was determined to spare was Atahualpa. One account has it that he personally defended the Inca King, even taking some blows for his courage. What actually happened at Cajamarca will probably never be known, but the numerical disparity between the forces and the unlikely nature of Pizarro's victory propelled him to the top rank of Spanish conquistadores.

With Atahualpa captured, the plunder could begin. The account given by Pizarro's personal secretary and chronicler, Francisco de Xeres, who returned to Seville the following year, demonstrates the extent to which a desperate Atahualpa offered to collect his own ransom. Xeres quotes him as begging his captors: 'I will give enough gold to fill a room 22 feet long and 17 feet wide, up to a white line which is halfway up the wall.' Xeres adds: 'The height would be up to a man's stature and a half. As for silver, he said he would fill the whole chamber with it twice over. He undertook to do this in two months.'

Tribute poured in from all over Atahualpa's empire. For weeks Incas from far and wide – men, women and children – filed faithfully to Cajamarca carrying on their shoulders precious gold and silver objects to fill the ransom rooms. Devotional objects, dishes, bowls, platters and urns taken from temples, sepulchres and palaces arrived from throughout the land. All the Spaniards needed to do was stay put. Pizarro's method of collection set a precedent for how tribute would be gathered in Spanish-occupied Peru. Three of his men were sent to Cuzco with a local contingent to speed up the consignment from the capital. This included seven hundred sheets of gold torn from the walls of a temple. Hernando de Soto, one of Pizarro's captains, found in the Inca military encampment alone eighty thousand pesos' worth of gold and fourteen valuable emeralds.[13]

From May to July 1533, under the conquistadores' watchful eyes, a team of local labourers worked at nine furnaces to melt down the gold. Extraordinary pieces of art were lost for ever. The gold was cast in bars, weighed, stamped with the royal seal and shipped back to Spain. For the conquistadores, it had little intrinsic value, or aesthetic or romantic allure; its value was determined by weight. Smiths were melting down sixty thousand pesos' worth of gold each day.[14]

A strict system of reward was imposed. Individual Spaniards were not supposed to pocket or steal any gold or silver items; everything was to be centralised, melted down and divided up as Pizarro dictated. Foot-soldiers got one share, roughly equal to forty-five pounds of gold and ninety pounds of silver. Horsemen received double these amounts, although each individual man's share was often altered depending on his personal role in the battles of the conquest. The lower orders rarely received their entitlement, but few complained. This was still more money than they would ever have seen in their lives before.

Francisco Pizarro took thirteen times a foot-soldier's share, plus Atahualpa's gold throne, which was worth another two. The four Pizarro brothers between them took 24 of the 217 parts of the treasure, a relatively democratic outcome.[15] They could have taken more, but they probably feared a backlash. At the heart of all the deals, from Columbus onwards, was the crown's kickback – the Royal Fifth that was cut into all loot from the colonies, no matter how it had been extracted. The arrangement was not dissimilar to the terms of engagement of modern Russia: we won't mess with you, as long as you keep the money coming into our coffers.

Gold was so common in Peru that Europeans would make transactions among themselves by just passing lumps around, without bothering to measure or weigh them properly.[16] Many of the conquistadores had racked up debts fitting out their expeditions, knowing that they could pay them as soon as the gold started to come in.[17] The wills of the many who fell to disease or died at the hands of Incas, or in the subsequent civil wars, show that sizeable portions of the worth of their estates were made up of money they were owed by their *compañeros*.

Pizarro's astonishing success in defenestrating Atahualpa made him an object of great respect, but also increasing envy. With gold production (or rather melting) in full flow, Almagro arrived with a force of 150 men. They had all missed out on Cajamarca, so they were eager for some booty of their own.[18]

Leaving Atahualpa as the official head of the Inca state was a smart move. It ensured that his word was followed and that the pace of gold procurement was maintained. Atahualpa thought the invaders would take their bounty and leave. He could not see how such a small number intended to settle his empire and take his land. He underestimated their resolve.

After the ransom had been collected, Pizarro had no further need for Atahualpa. The one person he needed out of the way was de Soto, who had befriended the jailed Inca leader – the two would play chess together. Pizarro sent Atahualpa's protector off on a spurious expedition upcountry, then, out of the blue, put the King on trial for the murder of his brother – something that had been known about, and tacitly agreed, long before. Pizarro had him strangled, but not before he was forcibly 'converted' to Christianity.

On his return, de Soto made clear that Spain had no right to put to death a sovereign leader in his own land. Pizarro shrugged his shoulders. Later, King Charles also expressed his annoyance at the idea of an illegitimate chancer from Trujillo being responsible for regicide: 'We have been displeased by the death of Atahualpa, since he was a monarch and particularly as it was done in the name of justice.' Yet Pizarro knew that, for all his manufactured anger, the King would soon forget the incident as he watched in awe as the riches kept gushing in. For good measure, he took Atahualpa's ten-year-old wife, Cuxirimay Ocllo Yupanqui, as one of his mistresses. She took the name Doña Angelina and would later bear him two sons, Juan and Francisco.

With the Inca Empire in turmoil, Pizarro began the process of formal settlement of Peru that the Spanish crown wanted to see. After installing a new puppet emperor, the Spaniards pressed on to Cuzco. Their captains moved into Inca palaces, throwing out the old nobility. Soldiers were given central plots of land, making the colonial quarter of the city easily defensible. The melting down of gold artefacts into currency began all over again. There was only half as much gold as at Cajamarca – much had already gone to pay Atahualpa's ransom – but the city contained four times as much silver. Almagro's men finally got their rewards. They demolished the Qurikancha temple, the most important place of worship to the Sun God in the entire kingdom. It contained a garden of plants with silver stems and gold ears – all were seized and melted. Cristóbal de Molina, a priest watching on, recorded: 'Their only concern was to collect gold and silver to make themselves all rich; what was being destroyed was more perfect than anything they enjoyed and possessed.'[19] Having stripped the temple of its gold, they covered it over with a church.

This was cultural theft on a grand scale. With Cuzco in Spanish hands, the conquest of Peru was complete. 'This city is the greatest and finest ever seen in this country or anywhere in the Indies,' Pizarro wrote to the King. 'We can assure your Majesty that it is so beautiful and has such fine buildings that it would be remarkable even in Spain.' Yet with Cuzco deemed an unsuitable location for the capital of the new lands, Pizarro founded the coastal city of Lima in January 1535. This was one of the achievements of which he was most proud.

Meanwhile, the first Peruvian gold, accompanied by Hernando Pizarro, started to leave for Spain. Four ships disembarked with more than 700,000 pesos in gold and 49,000 marks in silver.[20] The Pizarro family was acting together as a solid business enterprise, and Francisco happily trusted his brother with the loot. King Charles – for all his supposed concerns about the behaviour of the conquistadores – allowed some artefacts brought back in their original form to be displayed to an amazed public before they were melted down. One of the early returnees wrote: 'There were twelve of us conquistadores in Madrid and we spent a great deal of money, for the King was absent and the Court was without knights. We had so many parties every day that some were left with no money. There were jousts and hooplas and *juegos de cañas* all so lavish that it was a wonder to see them.'[21]

The point of these celebrations was not just to show off, but to convince the crown that further expeditions and reinforcements in the New World were worth the investment. The Pizarros also wanted to demonstrate that they could be trusted to rule the new lands. Hernando set about procuring provisions and specialist labour for his brothers in Peru. Men across Europe were beguiled by the conquistadores, seeing them as models, or mentors, for a career in the New World.

By this point, the crown was becoming increasingly suspicious of the Pizarros and men like them. The King was alarmed by the adventurers' braggadocio. Many Spaniards, dazzled by the amount of gold they had seen coming from Cajamarca and Cuzco, organised their own expeditions to push into the Amazon in search of loot. Other colonies were complaining that their small populations of colonists were being depleted by the gold rush to the south; the governor of Puerto Rico caught some Spaniards trying to leave his island and had their feet cut off.[22] The crown imposed new rules. One of these was a decree that only married men or wealthy merchants could leave for Peru. On the ground, this was largely ignored.

The Spaniards could usually intimidate local Inca rulers, from Atahualpa downwards, to do their bidding. In 1536, with the revenue from gold reaching a peak, the Inca leader Manco Yupanqui launched a rebellion. Initially, he had cooperated with Pizarro, procuring for the occupiers more gold treasure and young women. However, angered by his treatment at the hands of Francisco's brothers – who intermittently imprisoned him – he raised an army of tens of thousands of warriors, marched on Cuzco and laid siege to the city for ten months. Many of his men fell victim to smallpox; the remainder were met by the Spaniards and their allies at the nearby fortress of Ollantaytambo and routed. Manco retreated to the jungle where he remained nominal head of the resisting Incas until his death in 1544, which came at the hands of Almagro's supporters. No other ruler was able to repeat the scale of his rebellion.

Inca civilisation had been finally subjugated. The enrichment of the new colonial class and the impoverishment of the native population worked in synchrony. According to one estimate, the Gini coefficient for the region stood at 0.22 in 1491, before the Spanish conquest, denoting considerable equality. It rose steadily over the following centuries to reach 0.58 in 1790 – as high as the most unequal societies of the present day – before falling back slightly after Peruvian independence.[23] The money that flowed out of the Americas and into Spain would for centuries enrich only the top stratum of society. By the 1750s, the top 10 per cent had a share of national income that was fifteen times greater than the bottom 40 per cent.

The exploitation of resources may have been the motive for the conquistadores. But the Spanish crown had grander ambitions – to repopulate and 'civilise' the New World. To this end they needed to settle whole families, rather than leave the land in the hands of single and dissolute men. First he provided incentives for married men to travel. As early as 1502, Ferdinand instructed Luis de Arriaga, a *hidalgo* (knight) who had been on one of Columbus's first voyages, to found fifty new towns in the Caribbean with 'sound Spanish families'.[24] Men who moved with their families were rewarded with the free labour of Indian workers, depending on their social status. *Hidalgos* who moved to the New World with their wives were to be 'given eighty Indians, foot soldiers sixty, and even common labourers thirty'.[25] A strict ethnic policy existed. Jews and Muslims were banned from making the voyage west, while black Africans were allowed into the colonies only as slaves. This demarcation became ever harder to enforce. At least two men in Pizarro's 1530 expedition to Peru were of African descent, and the governor did not seem to judge them the worse for it.[26] Nevertheless, the early settlement voyages were planned meticulously; the crown wanted to transplant the social order of Spain, with its lords, *hidalgos* and priests, into its new territories.

The lightning conquests of Mexico and Peru changed this. They were undertaken by small groups of single men who found themselves lording it over vast lands with large populations, many living in developed urban centres. The crown could not stop the conquerors taking wives and mistresses and raping local women, creating a *mestizo* population of mixed ancestry. Francisco himself had four *mestizo* children with women who had been the wives of Inca nobles, but he was austere and abstemious compared to most. It was said that Cortés had a hundred concubines.

The legality of staking out territory was something that, formally at least, the Spanish wrestled with. Land parcelled out to the conquerors was run on the basis of the *encomienda*. This was a contract that granted the new lord the right to exploit free Indian labour. In Peru, while the land notionally remained in the hands of Inca rulers, its produce was handed over to the Spaniards as tribute.[27] The only obligation on the new self-styled lords of the manor was to look out for their workers' spiritual welfare by converting them en masse to Christianity.[28]

Encomiendas were common in Spanish colonies before the conquest of Peru; Pizarro already held one of the largest in Panama. A similar system, originating from the Spanish reconquest of Andalusia from the Muslims, had been used to divide up the land during Columbus's administration of the first colony on Hispaniola.[29] *Encomenderos* were supposed to live apart from their workers. They took up residence in the towns, becoming absentee landlords and employing enforcers known as *majordomos* – whose methods were often brutal – to ensure their tribute was collected. Some *majordomos* were old Inca chiefs who could regain a semblance of power – and become exempt from paying tribute – by doing the colonists' dirty work (similar to reeves in Norman England). Such acquiescence was another means of tax avoidance, albeit from a position of weakness rather than strength.

The Pizarro brothers were in a position to take the best estates in the most fertile valleys, and so they did. They divided up the land that had been the personal territory of the Inca ruler Huayna Capac, before they gave away anything else to their fellow adventurers.[30] They also used the system, and the patronage it offered, to neutralise the political threat posed by the old Inca aristocracy. Two grandsons of Capac were given *encomiendas*, as were daughters of the former emperors who married *conquistadores*.[31] So, while the Incas did not die out, in the sense that a large *mestizo* population developed with Inca ancestry, their culture was steadily emasculated.

Amid the brutality and the carnage lay a desire among the conquistadores for greater status. They enjoyed new titles – they were referred to as 'Don' by their peers, and had bestowed on them a coveted coat-of-arms.[32] Many of the higher-born *hidalgos*, who already enjoyed such privileges, were more likely to return home to Spain. Old money and old titles were disdainful of the *arrivistes*.

Although craving the rewards and titles he felt he deserved, Pizarro did not adapt his behaviour to that of the new gentry. He tended to fight on foot alongside the common men rather than on horseback, and on his own *encomiendas* he is said to have gone out to reap corn in the fields – a gross breach of the colonists' code of behaviour. He also personally supervised and worked on construction projects.[33] He seemed less concerned with the family name or legacy than his brothers, remaining every bit the rough adventurer to the end of his life. By 1540, up to thirty thousand locals were paying tributes on his and his children's estates – a sum that would have guaranteed a life of luxury.

The crown had long been discomfited by the idea of *encomiendas*. As early as 1512 – well before Pizarro had made his name in the Americas – a Royal Commission had declared the indigenous population to be, technically, free. 'It is not just for Christian princes to make war on infidels simply from a desire to obtain their wealth,' it noted. But the 'free' workers were not paid wages – only provided with clothing and housing. Their homes and villages were razed, to ensure inhabitants would live in the new Spanish towns or on plantations.[34] Concerned that the 'civilising', missionary task of the conquests was being undermined by what was essentially a system of slavery, King Charles outlawed the *encomiendas* in 1530. However, it soon became clear that this was the quickest and simplest way of purloining land and resources, and keeping the population subjugated. The business case was incontrovertible, and the practice was reinstated in 1534. From early in the Spanish settlement, one or two voices, usually from the Church, deplored the treatment of the local population in pursuit of profit. Some members of the Dominican order were outspoken opponents of the system. In 1510 a Dominican preacher, Fray Montesino, had made himself unpopular with his fellow settlers on Hispaniola by expounding from the pulpit:

In order to make you aware of your sins against the Indians, I have come up to this pulpit, I am a voice of Christ crying in the wilderness of this island. By what authority have you waged such detestable wars against people who were once living so quietly and peacefully in their own land? For, with the excessive work you demand of them, they fall ill and die or, rather, you kill them with your desire to extract and acquire more gold every day.[35]

Pragmatism usually prevailed. The Church had also benefited considerably from exploited labour and landownership alongside the conquistadores. The Pizarro brothers were particularly close to the Dominican order, and Hernando donated a hundred sacks of coca leaves per year to its monastery in Cuzco from his plantations. The value of the crop increased rapidly each year, ensuring huge trading riches for the clergy. The Dominican missionary Gaspar de Carbajal said: 'all that we have in this house was given to us by the Pizarros'.[36] The order's loyalty was guaranteed.

Diseases carried across the Atlantic by the settlers further threatened the survival of the indigenous population. Typhoid came first; the first outbreak of smallpox was reported in 1518, just before Cortés's final conquest of the Aztecs. Such was its impact that the chronicler Francisco López de Gómara wrote: 'the Aztecs later counted the years from it, as from some famous event'.[37] So quickly was the indigenous population declining that the colonisers began slave expeditions to other parts of the Caribbean to replenish their stocks of labour. Yet it wasn't easy to make up the numbers. Two-thirds of the slaves brought to Hispaniola in one of the first voyages died en route.[38]

Pizarro was also affected by epidemics during his conquest of Peru – they were not always unhelpful. The first Inca leader he had come across, Capac, was killed by smallpox carried by one of Pizarro's early expeditions. When he died, his body was carried through his empire to be venerated, which spread the disease further.[39] As many as 200,000 Incas, including much of the nobility, fell victim to such epidemics.[40] This caused the succession crisis that was engulfing the Inca Empire just as Pizarro's 1530 expedition appeared on the scene. It is impossible to see how the conquest would have been as straightforward without these outbreaks, which not only constituted a form of population control but debilitated and distracted the living. The economics of tribute depleted the population in other ways. Forced displacement of so many people took its toll. The sudden destruction of a way of life also reduced fertility rates. Spanish official and man of letters Hernando de Santillán described the lives of the Indians at the time:

> They live the most wretched and miserable lives of any people on earth. As long as they are healthy they are fully occupied only in working for tribute. Even when they are sick they have no respite, and few survive their first illness, however slight, because of the appalling existence they lead. Because of this they despair, for they ask only for their daily bread and cannot have even that. There are no people on earth so hardworking, humble or well behaved.[41]

Much of the population was literally worked to death, nowhere more than in the mines. A major breakthrough occurred when silver was discovered at Potosí (by an Inca). Pizarro made sure no time was wasted. Conscripted labourers were sent down the shafts; they worked there for up to a week at a stretch. The silver was combined with mercury and heated until the silver was pure, an extremely dangerous process.[42] Yet nobody objected – not the conquistadores, nor the Church, nor the crown. The output of Potosí provided a Royal Fifth of 1.5 million pesos per year, one of the largest and most consistent sources of revenue from the New World.

Hernando, the most business-minded of the Pizarro brothers, saw the mines as an investment with a long-term yield. He began stocking them with Spanish tools and bringing over a labour force of black slaves as early as 1536.[43] Hernando and Gonzalo supplemented the business in Potosí with control of the silver mines at Porco.[44] Pizarro-owned buildings dominated the town square and Porco became an early example of a 'company town', a model copied around the world in the centuries since. 'Your Highness has mines at Potosí worth more than Castile,' wrote one acolyte to Gonzalo.[45] Domingo de Santo Tomás, a missionary, wrote to the Council of the Indies: 'Some four years ago, to complete the perdition of this land, there was discovered a mouth of hell, into which a great mass of people enter every year and are sacrificed by the greed of the Spaniards to their "God". This is your silver mine called Potosí.'[46] But voices such as his were a tiny minority.

By 1570, the populations of Peru, Mexico and the rest of Central America may have been reduced by as much as 80 per cent from epidemics and forced labour.[47] In Peru alone, the number of inhabitants is estimated to have fallen from seven million to under two million in the fifty years following the conquest.[48]

The sheer volume of wealth, titles and land at stake, coupled with the lawlessness and 'might makes right' atmosphere of the new frontier, produced combustible rivalries among the conquistadores. The more lucrative the colony became, the more fragile were the deals that brought the protagonists there. Peru was particularly tense. Almagro was unhappy about playing second fiddle to Francisco and the other Pizarro brothers. Even years later he could not get over the fact of being absent from the looting at Cajamarca. (Compare that to a modern banker cut out of a deal, or an internet mogul bought out in the early days of a lucrative start-up.) Feeling that he deserved more for his role in lifting Manco's siege of Cuzco, in 1537 Almagro finally snapped. He had Hernando and Gonzalo Pizarro jailed, taking the city for himself. The conflict between Almagrists and Pizarrists erupted into civil war. At first, the Pizarro brothers toyed with the idea of reaching an accommodation with Almagro; Francisco proposed turning Cuzco over to the control of three 'neutrals'. Hernando consented – on condition that the neutrals were all Pizarros.[49]

When Almagro faced Francisco in person, Pizarro demanded: 'What is the reason why you took the city of Cuzco, that I won and discovered with so much toil?' Almagro replied: 'Watch what you're saying – that I took Cuzco from you and it was won by your person; you know very well who won it. And the land is the king's to give me, not a pasture of Trujillo.'[50] He was correct in that the vital question of ownership rights had not been settled.

Even though these two families had more gold and silver than they could ever know what to do with, the lust for yet more wealth led to their downfall. The Pizarros defeated Almagro's forces at the Battle of

Las Salinas in April 1538 and, in traditional fashion, they then had him garrotted. His son, Diego Junior, was stripped of his lands and left bankrupt.

Three years later, in June 1541, Diego exacted his revenge. One of the great moments of the Spanish conquest of the Americas was about to be played out. Twenty of his men stormed Pizarro's palace. Most of the courtiers fled; only a few remained to fight the intruders. Pizarro killed two attackers and ran through a third. While trying to pull his sword out of his assailant's body, he was stabbed in the throat. He fell to the floor and was repeatedly stabbed. As the legend goes, as he lay dying on the floor, he painted a cross in his own blood and cried out to Jesus: 'Come my faithful sword, companion of all my deeds.' Perhaps Pizarro went to his death convinced of the morality of his actions. The evocative final quote handed down is, in any case, an essential part of his legacy management.

The old friends and business partners who had sought their fortunes in the New World had finished each other off in their pursuit of it.

The murderers then tortured and killed Francisco's secretary to extract the whereabouts of the wealth that he had stashed away. They ransacked his townhouse, making off with jewels. Francisco's final testament, detailing his fortune and the heirs to whom it belonged, was stolen or destroyed by Almagro and his supporters. His children were hurriedly smuggled away into exile.[51] Almagro and his allies consolidated control, but only briefly. Hernando's forces regrouped, then captured and killed Diego.

Francisco was dead. Juan, the least-known Pizarro brother, had been killed at the hands of the Incas while defending Cuzco in 1536. Gonzalo took on the mantle for a while, becoming governor of Quito in the newly discovered Ecuador in 1541. He headed on from there into the Amazon basin with fellow *conquistador* Francisco Orellana (also from Trujillo and probably a relative) in search of the fabled lost city of gold they called El Dorado. Their adventure ended in failure, with many of the adventurers dying of disease.

By this point the Spanish occupation of the New World had taken on a greater sense of permanence. The crown saw the lands not just as sources of plunder, but in terms of an expansion of power and prestige. While the conquistadores' excessive use of violence might have been a touch embarrassing, and their free spirit more than a little annoying, they had served the royal family's interests perfectly. The newfound wealth derived from gold had allowed the monarchy to consolidate its absolutist power against internal rebellions, the most alarming of which was the Revolt of the Comuneros in 1520–1. Since then, the King and Queen had had more at their disposal to reward noble cliques. Cortés's and Pizarro's treasures were used to underwrite a credit boom to fund their imperial ambitions, stealing a march on Spain's European neighbours.

The wealth boom and the state's increasing thirst for income encouraged more Spaniards to declare themselves *hidalgos*. As well as enjoying higher status, nobles were exempt from many taxes on their lands (as was the case in France under Louis XIV, when the poorest bore the highest burden). With each new tax to pay for imperial expansion, more of the newly enriched batch of Spaniards, including those returned from the New World, set about fabricating claims to prove their nobility. By 1542, perhaps 12 per cent of the population had 'achieved' – or bribed their way to – *hidalgo* status. As *hidalgos* were not supposed to engage in 'vile and base professions', they did not engage in any productive work, which contributed to Spain's long-term economic decline from the seventeenth century onwards.[52]

In the Indies, the extreme brutality had served its purpose. In 1544 – conveniently late in the day – the New Laws were passed, in theory to protect the rights of what was left of the indigenous population. But mostly they were an attempt to stop a new autonomous class emerging thousands of miles from the political control of the royal court. They proposed to stop the granting of *encomiendas* and make them non-inheritable, so that a family like the Pizarros could not style themselves as aristocracy.[53]

Many of the conquistadores saw this as a threat to their business model, independence and even survival. With his eldest brother Francisco dead and eager to defend what he saw as the family's rightful possessions, Gonzalo Pizarro marched on Lima. He scored quick victories against those who remained loyal to the crown, culminating in the death of the King's first viceroy of Peru, Blasco Núñez Vela, in January 1546. Nearly five years after Francisco's assassination, the Pizarro family was firmly back in the saddle. There was even talk of crowning Gonzalo king of a new country, and elevating all his supporters to the ranks of aristocrats.[54] One of his supporters, Francisco de Carvajal, urged him to proclaim himself king because, if he did not, he would remain a vassal of the old crown and continue to be subject to Spanish justice for killing Núñez Vela. The only way to avoid such a fate was to break with Spain completely:

> No king can be a traitor. This land belongs to the Incas, their natural lords and, if it is not restored to them, you have more right to it than the King of Castile, for you and your brothers conquered it at your own expense and risk. I urge you, whatever may happen, crown yourself and call yourself king, for no other name befits one who has won an empire by his strength and courage. Die a king and not a vassal.[55]

Gonzalo resisted such talk. Perhaps, for all his ambition, he did want acceptance from Spanish society, as is often the case among those who suddenly find themselves wealthy. The roots of the conquistadores remained firmly in Extremadura and Castile.

Shortly after the death of Núñez Vela, the King's new man in Peru reached a deal with the colonists, offering to repeal the New Laws in return for their loyalty. Once that was secured, he had Gonzalo isolated and beheaded. So much for gentlemen's agreements, but the Pizarro brothers had more than once double-crossed others.

That left only one brother, Hernando, the legitimate and literate one. He was less prone to fighting, more to deal-making. He was described by one contemporary as a 'bad Christian with no fear of God and less devotion to the King'.[56] He regarded the Royal Fifth as nothing less than a scam. For some years he had been employing a full-time agent in Panama to find ways of bending the rules on customs duties and minimising his payments to the royal exchequer.[57] In so doing he created one of history's first tax havens, a lesson Caribbean islands such as Bermuda would learn for the future.

With all of his brothers now dead, and with the crown consolidating its position in Peru and across the new lands, Hernando returned to Spain. He knew punishment was awaiting him, but he was prepared to accept it in order to repatriate some of the family money. He was convicted at the Council of the Indies in Madrid for his part in the killing of Almagro. This was little more than an excuse to get him out of the way. Top priority for the King and his advisers was to consolidate their power over the conquistadores and to take more of their money.

Hernando spent twenty-one years in prison, mostly in the castle of La Mota in Valladolid, the same building in which he had stored the family's first fortune of gold after he had returned from the New World triumphant in 1534.[58] La Mota was more house arrest for celebrities than jail (one of the Borgias, Cesare, had been sent there thirty years earlier, but was said to have escaped by climbing down a rope). Hernando had access to pen and ink, and was able to acquire good food, all bought and paid for with Peruvian gold. Guests, including mistresses, were allowed to visit.[59]

The cycle of plunder, wanton destruction, death and punishment was complete. Francisco Pizarro had opened up one of the most important countries in the Spanish empire and, after enjoying certain luxuries out there in Peru, he had died without realising anything permanent for his family. The only one to survive and ultimately benefit was the wily Hernando.

The Pizarro family's creative accountants had been busy concealing their assets in the New World, minimising the family's exposure,[60] yet still they lost out. Many of the *encomiendas* were seized by the crown and given over to third parties. The judiciary even seized the townhouse that Francisco had built in Lima and used for his offices.[61]

Hernando spent much of his time inside and outside prison fighting off lawsuits. In 1563 the Council of the Indies pronounced that his lands had been ill gotten and that 'his' Indians should be transferred to the service of the crown. The protracted legal process meant that the Pizarro family continued to keep hold of, and benefit from, their possessions for some years. An order to sell off the mines at Porco, the most important pillar of the family fortune, was not carried out until 1580, by which time Hernando was dead. All in all, some of the wealth was forfeited, but much of it was kept. Pizarro also reaped the profits from the booming coca trade. His annual income of 32,000 pesos in and around 1550 was sizeable, and comparable to that of Cortés's family.[62] At the time of his release in 1561, Hernando was the largest landowner in Trujillo.[63] He returned to the family's hometown as a respectable, wealthy gentleman.

Yupanqui, Francisco Pizarro's mistress and widow of Atahualpa, took their daughter Francisca back to Spain, where she received her own large income from the conquered lands. At the age of eighteen, she married her uncle, Hernando, in order to keep the estates in the family – even though he was still languishing in prison at the time. She was later legitimised by imperial decree, taking the title Doña Francisca. Inca blood had married into Spanish nobility (albeit of the second order). She lived the rest of her life in Trujillo as a lady of high standing. Hernando lived into old age and died in comfortable circumstances.

The next generations consolidated the family fortune, but continued to struggle to fend off claims in the courts. In 1629, the next head of the Pizarro family, also called Francisco, was awarded by royal decree the title of marquis in Castile, in exchange for giving up the family's old claims of *encomiendas* in Peru.[64] He was also granted a decent yearly income. The Pizarros had traded some of their riches for status, becoming an established part of the Spanish nobility. New money acquired from conquest had become old money, as it usually does.

In the centre of the sleepy town of Trujillo, the palace built by Francisca Pizarro still stands today. On the other side of the Plaza Mayor is a giant statue of her father, Francisco, astride his horse in full regalia, the very picture of the *conquistador*. The statue's history is one of the many parts of the Pizarro story that are disputed. One probably mischievous rumour that is repeated in guidebooks for tourists says it is actually a monument to Cortés. The American sculptor, Charles Rumsey of Buffalo, tried to offer it to the Mexicans, but they refused it. So he offloaded it in Trujillo. Stories such as this infuriate the small but vociferous band of Pizarro aficionados. One of them is a naturalised

Belgian tour guide, Josiane Polart Plisnier, known locally as 'Susi'. She lays a wreath twice a year under the Pizarro statue to commemorate his patriotism and courage.

In the Extremadura city of Badajoz, the descendants of the family live on in the form of Hernando Pizarro, a civil engineer. His forebears are the original Hernando and a lady called Isabel who visited him in prison, and he bridles at what he says is the unfair treatment meted out to the Pizarros. He describes Francisco as 'brave and valiant', a man who inspires admiration for going to the other end of the world to seek wealth. He admits he had flaws, but decries the tendency among some historians and economists to transpose contemporary ethical norms to earlier eras. Spain is still grappling with legacies such as his, as is Latin America. In Franco's time, the conquistadores were fêted as heroes; in the 1980s and 90s, democratic Spain underwent a radical revision of its history, with politicians and diplomats apologising for the violence and appropriation of land, commodities and wealth.

Pizarro's renegade individualism, his tooth-and-claw colonialism, offended against the social codes of decorum back home. Yet the riches he brought back were gratefully received and subsumed into the mainstream. This process has been replicated many times over in subsequent centuries. The conquistadores were among the first to identify resource allocation and exploitation as a route to instant fortune.

After encouraging companies and private adventurers to take the huge risks involved in trade – and turning a blind eye to their excesses against indigenous populations – the Spanish, Portuguese, Dutch and British governments (and social elites) followed behind them. The colonies they established would provide political and economic power for centuries.

Francisco Pizarro and his brothers from a small town presided over one of the earliest gold rushes. The robber barons of the nineteenth century to the Russian oligarchs of today have learned much from their experiences. It is impossible to cast judgement on the conquistadores without reference to the many who succeeded them in the relentless search for riches from under the ground.

'He may have been the richest of them all': Roman politician and
property developer, Marcus Licinius Crassus

(Louvre, Paris, France / The Bridgeman Art Library)

Alain Le Roux swearing his allegiance to William the Conqueror and receiving the honour of Richmond in north Yorkshire

(British Library / Robana via Getty Images)

'So abundant is the gold which [is] found in the country that he is th[e] richest and most noble king in a[ll] the land': a detail from the 137[7] Catalan Atlas, showing Mansa Mus[a] with golden sceptre in one hand an[d] a large gold nugget in the othe[r]

(Bibliotheque Nationale, Paris, France[,] The Bridgeman Art Librar[y])

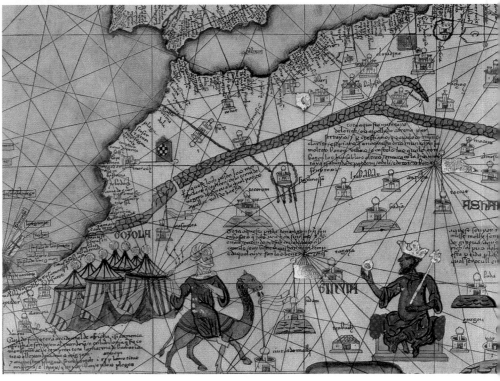

Uncrowned king of the
Florentine Republic and banker
to the pope: Cosimo de' Medici

Francisco Pizarro: an
illegitimate and illiterate boy
from south-west Spain who
became the cruel subjugator
of the Inca civilisation and
conqueror of Peru

'To hand the King his shirt in the morning or to take it from him in the evening was seen as the highest honour': Louis XIV, the absolutist Sun King and war-maker, Europe's longest-reigning monarch, a figure assured of his own divinity who left his country mired in debt

The Pharaoh Akhenaten,
who created his own religion

(Mary Evans / BeBa / Iberfoto)

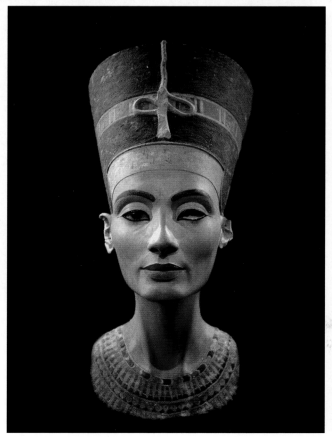

Akhenaten's glamorous
wife Nefertiti: 'the radiant
one has come'

(REX / Universal History Archive /

Universal Images Group)

'The ultimate commodities king': Dutch adventurer–capitalist and Governor-General of the Dutch East Indies: Jan Pieterszoon Coen

(Getty Images)

Robert Clive, the man who turned the East India Company
into a dominant force in global trade, enshrining British rule
over the subcontinent for two centuries

A backroom deal: Clive meeting Mir Jafar after the Battle of
Plassey, 1757, in a painting by Francis Hayman

Alfred Krupp: he built a corporate city around
his gigantic steel mills, controlling his workers
from cradle to grave

Arbeiterkolonie Westend, one of Krupp's settlements in Essen for his workers

CHAPTER 6

Louis XIV and Akhenaten – Sun kings

When you live for others' opinions, you are dead. I don't want to live thinking about how I'll be remembered.

Carlos Slim

What do you desire when you have everything from birth? You look for glory. What do you do when you have more worldly goods than you could possibly use? You build your own city. Louis XIV, the Sun King, commanded all the levers of French society for seven decades. He oversaw France's rise to Europe's pre-eminent power, consolidating a system of absolute monarchy that endured until the revolution. Everything revolved around Versailles, his palace, his creation and his power base.

Louis's extravagance was based on political and economic calculation. Versailles was not a mere vanity project but an essential part of his rule. By forcing his recalcitrant nobles to leave Paris, he ensured that they would be always beholden to him. He controlled men, their money and their wives. His state could not stop spending, however, both in the glorification of one man and in the pursuit of war with his rivals. All of that was paid for from one source – the taxation of the poor. And even then the sums didn't add up. At the time of Louis's death, France was deeply in debt.

This chapter is about hereditary wealth. Louis was not driven by the impulses of the self-made man. He did not see the need to prove himself. Nor did he see patronage as a means of bolstering a reputation that had been built during a clamber to the top. He sponsored some of the greatest artists and writers of his generation because that was what kings did. His reign – the longest in the history of European monarchy – was based on the fusion of power and wealth, and an unquestioning belief in his own divinity.

His closest parallel pre-dated him by three millennia. The story of the ancient Egyptian pharaoh Akhenaten only became known thanks to historians in the nineteenth century. Akhenaten, whose name translates as 'the living spirit of the sun disc', ruled at the peak of Egypt's wealth in the late eighteenth dynasty (1353–1336 BC). He too built his own city, Akhetaten, in what later became known as el-Amarna. Not satisfied with that, he sought to create his own religion. Within five years of coming to power, he had replaced millennia of polytheistic tradition with a monotheistic religion, eclipsing the multiple gods and mythologies of his nation with a single ascendant sun god, the Aten.

Both men created personal cults based upon solar imagery. They did so by constructing new cities, bringing the elites to orbit around them. From the palaces of ancient times and the seventeenth century to the monumental skyscrapers of today's global cities, what greater demonstration of status can there be than to manufacture a city in your name?

Louis XIV was a divine gift. His parents, Louis XIII and Anne of Austria, had been married for twenty-three years and had endured four stillbirths. So when the heir to the throne arrived on 5 September 1638, chroniclers described his birth as a miracle of God. He was called Louis *le Dieudonné* – Louis the God-given. His birth on a Sunday was regarded as particularly auspicious, and was celebrated with bonfires, fireworks, poems and speeches.

At the age of five Louis assumed the throne, but under the aegis of his mother, who in turn entrusted power to her chief minister, the Italian Cardinal Mazarin. This arrangement held, but over this period France was convulsed by a rebellion known as the Fronde. Frustrated by the assertiveness of a new breed of political officials, a large number of small-time aristocrats rose up to protect their feudal privileges. In 1648, just as the Thirty Years War was coming to an end, Paris erupted in fighting, with a mob breaking into the royal palace and demanding to see their nine-year-old King. According to legend, Louis pretended to be asleep. The mob departed contented, firmly believing that they answered not to self-appointed royal bureaucrats, but only to the King, 'this shining star, this radiant sun, this day without night, this centre, visible from all points of the circumference'.[1] Four years later, following the final victory of royalist forces, the teenage King took the lead role in a celebratory ballet, dressed as Apollo, with his hair gilded and braided to represent the rays of the sun.

Louis finally assumed all the reins of power in 1661, at the age of twenty-three. For all the protestations of loyalty to him, the periods of disorder were salutary for the young King. The Fronde had discredited the nobles, so France turned to Louis with an enthusiasm born of a sense that the monarchy alone could maintain order and ensure prosperity. The unpopular Mazarin had died the same year. Louis decreed that he would not be replacing him. He intended to be his own first minister and insisted that his ministers were to address themselves directly to him. His announcement was received with amusement and incredulity. Not since Louis's grandfather Henry IV had died in 1610, half a century earlier, had the king sought direct control over the affairs of government.

In order to establish the hegemony he sought, Louis needed to see off his rivals quickly. The most important of these was Nicolas Fouquet, Marquis of Belle Île and superintendent of finance during Louis's regency. As well as maintaining a small private army Fouquet had constructed a huge palace at Vaux-le-Vicomte, south-east of Paris. The project involved 18,000 labourers, cost 18 million livres and required the demolition of three villages. From this lavish base, he established a near monopoly over the patronage of celebrated artists and writers. On the King's assumption of the throne, Fouquet invited six thousand guests to dine at his chateau and watch a play by Molière. The evening finished with a spectacular firework display.

Louis did not appreciate the prospect of being outshone by a mere marquis, so he had Fouquet arrested and charged with treason and embezzlement. His real crime was to have sought to compete with the King in terms of splendour and wealth. He was imprisoned in a fortress where he died nineteen years later.[2] Louis seized 120 tapestries, plus the statues and orange trees from Fouquet's estate. The message to any future competitors for power, prestige and patronage was clear. As Voltaire wrote: 'On 17 August, at six in the evening Fouquet was the King of France. At two in the morning he was nobody.' For sure, Fouquet had exploited the Fronde to amass a fortune. But he was in good company; most of the nobles were doing it. His mistake was not to appreciate quickly enough the shift in power.

One man who did was Jean-Baptiste Colbert, who had ordered Fouquet's arrest and succeeded him as the man in charge of the nation's finances and the royal reputation. He was finance minister, central bank chief and spin-doctor rolled into one. Yet no matter how powerful he was compared to others, he made sure that he never gainsaid his King.

Following Fouquet's arrest, all the writers and artists in his service passed to the royal household. In June 1662, Louis XIV organised a grand two-day *Carrousel* at the Tuileries, surpassing his former rival for spectacle and extravagance. Five teams of noblemen jousted and fenced – dressed as Romans, Persians, Turks, Indians and Americans – with the victor on each day receiving a diamond and a portrait of the King set in a frame of precious stones.[3]

Colbert ordered the poet and critic Jean Chapelain to produce a report into the uses of the arts 'for preserving the splendour of the king's enterprises'.[4] The task was nothing less than the reorganisation of culture to construct an image of absolute royal power. The academies established during Louis's reign were crucial instruments of control. A precedent had already been set. In 1634 Cardinal Richelieu, chief minister to Louis XIII, had discovered a group of intellectuals holding secret meetings in Paris. In order to neutralise this source of possible cultural autonomy and dissent, Richelieu had founded the Académie française to bring the intellectuals under the financial sponsorship of the crown in return for their political loyalty. The cardinal stated: 'matters political and moral shall be treated in the Academy in conformity with the authority of the Prince, the state of the government, and the laws of the realm'.[5] Louis XIV and his ministers extended this principle, establishing academies for disciplines ranging from painting and sculpture to science, music and architecture.

The economy was recalibrated to one end: the projection of the King's majesty. In 1663 a factory was established, in Paris's Avenue des Gobelins, employing two hundred workers to produce furnishings and tapestries for the royal palaces. By 1671 almost all branches of high culture had been brought under state control. The financial patronage and enhanced status offered by the academies meant that any artist with ambition (or an instinct for self-preservation) offered himself into the King's service – from Racine to Molière, from the painter Charles Le Brun to the composer Jean-Baptiste Lully. The academies commissioned work and ran competitions; in 1663 the Academy of Painting and Sculpture established a prize for the best painting or statue depicting the heroic actions of the King. Chapelain, who oversaw the literary sphere, wrote in a letter to the Italian poet Girolamo Graziani: 'It is necessary for the honour of His Majesty that his praises should seem spontaneous, and to seem spontaneous they have to be printed outside his realms.'[6]

The manifestation of glory and the exercise of control underpinned Louis's rule. Having sidelined or punished those who sought to assert their independence during his regency, he projected his power across his realm and beyond. Alongside culture, architecture and warfare were central to this task. The only area where the King delegated some control was over the nation's finances. In his defence, he had inherited a fiscal mess from his father, and the hiatus that led to the Fronde had made matters considerably worse.

Colbert sought to make France, in spite of its feudal and militaristic traditions, a more commercially oriented state. He undertook a major reorganisation of the nation's industry and navy, improving canals, roads and other parts of its infrastructure. He sought to compete with England and Holland in foreign trade, establishing the French East India Company by royal edict in 1664. Louis was excited by the prospect of France's modernisation and heightened status and took a keen interest in these plans. He was less troubled by the state of the nation's finances, leaving the task in its entirety to his trusted lieutenant.

Colbert's main problem was to stem the budget deficit. If he couldn't keep a handle on spending (or at least the King's), then he had to increase revenue. In an early memo to Louis's regent Mazarin, Colbert complained that only half of all the taxes paid by the people reached the treasury. Tax exemptions for the wealthy, as ever, were a problem.

The most contentious levy was the *taille*, a land tax established two hundred years earlier under Charles VII. Nobility, clergy, court and government officials were exempt. Boisguilbert, a noble, judge and early economist, estimated that during Louis's reign no more than a third of the population paid the *taille* – and that was the poorest third. The method was unduly complicated, but it boiled down to local officials being personally responsible for the collection of the sum decreed. This created a wealthy class of middlemen tax collectors who took a cut on the monies they eked out. Along with the carrot came the stick: failure to collect the full amount was punishable by imprisonment. In one city alone, Tours, in 1679, fifty-four tax collectors were imprisoned. The rhetoric was designed to invoke a sense of patriotic duty. Taxes paid to the King were a *don gratuit* – a gift or an act of benevolence.

The more Louis spent, the more the coffers dried up, and the more the squeeze was applied on the lower orders to hand over whatever they had. The violence was extreme, but it was applied far away, out of sight and out of mind. The issue was not raised at court, or at least not in the presence of the *grand monarque*.

The Duc de Saint-Simon, a member of that court, describes in his memoirs the troubles accompanying the 'history of losses and dishonour' in war, as well as the hardships of famine.[7] His chronicles provide a valuable and critical account of the taxes imposed to meet the King's super-sized ambitions and increasingly desperate need for revenue. They were published after his death – it would have been impossible for him to survive if he had been so outspoken during his lifetime. The taxes, he wrote, 'increased, multiplied, and exacted with the most extreme rigour, completed the devastation of France'.[8] They included an 'onerous and odious' tax on baptism and marriages. When the poor tried to evade this by holding unofficial wedding and baptism ceremonies, the authorities sent in the troops.

When they had nothing left to lose, the peasantry sometimes fought back. In the Vivarais region in the south-east of the country, peasants were required to pay ten livres for each male child born and five for each female, plus three livres when they bought a new coat, and five when they bought a new hat. Their uprising was not suppressed until a force of nearly five thousand men had been dispatched.

One reference is made in a letter in 1675 from Madame de Sévigné, a well-known aristocrat and prolific writer, to her daughter, in which she refers to riots in Brittany. She begins and ends her note with trivia about the smell of wine and other 'pretty things', but in between she asks:

> Do you wish to hear the news from Rennes? A tax of a hundred thousand crowns has been imposed upon the citizens; and if this sum is not produced within four-and-twenty hours, it is to be doubled, and collected by the soldiers. They have cleared the houses and sent away the occupants of one of the great streets and forbidden anybody to receive them on pain of death; so that the poor wretches (old men, women near their confinement, and children included) may be seen wandering around and crying on their departure from this city, without knowing where to go, and without food or a place to lie in. Day before yesterday a fiddler was broken on the wheel for getting up a dance and stealing some stamped paper. He was quartered after death, and his limbs exposed at the four corners of the city. Sixty citizens have been thrown into prison, and the business of punishing them is to begin tomorrow. This province sets a fine example to the others, teaching them above all that of respecting the governors and their wives, and of never throwing stones into their garden.

Louis saw glorification of his majesty as an obligation. The people, he insisted, expected nothing less of him. Initially, he focused on Paris, demanding the reconstruction of two of his palaces – the Louvre, beginning in 1663, and the adjoining Tuileries, in 1664. He created temples to Apollo, dripping with sun-king imagery. His thoughts soon turned elsewhere, moving on to a grander scale.

Versailles was little more than a chalet twenty kilometres south-west of Paris, the 'most ungrateful of all places',[9] where Louis would go hunting with his father. Situated on mosquito-infested marshland, it was an unpropitious spot on which to build. In spite of that, or because of that, the King was determined to create a palace there to outshine anything else on earth. The location was chosen to make nature bend to his will, just as his subjects were required to do. Colbert urged caution, suggesting that the initial architectural plans were 'more concerned with Your Majesty's pleasure and diversion than with your glory'.[10] Louis ignored him, so he fell into line and freed up funds for the *grand projet*.

The palace was conceived and built in four stages over several decades. Such were the mortality rates among construction teams that corpses were removed at night so as not to demoralise the workforce. The ten years of relative peace initiated by the signing of the Treaty of Nijmegen in September 1678, which brought to an end the long Franco-Dutch War, marked the third and most important period, transforming it largely into the palace that is seen today.

Every aspect of the design revolved around the glory of the King. Louis would take mass every morning, looking down from on high on the royal tribune, facing the altar and the organ across the marble-lined chapel. Yet, tellingly, the chapel was not located in the heart of the palace. The central axis, through the *cour d'honneur*, took visitors to the Hall of Mirrors, a remarkable chamber, facing the landscaped gardens, in which the mirrors reflected the natural light. The King would sit on his throne to welcome ambassadors and other visitors, exhausted by the long walk up the stairs and through the many corridors. On their long walk they would have been required to marvel at the grand paintings, tapestries and sculptures that adorned each room. The message was clear: France, in art and culture, was now more than a rival for Venice and other centres in Europe. Christian images were rare in the palace: solar imagery dominated. The Salon of Apollo – or throne room – was graced with a painted ceiling depicting the god in his chariot, accompanied by the seasons. Apollo was the most dominant image, in the gardens and in the palace: frescoes, statues, mosaics, tapestries and portraits were dedicated to his manifold achievements. The sun as a motif was highly significant: it gave light and life to all. The Sun King was the universal benefactor, bestowing largesse to all his subjects, irrespective of wealth and rank (not that one would know it from his tax policies). Colbert, for all his attempts at fiscal reform and austerity, reinforced in the King a view of the practical and financial merits of Versailles: 'Nothing does more to signal the grandeur and intelligence of princes than buildings,' he declared, 'and all posterity measures them by the yardstick of these superb palaces which they construct during their life-time.'[11]

In 1682 Louis moved his entire court to its new home, together with the central administration of government. At its height, the court at Versailles numbered 20,000 people, with 1000 nobles and 4000 servants living in the palace complex proper and another 4000 nobles and their servants housed in the town. It was a self-contained society of the elite. It represented a clean slate, far from the cluttered and competing architecture of the capital and the site of Louis's childhood trauma during the Fronde.

The relocation had a direct political purpose. By removing the elite from the traditional arenas of power and politics, the Sun King forced the nobles to orbit around his new centre of power, dependent upon him for promotion, favour and gifts. The aristocrats populating the court at Versailles were subject to crippling costs as they sought to outdo one another in extravagance. A single noble at Versailles with a staff of twelve servants would require twelve thousand livres per year to finance his lifestyle. Only a few could afford this sum; the rest were dependent upon the crown for a royal pension to supplement their income. In 1683, 1.4 million livres were paid over in such pensions, representing around 1.2 per cent of all government expenditure.

These financial rituals were one part of Louis's system of patronage and control. The nobility was indulged in court, but largely excluded from government. The great ecclesiastics were no longer admitted. Louis had four councils, small groups advising him on finance, foreign affairs, internal affairs and judicial issues. Most of the members were men of middle-class birth, often lawyers (*gens de la robe*), who owed everything to the King and could not possibly be independent of him. Meetings were held in the royal apartments. All members could take part in discussing the issues in question, but all decisions rested with one man. No minutes were taken and no record was kept. Louis's will was as he decreed it.[12]

Versailles became the theatre set on which the King acted out his royal duties. His early training as a ballet dancer prepared him well for the public stage. As Saint-Simon observed: 'Louis XIV was made for a brilliant Court. In the midst of other men, his figure, his courage, his grace, his beauty, his grand mien, even the tone of his voice and the majestic and natural charm of his person, distinguished him till his death.'[13] Voltaire also attested to the King's pre-eminence, in spite of his stature (he was just five feet three inches tall): 'Above all his courtiers Louis rose supreme by the grace of his figure and the majestic nobility of his countenance. The awe which he inspired in those who spoke with him secretly flattered the consciousness of his own superiority.'[14] The King's prelate, Bishop Bossuet, saw Louis's glory as giving the populace a purpose in life and bringing order to society: 'God forbade ostentation inspired by vanity and the foolish display bred by the intoxication of riches: however, it was also his wish that the courts of kings should be dazzling and magnificent to inspire respect in the common people.'[15]

Even the most intimate and mundane aspects of Louis's everyday life were ritualised and charged with symbolic meaning. The *lever* and *coucher* – the rising and setting of the Sun King – were high points in the day of the court and the nation. The King's bedroom was the focal point of Versailles, commanding the central axis of the entire palace. The intimacy of the location and the occasion reinforced his authority. Each morning an invited elite gathered in the bedroom to observe and assist Louis as he arose, prayed, washed and dressed; in the evening he was similarly attended as he prepared for bed. Even these rituals were subdivided into two hierarchical parts: the full court in the gallery attended the *grand lever* outside the King's bedchamber, while the *petit lever* was a less formal affair, in which only a select group of courtiers attended to him. To hand the King his shirt in the morning or to take it from him in the evening was seen as the highest honour. This was deference by humiliation. Louis had succeeded in his task of making the haughtiest aristocrats bend to his will. The uppity rebelliousness of the Fronde was a thing of the past.

Divide and rule was essential. In this claustrophobic micro-world of Versailles everyone knew everyone. Gossip and sniping came with intense rivalry and boredom. Access to the King was carefully controlled and was used to denote who was in favour and who was not. Strict rules dictated who could see him, when and where, and what role they would be allowed to play. Some courtiers waited for years just to be acknowledged with a peremptory wave of the hand. Such rituals were mirrored at mealtimes. A small number of carefully chosen members of the public were permitted into the palace late in the evening to watch the King's last meal of the day, the *grand couvert*. Louis would pick at the many dishes laid out at his large table, a gesture of approbation for France's agricultural industry. Sometimes he would open his apartments to the nobles for diversions such as cards and billiards.

Sex was another of Louis's pastimes. During his reign he had one wife and three serious mistresses, alongside casual dalliances whenever he was in the mood. His marriage to the Infanta Maria Theresa was entirely political. Young Louis had originally been attracted to Maria Mancini, the niece of Mazarin, but he realised the importance of a peace deal with Spain. His first mistress was Mademoiselle de la Valliére, who was only seventeen at the time. He was infatuated with her until after a few years he became bored with her. In 1674 she retired to a Carmelite monastery. Madame de Montespan, who had been intriguing against mistress number one for some time, held the top spot in the King's affections for nine years, though not without occasional rivals. She was given a suite of twenty rooms in the palace, nine more than the Queen. She had nine pregnancies and bore Louis seven children. Their education was entrusted to a certain Madame Scarron (or the Marquise de Maintenon, as the King decided she be called from 1678). She was the grandchild of a famous Protestant leader but the daughter of a workless spendthrift. Born in the antechamber of a prison and orphaned at the age of seven, Scarron was an unlikely choice as governess. Her low birth made her selection as the King's third and final mistress all the more unlikely. But nobody would be so reckless as to say as much.

Across the court, Louis dispensed favours in return for absolute loyalty. He was happy to indulge his nobles, as long as they did not attempt to outshine him. For the marriage of the Duc de Bourgogne to the young Princess of Savoy, which coincided with the end of the War of the League of Augsburg, the King announced that he wanted to see a magnificent court. As ever, no expense would be spared: 'no one thought of consulting his purse on his state: everyone tried to surpass his neighbour in richness and invention. Gold and silver scarcely sufficed: the shops of the dealers were emptied in a few days; in a word the most unbridled luxury reigned over Court and city.'[16] The King was honoured with a huge diamond, the size of a 'greengage plum'. This would be paid for by the state (or rather, by the poor). 'He must consider the honour of the crown, and not lose the occasion of obtaining, a priceless diamond which would efface the lustre of all others in Europe ... it was a glory for his regency which would last forever,' noted Saint-Simon.[17] 'He liked splendour, magnificence, and profusion in everything: you pleased him if you shone through the brilliancy of your houses, your clothes, your table, your equipages. Thus a taste for extravagance and luxury was disseminated through all classes of society.'[18]

Versailles might have brought the nobles under his watch, but it also led to Louis's almost complete isolation from his people. Apart from a few weeks at his palace of Compiègne in the summer and Fontainebleau in the autumn (hardly slumming it), Louis spent his entire time in Versailles. In his later decades, he almost never ventured out into the rest of France. The splendour of the palace reinforced the notion of divine infallibility. In the regions, however, out of sight and largely out of mind, rebellions continued. Local nobles – from Bordeaux to Grenoble, from Rennes to Metz – saw the powers of their *parlements* and governors emasculated. The King's authority was vested in his royal *intendants*, men he chose – often from the ranks of lesser merchants – to ensure that everyone bent to his will.

The second half of Louis's epic rule was characterised by unbridled spending, self-veneration, absolutism and almost continual warfare. He fought three major, and largely unsuccessful, military campaigns – the Franco–Dutch War, the War of the League of Augsburg and the War of Spanish Succession – not to mention a number of smaller escapades.

The realm might have been exhausted, but the scale of his extravagance only increased. This was the cross his people had to bear. The Revocation of the Edict of Nantes in 1685 and persecution of the Huguenots took the King from the realm of smart political and business leader into zealot. He fell increasingly under the influence of Madame de Maintenon, a dour and devout woman. The good times, the partying, were declared over. In any case, thanks to the various wars, the finances of the state, and the court, were hopelessly depleted.

Colbert's death, a year after the move to Versailles, marked a turning point in the fortunes of France. It removed from the court the one man with the authority to challenge the King; his successor and former rival, the Marquis de Louvois, was far more pliant. The death in the same year of Maria Theresa allowed Louis to marry Madame de Maintenon. She was wife and queen in all but name. For all his unbridled power, Louis did not want to set a precedent by being seen to marry a woman from the lower orders, so their marriage was never formally consecrated.

Twice France was struck by famine during Louis's reign, in 1693 and 1710. An estimated two million people perished. In Louis's mind, such hardships provided another opportunity for taxation. When the Great Freeze of 1709 led to a failed harvest, corn was collected into large granaries by the authorities; prices were fixed and food was rationed. Saint-Simon described the decision as resulting 'in an oppression so enduring, so sure, so cruel', suggesting that on Louis's orders a shortage was deliberately engineered: 'Many people believed that the finance gentlemen had clutched at this occasion to seize upon all the corn in the kingdom, by emissaries they sent about, in order to sell it at whatever price they wished for the profit of the King, not forgetting their own.'[19]

By then, Louis had been searching for ways to raise more cash for over two decades. In 1687, a year after the League of Augsburg was formed, an alliance of most of the European powers to resist Louis's expansionist plans, he was persuaded to sell the family silver. From his bedroom, a silver side table, weighing 350 kilograms, was identified, alongside an even heavier mirror, plus stools, vases for orange trees and even incense burners. Some twenty-one tonnes were melted down in all for the war effort. This was a humiliation Louis sought to conceal. Nobody commented on it, at least not in public.

Louis also devalued the currency by a third, enabling him to pay back his debts more easily: this 'bought some profit to the king, but ruin to private people and a disorder to trade', noted Saint-Simon.[20] Many around him saw his actions as cruel and economically foolhardy, but they were powerless to act. The King's finance and war minister, Michel Chamillart, wrote to him begging to be relieved of his duties. Everything would 'go wrong and perish due' to the intense pressure he was under, he complained. Louis replied: 'Well! Let us perish together.'[21]

Saint-Simon summarised the plight of the economy best when he wrote:

> People never ceased wondering what had become of all the money of the realm. Nobody could any longer pay, because nobody was paid: the country-people, overwhelmed with exactions and with valueless property, had become insolvent: trade no longer yielded anything – good faith and confidence were at an end. Thus the king had no resources, except in terror and in his unlimited power, which, boundless as it was, failed also for want of having something to take and to exercise itself upon. There was no more circulation, no means of re-establishing it. All was perishing step by step; the realm was entirely exhausted.[22]

Louis died at Versailles in 1715, four days before his seventy-seventh birthday. Even his slow demise, in which his courtiers would monitor the passage of gangrene up his leg, was a public performance. Like other members of the super-rich, whether self-made or blue-blooded, in later life he spent many hours thinking agitatedly about his legacy. The succession was anything but clear. Nor, he feared, was the historical and religious reckoning. His words to his great-grandson, the dauphin and heir apparent Louis XV, are etched into French history: 'I have loved war too much.' As with Crassus in the Roman Republic, Louis's military escapades were his undoing. He left a country mired in debt, some two billion livres – about £160 billion in today's money. He never once balanced the books or paid for Versailles.

Yet, the opulence of his reign was deemed a duty, not a lifestyle choice. He may or may not have said (as is ascribed to him without historical evidence): '*L'état, c'est moi*' – I am the state. Virtually his whole life he had been on the throne. He knew nothing else. France knew nobody else. He was buried in the basilica of Saint-Denis, outside Paris, the resting place of kings. Eighty years later, when revolutionaries executed his descendant Louis XVI, the Sun King's body was exhumed and destroyed.

Few eras have witnessed such wealth showered on one individual. Louis indulged himself, and was indulged, while most of his countrymen suffered wars and privation. Yet the ceremonies and the glories were not merely ostentation. The earth orbited around the Sun King, absorbing his rays. He commanded and he received. He himself explained it this way:

> Those people are gravely mistaken who imagine that all this is mere ceremony. The people over whom we rule, unable to see to the bottom of things, usually judge by what they see from the outside, and most often it is by precedence and rank that they measure their respect and obedience. As it is important to the public to be governed only by a single one, it also matters to it that the person performing this function should be so elevated above the others, that no-one can be confused or compared with him; and one cannot, without doing harm to the whole body of the state, deprive its head of the least mark of superiority distinguishing from the limbs.[23]

For all the grandiloquence and hubris, for all the financial profligacy, Louis arguably was the first leader of a modern French state seeking to rationalise and centralise its practices, and elevating high culture to a national mission. This was, as Voltaire dubbed it, *le Grand Siècle* – the Great Century.

Rewind three millennia, and the parallels are uncanny – a semi-divine leader, a sun god, the creator of a new city and, in Akhenaten's case, the promulgator of a new religion.

He was born Amenhotep IV, a pharaoh in the eighteenth dynasty of ancient Egypt. His father had established an empire stretching from Syria in the north to Nubia in the south, first by military force and then consolidated by diplomacy and trade, with gifts and tributes pouring in from foreign lands.[24] This was a time of stability and prosperity, but the new ruler – son of Amenhotep III and father of Tutankhamen – was determined to leave an indelible mark on history. In the fifth year of his reign, he abandoned the traditional spiritual capital of Thebes, where he was crowned, to construct an entirely new city two hundred miles to the north in a remote, unpopulated site on the east bank of the Nile. It was to be dedicated to the Aten, the sun disc, and would be called Akhetaten (now known as el-Amarna). A month before he arrived at the site, Amenhotep changed his name to Akhenaten, 'the living spirit of the Aten'.

Akhenaten was a radical. He was prepared to ride roughshod over tradition and humiliate Egypt's power brokers in his eagerness to leave a mark. In a matter of a few years, he wrested control from the priests of Amun, placing the Aten, and himself, at the centre of a solar system of wealth and power. Akhenaten used the vast apparatus of Egyptian theology to construct his own supreme authority. The polytheistic mythology of ancient Egypt did not occupy a distinct religious sphere; it permeated all aspects of daily life. By reinventing the gods, Akhenaten controlled his people.

The construction of solar mythology required a vast canvas upon which the sun kings could write themselves large. As one historian has written of Versailles, 'only the most splendid building in Europe could accommodate a solar system of metaphors', and the same applied for Akhenaten.[25] The Aten was a cipher for the magnificence of Akhenaten and Akhetaten was the city in which he constructed his power. Akhenaten declared his intention on two stelae – large tablets – he erected after his first visit to the still-empty desert site: 'I shall make Akhet-Aten for the Aten, my father, on the orient of Akhent-Aten – the place which he himself made to be enclosed for him by the mountain, on which he may achieve happiness and on which I shall offer to him. This is it!'[26] These stelae were designed to give the new inhabitants a sense of identification with the city. Akhetaten was ringed with sheer limestone cliffs and divided in half by the Nile along its north–south axis. The west bank was used for cultivation and the east for construction. This was a new sacral landscape that would stop families from returning to their traditional religious observances.

At its height Akhetaten may have been home to a population of over twenty thousand. Temples and palaces were surrounded by administrative offices, structures for the production and storage of goods, and housing for the community. Buildings identified include a record office, barracks for troops, and granaries and bakeries. At the periphery were the tombs of the royal family and high-ranking officials. Temples were not only spiritual institutions but temporal powerhouses controlling vast material assets – cultivated land, huge stores of grain, precious metals and slaves. The offerings needed to sustain the gods also sustained an entire economy on earth. Each temple ran its own micro-economy, ever mindful of the demands of the pharaohs. Huge warehouses were built within temple premises, partly as protection against bad harvests. Grain was wealth, and great stores of it were there for shipping around the country and even abroad for the realisation of grandiose royal schemes. The major temples were the reserve banks of their day.[27] The autonomy of the temples depended on their loyalty. The larger ones owned fleets of merchant ships; others were granted rights to exploit gold mines. For their part, the pharaohs would give direct gifts of precious metals and jewels to the temples as an expression of piety; often the excess of the booty from foreign campaigns.

As with palaces in Louis XIV's time, temples were the sources, and projections, of power. But it was not all one way. The temples had their own power bases, outlasting the reigns of individual pharaohs, and could legitimise the reigns of certain pharaohs in return for patronage, as the cult of Amun did for Queen Hatshepsut. The power of deities, and their associated temple institutions and priests, rose and fell, masked behind the myth of the eternal. Akhetaten was not dominated by temples to the Aten, but by the palaces of the royal family which lined the bank of the Nile and, in particular, the 'royal road' – the axis of the city which ran parallel to the river, linking the palaces. The Great Palace was the largest, covering an area of over fifteen thousand square metres, and served the official needs of Akhenaten as head of state. Scholars have speculated that the royal family lived in the North Riverside Palace, with a further North Palace serving as a ceremonial building or potentially the residence of Princess Meritaten, the eldest child of Akhenaten and his wife Nefertiti, whom he had married at the very start of his reign. The Great Palace contained an enormous courtyard surrounded by large statues of Akhenaten, and a complex of halls, smaller courts and monuments arranged formally along parade routes. At the southern end of the palace was a huge hall built for Akhenaten's immediate successor, Smenkhkara, containing 544 brick columns and walls encrusted with glazed tiles. This palace provided Akhenaten 'with a sumptuous semi-religious setting which advertised his new religion and art'[28] to important guests, perhaps including foreign envoys.

As with Louis, Akhenaten sought to ensure that the elite was beholden to him. He and the royal family would greet and reward loyal subjects in a ritual at the Window of Appearances in the Great Palace. This patronage was depicted in stone carvings in the tombs of high-ranking officials at Akhetaten. Osiris and the perilous journey to the underworld, with its mythology of the weighing of the heart against the feather of Ma'at, were replaced with vignettes of the royal family and an earthly existence where the dead basked in the rays of the sun during the day, received offerings from the temple, and returned to the tomb at night. Scenes centred upon the relationship of the deceased to the royal family. The power of the Pharaoh's patronage was expressed in the tomb of May, the 'fan bearer at the King's right hand', where it was stated: 'I was a poor man on both my father's and my mother's side – but the ruler built me up, he caused me to develop, he fed me by means of his Ka [one of the essences of the soul] when I was without property.'[29]

The ceremonial display of power was also crucial to Akhenaten's reign. He was frequently depicted on a horse-drawn chariot, travelling along the royal road, mimicking the traditional display of divine images during religious processions as well as the passage of the sun through the sky. Akhenaten, the royal family and the Aten became the primary subjects of imagery, reflecting a completely new approach to iconography. The Aten had no representation in the form of other gods or animals, but was worshipped only as the sun. Yet a connection between sky and earth, the intangible and the revealed, was necessary. Thus the Aten's rays terminated in human hands caressing Akhenaten and Nefertiti, and offering them the symbol for 'life', the *ankh*, while the Pharaoh offered the Aten food and incense. One result of the rejection of polytheism was that the royal family were imbued with a divinity over and above the traditional concept of the Pharaoh as the son of Re. Akhenaten, his queen and their children assumed the role of a divine family, carved more deeply than other subjects, giving them special prominence when viewed in bright sunlight. Nefertiti, 'the radiant one has come', was said to be both glamorous and intelligent (although it is unclear whether the depiction of her beauty was real or idealised). She certainly was fertile, bearing for her husband six daughters (the number of sons is not recorded). She was also imbued with a distinctive prominence for a great royal wife, reflecting the role of the royal family as divine triad. Iconography previously restricted to pharaohs was extended to her, showing her smiting enemies or in the presence of bound captives. When portrayed alongside Amenhotep IV in Karnak she was depicted as smaller than him, but in the fifteen stelae carved at Akhetaten she was accorded equal prominence with Akhenaten.

Another unique theme was the naturalistic portrayal of daily life – a revolutionary break with past visualisations of pharaohs, conveying affection, movement, work and nature. For the first time a pharaoh was depicted informally, in family poses. Man and wife were seen tenderly, and affectionately holding their children. Grief was also depicted in the royal tomb, with Akhenaten and Nefertiti shown bent in sorrow at the death of their second daughter, as the Pharaoh reached to comfort his queen. Akhenaten was breaking with tradition in life, as he was with divinity.

The rise of the Aten, and his usurpation of all other gods, had taken place over time. In the eighteenth dynasty, the sun god Re was merged with Amun, the ancient god of Thebes, to create a deity commonly referred to as 'Amun-Re, King of the Gods'. His seat of power was Thebes, which became the theological and political centre of power – until abandoned by Akhenaten. Unlike other anthropomorphic gods, Amun was seen as transcendental: 'he is hidden from the gods, and his aspect is unknown. He is farther than the sky; he is deeper than the

Duat [underworld]. No god knows his true appearance ... He is too secret to uncover his awesomeness, he is too great to investigate, too powerful to know.' Re represented the revealed aspect of divinity, the visible light and source of life upon which all creation depended. As Thebes grew in status and wealth, Amun-Re became the nation's supreme creator god, reaching the peak of his power during the reign of Hatshepsut and assuming the traditional myth of the divine birth of the king.

Nonetheless, this new concept of the divine made no explicit attempt to eclipse the constellation of deities that populated Egyptian mythology. Amenhotep III, Akhenaten's father, actively connected himself with a multiplicity of deities. So Egypt's traditional polytheism continued to coexist with an emerging monotheistic strain of theology.

A new solar theology was also emerging. Focused on the sun and its light and movement as the source of creation, vision and time, this new doctrine rejected the traditional mythology and iconography. It represented a universalism of vision correlating with Egypt's position as a world power, with ever-broadening political horizons. The worship of the sun disc Aten had begun in earnest during the reign of Thutmose IV (Akhenaten's grandfather).[30] The Hymn of Suty and Hor in the reign of Amenhotep III presented the Aten as a god with the attributes of Re, and familiar deities were presented as manifestations of the Aten:

Hail to you, Aten, Sundisk of the day
Who have fashioned all things and made them to live;
Great Falcon with many-hued plumes,
Scarab who raised himself up by himself,
Who came into existence all by himself, not being born,
Elder Horus in the midst of the sky.[31]

Akhenaten claimed to be the 'dazzling sun disc',[32] the merging of person and deity. In effect, he was the Son of God. While Louis XIV's solar imagery sat alongside Catholicism, for Akhenaten the theological shift was more fundamental. The Aten came to eclipse the constellation of deities that had hitherto populated ancient Egyptian religion.

Akhenaten set about creating the physical manifestation of the pre-eminence of the Aten on earth in earnest. He started with a building project of unprecedented scale at Karnak in Thebes, creating eight temples dedicated not to the traditional god, Amun, but to Re-Harakhty, the falcon-headed sun god. The largest temple that he built there, Gempaaten (or 'Aten is found'), was open-air and oriented towards the sunrise. It bore many of the hallmarks of Akhenaten's later doctrines and radical artistic style, and historians have speculated that this was the time when he was formulating his 'teaching', or the doctrine of the Aten.[33] At first, the Aten seemed able to coexist as a bright star within a constellation of other gods. However, by year three of Akhenaten's reign, the sun disc was being depicted on his own: monotheism was inexorably being imposed.

Akhenaten used religion, art, language and literature to assert his supremacy over all others, including his predecessors. After changing his name, he removed all references to Amun, Thebes and Karnak from his royal titulary. He wanted no rivals. The cult of Amun was effectively eliminated. Aten began to be established as the only god, to the exclusion of all others. Akhenaten's teaching is best understood through the 'Great Hymn to Aten', described as one of the most significant pieces of poetry to survive from the pre-Homeric world.[34] It was 'spoken' by Akhenaten, pointing to the role he assumed for himself as theologian-in-chief:

> *You are the one God,*
> *Shining forth from your possible incarnations*
> *As Aten, the Living Sun,*
> *Revealed like a king in glory, risen in light,*
> *Now distant, now bending nearby.*
> *You create the numberless things of this world*
> *From yourself, who are One alone –*
> *Cities, towns, fields, the roadway, the River;*
> *And each eye looks back and beholds you*
> *To learn from the day's light perfection.*[35]

Amun and his priests were the most direct victims of Akhenaten's lust for supremacy. From year three of his reign, he closed the temples of traditional deities in Thebes, dismissing or re-indoctrinating the priests. In year four, the high priest of Amun was sent into the desert on a quarrying expedition.[36] Following the pronouncement of Aten as the only god in year nine, Amun's name was systematically hacked off all monuments and temples. All references to plural gods were expunged. The boundary stelae in the cliffs surrounding Akhetaten refer to 'bad things' Akhenaten had heard in the early years of his reign. The king is depicted on *talatat* – stone blocks – surrounded by soldiers from Thebes, and in rock tombs at el-Amarna, signifying the brute force underlying his radical religious reforms. Akhenaten was the only founder of a religion to have all the instruments of state power at his disposal, and we should assume that he employed them ruthlessly to realise his ideas.[37]

In some ways, he was only following precedent. Ancient Egyptian kings and queens all rewrote history. They portrayed themselves as lighting the world with their great deeds, from the building of colossal monuments to the conquering of foreign lands and enemies, displaying their limitless power and wealth. When a pharaoh ascended the throne, he was required to outshine the reputations of his predecessors, or, better still, to destroy their legacy. Amenhotep II is thought to have attempted to eliminate the legacy of his grandmother, Queen Hatshepsut, at the beginning of his reign by chiselling her image and name from stelae and smashing her statues and burying them.

The supremacy of the Aten did not survive Akhenaten's journey to the underworld. His cult of personality was unceremoniously dismantled, and his successors abandoned the city of Akhetaten and restored polytheistic religion. His temples were demolished, his art defaced, his tomb desecrated. Akhenaten's successors did an even more comprehensive job than the French revolutionaries in exacting revenge on the excesses of a past leader. The apex of wealth that had marked Akhenaten's reign was never again attained as the power of the eighteenth dynasty waned. In archival records, he was referred to as 'the criminal of Amarna'.[38] His name was excised from the official lists of pharaohs. He was obliterated from history – until the late nineteenth century, when archaeologists rediscovered the site of his great city.

The process of rehabilitation then began. His tomb was unearthed in 1907, prompting frantic excavations and a wave of academic study about his life and legacy. In the 1930s, the renowned American archaeologist and Egyptologist James Henry Breasted called him 'the first individual in human history'. Around this time, psychologists, theologians and politicians vied for his inheritance. In his 1937 book *Moses and Monotheism*, Sigmund Freud makes the unlikely claim that the 'Hymn to Aten' was a tribute by the Jewish people to Egypt for the gift of monotheism. Akhenaten has since been lauded as a precursor to both Christianity and Judaism. The radical Mexican artist Frida Kahlo took up Freud's celebration of the Pharaoh's *Geistigkeit* – his spirituality and intellect. In one of her diaries she links herself and her husband, the painter Diego Rivera, to Akhenaten and Nefertiti. According to the *Paris Review*, Kahlo used to call herself and her partner *'pareja extraña del país del punto y la raya'* (strange couple from the land of dot and line): 'In her diary, she draws them as Nefertiti and her consort, Akhenaten. Akhenaten has a swollen heart, and ribs like claws around his chest. He has testicles that look like a brain, a penis that looks like his lover's dangling breast. Below is written "Born to them was a boy strange of face." Nefertiti carries in her arms the baby Frida couldn't have.'[39]

The story has inspired filmmakers and writers. One of Agatha Christie's least-known works is a play she wrote in 1937, after being introduced to the discoverer of Tutankhamen's tomb at the Valley of the Kings in Luxor. *The Egyptian*, an epic tale of the life of Akhenaten's physician by the Finnish novelist Mika Waltari, was denounced as obscene when it was published in the United States in 1949. It flew off the shelves, becoming the biggest seller that year; a few years later it was turned into a Hollywood movie. The modern composer Philip Glass has written an opera about Akhenaten. Thomas Mann's 1943 novel, *Joseph and His Brothers*, takes particular interest in the disputed question of the Pharaoh's sexuality, even his sexual biology. German magazines during the Nazi era attempted to claim Akhenaten as one of their own, his half naked body apparently displaying healthy Aryan tendencies.

These interpretations might seem a stretch, but they testify to popular fascination with Akhenaten's extraordinary cultural afterlife. A new burst of Akhenaten fever occurred only a few years ago when DNA

tests provided evidence that he was, after all, the father of Tutankhamen. Historians argue feverishly over his legacy. Some regard him as
a modernising reformer, instituting a rational religion of the sun as life-
giver,[40] while others point to his megalomania and brutality.[41] The one
point of agreement is fascination at his lost Utopian city.

Unlike with other protagonists in this tale of the super-rich over the
ages, interest in Louis and Akhenaten does not revolve around the
acquisition of wealth. That was synonymous with title and power. What
sets these two kings apart, in their different eras and locations, is the
emphasis on glory, iconography and legacy. Presented as omniscient and
godlike, both gained a mythical status within their own lifetime. As
Montesquieu wrote over twenty years after Louis's death: 'the magnificence and splendour which surround kings form part of their
power'.[42] The infinite representation of wealth and glory was no vanity
project; it was innate to all they did.

Yet, in that final test, legacy, they both failed. Immediately on
Akhenaten's passage to the underworld, monotheism was obliterated.
The demise of Louis XIV's vision would be slower, but in the revolution that came in 1789 his rule would be denounced as the monarchy
was removed. Versailles, while damaged, was spared. It stands as testament to a king's ambition, to the use of architecture for the projection
of national pride and self-veneration. Just as the ancients had done, so
the model would be repackaged for our contemporary times.

CHAPTER 7

Jan Pieterszoon Coen and Robert Clive – To the traders, the spoils

A rising tide lifts all boats.
President John F. Kennedy

The English and Dutch East India companies represented a new way of getting rich. The activities of the first trading corporations from the late sixteenth to the eighteenth century went beyond the old-fashioned smash-and-grab conquests of the Spanish and Portuguese adventurers, the likes of Francisco Pizarro. The Dutch and then the English created entirely new economies, based on monopolies in the trade of expensive goods, such as spices.

This marked the beginning of globalisation and these were the first multinationals. In the case of the Dutch, it also marked a brief experiment with popular capitalism and a shareholding democracy. Any citizen, down to a street seller, could buy stock in the company bringing home riches from the East. Many did. Both the Dutch East India Company in Indonesia and the English East India Company in India were prepared to use extreme violence whenever necessary. They possessed their own military forces and acted as if they were states.

This chapter focuses on two men. They came from different countries, companies and generations, but they shared a mission to open new trading fronts. Jan Pieterszoon Coen, the most prominent figure in the early expansion of Dutch power in Asia, was the ultimate commodities king in an era known as the Golden Age. He gave short shrift to anyone who questioned his methods. He wrote to the seventeen directors of the company: 'we cannot make war without trade nor trade without war'. Robert Clive – Clive of India – built English power through a series of military victories against armies that were vastly superior to his in number. Along the way he lined his pockets in deals with local rulers that would stymie his political ambitions back home.

In the eyes of these men, military force was a vital tool for subjugation and the extraction of resources. As they were operating thousands of miles away from their superiors, and communication took months, they could present their actions as faits accomplis to the authorities back home. Both men fulfilled their dreams. Both became rich, yet failed to win the respect of those who had profited from their endeavours. The British and Dutch elites were delighted with the wealth that the traders sent home, but in public they expressed discomfort at the ruthlessness, corruption and extortion. High society shunned the gauche Clive and, after a brief political career, he died in unhappy circumstances, possibly committing suicide. Coen died from dysentery in his adopted distant land, an event that passed with barely a mention back home. Ever since then the Dutch have struggled to come to terms with the actions that underpinned the enrichment of their country, as have other Europeans with similar legacies.

In a nondescript small town in Holland stands a statue to a man and his money-making machine. Jan Pieterszoon Coen was born in 1587 into a professional, Protestant family in the northern port of Hoorn. His father was a trader, the occupation of choice, a former brewer who bought and sold everything from herring to cloth. The family was by no means wealthy, but in one important respect Coen was fortunate. He had been born in the right place at the right time. Hoorn was one of the most important departure points for the Dutch merchant fleet. This was a time of great optimism, the start of the Golden Age in a republic that was breaking away from the Habsburgs' Spanish Empire. This was a period of great science, law, philosophy and most of all the art of Rembrandt and Vermeer; this was the period that saw the height of the Netherlands' global power.

Dutch seafarers were already challenging the hegemony of the Spanish and the Portuguese. In England, Sir Francis Drake had set off with his flotilla to circumnavigate the globe and seek out the fabled Spice Islands of what is now known as Indonesia. He came back laden with riches. Across Europe everyone wanted to get in on the act. The Dutch were venturing to the West Indies and southern Africa, and they would soon land at New Amsterdam, the location of what would become New York. Jan Huyghen van Linschoten, a Dutchman who had worked for the Portuguese Catholic Archbishop of Goa, published a book that aroused considerable interest. Its title was *Itinerario* and it documented in detail the spice plants and resources in the part of the world that would most fixate his countrymen: the islands of the East Indies. 'If I possessed only 200 to 300 ducats they could easily be converted into 600 or 700,' Linschoten wrote. The optimism, the braggadocio, of these seafarers was not unlike that of their successors on the computerised trading floors of contemporary times. Money was there to be made; all you needed was guts and for meddlers not to stand in your way.[1]

Spurred on by Linschoten's predictions (which turned out to be conservative, given the prices which spices ended up fetching) and his navigational charts, four Dutch businessmen clubbed together to form the Company of the Far Lands. Its agents set off on their first voyage to South-east Asia in 1594 with a fleet of four ships and 249 sailors. Only eighty-nine men returned, such were the rudimentary conditions on board for the long voyages across stormy seas. They came back with a small amount of pepper and no spices. Even so, they still made a handsome profit.

Second time around they were more lucrative still. Even though only eight of the company's twenty-two ships made it home, the profit margin rose to a staggering 400 per cent. When the first of the ships returned to Amsterdam, such was the excitement that the church bells pealed. The commander, Jacob van Neck, declared that his aim was

'not to rob anyone of their property but to trade uprightly with all foreign nations'. As with contemporary examples of a rampant free
market, such strictures about good behaviour were quickly cast aside.[2]

The tales of derring-do, of drama on the high seas, led to a queue
of ambitious young men desperate to try their hand at nautical hero-
ism. Some of the stories, adorned by the imaginations of excessively
fertile minds, came replete with sea monsters and mutant humanoids.[3]
Older traders warned of the potential for chaos if fleets of unregulated
and unseaworthy vessels left the Dutch ports. In 1602, a merchant of
renown by the name of Johan van Oldenbarnevelt pushed six competing companies to merge into the Verenigde Oost-Indische
Compagnie (VOC). This was the Dutch East India Company. A board
of directors known as the Heeren XVII, the 'Seventeen Gentlemen',
drawn from the great and the good, the *regenten*, would oversee the new
company. The terms were extraordinary: an initial twenty-one-year
monopoly on all trade between the Cape of Good Hope in South
Africa and the Straits of Magellan, which divide the Pacific and the
Atlantic at the southern tip of South America. For two decades, the
company had half the world at its disposal. It was no surprise that the
most ambitious men rushed into its employ.

Coen's parents spotted the opportunity early; in order to boost their
son's prospects, they sent young Jan to Rome to train as an accountant
and merchant and learn the vital art of double-entry book-keeping that
had been established long before in southern Europe, but was still relatively unknown in the north. He lived with an influential Flemish-Italian
banking family, the Visschers, for seven years – his whole teenage life.
In his spare time, alone in his quarters, the young man read voraciously.
He particularly enjoyed Machiavelli's *The Prince* (not the only subject in
this book to do so). By the time he returned to Hoorn, his father had
died. The VOC was sending its first expeditions to the East Indies in
search of spices and was looking for talented young recruits. He took his
initial voyage east, as an assistant merchant, in 1607, and stayed in the
East Indies for three years. He was only twenty years old, part of the first
wave of Dutchmen to make the trip.

He soon became a man to watch; ahead of his second trip in 1612,
he was promoted to a senior merchant, with command of two ships.

During his stay out in Asia, the precocious trader wrote a business plan for the VOC and sent it to the Heeren XVII. This *Discoers Touscherende den Nederlantsche Indischen Staet* became standard reading. Coen made two important points. First, the VOC should prioritise its destinations and commodities. It should focus exclusively on establishing monopolies in nutmeg, cloves and mace, which were highly prized cooking ingredients and also important for medicinal purposes. This was where the big money was to be made. Second, all means necessary should be deployed to secure this objective. No native and no rival company should be allowed to get in the way.[4] He wrote: 'Your Honours should know by experience that trade in Asia must be driven and maintained under the protection and favour of Your Honours' own weapons, and that the weapons must be paid for by the profits from the trade; so we cannot make trade without war, nor war without trade.'[5]

It was a chilling piece of work that would set the benchmark for the VOC's activities.

Spices, which had hitherto been transported only in small quantities, usually overland through the dangerous routes of Central Asia, could fetch massive profits when sold in European cities. Ten pounds in weight of nutmeg could be bought for less than one English penny in Asia and sold for more than eight hundred times that amount in Europe. Cloves would have increased in value by a hundred times by the time they reached India, and 240 times on reaching Lisbon.[6] The profits made by the VOC were such that, between 1630 and 1670, its shareholders enjoyed annual dividends of 10 per cent or more. Few ventures over the centuries have matched that return.[7]

Coen became accountant-general in 1613. The following year he was appointed head of the VOC's plantations and trading operations in Bantam, in the west of Java. His rise up the ranks was effortless. He became director-general of VOC trade (the seventeenth-century equivalent of a chief financial officer), before securing the top job of governor-general of the East Indies in 1619.[8] He served two terms in the latter office, establishing many of the routes that the VOC would follow for nearly two centuries. He drew up a grand plan for intra-Asian trade to be self-financing, by exchanging Indian textiles for pepper on Sumatra, Chinese goods for silver in Japan, and sending elephants from Ceylon to Siam. Coen wrote, bluntly as ever, to his directors: 'Send enough money until the marvellous native trade has been reformed.'[9]

One of his early decisions was to approve new instructions for sailors to the Indies that would give them an edge over their English rivals. They were to sail from the Cape of Good Hope on the 'roaring forties' – strong winds that blew all the way across the Indian Ocean, bearing north to Java. This route took only eight months, a considerable improvement on the voyage around India that lasted over a year.[10]

The VOC was an ultra-efficient, multinational trading machine, maximising its assets at all times. In a normal year, three fleets would depart Holland for the Indies, with metronomic regularity, on expeditions lasting eighteen months. The largest would leave around Christmas. Fitting the fleets was easier in the winter, when more men were out of work and willing to take their chances as sailors.[11] The ships returned with such vast quantities of spices that they ran the risk of flooding the market and depressing the price. A deal was reached allowing them to sell their entire cargo for a fixed price, on the promise that they would not sell any more for a set number of months. This was called the *stilstand*.[12] Guaranteed high prices and low risk made the spice trade an attractive proposition for potential investors.

The Dutch were the leaders in the field, not just in terms of the quality and quantity of their products, but also in the structure of their businesses. The English East India Company was run on traditional lines, answerable ultimately to the King. Decision-making tended to be formal and cumbersome, making it harder to respond to instant market opportunities. The Dutch were more nimble. The ships in the Indies were rarely idle. The ownership structure was more modern. Remarkably for the time, shares in the VOC could be bought by anyone, including foreigners.[13] The credit market that already existed in the Netherlands in the seventeenth century allowed relatively poor people to buy ⅓2nd or ⅙4th shares in VOC ships.*

---

* These sales could be likened to the 'popular capitalism' of the 1980s era of privatisation under Margaret Thatcher. An illusion of broad ownership was created – the prospect of instant profit was exciting enough to tempt hundreds of thousands of people to dabble in stakes in companies they knew little about.

The VOC's popular investors could make money, but their tiny holdings afforded them no say in the running of the company. The advantage for larger, richer investors was that they could spread risk across a number of convoys and trade routes by buying shares in different ships.[14] As with more recent examples, richer shareholders ended up consolidating their ownership as small shareholders sold up quickly after realising their instant returns. The VOC could not be said to constitute a stakeholder democracy, but it was a departure from anything that had gone before.

The company became a global conglomerate. It was simultaneously producer, consumer, middleman, cargo-carrier and seller, employing up to fifteen thousand people as early as 1625, at a time when a workforce of a few hundred was deemed large. Dutchmen staffed wharves and offices in the Netherlands. Company soldiers were recruited mainly from Germany and France – usually impoverished men fleeing the war-ravaged Holy Roman Empire. Some became permanent émigrés, but many died on board the ships or in the company's campaigns. Over half of the million men who embarked from Holland's wharves for the East never returned.[15] The lack of opportunities elsewhere made such risks worth taking. The VOC also created its own long-term pool of labour: by 1700, perhaps one-sixth of its workforce was made up of Asian-born children of employees. Dutchmen were not allowed to take their local wives home, so some chose to settle in Asia.[16] Ordinary shipmen received a wage comparable to that of a low-ranking soldier. The biggest draw was the prospect of three years of uninterrupted employment at a time when some economic activity back home was still seasonal. Promotion prospects were helped by the high mortality rates on the long voyages; petty officers on ships had to be replaced. Those who re-enlisted after one voyage to the Indies would take positions of greater responsibility. Locals and indentured workers had no prospect of such advancement, however. They were moved from plantation to plantation, forced to buy their foodstuffs through the VOC. This was part pure slavery, part a precursor of the early twentieth-century American 'company towns' that employed miners and steel workers.

With each voyage, the scramble for economic and military supremacy became more intense. Armed exploratory parties were dispatched to strategically important outposts. Flags were raised, territory was claimed; low-level conflict with indigenous populations and between arriving Europeans simmered, and frequently erupted into open war, particularly between the English and the Dutch.

One of Coen's first decisions as governor-general was to seek a new headquarters for the company, away from Bantam, which he considered too far from the main spice production centres. In 1619 his forces stormed the settlement of Jacatra some forty miles to the east (site of the modern-day Indonesian capital of Jakarta), setting it ablaze and driving out its inhabitants. This tactic of forcible expulsions would become standard practice. The Dutch rebuilt the town and proclaimed it the capital of the Dutch East Indies. Coen had wanted to rename the city 'New Hoorn', after his birthplace, but the Heeren would not allow it.[17] Instead, they chose Batavia, the old Roman name for Holland, to evoke a stronger sense of nationhood in the colonies.

This was one of many disputes Coen had with his bosses back home. He wanted to build a model city to serve as the headquarters for the model company, a replica Dutch town with churches, a municipal hall and typical wooden, gabled homes. In repeated letters to the Heeren, he insisted that Dutch interests in the Indies would be improved by mass emigration from Holland. They refused to back his grandiose ethnic ambitions.[18] The reality on the ground was hardly propitious. Batavia became known as the 'graveyard of Europeans'; its swamps were a breeding ground for mosquitoes. Many Europeans died there and some of the survivors clamoured to be repatriated back home; but others stayed put, prepared to put up with anything for profit.

Throughout his two terms as governor-general, Coen's relations with the Heeren were decidedly tetchy. Class had something to do with it: Coen came from a more humble merchant background rather than the city fathers who oversaw the company.[19] He also had no experience of municipal politics, having gone abroad as a young man. From the tone of his correspondence with the Heeren, it is clear that he was constantly frustrated by these men who lived comfortable lives at home, and who, in Coen's view, did not appreciate the dangers and opportunities of the Indies.

Coen despised those who tried to hold back his ambitions. His hatred of the English started early. The Anglo–Dutch rivalry for control of the Spice Islands was intense, but rather than see it as healthy competition, Coen took it personally. Back in 1609, at the start of his career, he had an early initiation into the duplicitousness of the English (or so the Dutch thought). The inhabitants of a small volcanic archipelago known as the Banda Islands had given an English captain permission to open a factory on the island of Neira – breaking the terms of contracts they had signed giving the Dutch a monopoly. It is not known whether the Bandanese failed to understand the nature of the contracts, or whether they were persuaded or threatened by the English to break them.[20] The VOC dispatched a small naval force to re-establish Dutch hegemony over the islands, but they were seen off, their bodies dumped in the sea. Coen was part of a rescue party that arrived too late to save them. This would leave an indelible impression on him.[21]

Time and again over the next decade and more, he asked the VOC's directors for more financial and military support to go after the English. This put him at odds with the government back home, the States-General, which favoured an alliance with the English against the Spanish.[22] Coen regarded Spain, the traditional military enemy of the Dutch, as less of a threat than England, his new commercial rival. After the humiliation of Neira, he suffered further indignity during an altercation with an English captain, John Jourdain, on the nearby island of Ambon in 1613. He challenged the Englishman to produce his captain's commission, to which the ill-tempered Jourdain rejoined: 'His long beard (for he had none at all) could not teach me to followe my commission.'[23] This obvious jibe – Coen had a handlebar moustache rather than a beard – would not be forgotten. Six years later, Jourdain was caught in a skirmish with Dutch ships and shot in the heart while attempting to surrender. It is not known whether Coen ordered the killing, but he rewarded the captain of the Dutch party, and the man who fired the fatal shot, with gold.[24]

By 1619 the two governments had become increasingly concerned at the skirmishes, leading King James I and the States-General to conclude a truce – the Treaty of Defence. The market in spices would be divided between them in a fixed proportion of two to one (favouring whichever company was occupying a particular island at the time). A council was established locally to oversee the merchants of both companies, who were required to share trading posts. It took nine months for news of the agreement to make it all the way to Coen. He denounced it, complaining that he was being forced to 'embrace the serpent'.[25] Furious that the treaty guaranteed the English a larger share of the spice trade than they had been able to capture for themselves, he wrote to his directors:

> They [the English] owe you a debt of gratitude, for they had rightly helped themselves out of India, and now your gentlemen have put them straight back in again ... And why the English have been allowed to have one-third of the cloves, nutmeg, and mace I cannot fully understand. They could not pretend to lay claim on a single grain of sand of the beaches in the Moluccas, Amboyna, or Banda.[26]

With each year in the Indies, Coen became more bellicose. He wrote to the Heeren: 'If you, gentlemen, want great and noble deeds in honour of God and for the prosperity of our country, so relieve us of the English.'[27] One of his tactics to outfox his enemies was to bombard them with legal hurdles. Every time the English asked for their share, the Dutch retaliated by presenting them with the bills of the costs made in defence of their forts and the waters around the Spice Islands and Java. These comprised every guilder spent on the garrisons, food and clothing for soldiers, sailors and other VOC personnel, and the provision of everything from gunpowder to the cloth used for bartering.[28]

Coen's ultimate goal was the total expulsion of the English from the region. Force was the safest bet. In 1621, he led an attack on the Banda Islands, to teach the natives a lesson for violating their contracts and trading with the English. The local leaders on the mountainous island of Lonthor – called *orang kaya*, or rich men – were forced to sign an agreement with the Dutch for the exclusive production of spices in amounts that they could not possibly meet. When they failed to achieve the numbers required, they were starved, tortured or chopped down – or a combination of all three. Their bodies were strewn around the island for all to see. Out of a population of some fifteen thousand, it is said that only around a thousand survived. Some Dutch historians dispute this figure, arguing also that many of the deaths would have been caused by disease. Either way, eight hundred of the survivors were forcibly removed to Batavia, their places taken by slave labour from other islands. Coen had hired Japanese mercenaries to kill the island's forty-four *orang kaya* and impale their bodies on bamboo spikes, an atrocity that is still remembered on Lonthor with an annual commemoration.[29] Devoid of their 'surplus' population, Coen was able to refashion nutmeg plantation on the islands on an industrial scale, creating precise land parcels that would be handed to Dutch planters and worked by slaves, prisoners and indentured labourers brought in from neighbouring islands. He saw the people themselves as economically expendable. While news of the clearing left some of the Heeren squeamish, Coen had no such qualms. He would do whatever it took to serve the interests of the spice monopoly.[30]

The conflict with the English came to a head two years later, in 1623, when ten English East India Company employees and ten foreign employees of the VOC (nine Japanese mercenaries and a Portuguese) were arrested on Ambon, where the English and Dutch shared a trading post. One of the Japanese confessed under torture – a standard Dutch procedure of having water poured over the head until close to drowning (similar to the modern technique of water-boarding) that invariably brought the desired confession. All were convicted of spying on Dutch fortifications, sentenced to death for treason, and beheaded. The head of the English captain was impaled on a bamboo pole in the main square. It is said that the Dutch sent the English the bill for cleaning the blood-spattered carpet from the executioner's block.

Even though Coen had already left the Indies, having completed his first term as governor-general, this did not stop English merchants suspecting him of ordering the executions. Certainly, he approved of the Amboyna Massacre, as it came to be known, when news of it reached him in Europe.[31] For years, successive commissions of inquiry, some by the English, others by the Dutch, ended in acrimonious disagreement, and the affair would sour relations for generations. The massacre, coupled with Jourdain's death in 1619, made Coen a bogeyman for the English. So incensed was King James that he said Coen was 'deserving of hanging'.[32] At home, too, Coen was not impervious to criticism. One of his Dutch superiors reminded him: 'there is no profit at all in an empty sea, empty countries, and dead people'.[33]

Yet, with so many people making so much money – from the small investor to the company director as well as the various groups with a stake in the supply chain – it seemed perverse to complain about the treatment of natives. As for those on the ground, the opportunities for enrichment bore little resemblance to official salaries, which company employees regarded as something between mean and derisory. Formal pay differentials were small – the governor-general earned only seven times more than the lowliest employee. In reality, it was much greater than that, as the more senior the official, the more opportunity he had to make money through 'private trade' (corruption). The figures at stake were enormous: a governor-general (nominal salary 700 florins a month) could take home a fortune of 10 million florins. One junior merchant was ready to pay 3500 florins to the Appointments Board for a post that paid 40 a month but yielded 40,000.[34] This sort of remuneration package might even outstrip the bonuses accrued by modern-day CEOs and bankers. Corrupt practices were rife. One of these was to dilute the cargoes of precious metals that were stored in warehouses.[35] Officials at Batavia's port would, at a price, wave through the loads. They would accept handsome payment for unauthorised cargoes to be loaded on to company ships and unloaded at company ports. The black economy thrived.

A solemn type, Coen abhorred the customary practices of adventurers, be they Dutch, English or Spanish – the whoring, drinking and siphoning off of money and goods. The first governor-general, Pieter Both, described him as 'delightful' and 'modest' in his habits.[36] He tried to stamp out ill-gotten gains, but only to an extent. Overall, the exchequer back home received only a fraction of the total value of the spices, but it was felt that heavier regulation and supervision would dampen the entrepreneurial spirit. It was not until the late seventeenth century, long after Coen and the first generation of Dutch traders had departed the scene, that the company began to tackle graft seriously. The evidence suggests Coen's professed asceticism may have been more for show. In one of his many broadsides against the Heeren, Coen admonished them over his pay: 'I thought my services were more valuable than what you offer.'[37] His complaint may have had more to do with recognition and status than personal profiteering.

Whatever the tensions with the Heeren, Coen returned to Amsterdam in 1622 to a hero's welcome – the admirable and tough man of finance in search of riches for his fellow Protestant compatriots. He was largely in tune with his times, a mixture of piety and acquisitiveness that allowed for atrocities to be carried out against the lesser orders, as long as they were not mentioned. The Dutch Reformed Church had a similarly ambivalent approach to violence in the service of profit as did the Catholic Church in Spain and Portugal. The Dutch approach, however, was more risk-averse. The object was to pre-empt competition, monopolise supply and control all the conditions of trade, from production of raw materials to point of sale. Confrontation might be required to make the first breakthrough, but once that was achieved, consolidation was the order of the day.

Dutch primacy in world trade sharply lifted living standards back home. This period marked the arrival of the middle class as a political force and new market for consumer goods. The *regenten*, or regents, included not only merchants but brewers and shopkeepers. These were the people who formed the majority of VOC's investors in its early years.[38] Others to benefit from colonial expansion included jewellers, printers and dyers.[39] All this combined to produce a trickle-down effect; wages in seventeenth-century Holland were much higher than elsewhere. Inequality lay less between different strands of urban society than between country folk and people living in the trading cities.[40]

The cities of the Low Countries became some of the main centres of European culture. Still-life painting was the means by which the exotic commodities plundered from the Indies could be shown off and preserved for posterity. Those who could afford to invest in paintings would find a fashion for depictions of spices, fruits and birds from Asia and Africa.[41] Throughout Enlightenment Europe, a public debate emerged around the notion of luxury. Was it good or bad for the health of a nation? Thinkers from Bernard Mandeville to Jean-Jacques Rousseau tackled the question. Popular perception in the Golden Age shifted from hostility against 'old luxury' – the established rich –

towards acceptance of a 'new luxury' – a consumer culture in which at least a large minority of the population could participate.[42] Mandeville, a Dutchman who emigrated to England and wrote *The Fable of the Bees* in praise of individualism, summed up the attitude of the emergent, aspirational middle class:

> *Thus every part was full of Vice,*
> *Yet the whole Mass a Paradise.*

This was the Netherlands that Coen had helped transform.

One of his first tasks on his return home was to find a woman to marry, preferably upwards in social rank. His bride, Eva Ment, was suitably young (only nineteen), and crucially she came from a respected family. Their wedding was a grand event, as portraits of bride and groom testify. Life in their townhouse on Warmoes Street, in a fashionable part of Amsterdam, gradually became tedious for someone of his drive. Coen agitated to be sent back to the East Indies, but the Heeren did not want to antagonise the English. Eventually they relented – business was business, after all – and he returned for his second stint as governor-general in 1627.

The plan was for him to travel back incognito, so as not to inflame the English. Coen took Eva and several members of her family with him, as a demonstration to the rest of society of a settler's determination to build a new life in the far-flung colonies. He had been given a new brief to expand trade beyond the East Indies and into India and China. He struggled to do so, as much of his time was spent defending existing territory. Batavia twice came under attack from Sultan Agung of nearby Mataram, who had refused repeated demands from the Dutch for permission to build a new trading post on the north coast of Java. Both of Agung's incursions were repelled, but during the second siege, in 1629, Coen died from dysentery caused by poisoned water. He was only forty-two years old. One of his daughters also died during the siege. Eva returned to Holland, only for the baby girl to die on the voyage home.

Coen did not have time to enjoy the material fruits of his endeavours. He had established a system of exploitation of resources that would be emulated by other countries long after the Golden Age had passed. The world's first giant corporation had been established over the dead and mutilated bodies of thousands of local inhabitants of the Spice Islands. The VOC went bankrupt in 1800, but by then the wealth of Holland had been established. Batavia became a multinational city of seventy thousand, populated by Dutch, other Europeans, Chinese and Japanese. It remained the most important trading post in the Far East for two centuries, until Stamford Raffles founded Singapore.

For years after his death, Coen was largely forgotten; it was only in the late nineteenth century that he enjoyed a semblance of rehabilitation. The town of Hoorn had fallen on hard times, its trading status usurped by other ports at home and abroad. But the unveiling of a statue to him in the main square in 1893 attracted the great and the good from around the country. Staring operatically into the distance, a cannon behind him and a sword to his side, Coen appears to be dismissing his critics with disdain. Under him is carved his famous exhortation that he made in a letter to the Heeren in 1619: 'Dispereert Niet' (Do Not Despair). The saying continues: 'God is on our side.' One of the unresolved issues for the super-rich is the extent to which their success is ordained by a higher power, or the extent to which it is the product of human skill and endeavour. Cosimo de' Medici was tormented by the question. Others, such as the contemporary banker Lloyd Blankfein (see Chapter 14), seek to make light of it.

Coen has remained a figure of intense controversy in Holland and Indonesia. An evocative black-and-white newsreel from 1944 shows Indonesians in Jakarta angrily tearing down a monument to him, shortly before their country gained independence. The discomfort in the Netherlands has been intense; in the 1970s demonstrations against Coen and his sort were regular occurrences. The Dutch school curriculum teaches children about colonisation, but this is a period of the nation's history many would rather forget. Yet how can this be reconciled with the economic wealth of the nation that was predicated on the risks taken by such adventurers? The modern liberal Dutch may be trying to have it both ways. In their business model and motivations, is there much to differentiate early colonial commodities traders from their contemporary equivalents?

It took a moment of bathos in Hoorn to bring matters to a head – a lorry putting up lights smashed into Coen's statue in August 2011. Its removal for several months of repairs coincided with a growing national debate about his legacy. Next to the statue on the main square stands the Westfries Museum, which for more than a century has told the history of Dutch traders from the region, notably Coen and the VOC. As the local council discussed the future of its most famous son, the museum decided to 'put him on trial'. Two well-known academics made the case for and against the reinstatement of the statue, while a television personality summed up as judge. This was relayed on a video screen to visitors to the museum. A glossy magazine was also produced entitled *Coen: Held of Schurk?* (Hero or Villain?). It presented the arguments and celebrated some of the art the debate had aroused, including a mock-up of Coen as Hitler. The museum received a European Union award; its handling of the case was held up as a model for how cultural institutions can contribute to the debate about history, wealth creation and the super-rich.

By two to one, visitors decided to restore Coen to his place in the centre of the square, but with a panel on the side of the plinth explaining his 'controversial' role in history. A very Dutch compromise had been found. Just as the furore was quietening down, in October 2013 the Indonesian Ambassador to the Netherlands was invited to Hoorn. Her minders asked that she avoid the Coen statue and visit a different monument to the Golden Age. The official explanation was that she didn't want to stir up trouble. Perhaps she simply couldn't face the man himself.

A century and a half after Coen's birth, a young Englishman would follow a remarkably similar path. Born in 1725 in the village of Styche, Shropshire, Robert Clive did not come from poverty, as some historians have suggested; but nor did his family possess anything approaching the wealth that he would amass for himself over the course of his lifetime. His father, Richard, was a landowning lawyer, straddling the boundary between old gentry and the new professional classes. During Robert's childhood his parents fell on hard times, and the estate fell into disrepair. He was sent for a while to live with his mother's sister in

Manchester, who spoiled him. By the time he returned home the young man was out of control. He was sent to a number of schools, and also received education from private tutors, but no matter who was instructing him, he always struggled academically.

The eldest of thirteen children, Clive showed attributes as a teenager that would stand him in good stead for his trading adventures – aggression, determination and an acute business brain. For several months he led a gang of boys who ran their own protection racket in the nearby town of Market Drayton; they perched on gargoyles to frighten passers-by and broke shop windows if the owners refused to give them money. A hellraiser, he was, in the words of one Victorian biographer: 'the leader in all the broils and escapades of schoolboy life; the terror of the masters; the spoilt darling of his schoolmates'.[43]

Richard Clive concluded that his son was not going to make his way in the respectable professions, so he secured him an interview in Leadenhall Street for the position of clerk in the East India Company. Accountancy was the one formal skill Robert had picked up during his schooling, passing the test with comparative ease.[44] At the age of seventeen, he was on his way aboard the *Winchester*, destined for a career as a bureaucrat in the company's Indian settlements.

Like Coen before him, Clive had little experience of adult life when he first made the trip to Asia. In the course of his perilous fourteen-month voyage to Madras, he ran out of money and was forced to borrow from the ship's captain. He arrived at the small settlement of Fort St George with only the clothes on his back. However, even as an entry-level clerk for the East India Company (EIC) on a salary of £5 a year, Clive kept three servants, paid for out of his living expenses.[45] Despite a lifestyle of relative comfort, he wrote home a year after his arrival: 'I have not enjoyed one happy day since I left my native country.'[46] He was prone to episodes of depression that would afflict him throughout his life. His work did not help lift his gloom – he was little more than an assistant shopkeeper, charged with haggling with suppliers.

The India into which Clive stepped was fractured. After the death of the Mughal Emperor Aurangzeb in 1707, a number of subordinate states with their own kings and political structures had begun to break free of central control.[47] From the 1720s, rich provinces such as Bengal had moved towards *de facto* independence, opening up new opportunities for outside traders, most of all the English. Initially, at least, the leaders of these provinces, the *nawabs*, were at least as powerful as the European merchants. They needed to be wooed – that invariably meant a share of the spoils.

The Governor and Company of Merchants of London trading into the East Indies, or the Honourable East India Company, as it was variously known in its early years, was granted a Royal Charter by Queen Elizabeth I in 1600. While playing second fiddle to its better-organised Dutch rival throughout the seventeenth century, the EIC focused its operations on the Indian subcontinent instead of the Spice Islands. In place of spices, it developed successful businesses in commodities like indigo and saltpetre, and especially textiles. The company quickly became a major force at home and abroad. The government, supposedly its political master, was by the middle of the century £4.2 million in debt to the EIC. The power relationship was uneasy.[48]

The company chose its allies carefully. The Mughal Emperor was keen to encourage an interloper to rival the Dutch, Portuguese and French, so he granted the British licences for 'factories' (trading posts, run by 'factors', or head merchants) as early as 1617.[49] The fracturing of Mughal authority laid these factories open to raids and led the company to arm itself to defend and extend its holdings. To protect its forts in the coastal outposts of Madras, Bombay and Calcutta, it recruited bands of soldiers from the streets of English towns. It was this small, insular but well-established expatriate community that Clive encountered when he arrived in 1744.

Clive's rise in the EIC was as rapid as Coen's had been in the VOC. His first taste of military-trading hostilities came in 1746 when the Compagnie française des Indes drove the British from their settlement in Madras, during what is known as the First Carnatic War. Having survived a duel with a company officer, whom he had accused of cheating while gambling,[50] Clive hastily enlisted to join the army, for no pay, as long as he was given the rank of captain.[51] He distinguished himself in the successful defence of the fort of Madras, coming to the attention of the new commander of British forces, Major Stringer Lawrence. By the time Madras was returned to the English in 1749, in return for the restitution of Louisburg (in what is now North Carolina) to the French (a mutually expedient early version of global trading), Clive appeared set for a military career. Lawrence said of him: 'he behaved in courage and in judgement much beyond what could be expected from his years'. The two officers became good friends: the ambitious young man and his mentor. At the same time, Clive made considerable profits from contracts to supply the company's armed forces.

Despite a formal peace treaty between the British and the French in 1748, a proxy war continued in India. The tactics deployed by the two nations in the south of the country were similar: find a local potentate and buy his loyalty. Divide and rule was to prove a cost-effective route to economic, and later political, hegemony. In 1751, the Carnatic Wars erupted again when the French and their ally Chanda Sahib targeted the strategic town of Trichinopoly, south of Madras. Knowing that they were outnumbered by the French forces, the British were on the point of giving up on the territory. Clive had other ideas, convincing his superiors to allow him to lead an expedition against the French. For a twenty-five-year-old still with much to prove, this was a supreme act of bravado.

The British were in disarray and, with Lawrence back in England haggling over a pay dispute, there was little appetite to take on the enemy. Clive rose to the challenge. He marched a small force to Arcot, the Carnatic capital, in the knowledge that the majority of Chanda's army was several hundred miles away, besieging Trichinopoly, and took it without a shot being fired. Chanda immediately dispatched his son, Raza Sahib, and a force of some 7500 to retake Arcot. But Clive stood firm, repelling the assault with just five hundred men (two hundred British and three hundred local sepoys). This was the sort of imperial deed that was beginning to capture the public imagination back home. 'It may have been luck, it may have been bungling on the part of the enemy,' wrote one of Clive's biographers, 'but it created the legend of English courage and invincibility which was to carry English arms in India from one success to another.'[52]

Arcot began to convince the British government that, as well as securing the EIC's commercial interests, it could start to stake a formal claim for territory.

Clive returned to England for the first time in 1753. He was showered with praise and invitations to dine at top tables, but gradually
doubts about his 'character' emerged among the upper classes. His
wealth was estimated at £40,000, a huge amount for a man of his station. Some, including key figures inside the company, were beginning
to wonder how he had become so rich, so quickly.

He brushed aside the sniping and planned his spending carefully. His
first task was to pay off his family's various debts. Then he pumped
money into becoming a Tory MP for the seat of St Michael's in Corn-
wall, which he achieved with consummate ease. However, a year later,
a parliamentary petition rejected the result.[53] Such objections were
common tools in the politics of the eighteenth century, where pretty
much any election was open to a petition from the losing candidate.
The episode provided Clive with a lesson in the chicanery of the political system. Without friends in the right places, it was hard to achieve
your ends. This experience contributed to his later support for the
rakish radical MP John Wilkes, whose campaigns for electoral reform,
freedom of the press and American independence posed a direct challenge to the opaque old order.

Clive's true interests lay in India. There he could grow his fame and
fortune unencumbered by rotten boroughs (corrupt mini-fiefdoms usually with tiny numbers of voters and passed down from father to son)
and the other assorted rotten practices back home. He accepted a lieutenant colonel's commission with the company and returned in 1755 –
partly because he was close to running out of money again. This time
he took with him his new wife, Margaret Maskelyne, the seventeen-
year-old sister of a friend and a member of a powerful Anglo-Indian
family.

Bit by bit, he was acquiring the accoutrements of success and
respectability. He developed his own public relations strategy for his
next stint abroad, keeping up a regular correspondence with major society figures such as the Archbishop of Canterbury.[54] He had learned that,
if he wanted to be respected in society, telling the story of his heroic
actions was just as important as undertaking them in the first place. He
constructed a network of friends and family who would represent his
interests: advisers and spin-doctors.[55]

Clive stepped off the ship at a time of great political turmoil, and opportunity, in India. The Nawab of Bengal, Siraj-ud-Daula, saw the increasing military presence of the EIC as a threat; he decided to strike first. In 1756 he seized Calcutta, determined to drive out the Europeans. Captured Englishmen were placed in an overcrowded and sweltering cell where dozens suffocated (the number of deaths is disputed). The episode of the 'Black Hole of Calcutta' would feature prominently in imperial propaganda. Portrayed as a deliberate act of savagery by Siraj, when in fact it may have been more to do with the negligence of his soldiers, the horrors of the Black Hole were repeated and embellished for the domestic British audience.[56] The incident provided a useful pretext for the subsequent expansion into Bengal; proof of the supposed barbarity of the native population. In later years the high priest of Victorian imperialism, Lord Curzon, would describe the deaths as 'practically the foundation stone of the British Empire in India'.[57] In the immediate term, the fall of Calcutta was viewed as a disaster. Clive reckoned it cost English traders about £2 million, not just from the loss of the town itself, but also because Indian traders would be more reluctant to do business if it looked like the English were on their way out.[58] The EIC had to act quickly to recoup its losses. This view of trade backed by military power was identical to Coen's in the previous century.

Clive recaptured Calcutta and advanced on the Nawab's army, which was camped at Plassey. The Nawab's forces numbered thirty thousand and included a contingent of French artillerymen – loaned by the French governor Joseph-François Dupleix, who was alarmed by the growth of the EIC's power. Clive's army was about a tenth the size, a mix of Europeans and Indians. His victory, on 23 June 1757, against all the odds, boosted the reputations of both British invincibility and Clive the empire-builder.

The spin was more heroic than the substance. Clive had made a deal with one of the Nawab's generals, Mir Jafar, and a disaffected section of his court, to oust Siraj. Mir Jafar, who had been in charge of thousands of the Nawab's infantry, held them back from the battle, helping Clive to win. The following day, the Englishman met with Mir Jafar, embraced him, and hailed him as the new ruler of Bengal. Clive reported back to his bosses that he had presided over a 'revolution'. The British, he said, 'shall return to Calcutta and attend to trade which was our proper sphere and our whole aim in these parts'. French influence waned quickly. Its own East India Company had amassed two million francs in debt and was reliant on bail-outs from the treasury; in contrast, the EIC was becoming so rich that it was making annual loans to the government in London to help fund military campaigns elsewhere. Dupleix was sent home and died in ignominy – although later French historians laid the blame on the faint-heartedness of King Louis XV, who had refused the governor reinforcements.

In 1759 Clive wrote to the Prime Minister, William Pitt the Elder, advising him that the potential of India was too great for a single company to tap into. The country, he said, was ripe for conquest.

> So large a sovereignty may possibly be an object too expensive for a mercantile company; and it is feared that they are not themselves able, without the nation's assistance, to maintain so wide a dominion. I have therefore presumed, Sir, to represent this matter to you, and to submit it to your consideration, whether the execution of a design, that may hereafter be still carried to greater lengths, be worthy of the Government's taking into hand. I flatter myself I have made it pretty clear to you, that there will be little or no difficulty in obtaining the absolute possession of these rich kingdoms.

The foundations of the Raj had been laid. And yet, it was due less to valour and more to a backroom deal with Mir Jafar, an up-and-coming general who saw the financial benefits of siding with the foreign power most likely to succeed.

With characteristic brashness, Clive had forged the signature on the treaty of his superior Admiral Watson, who was not party to the negotiations. When he found out, Watson was not pleased, but his anger was softened by the prospect of a share in the spoils. Clive estimated that Mir Jafar repaid various servants of the EIC a total of thirty million rupees (over £3 million) for helping to install him as Nawab.[59] Presented with copious gifts in Murshidabad, the city nearest to Plassey, which Clive found to be 'as extensive, populous and rich as the City of London', he said: 'Please Allah, I do not want your wealth. I seek only your assistance in establishing a new government.'[60]

Clive's reception convinced him that the English had only scratched the surface in Bengal; there was far more money to be made. There were some there, he wrote, who possessed 'infinitely greater property than any in [London]'.[61] He was waited upon by Mir Jafar's eldest son,[62] a sure sign of his power in the new order of things. And he saw to it that his co-conspirators in the agreement to remove Siraj were handsomely rewarded. Watson received a sapphire, a ruby and pearls.[63]

Clive amassed his personal wealth by a number of means, of varying legitimacy. The scale of his military victories, and his distance from any other authority, ensured there were few rules governing what he could and could not get away with. After Plassey, he paid himself 'expenses' and then treated himself to 1.25 million rupees (about £160,000) from the defeated treasury.[64] This was small change compared to one of the most lucrative scams cooked up by the new Nawab on behalf of his English boss. He presented Clive with a *Jagir*, an annuity on the company's estates, of a massive £27,000 per year for the rest of his life. The EIC was listed as the official revenue collector for the land but it took only a 10 per cent cut – the rest went to one man.[65] With one eye on how he wanted to be received as a gentleman when he chose to return to England, Clive wrote home after Plassey, asking a friend to buy him '200 shirts, 3 large of the finest stockings, several pieces spotted muslin and plain 2 yards wide for aprons'. This all had to be 'the finest and best you can get for Love or Money'.[66]

When it came to graft, there was little to choose between the English and the Dutch, but the English probably edged it. From the early eighteenth century, the company's servants in Bengal abused the privileges granted them by the local ruler by forging and selling *dastaks*, passes that exempted them from tolls and taxes.[67] Some were sold to Indian merchants. Long-standing national rivalries melted away when it came to personal gain. In the 1750s, Clive was a friend of the VOC's chief agent in Bengal, Adriaan Bisdom. The Dutch provided him with a ship to bring some of his fortune back via Batavia, where it was less likely to be detected. Clive is estimated to have shipped over £50,000 in this fashion. So common did the process become that he was forced to launch an inquiry into the conduct of his underlings. This was a win–win for everyone – the Dutch charged handsomely for their laundering services.[68]

The image for public consumption was something quite different. Clive would, without a trace of irony, denounce the previous practices of the government of Bengal before it was cleaned up by the English: 'I shall only say that such a scene of anarchy, confusion, bribery, corruption and extortion was never seen or heard of in any country but Bengal; nor such and so many fortunes acquired in so unjust and rapacious manner.' He saw no contradiction between his own wealth and his public attempts to stamp out corruption, for example by making it illegal for company employees to accept gifts worth over a thousand rupees without the express permission of the governor. He knew he had to have a financial power base if he wanted to make another play for political power and legitimacy at home, and his moves against (others') corruption were motivated by the need to manage his reputation carefully. While Clive was no doubt corrupt by any standard, Mir Jafar argued – with some justification – that whoever might replace him would not be able to exercise the same authority and restraint over the EIC's officials, both English and Indian.[69]

When Clive arrived in England again in July 1760, he was desperate to buy himself the status of an English gentleman. Pitt, who had been impressed by the tenacity of this self-made trader and officer, praised him in Parliament as 'a heaven-born general'.[70] He had come to be known as Clive of India. King George II, when discussing where to send one of his young courtiers to gain a military education, exclaimed: 'If he wants to learn the art of war, let him go to Clive.'[71]

After his unfortunate experience in politics first time around, Clive was determined to secure himself a seat, and keep hold of it. 'If I can get into Parliament I shall be very glad, but no more struggles with the ministry,' he wrote to his father.[72] He begged his father not to make too much of his bid. Understatement was a better route to success: 'I desire you will endeavour to moderate his expectations, for altho' I intend getting into Parliament and hope of being taken some notice of by His Majesty, yet you know the merit of all actions are greatly lessened by being too much boasted of.'[73] With his greater public status, surely this time nobody would stand in his way? In 1761 he was duly elected MP for one of Shrewsbury's two seats. He was given the title Baron Clive of Plassey in the same year, although he was disappointed to have been awarded an Irish rather than an English peerage, which precluded him from sitting in the House of Lords.[74] He saw his country seat as key to establishing his stock as a gentleman: bucolic splendour, hunting, fishing; new money desperate to be accepted by old money.*

Clive was keen to buy not just his own but others' routes into Parliament. He secured a seat for his brother William at Bishop's Castle, as well as for trusted confidants from the EIC, such as Sir Henry Strachey and John Carnac. Yet just as he was securing his power base, his relationship with company bosses turned sour. In 1763, a ferocious argument erupted. Initially about the means by which company servants transported their money home, it became a personal clash between Clive and his rival Laurence Sulivan. As Sulivan was a fellow MP, the row was brought to the heart of Westminster. Sulivan attacked Clive's *Jagir*, his annuity, as immoral on the grounds that the EIC had deposed the man who had granted it, Mir Jafar, only a year later, in 1760. Clive condemned the company for its ingratitude to him and defended his hard-won booty. Desperate to preserve his primary (and extremely generous) source of income, he agreed to cease his involvement in company politics in return for recognition of the *Jagir*. The matter was taken to the general court of the company, a body where each man who owned stock of £500 or more was entitled to a vote. After a tortuous legal battle the court agreed to grant Clive the *Jagir* income for ten years.[75] Sulivan insinuated that Clive and his supporters had been 'splitting' their stock, loaning £500 worth to friends for the duration of the meeting to increase their voting power.[76]

Clive made one final trip to India, serving as Governor of Bengal between 1765 and 1767. Even though India's internal politics remained

---

* Some 250 years later, the tiny stratum of global super-rich flocking to Britain would take a similar approach to reputation management. Buy into the English country, then try to learn its customs, and finally ingratiate yourself with as much blue blood as can be found.

turbulent, and external threats persisted, the company continued to provide attractive investments. Clive used insider knowledge to maximise his returns. In private letters to important individuals, he dramatically overestimated the amount of money the EIC would make through its tax-collecting rights in three provinces and downplayed the difficulties involved in transporting that money back to England.[77] The figure of £4 million per year was soon floated in the press. Clive advised his friends and his own agents to buy stock, suggesting it would double in value within three years. All this created a speculative boom in the company. John Walsh, Clive's representative in London, would later admit that he had 'spoke of [EIC stock] to many persons as a very beneficial thing, some of whom, as he understood, bought in consequence'.[78] Clive's followers voted with the speculators to increase the dividend at the general court, inflicting a defeat on the company's directors and earning Clive a cool extra £7500 annual return on his own stock. The chairman wrote to Clive that this behaviour 'appeared strange to all the real and old proprietors who were in general our friends'.[79] In 1767 Parliament stepped in to put limits on the dividends the company could pay, a move that sparked outrage among stockholders.[80] Opposition among the wealthy to state intervention, even when entirely justified, took hold early on in Britain.

That year, Clive returned to England for the third and final time. He had secured the company's position in Bengal, consolidating the government's long-term prospects. He hadn't done too badly for himself, either. He presented diamonds to Queen Charlotte worth £12,000 and ornamental swords and other artefacts to King George III worth £20,000.[81] These gifts were compared unfavourably, however, with the million-pound fortune that he kept for himself.

Clive felt confident enough about his achievements to be more up front about his wealth. He brought back exotic animals from the subcontinent, to be kept as pets by his newly acquired aristocratic friends. The 'Marlborough Tyger', kept at Blenheim Palace, was 'finely ornamented with variegated Stripes, from the Point of the Nose to the Very Extremity of the Tail'. The wildcat that Clive gave to the Duke of Cumberland's uncle came with a keeper: 'when he speaks to it in the Indian language, it will do anything he bids it'.[82] There was something rather desperate about Clive's desire to bestow presents upon friends and allies. But some of his gestures seemed genuine. He made sure all of his sisters had generous annual allowances, and did the same for former military comrades such as Stringer Lawrence.

Clive's property portfolio would rival that of any modern developer. He kept most of his houses for private use. He shuttled between his three seats of Walcot, Claremont and Oakly, as well as the former family home at Styche Hall, which he refurbished. When in London he would stay at his townhouse in Berkeley Square, whose frontage was designed in the latest affluent Palladian style.[83] He was meticulous with his purchases and renovations. Walcot was poached from an MP who had got into financial trouble, for the staggering sum of £90,000.[84] Claremont cost £25,000, only for Clive to spend four times that amount doing it up, employing the talents of the famous landscape architect Capability Brown to sculpt the gardens. He never actually bothered to live there.[85]

Flashing cash in such a manner brought criticism from many quarters. The nabob (a play on the word 'nawab') became a figure of fun – the vulgar trader returning from his adventures. R. Tickell's theatrical character Sir Peter Pagoda typified this on the London stage to great hilarity. Perhaps the cruellest depiction was in Samuel Foote's 1768 play *The Nabob*, which featured a character who had to learn from a waiter how to throw dice in order to be accepted at society gaming tables.[86] Audiences had a good idea who the character was based on.

Rumours gathered pace about the extent of Clive's wealth. Burke's *Annual Register* in 1760 reported his fortune at £1.2 million in cash and jewels, plus £200,000 worth of jewels owned by his wife. His annual income was estimated at £40,000 per year (putting him among the richest men in the land), plus his tax-collecting entitlement in Bengal. He made little effort to scotch the stories. Nor did he see the need to respond. As time went on, resentment grew. The election of 1768 saw nineteen of Clive's nabobs returned to Parliament, many representing rotten boroughs that, as a reformer, he might have abhorred.[87] In the eyes of much of the political class, the scandal was not so much how these men had got elected. Corrupt practices were the norm throughout the eighteenth century. The problem was Clive's openness, his vulgarity, which was bringing the system into disrepute. In the 1774 election, when John Walsh managed to buy his way into Parliament at Worcester, the public outcry was so great that Clive was burned in effigy in the street. Walsh's rise was distasteful to the establishment. After joining the EIC at the age of fifteen, he had become Clive's private secretary. On his return to England, his fortune was estimated at £150,000, a financial gain inextricably linked to that of his boss.

Much of Clive's final years in the spotlight was taken up fighting his many enemies. While he was indeed incredibly rich, he rarely had time to enjoy his wealth. He grew bitter and paranoid. His attitude to the bosses of the East India Company sometimes mirrored Coen's feelings towards the Heeren back in Holland. They both resented pampered men sitting in the comfort of their European cities who did not understand the trials of a man in the colonies and the decisions he had to take. Clive's rows with the EIC became ever more furious. He often prevailed through a mixture of compelling oratory and the time-honoured tactic of buying up MPs. Those loyal to him were dubbed the 'Bengal squad'; they were fiercely independent and dismissive of the old order.

Both sides used developments within India itself to undermine the credibility of the other in Parliament. The Whig politician, and son of the first Prime Minister, Horatio 'Horace' Walpole, wrote in 1772 of a famine in Bengal: 'They starved millions in India by monopolies and plunder, and almost raised a famine at home by the luxury occasioned by their opulence, and by that opulence, raising the price of everything, till the poor could not afford to purchase bread.'[88] He added, acerbically: 'The groans of India have mounted to heaven, where heaven-born General Clive will certainly be disavowed.'[89] Edmund Burke, a fellow Whig and political theorist, later took up the cudgels, accusing the nabobs of profiting from a corrupt regime in India and exporting that criminality back into English public life.

It became open season against Clive. A parliamentary motion accused him of embezzling money and treasure worth £254,000 during the conquest of Bengal, 'to the evil example of the servants of the public, and to the dishonour and detriment of the State'.[90] In the final ignominy, he was called to appear before a parliamentary inquiry. In light of the opportunities that had beckoned, what, he asked his fellow MPs and would-be inquisitors, would they have done? He denounced their impertinence, complaining that he was being questioned 'more like a sheep-stealer than a member of this House'.[91] He added:

> Consider the situation in which the victory at Plassey had placed me. A great prince was dependent on my pleasure; an opulent city lay at my mercy; its richest bankers bid against each other for my smiles; I walked through vaults which were thrown open to me alone, piled on either hand with gold and jewels. Mr Chairman, at this moment I stand astonished by my own moderation.*[92]

Although the House rejected a motion of censure against Clive, even acknowledging his 'great and meritorious services to his country', he took the insult intensely personally. He felt he had dedicated the best years of his life to opening up India for British profit, only to be publicly humiliated. The bouts of depression that afflicted him at moments during his life overwhelmed him in his later years. He was not only politically isolated; he had no means of recovering his reputation. He could hardly go back to India and fight another war with his advancing age and growing health problems.

Clive died in mysterious circumstances. In November 1774, he was laid low by fever and was taking morphine to cope with the pain. While playing a game of cards, so the story goes, he suddenly excused himself. Shortly afterwards he was found dead on the floor of an adjoining room. He had died from an overdose. Was it suicide or accidental

---

* Rarely has a sentence from a member of the super-rich been more apposite – or more candid. It encapsulates so much of their psychology – a sense of just deserts for being more successful than others and a frame of reference not with the rest of society but with others of their type. Because Clive could always have made a little more, because he could have made even more money, he felt that the fact that he stopped where he did gave him moral exoneration. Fast forward to the present day, and the various inquisitions of Bob Diamond, Fred Goodwin and the other early twenty-first-century bank bosses over rate fixing, bonuses and presiding over disasters. MPs enjoyed their rhetorical moments in the sun, but invariably failed to elicit much in the way of contrition. Instead, those who were asked to explain themselves were imbued with an overriding sense of self-pity and injustice for having even to answer for their actions.

over-medication? Other versions of the story have him cutting his own throat with a penknife.[93] His body was hastily buried without an inquest to avoid a scandal.

Clive's legacy has been the subject of intense argument. He was made scapegoat for what was regarded as an increasingly corrupt and incompetent regime in India. He was by no means the only, or the last, company servant to return from India and splash the cash in British society.[94] For many years, his reputation was in tatters. The first biography published after his death was written under a pseudonym, Charles Caraccioli. It painted Clive as both cruel and corrupt, and was probably assembled collectively by a number of his enemies in the company's military.[95] One poem written on his death summed up the mood:

Life's a surface, slippery, glassy,
Whereon tumbled Clive of Plassey.
All the wealth the East could give,
Brib'd not death to let him live.
No distinctions in the grave,
'Tween the nabob and the slave.[96]

In the early nineteenth century, as the British emerged triumphant as undisputed masters of India, Clive's life and legacy again became a battleground. For the radical James Mill, he was the embodiment of the corruption that marked the company's abandonment of 'civilised' methods in India for more 'barbarous' ones. Clive, argued Mill, subverted the company's original trading mission because of greed and a desire for power. But the Tory colonial administrator Sir John Malcolm, whose biography of Clive was published in 1836, argued that his conquest of Bengal followed the logic of commercial competition with the French.[97] Later Victorian biographers, writing in the flush of Britain's high imperial age, were more fulsome in their praise. Writing in the 1880s, a historian and one-time officer in India, Colonel George Malleson, described Parliament's inquiry as 'this persecution of a man who had rendered the most magnificent services to his country'. Clive's crime, in the eyes of his enemies, was 'that he had become rich himself, and prevented them from fattening on the plunder of the country he had conquered'.[98]

Through his son's marriage into the family of the Earl of Powys in the early nineteenth century, Clive posthumously achieved proper English ennoblement for his family. By this time, the power of the East India Company had waned. A series of Charter Acts took away its trade monopolies and opened the field to competitors.[99] The turmoil of the great Indian revolt of 1857 gave the state the excuse to abolish the company and replace it with official imperial structures. The EIC came to be seen by the establishment, just as Clive had been, as getting a bit too big for its boots.

Just a few months before Clive's death, Warren Hastings, one of his acolytes who had served under him at Plassey, became the first British governor-general. The Raj was established. Clive became seriously rich, but like Jan Pieterszoon Coen he failed to achieve the respectability he craved. A man dismissed as brash and vulgar, he established a bridgehead for imperial power and wealth that for two centuries would see Britain rule the world.

CHAPTER 8

The Krupps – Manufacturing patriotism

I knew everybody's licence plate, I could tell you when they drove into the parking lot, when they left, so it was kinda extreme.

Bill Gates

The family firm and the self-made man: these two terms evoke a romanticised view of the individual who has become rich through personal endeavour. Their roots lie in the Industrial Revolution, in the development of a business class with few links to the landed gentry who had dominated European politics and business until then. The revolution, which began in northern Europe in the late eighteenth century, created a new generation of wealthy. Out of the coalfields, mills and shipyards stretching from Scotland to the north of Italy emerged the craftsman–innovator, the man of means, bulwark of society.

The Krupp family, of Essen in the Ruhr area of Germany, epitomised this new breed. Theirs is a story of a company rising out of obscurity to symbolise a nation's ambitions and values – for good and ill. The man who transformed the firm into a global monolith was Alfred Krupp. When, at the absurdly young age of fourteen, he took over after the sudden death of his father, the company employed five men. When he died sixty years later he presided over a corporate city-state that housed, fed and controlled the lives of tens of thousands of workers. Alfred Krupp was more than a company owner; he was an overlord who made huge profits from selling weapons to all comers. He was a mechanical engineer and a social engineer who was obsessed with controlling his workforce.

His was a dynasty that would last more than a century. On the eve of the First World War, amid a lucrative arms race, the company's owner, Bertha Krupp von Bohlen und Halbach, was richer than the Kaiser.[1] A decade later, Adolf Hitler, in *Mein Kampf*, exhorted Germany's youth to be 'hard as Krupp steel'.[2] Germany was Krupp, and Krupp was Germany. After the Second World War, Krupp's senior managers were sentenced at the Nuremberg trials for crimes against humanity for their use of slave labour. Within a few years their sins were forgotten. The Americans needed Krupp to help bolster West Germany against the threat of communism from the East. The company was too important to ignore.

The most controversial episodes of the dynasty's past have not been ignored, but nor are they particularly emphasised. Instead, official corporate accounts focus on the firm's folkloric origins. Villa Hügel, a 269-room mansion that Alfred built late in life, was a monument to power and wealth, a home and headquarters at which industrialists and politicians the world over would pay homage. It now serves as a cultural institute for the regional government. It is a reminder that throughout the two-hundred-year history of Krupp, the interests of private business and the state have been intertwined.

The rise was steady and unspectacular. The first recorded mention of a Krupp came in 1587, when a certain Arndt Krupp joined the merchants' guild in the free imperial city of Essen, which was a centre for silver and coal mining and for the munitions industry. Gunsmiths made a hearty profit there; thousands of rifles and pistols were produced each year. The Krupps, from their earliest days, proved adept at exploiting adversity. Arndt arrived in the city just before the Black Death struck; in an echo of Crassus and the Roman Republic, he bought up a number of properties at a snip from families desperately fleeing the plague. During the Thirty Years War in the early seventeenth century, his son Anton acquired instant riches by producing weaponry for Catholic and Protestant states alike.

The Krupps became pillars of the local establishment, members of guilds and important figures in the municipal authority. During the eighteenth century the family built up a trade in colonial goods, such as tobacco. At the turn of the nineteenth century the family's matriarch, Helene, bought an ironworks, and so the Krupps moved from trading to manufacturing. On Helene's death in 1810, her son incorporated the firm Friedrich Krupp (which he named after himself), a name that was to be inextricably linked with the fortunes of Germany from that point on. But Friedrich was a failure as a company boss. When he died of tuberculosis in 1826, aged thirty-nine, his entire inheritance of 42,000 thalers from his mother was gone.[3] The firm had lost money consistently for the first twenty-five years of its existence. As a result of his less than impressive business reputation, Friedrich was stripped of the public offices he held in the city. The family that survived him had to move away from one of Essen's more upmarket squares and live in the foreman's house on the ironworks – a move that was, in later years, to become a central part of the Krupp myth.

It fell to young Alfred, barely into his teens, to pick up the pieces. Sixty years later, he would contend that he was simply lucky where his father had been unlucky; this sense of the precariousness of his position and wealth spurred him on to try to expand the company at every opportunity.

Alfred's intelligence had been remarked upon by his tutors, but after inheriting the company he had to put a stop to his learning. Instead, he devoted himself to the manufacture of steel. He would later say: 'the anvil was my desk'.[4] With most of the savings misspent by Friedrich, the family had to live frugally. With only a handful of employees at first, Alfred had to shoulder much of the work himself. The pouring of the molten metal had to be done at exactly the right moment or it would cool too quickly or too slowly, and the process would be ruined. His one major customer, the Düsseldorf mint, sent back several consignments that were deficient.[5] Alfred would not stop until he had achieved exactly the right manufacturing process, pressing his workers to labour until after sunset.

Diligence was accompanied by guile. He wrote to prospective customers exaggerating the size of his plant in a desperate attempt to impress and to land that one game-changing big order. He traipsed across Europe to woo potential buyers. From an early stage he saw his personal reputation and the fortunes of his company as indistinguishable. When he perfected a rolled-steel musket barrel he took it down to an army barracks on horseback to show the officers, only to be turned away by the guards. Undeterred by such setbacks, he toured the states of the newly formed Zollverein (Customs Union) with his younger brother Hermann to take advantage of the growing markets of the 1830s.[6] He took his guns and cannon around city fairs in search of the elusive prize: brand recognition.

It finally worked. And when it did, progress was rapid. Within a few years Krupp products were being sold as far afield as Brazil. Another breakthrough came in 1841 when Hermann invented the spoon-roller for making cutlery. Each new invention – from heavy machine tools to home goods – was patented, enabling Alfred to reinvest the money in expansion. In these early years, when each major contract could make or break the firm, Alfred made it his mission to crack emerging markets and source supplies from wherever possible.

By the time of the Great Exhibition in London's Crystal Palace in 1851, Alfred was banking on a single breakthrough to make him stand out from the crowd. He got it, displaying a single steel ingot more than twice the weight of anything produced by his British competitors, and winning the exhibition's gold medal. Not content with that, he unveiled his steel-barrelled cannon, displayed under the national flag and shield of Prussia, gaining worldwide plaudits. At the same time, he branched out into the lucrative railway business of the United States, producing a new form of wheel for trains. This generated a spectacular source of revenue from the newly emerging class of American industrial barons (see Chapter 9).

Even as he was creating a sensation abroad, Alfred was still relatively unknown in his hometown, where the police commissioner mistakenly referred to him by his father's name.[7] His unassuming personality masked a fierce ambition. Alfred was desperate to be in the lead on each technological development, seeing himself in round-the-clock existential competition with his rivals. While working on one production process, he wrote to a subordinate: 'We must follow this chance, and not let it escape – we must be the first, if it is good.' Two principles guided Krupp throughout his long business life – secrecy and the search for expansion. There was no market he would not try to conquer. Nearly two hundred years on, the technical rivalry of the nineteenth-century steel industry has been replicated by the Silicon Valley tech giants, with their fierce competitiveness, secrecy and battles over monopolies and patents.

Most of Krupp's attention was directed towards Britain, the birthplace of the Industrial Revolution. From afar, and to Krupp's eyes, the country was teeming with mechanics and inventors, designing ever more effective pumps and pulleys. Since the mid-eighteenth century the British had been leading the way. The crucible technique in steelmaking pioneered by Benjamin Huntsman, a clockmaker from Sheffield, had given the British an inherent advantage since the latter part of that century. In this method, iron was placed in a furnace inside clay crucibles, and would be melted at extremely high temperatures and charged with existing steel to remove impurities. Alfred's attitude towards Britain was a mix of admiration and rivalry: men such as John Smeaton, sometimes called the first engineer, Joseph Bramah, the originator of hydraulic power, Richard Arkwright, with his spinning frame that revolutionised the production of cotton, and Thomas Newcomen, with his steam engine. These self-made engineers became masters in their fields; they were respected inventors, but only some of them (such as Arkwright) became substantially wealthy. Alfred Krupp and the American robber barons were different. They marketed their skills for great personal wealth and global recognition.

A shy man who liked to keep people at arm's length, Krupp appreciated the English traits of reserve and formality. On his first visit in 1838, he anglicised his name from Alfried to Alfred, just as William (born Wilhelm) Siemens had done. Both thought they would fit in better if they sounded less Teutonic. He spent several holidays in England, taking in the sea air at Torquay. Back home he dressed like a quintessential Englishman with his top hat and tails.

But business was business and he was desperate to catch up with English technology. Such was the global competition that industrial espionage was central to Krupp's work, and that of his rivals. He developed sophisticated networks of agents across Europe and North America to keep an eye on the competition, and insisted they reported to him directly. Sometimes he did the work himself. He gave himself the pseudonym Schropp to disguise himself to English industrialists, in the hope of winkling out some of the secrets of their steel-making. Touring Sheffield, Stourbridge and Hull, he met Friedrich Sölling, who would remain a lifelong servant to the company. Krupp left behind the long-serving Englishman Alfred Longsdon to keep abreast of technological developments in the country, a role that would be filled by others in Paris, St Petersburg and New York.

Even his hapless father, Friedrich Krupp, had been an early globaliser, toying with the idea of setting up a factory in Russia back in 1820.[8] Alfred was constantly threatening to move the whole works to Russia whenever he fell foul of the German authorities' conservative attitudes towards his wares. The Russians offered him 21,000 roubles to build a factory in St Petersburg in 1849, but nothing came of the idea.[9] Operating abroad had its attractions. For a long time, Alfred's steel cannon were regarded as something of an expensive joke by the Prussian officer corps. They were interested only in improving their existing bronze-barrelled weapons.

European politics came to the aid of the Krupps, allowing Alfred to demonstrate the technical superiority of his products. He was returning from another fact-finding mission to England through Paris when street fighting broke out. This was 1848, a year when revolutions engulfed Europe. Initially he took no interest, writing: 'In the Devil's name, let them break each other's heads.' He regarded war and upheaval as bad for business, a curious attitude given the fortune he would later make in the arms trade. 'If only peace could be restored in France,' he lamented, 'and normal, lucrative business for us resumed.'[10] But the urban insurrections increased the demand for artillery from every royal court in Europe. Krupp's cannon, untested by the Prussian War Office in 1847, was by 1852 being put on display to impress the visiting Russian Tsar. Even the spoon factory in the Austrian town of Berndorf changed its production to sabres in these years, as the firm became increasingly geared towards producing war materiel.

That same year, 1848, Alfred finally took ownership of the company from his widowed mother, but it came at an inopportune moment. In the midst of economic crisis across Europe, he decided to melt down the family silver to ensure he had enough cash flow to pay the workers' wage bill (just as Louis XIV had done to pay for his wars).[11] This became another element in the enduring Krupp myth – the selfless patriot who sacrificed his personal wealth for the wellbeing of his *Kruppianer*.

Frustrated by the Prussian War Office, which was still reluctant to buy his wares, Krupp looked elsewhere for customers. It was an uncomfortable truth for the company in its later, ultra-patriotic years that Alfred did deals, or came close to doing deals, with most of Prussia's rivals. In 1860, when he developed a breech-loading cannon, rather than the traditional muzzle-loaded artillery pieces, he threatened to sell it to Britain and France unless Prussia agreed to place an order. War Minister Albrecht von Roon, a long-term detractor and one of the towering figures of the Prussian government, backed down only when the British and French governments approved Krupp's patents in their own countries.[12]

In 1862 Alfred opened the first Bessemer works in continental Europe. The Bessemer process, again developed in England, was another step forward in production, allowing impurities to be removed from iron by oxidation – blowing air into the molten metal. Longsdon, his English confidant, had used family connections to secure the German patent. Alfred kept the information strictly in the hands of a few trusted colleagues.[13]

In the *laissez-faire* atmosphere of the mid-nineteenth century, it was common practice for arms manufacturers to sell to countries outside their own. But Prussia was about to embark on so many wars that patriotism and good business were bound to come into conflict. Alfred almost sold a large order of cannon to the Austrians not long before the Austro-Prussian War of 1866. When questioned by von Roon, he replied: 'Of political conditions I know little. I go on working quietly.'[14] It took a personal aside from the King for Krupp to reconsider his duty – plus an agreement by the Prussian government to pre-pay for its cannon.[15] With Franco-Prussian tensions on the rise over Napoleon III's

attempts to add Luxemburg to his empire in 1868, Alfred sent a cata-
logue of his wares to the French Emperor.[16] Krupp's French rivals, the
Schneider brothers, inadvertently did him a favour by convincing their
War Ministry to 'buy French'.[17]

Alfred took the hint, faithfully producing shells for the war effort,
declaring – with all the portentous patriotism he could muster – that
such was his devotion to the cause he didn't care if he was paid the full
amount. On the quiet, he was prepared to turn his factory over to the
French if, as most Germans feared, they successfully invaded the Ruhr.
'We will offer them roast veal and red wine,' he wrote in his diary, 'otherwise they will destroy the factory.'[18] The gifts of cigars and brandy
he sent to the Prussian front line went only to those members of the
officer corps who had supported plans for the army to buy his steel
cannon. He did, however, set aside 120,000 thalers for a foundation for
wounded soldiers, including a hospital that would later become the
company's own, providing help for injured workers.

The Franco–Prussian War of 1870–1 – which ended with the surrender of France and the unification of the German states – was the
making of Otto von Bismarck, and Alfred Krupp. To reward him for his
military and diplomatic triumph, Kaiser Wilhelm I gave Bismarck
unbridled powers. The Iron Chancellor was now master of all foreign
and economic policy, seeing the growth of industrial production as at
the heart of German power. Recalling the chaos of the revolutions that
had afflicted Europe, he famously declared: 'The great questions of the
time will not be resolved by speeches and majority decisions – that was
the great mistake of 1848 and 1849 – but by iron and blood.' The Iron
Chancellor ensured that Krupp became the company of choice across
all government ministries. Alfred's workforce tripled to ten thousand as
a result. He could now rely on regular contracts from the German state
to keep his business expanding.

Iron, blood and war were the Krupp business model. Sales of armaments expanded around the world, so much so that they accounted for
two-thirds of turnover. Krupp was one of the world's first global business leaders and one of the first to see the importance of combining
modern technology with marketing.

Krupp had made his money, and his global name, selling anything to anyone at any time. Before the 1870s, Russia, not Germany, had been the company's biggest client. In the 1860s Krupp was convinced that China was the next superpower-in-waiting. The Chinese government's first diplomatic mission to Europe included a visit to the Essen works in 1866. Soon after, Alfred appointed a merchant, Friedrich Peil, to be the firm's representative in China and Japan.[19] This paid off in 1871 when the Chinese government placed a large order for 328 artillery pieces. During the Russo-Turkish War of 1877–8, which threatened to smash Europe's fragile balance of power, Krupp guns pounded soldiers from both sides. Satisfied with his work, Alfred produced a brochure for distribution in Britain, with glowing testimonials from the two warring parties.[20] Governments and international buyers of all kinds were invited to Krupp's *Völkerschiessen* – an outing to the company's shooting range in the nearby town of Meppen, where they could see the latest cannon and other armaments fired across fields (and would be heartily fed and watered as they watched admiringly).[*]

In 1885, the Turks placed a huge order for nearly a thousand artillery pieces, including massive coastal defence guns. The armies of the Tsar and the Sultan were once again facing each other armed with Krupp guns. The same applied across the Balkans as well as in South America and Asia. There were, according to one historian, 25,000 Krupp cannon pointing at each other around the world in the 1880s.[21] Krupp had produced economies of scale. But the quantity was accompanied by quality. Only once in a while does a single piece of military kit gain ubiquity, and Krupp cannon achieved that accolade. The next such occasion, and perhaps the only one since, was the Kalashnikov semi-automatic rifle. (Prior to his death in December 2013, Mikhail Kalashnikov, the inventor of the eponymous AK-47, left a note to the Russian Orthodox Church seeking to repent for the deaths his weapon had caused. Krupp would do no such thing.)

---

[*] He was keen to spend money on new processes and the best-quality raw materials. Creating showcase products took time and money, but it paid off in the end. In 1873 Alfred wrote: 'the gun maker must be a spendthrift. He must make only the best, regardless of the cost.' This approach could be seen as a precursor to the German emphasis on long-term research and development that underpinned the *Wirtschaftswunder* – the economic miracle of the post-Second World War years.

Governments expressed their gratitude, showering Krupp with honours and invitations. By the time of his death he had accrued forty-four prizes, including the Order of Vasa (Sweden), the Order of the Rising Sun (Japan) and, most prestigiously, the Légion d'honneur from Napoleon III.[22] He didn't set much store by the various medals he received. What he wanted was large orders for his company, not what he called 'little crosses and stars and titles and similar shabby baubles'.[23] In his own country, he refused ennoblement, saying he had no desire to bear any name other than his father's.[24] He did appreciate gifts, though, and was disappointed on the rare occasion when he received nothing in return for sending showpiece cannon to a king or an emperor. These gifts, he contended, should denote respect, not ostentation; he did not appreciate a lavish jewel sent from the Ottoman Sultan. Nevertheless, he knew that accepting such things was good for business. 'The commercial manufacturer', he wrote, 'must be a waster of money in the eyes of the world.'[25]

Krupp felt he did not have to choose between business and patriotism. He had made his business indispensable to the nation, especially in times of war, just as the nation's wars were indispensable for his business.

As Germany expanded under the rule of one Kaiser, so the firm expanded under the rule of one boss. Bismarck intervened on Krupp's behalf to smooth the path for a number of takeovers. Rigid control of the company was Alfred's consistent policy. He resisted raising capital from banks; he was suspicious of subcontracting. One of the reasons he was keen to keep everything in house was his obsession with corporate confidentiality. Personal, and family, connections were crucial to keeping his company one step ahead of its rivals technologically. After his marriage to Bertha Eichhoff in 1853, her brother was placed in charge of the puddling process, whereby molten iron was stirred in a special furnace, which meant steel could be produced without the use of charcoal. The occupation of puddler was highly skilled, and the process was one of the most secretive parts of cast steel production at the time.[26]

Alfred saw financiers as a lower form of economic player, seldom to be trusted. He would not have been an admirer of contemporary corporate practice, with its emphasis on quarterly profit figures and dividends. He was desperate to keep his company private. 'The secrets are our capital, and that capital is squandered as soon as the knowledge is released to others.' This attitude contained no little anti-Semitism: 'Industry today has become a field for speculators, Jews of the bourse, stock swindlers, and similar parasites.'[27] He vehemently resisted the idea of turning the firm into a public company, unlike some of the rival ironworks. His close allies, such as his old friend Sölling, were urging him to loosen the reins in order to secure much-needed cash for the firm. Krupp's refusal to go to the markets stood in the way of his expansion plans, so he did the next-best thing: he went straight to King Friedrich Wilhelm (Kaiser Wilhelm's father) and received an extension of credit on the grounds of his great 'patriotism'.[28]

The European stock market crash of 1873 put the company in even more trouble. As demand dried up, the firm was overstretched and exposed. Debts more than doubled in two months; then, a year later, they doubled again to sixty-four million marks.[29] This time a personal appeal to the Kaiser came to nothing; once was enough, Bismarck told Krupp, particularly for a firm whose nationalist credentials were prone to fluctuation. This made Krupp so furious, and ill, that one doctor diagnosed him as having 'hypochondria bordering on insanity'.[30] Instead of heeding the advice, Krupp sacked the doctor.

Eventually, a group of banks clubbed together to bail him out.[31] The terms gave the bankers a seat on Krupp's management board, a development he saw as shameful. The injection of credit stabilised the firm and, in spite of his fears, the consortium did not intervene on operational decisions. The Krupp style of doing business had become too valuable to risk disruption. The company was deemed too big to fail.

Alfred's suspicion of outsiders turned into paranoia. 'I hate the idea of fraternisation with our competitors,' he wrote, 'since nobody will do anything for us, and everybody just wants to derive some benefits from such fraternisation.'[32] He could not abide the idea of workers leaving the company. When a foreman resigned in the 1870s to take a job in Dortmund, Alfred chased after him and tried to convince the police to have him arrested, wanting to 'attack him with damage suits and public stigma as long and as much as the law allows'.[33] Of wages, Alfred said:

'Our workers shall receive the maximum that industry shall afford' – so that they would not need to seek employment elsewhere.[34]

Krupp was not just rich; he was not just an inventor and industrialist. He wanted to create a new corporate ethic. The company name would become synonymous with more than steel; it would be equally famous for the social welfare programmes it provided for its workers, and for its attempts to control their lives. A voluntary health insurance scheme dated back to 1836. Pensions came in 1853. These funds would be topped up periodically by the private wealth of the Krupp family themselves.

Not all of these social measures were particularly innovative: sickness insurance, for example, had been briefly instituted during the Napoleonic occupation of the Rhineland in the early nineteenth century. Mine owners in the Ruhr had been paying profits into workers' insurance schemes since the eighteenth century. But the legislation the German parliament passed from 1881 enshrining accident and sickness insurance, and eventually pensions, paved the way for a new social and employment model. The idea was simple: a worker who felt more secure for himself and his family would be more productive. The scale of the Krupp schemes was unprecedented. Sick pay, though dispensed only from the fourteenth week of an illness, gave the worker two-thirds of his salary, which was generous for the time.[35] Business and government saw eye to eye. Bismarck saw no need to impede the manager or owner of a company by restricting the hours of work or introducing other forms of regulation. But 'the real grievance of the worker', he said, 'is the insecurity of his existence':

He is not sure that he will always have work, he is not sure that he will always be healthy, and he foresees that he will one day be old and unfit to work. If he falls into poverty, even if only through a prolonged illness, he is then completely helpless, left to his own devices, and society does not currently recognize any real obligation towards him beyond the usual help for the poor, even if he has been working all the time ever so faithfully and diligently. The usual help for the poor, however, leaves a lot to be desired, especially in large cities, where it is very much worse than in the country.

The expansion of the works, as was the case with so many towns during the Industrial Revolution, changed Essen beyond recognition. Its population grew from seven thousand in 1850 to fifty thousand two decades later, most of them deriving their living from the Krupp works, directly or indirectly. Germany, particularly cities in the Ruhr area in the north-west of the country, was in the throes of urbanisation – a process that many towns and cities in Britain and the United States were also undergoing. Overcrowding was endemic. In Berlin, for example, one-fifth of the population lived in cellars. The staple diet for many working people was potatoes, thin soup and black bread.[36]

By 1890, Essen had grown to eighty thousand citizens, with the *Kruppianer* and their families accounting for fifty thousand of these.[37] This created a huge housing problem, with many workers and their families living in squalor – yet this existence was still preferable to working on the land. Although a later official history of the firm would claim that Alfred's desire to build houses was 'not forced on him by a scarcity of local dwellings', the average number of people per house in the town had increased to over fifteen by 1864, at which point the company undertook its first concerted house-building programme.[38]

Two new colonies, Schederhof and Cronenberg, were built. The first houses near the factory were relatively comfortable dwellings for foremen and their families. A more austere barracks for single workers was constructed, eventually housing six thousand of them. Entire neighbourhoods were built around Essen, often named after Krupp ancestors. The new houses just about managed to keep pace with the population explosion, but did little to reverse the overcrowding. There was still an average of sixteen people per house in 1890.[39]

Death rates would later drop as strict public health codes were enforced. The largest colony, Cronenberg, housed eight thousand people. As well as houses, the estate contained 'a parsonage, two school buildings, a Protestant church, several branches of the co-operative store, an apothecary shop, a post-office, and a market-place one-third of an acre in size, a restaurant with games, bowling alley and a library with a large hall for workmen's meetings'.[40]

Krupp arranged his city according to the needs of the business. Rents in company homes were up to 20 per cent cheaper than those for private rooms in town; this was designed to tie in his labourers. The policy at least had the merit of transparency: a new worker was told that if he left the firm for another job, he would lose his accommodation. His rent came straight out of his wage packet and went back into the company. He would spend his money in the Krupp stores, handed over to the firm by the Essen Co-operative Society in 1868. Soon, according to one historian, there were fifteen retail grocery stores located throughout the various settlements, nine branch stores for manufactured goods, one shoe factory and three branch shoe stores, one hardware store, one mill and bakery, with six bread stores, a slaughter-house, with seven retail meat stores, two clothing establishments, seven restaurants, one wine store and an ice company, one coffee house, a brush factory, a laundry and a weekly market for fresh vegetables brought in from the surrounding countryside.[41] The transformation of Essen into a company town was complete by the mid-1870s, as one visitor noted: 'Everywhere the name of Krupp appears: now on the picturesque marketplace, on the door of a mammoth department store, then on a bronze monument, on the portals of a church, over a library, numerous school-houses, butcher shops, a sausage factory, shoemakers' shops and tailoring establishments.'[42]

Krupp's dream was for workers to spend their lives from cradle to grave in the control of the company. From bathhouses, to schools and doctors' surgeries, this became a state within a state. Even in death, the firm presided, with support for widows and orphans.

Spared the responsibility to shareholders under which public companies laboured, Alfred Krupp was responsible only to his wallet and his conscience. The firm would remain a paternal enterprise demanding absolute obedience: 'We only want loyal men, who are grateful to us in their hearts and lives for giving them their daily bread.'[43] Such duty would be rewarded at the end of a working life, as Alfred made clear: 'If a man was engaged one day and disabled on the morrow, not from constitutional delicacy or his own carelessness, but by an accident occurring to him while at work, the works should be held responsible; or when a man has devoted his strength and unflagging efforts for long years to me, he should be enabled to spend his declining years without working or starving.'[44]

Writing of one worker in 1873, who had been injured on the job, Krupp said: 'My principles in these matters are well known and I ask not to pinch pennies. It will strengthen the fidelity and attachment of all others to the establishment.'[45] He signed off on an annual bonus for a skilled fitter named Bungardt 'since he is a capable man whom I would like to fetter'.[46]

Earlier in his career, Krupp had addressed his workers as fellow craftsmen, prefixing his letters to them 'Gentlemen of the Collegium'. As the business expanded and technology advanced, the idea of the firm as a collaborative enterprise between professionals was dropped. In September 1872, between the triumph of the Franco-Prussian War and the disaster of the economic crash, Alfred penned his *Generalregulativ* (General Regulations), which would govern the firm's employment policy until the end of the Second World War. This remarkable piece of work, twenty-two pages and seventy-two clauses in all, is one of a treasure trove of documents held in the Krupp archive. It is the hallmark of the extreme Teutonic patrician, or, to use modern parlance, someone with obsessive-compulsive disorder. Alfred would leave nothing to chance. The document sets out the hierarchy of the company from Alfred all the way down to the shop floor. Under its constitution, the firm was a sole proprietorship, inherited by primogeniture (succession by first-born son).

The *Generalregulativ* demanded the undivided loyalty of the workers and their obedience to the company above all 'prejudicial influences from the outside'.[47] They were not, in other words, allowed to concern themselves with politics. Current official histories of the company play up the welfare side of the *Generalregulativ* and ignore its more dictatorial aspects. The Krupp company website even places it in the tradition of 'Ideas Management', whereby workers can suggest improvements to the way the company operates.[48] Post-war German firms have been keen to emphasise what they see as their more collaborative approach towards employer–employee relations (with employee representatives elected on to a *Betriebsrat*, or works council), contrasting this with the more confrontational model ascribed to their Anglo-Saxon counterparts. The romanticised Krupp legend is seen as setting a trend.

Yet Alfred's approach could hardly be described as consensual. He sought to control every aspect of his workers' lives and worked them hard. In the mid-nineteenth century the average working day in German industry was between thirteen and sixteen hours, and eleven to twelve hours for children. Working on Sunday became commonplace as the factory system grew. Some workers would resist this by staying away from work on Monday mornings, a tradition known as 'Blue Monday'. However, strict factory rules like those introduced by Krupp eventually put a stop to this. Around 10 per cent of Krupp's workforce were white-collar, including overseers, draftsmen and administrative staff. Those higher up the chain were paid monthly – a sure sign that they had made it in the company and a reward that could be taken away if an employee failed to impress. White-collar employees were set apart from the rest; they were subject to a different code of factory rules and were entitled to better sick pay and a longer notice period. Krupp made sure there were plenty of internal vacancies and opportunities for advancement within the firm to keep the staff competing against each other, and he moved them around sites to undermine any collective feeling: personal incentives, carrot and stick, according to the modern business manual.[49]

From a particular vantage point in his house in the middle of the works, Krupp would watch out for late workers. He planned to institute a military-style uniform with insignia based on seniority and craft superiority, but was dissuaded from doing so. As late as the 1870s, he was still producing handwritten missives on what the workers should be wearing.[50] Two stories relate to the use of toilets. One has it that each worker needed the written permission of his foreman to relieve himself. According to another, the factory employed a man whose sole task was to prevent workers from staying in a cubicle too long. The bathroom was often a place where workers could have a chat, exchange information and leave flyers which announced illegal and unofficial meetings.[51] The Krupp archive denies that the man himself was as fanatical as that. Other, perhaps more likely, forms of control included a ban on socialist and Catholic newspapers; any worker caught reading such literature in their homes or barracks would face eviction. Krupp-sponsored libraries were not allowed anything of a religious, philosophical or political nature that might constitute a threat.[52]

Unions and other workers' associations were anathema. Krupp respected his most experienced craftsmen but was wary of any influence they might wield in an organised collective: 'I demand that the best and most skilled worker or master is removed as soon as possible if he even appears to incite opposition or to belong to an association.'[53] In 1872, when the young Social Democratic Party called a coal strike in the Ruhr, including at mines owned by Krupp, Alfred was adamant: 'Neither now nor at any future time should a former striker be taken on at our works, however shorthanded we may be.'[54] When the SPD entered parliament for the first time in the election of 1874, Krupp summarily sacked thirty workers for 'spreading socialist doctrine', calling a vote for the party a vote for the 'idle, dissolute, and incompetent'.[55] His crusade against socialism informed many of his actions in the works and in public life. In a letter to the company's board in July 1878, he advocated the building of a new school in a deprived area of Essen: 'Should we not decently make capital out of it against the Social Democrats, who ignore everything that is done for the workers or at least try to explain it away as egoism?'[56]

Alfred would have liked to remain above party politics, but the politicisation of the workforce forced him to enter the fray. In 1878 he stood as a National Liberal candidate in the elections to the Reichstag. An umbrella organisation of patriotic liberal groups, the National Liberals tended increasingly to right-wing politics and became avid supporters of the expansion of the German fleet. As a steel manufacturer and builder of parts for warships, Krupp's business and political interests were aligned on this, as he ensured they were in all the decisions he took. He narrowly lost to the Catholic Centre Party – largely because Essen was a heavily Catholic city. He was aggrieved and alarmed that a town almost totally controlled by his firm could not produce the correct result at the ballot box. However, the next year Bismarck passed his Anti-Socialist Law, proscribing the SPD and similar organisations, thus achieving many of Alfred's political goals by different means.

For all his antipathy to organised socialism, Krupp was not an uncritical advocate of the market. Even then, early on in the Industrial Revolution, the German and broader continental European approach had begun to diverge from those of America and Britain. In the United States, in thrall to Herbert Spencer and the theories of survival of the fittest (see Chapter 9), inequality was regarded by many in business as part of the natural order of society. Krupp and his fellow German industrialists did not flaunt the 'goodness' of inequality or the business sense behind pay differentials, but nor did they shy away from them. Around the 1870s and 1880s, average yearly income in Germany was about 740 marks (women received two-fifths of that, on average). Set against that was the estimated annual income of the wealthiest 1600, mostly landowners and industrialists, which exceeded 100,000 marks – some 135 times higher than the mean.[57] In spite of the more communitarian language, the gap was stark.

In February 1887, the Krupps made a second attempt to enter parliament. Aged seventy-five and with his health failing, Alfred left it to his son Friedrich, the heir apparent to the company. He too lost, again to the Catholic Centre. His defeat was all the more remarkable given that voting at the plant had long been done under the supervision of company officials.[58] Alfred had issued a grand pronouncement to his workforce before the election, arguing that a defeat for the Nationalist government would weaken the military and lead to war: 'For everybody's sake I can only hope that no one will allow himself to be misled into having any share in such disaster by voting against the Government. If, however, everyone does his duty, I shall gladly strain every nerve to increase the activity in all the Works, to lay down new plant, and to provide the means of living for more men.'[59]

His mix of bribery and blackmail proved to be in vain. Just a few months later, on 14 July 1887, Alfred suffered a heart attack and died, collapsing into the arms of his valet in the Villa Hügel, the mansion that stands as the great monument to his dynasty. It is here where the battle for his legacy continues to be played out.

For most of his career, Krupp had lived in more humble surroundings – in the old foreman's house on the works site. His wife, Bertha, repeatedly suggested that they move to somewhere more appropriate for one of Germany's great industrialists. She wanted somewhere out in the countryside. She took herself and their only son off for long periods to resorts and spas in Switzerland or the south of France to escape the smog that engulfed Essen. Alfred relented; the more he planned the new home, the more immersed he became in the detail. This was to be his grand architectural project, to proclaim the name of Krupp around the world – as ever with the super-rich and super-successful, compulsive competitiveness took over. He wanted a home and an office spectacular enough to impress politicians and industrialists; he wanted it built in the style that he so coveted – that of a grand English country home. Unlike others, however, he also wanted it on the cheap.

The project was fraught from the outset. The Hügel remained without a roof for months because Alfred personally chose French building materials, and the Franco-Prussian War made those imports hard to come by.[60] During the decade of planning, Krupp had hired and fired nine architects, often preferring his own drawings to theirs. Once completed, in 1873, the building contained a number of flaws. The heating never worked properly and, in any case, the steel skeleton of the structure leaked warmth, leaving the place cold throughout the winter months. He feared that excessive amounts of wood would cause a fire hazard. But his reasoning lay less in health and safety concerns and more in the emotional bond that he had developed with steel (just as Mansa Musa had with gold): 'Steel has finished being the material of war, it now has a milder destiny, it should be used for the first monument of victory, for monuments of great deeds and great men, as the expression of external and domestic peace, it should ring in church bells, be used for ornaments and commercial purposes, and in coinage.'[61]

The building may have been austere. It was formal. But it was a magnificent projection of power, an impressive venue for entertaining the many crowned heads who visited the works hoping to secure an artillery contract or wishing to bestow a medal on the manufacturer. The Kaiser had his own suite of rooms; the Shah of Iran and the Emperor of Brazil were guests who could avail themselves of the villa's riding stables and copious grounds. By 1890, the house had its own railway station. Maintenance of the building ended up absorbing up to 15 per cent of the company's profits, and yet in Alfred's time it could not be said to be ornate.

His son and subsequent generations refurbished it, adding ever more grandiose furnishings and artworks.[62] From the outset the Hügel made its desired impression on visitors, and was likened by many to the palace or embassy that in many ways it was. The German-English Baroness Deichmann wrote: 'Herr Krupp lived in princely style at an enormous country house with a very large guesthouse. It could be compared with a large embassy, for people from all parts of the world came to persuade him to make business arrangements with their governments. Thus there were a great many large dinner parties, and once we arrived to be told that many hundreds of people were expected at a ball that evening.'[63]

Alfred Krupp's obsession with self-reverential architecture put him in good company. Indeed, from ancient times to now, there are very few exceptions to the practice among wealthy entrepreneurs. Like him, they have usually attempted to explain away the palace or mansion as essential to business dealings.

When Krupp moved into the Hügel, he left the old family home standing in the works so that 'my successors, like myself, may look with thankfulness and joy at this monument; may it be a warning not to despise the humblest thing, and to beware of arrogance'. The meticulous preservation of the original family home may be seen as a sign of nostalgia from a man in his final years. Perhaps it was, but it was also a shrewd move, a piece of spin in the creation of the Krupp folklore. It reminded everyone of the stories of Alfred's father Friedrich, and how he pitched in with any work in the first small workshop, standing at the furnaces until late into the night.[64] The house enabled Alfred to play on his own humble origins, passed down from one generation to another:

I worked all day, and at night I worried over the difficulties that encompassed me. And while working as I did, sometimes all night long, I lived only on potatoes, coffee, and bread and butter, without meat, with the cares of the father of a family upon me, and for 25 years I held out, till, as my circumstances gradually improved, I could lead a more tolerable life.[65]

It scarcely mattered that, from his sixties onwards, Alfred barely bothered to visit the works personally.[66]

The tiny house still stands today, dwarfed by the huge ThyssenKrupp offices that dominate the city. The management of the Krupp reputation, the 'self-made' entrepreneur, could have been written for the modern-day American internet titan or the Russian oligarch who started his business in a garage or by hawking second-hand items on the street. What matters as much as the original version are the efforts that have gone into the telling and retelling of the story of Alfred Krupp, his descendants, and the modern-day company.

The villa today has been encroached upon by the *gemütlich* detached homes of a suburb of Essen. It serves now as part foundation, part archive and part museum and garden for the public. The story it tells is an important element in the Krupp legacy, a legacy that continues to be disputed, with the official version of a number of events sometimes at odds with those of individual historians. Disagreements are plenty – from the extent to which Alfred sold weapons to all and sundry to, inevitably, the role of the family during the Nazi era. Some of the differences are over tales of individual quirks, peccadilloes or scandals.

The museum tells the story, together with audio-visual guides, of Alfred Krupp, 'the constructor, inventor and visionary'. It is not uncritical, yet throughout it subtly gives the company the benefit of the doubt. Krupp's original drawings, small machine parts and even his first business cards are on display. One of the most fascinating of the many documents that have been preserved is his *Notizbuch*. This is the exercise book in which he recorded the performance of workers. Some have a plus, some have a minus, denoting that the sack will not be long in coming, alongside handwritten observations such as 'plump', 'clumsy' and 'dishonest'. On an upstairs floor his large desk is on display, alongside a bar stool from which he would work, looking out of a large window and into the town. Alongside is a small statue, with the inscription that was his motto: 'The purpose of work should be the public benefit'.

The villa's archive helps to shed light on the tense relationship between the Krupp history and contemporary Germany. This one man epitomises so much of the good and the bad of the nineteenth and twentieth centuries. He was an obsessive authoritarian, yet at the same time an early advocate of welfare; a man who claimed to abhor ostentation who built a mansion of outlandish size; a man who disdained financiers but would do everything he could to maximise the bottom line. His successors would be less contradictory in their pursuit of profit.

The wealthy fret constantly about their inheritance. Would Alfred's son live up to the name of Krupp and do the company proud? Friedrich, commonly known as Fritz, inherited one of the world's biggest business empires. But he was a reluctant heir: he had led a comfortable life. He was not hungry for industrial success. In short, he wasn't passionate about steel. As a young man, he had been taken ill and was sent with a doctor to Egypt, where the hot climate was intended to aid his recovery. While Alfred wrote him many long letters about the steadfast qualities he would need to run the firm, Fritz disappeared on a sightseeing trip for months without making contact. He was something of a dilettante, spending much of the family fortune on Italian art, including a dozen different busts of Dante.[67] Unlike his father, Fritz revelled in titles, honours and baubles. Kaiser Wilhelm II conferred upon him the title of *Excellenz* and made him a privy councillor.[68]

He was a more natural networker, enjoying the company of foreign businessmen while on his travels, not least the American robber barons. He developed a warm relationship with Andrew Carnegie, who gave him advice on how to manage his business. In one letter, dated 26 March 1898 and sent from a villa in Cannes, Carnegie wrote: 'I hope some day you will come over and visit us, but failing that, next year do come and yacht in the West of Scotland and then visit us at Skibo, where a Highland welcome awaits you and Madame Krupp.' The peripatetic lifestyle of the super-rich, the mansions and the yachts are not the preserve of the twenty-first century.

Fritz had ambitions in politics. He patronised and funded mass organisations that reflected good business for Krupp – the Navy League and the Pan-German League. The aim of the former was to promote the expansion of the fleet. By the turn of the century, it had a quarter of a million members. The Pan-German League was particularly popular among the middle class and business community, fostering expansionist patriotic sentiment and defending the rights of ethnic Germans beyond the country's borders. Fritz also helped establish a nationalist newspaper, and ran for parliament for a second time, after being persuaded by the Kaiser. This time he narrowly defeated the Centre Party candidate and sat as deputy for Essen between 1893 and 1898.[69] Fritz's politics are in part disputed in the official version of the Krupp family history, suggesting a less overt nationalism and ambition.

The company continued to grow. Fritz may not have been a natural corporate chief like his father, but he became skilful at mergers and acquisitions. In 1890 the firm developed nickel steel, and two years later it took over a company manufacturing armoured plating and ships' turrets. In 1896, in one of its most important coups, it bought the huge shipbuilding firm Germaniawerft, based in the northern port of Kiel. This became Germany's main warship supplier, including the first U-boats in 1906.

For all the power of the company, a scandal erupted in 1902 that threatened to destroy it. Fritz had been staying at a hotel on the Italian island of Capri, where he is said to have hired out a floor for himself and paid the hotel managers to send him (sometimes under-age) male prostitutes. He paid a Berlin hotel to employ some of these Italian boys as waiters so that they could 'accompany' him when he was in town. At the end of the summer he left Italy in unknown circumstances – it was said that the authorities there had politely but firmly ordered him out. Rumours began to circulate in the German press about an unnamed industrialist with a 'harem' of men and boys in Italy. The Kaiser refused to believe that this could be his friend Fritz. It was the Social Democratic newspaper *Vorwärts* that finally named him as the businessman in question. The Kaiser immediately ordered copies of the paper to be confiscated, and a criminal lawsuit to be brought against it. Fritz's already nervy wife Margaretha, on hearing the story, was committed to a psychiatric sanatorium.*

* The use of the legal system by the Krupps and their political allies to silence an inconvenient investigation is standard practice. The super-rich have been deploying this tactic since the advent of the printing press. In contemporary times, they have found a happy home in London, where the libel laws are among the strictest in the world. At the turn of twentieth-century Germany, what the Kaiser willed, the Kaiser received. A libel action was slapped on *Vorwärts*. But the night before he was due to confer with doctors on the fate of his wife, Fritz took dinner in the Hügel as normal,

The Capri scandal and Fritz's death brought to the fore two alternatives which Alfred had wanted to avoid: to end the family's leadership of the company, or, even worse in the eyes of some directors, to put it under the control of a woman, Fritz's young daughter Bertha. The problem, if indeed it was a problem, was that Bertha had just inherited all but four shares in the company. In so doing, she had instantly become one of the richest women in Europe. It was fortunate that, on a trip to Rome, she was introduced to a certain Gustav von Bohlen und Halbach, a well-born Prussian and the grandson of an American Civil War general. They were married in October 1906 in the presence of Kaiser Wilhelm who, by imperial proclamation, bestowed on Gustav the additional surname of Krupp. Primogeniture had been deftly manufactured. Germany's corporate champion would remain in the hands of a man.

Gustav continued where Alfred and Fritz had left off, branching into the construction of everything from barbed wire to stainless steel. The dilemma of reconciling global business interest with national sentiment had become ever more acute. When the Chinese had deployed Krupp guns against German troops in the 1880s, Alfred survived an attempt by members of the officer corps to paint him as unpatriotic. By the end of the century, Krupp had been charged with building Germany's navy, for which it had been able to fix profit rates at 100 per cent.[70] Although this outraged some on the naval staff, the Kaiser nodded it through, even removing Admiral Tirpitz in the ensuing political struggle. This was a measure of how far the company had come, and how indispensable it was to the military project of the German state by 1900. As Fritz's father had taught him, war and (when required) loyalty made good business sense. H.G. Wells blamed the outbreak of the First World War on 'Kruppism, this sordid, enormous trade in instruments of death'.[71]

then retired to his bedroom, where he committed suicide. Despite the Kaiser's initial bluster, the Public Prosecutor quickly dropped the case against *Vorwärts* after Fritz's death.

Again differences emerge. The official version has it that the sexual exploits of Fritz were an invention of left-wing newspapers hostile to the Krupps, and that no proof was ever found. The suicide is also disputed, with an alternative story of a stroke produced. No post-mortem was ever carried out.

Krupp enjoyed a seat at the political top table, while still making money out of Germany's potential enemies. In 1902, the firm concluded a deal with the English firm Vickers that allowed the latter to use Krupp's patented fuses in its shells. These shells were even stamped with a Krupp copyright.[72] As a result, during the First World War, artillery shells with Krupp fuses would kill and maim German soldiers. This was something future German leaders would not let the company forget.

Straight after the war, with the Versailles Treaty imposed and Germany's military emasculated, Krupp was forced to lay off tens of thousands of workers. Gustav did his best to soften the blow by maintaining generous severance deals. He also, with the help of the government, acquired companies in Sweden and the Netherlands, using them as fronts to continue some of the company's production in secret. Astonishingly, he was able to hide his operations from Allied inspectors, whose job it was to ensure that Germany could never regain its military prowess.

The firm recovered its reputation with a display of unquestionable patriotism. In 1923, the armies of France and Belgium occupied the Ruhr in order to seize goods and raw materials in place of war reparations unpaid by the Weimar government. Bosses and workers united in passive resistance. When a detachment of troops arrived at the works, they fired on the crowd, killing thirteen. The funerals saw a procession of union banners and hammer-and-sickle wreaths alongside top-hatted company directors and uniformed military personnel.[73] Rather than try the soldiers, the French court-martialled Gustav, accusing him of provoking the incident. He was sentenced to fifteen years in jail but was released after seven months as part of a normalisation of Franco-German relations.[74] This prison stint did much to restore the firm's national credentials.

As the fragile Weimar Republic began to disintegrate, a group of German industrialists began to move over to the Nazis, at first discreetly, then more openly. Gustav had been reticent to support Hitler; he and Bertha considered him somewhat gauche. Nor, as is the way of business leaders hedging their bets, did they oppose him – either before or after he had established his power. After being appointed by the Führer as head of the Federation of German Industries in 1933, Gustav quickly expelled the organisation's Jewish members.[75] He supported the

Adolf Hitler Endowment Fund for German Industry, soliciting contributions from other German businessmen.*

As Hitler's secret rearmament programme gathered pace, the company was there to fulfil the contracts. The firm grew again, from 35,000 to more than 100,000 employees. The Nazis provided a ready pool of low-paid workers – or, to be more precise, slave labour from the acquisition of factories in conquered lands in Eastern Europe.[76] Factories owned by Skoda in Czechoslovakia and Rothschild in France transferred to the German company. Up to 40 per cent of the labour force came from prisoners of war or inmates from concentration camps, including Hungarian Jewish women from Auschwitz. Gustav Krupp visited the camps to select labourers. This would form the basis of the accusations against him, and his son Alfried, at the Nuremberg Trials. Gustav – the only German to be accused of war crimes after both world wars – was deemed too ill to stand trial and died during the proceedings. Alfried denied active complicity, telling the court: 'We Krupps never cared much about [political] ideas. We only wanted a system that worked well and allowed us to work unhindered. Politics is not our business.' He was found guilty of crimes against humanity and sentenced to twelve years in prison and the confiscation of all his personal wealth. (After the Battle of Stalingrad in 1942, fearing for the progress of the campaign, Alfried began squirrelling some of his money out of the country.)

After the war, the Allies vowed, as they had in 1918, that the Krupp factories would never work again. They considered schemes for the 'de-concentration' of the German steel industry to prevent too much economic power falling into too few hands. This meant different things to different people: the United States wanted a free market whereas the Labour government in Britain advocated some form of socialisation. In the British sector of West Germany, which included the Ruhr, they set

---

* By this point, the Villa Hügel had undergone a number of refurbishments, each more elaborate than the one before. In his 1969 film *The Damned*, Luchino Visconti paints the scene of a patriarchal industrialist family, called the von Essenbecks, in league with the Nazis. This soap opera of sexual decadence and scheming in the dark but opulent drawing rooms and banqueting halls of their Valhalla was a thinly veiled portrayal of the Krupps.

up supervisory boards in factories with equal representation of management and workers.[77] Krupp was to be cut down and some of its assets sold off. The head of the firm – Alfried, even while serving time – was entitled to the proceeds of these sales, so long as he did not invest them back into the steel or coal industries.[78]

It should be said that while the Krupps' support for the Nazis was incontrovertible, they were by no means alone. Industrialists such as Fritz Thyssen and Friedrich Flick lined up to support Hitler; most notorious of all was the chemicals giant IG Farben, which provided gas to the extermination camps. The directors of the American branch of that firm included top figures from the Ford Motor Company, Standard Oil and the Federal Reserve Bank of New York.

Realpolitik soon took over: the big corporations were deemed too important to fail. The Americans rejected British proposals to nationalise the steel industry in the Western zones, and, as part of efforts to build a stable and economically powerful West Germany to counter the new Soviet East, Krupp was returned to its pre-eminent position in the national economy. Alfried – who had joined the SS as early as 1931 – and the other defendants at the Krupp Trial were granted amnesties in 1951, and by transferring his assets to his siblings the family avoided losing most of its wealth.

The process of rehabilitation was swift and memories were encouraged to be short. Alfried cultivated close ties with West Germany's first post-war Chancellor, Konrad Adenauer. The firm once again went into export overdrive, identifying new markets in the Eastern Bloc and everywhere from Mexico to Egypt to Iran. As part of the settlement with the Allies, Alfried was supposed to sell his shares in the company. But this stipulation was rendered meaningless by a succession of twelve-month extensions to the deadline, which continued right up to his death in July 1967.[79] Business and politics were looking after their own.

By then, Krupp had recovered its position. It had become the fourth-largest firm in Europe and it was finally time for the family to give up control. Initially a foundation took ownership of its shares, putting in charge someone who did not bear the name Krupp. The choice was inspired. Berthold Beitz, who died in 2013 at the age of ninety-nine, had run a Shell oilfield during the Second World War (in what was then Poland and is now Ukraine) and saved hundreds of Jewish workers by claiming that they were indispensable to the running of the operation. Honoured at Israel's Holocaust Memorial at Yad Vashem, Beitz was the perfect antidote to the company's wartime crimes.[80]

Another reason for the company's change of course was that it had run out of Krupps. There was one more son, Arndt, an avowed jet-setter, homosexual and alcoholic who divided his time between Florida and Morocco, ending up in considerable debt. He was persuaded to waive his inheritance in 1968 in return for an annual stipend from the company, and died in 1986 at the age of forty-eight. The Krupp name was no more.

Beitz headed the foundation and secured sources of funding in the difficult 1970s, when he persuaded the Shah of Iran to take a 25 per cent stake in the company, which subsequently passed to the Islamic Republic. As an astute businessman and humanitarian, Beitz's name is now the one that the company raises above others, ironically relegating the name Krupp itself down the ranks of the family's own firm. The company press release on his death stated: 'His great acts of humanity also shaped the corporate culture and social relations at Thyssen-Krupp. This included in particular his good relations with employees. For him, social partnership was of great importance.'[81]

The story of Krupp, and particularly its nineteenth-century patriarch Alfred, is one of industrial dominance – a corporate power that knew how to play domestic politicians while seeking perpetual international expansion. Alfred became hugely wealthy, as did his successors. He was not ostentatious, in a material sense, but through his villa and his formal relations he required the acknowledgement of his status. He was not a philanthropist in the same sense as many of the protagonists in this book; instead of offsetting a proportion of his wealth to outside causes, he saw his duty as ensuring reasonable conditions for his workers – in return for absolute obedience.

Krupp's history could be seen as a story of corporate public relations. Through economic crises, personal scandals and the repeated dilemma of patriotism versus the free market, Alfred and his descendants had to negotiate an intricate path. They did so usually with considerable success, not least the rehabilitation of a company complicit in Nazi war crimes.

Visitors wandering through the exhibits at the Villa Hügel today might be forgiven for wondering what all the fuss was about. The family firm has been adapted for each generation and scrubbed up to protect its legacy.

CHAPTER 9

Andrew Carnegie – Darwin and the robbers

There's class warfare all right. But it's my class, the rich class, that's making war, and we're winning.

Warren Buffett

Flashy, ruthless and possessed of an implacable self-belief, America's industrial titans of the late nineteenth century earned the soubriquet 'the robber barons'. The dominant figures of the era – John D. Rockefeller, Cornelius Vanderbilt, Andrew Carnegie and J.P. Morgan – are key to any understanding of global wealth and power through the ages. All except Morgan were born into relative poverty. This was, as satirised by Mark Twain, the Gilded Age.

The reputation of these men has fluctuated over subsequent generations. Historians initially denounced them as an amoral plutocracy, arguing that their greed contributed to the two 'panics' of 1873 and 1893, and later to the Great Depression of the 1930s. This highly negative depiction continued for a century, but in the *laissez-faire* 1980s they started to be portrayed as patriots and geniuses, maligned and misunderstood. After the financial crash of 2007–8, the criticism returned. They were seen as precursors to the reckless bankers of the contemporary age. The historical reckoning provides a mirror for each generation.

The way the robber barons spent their fortunes has divided opinion even more than the way in which they became rich. Some of their wealth was frittered away on ostentatious mansions and parties. But much of it was dispensed into charitable, artistic and educational foundations. Great art galleries, music halls, libraries and seats of learning bear their names. These men assumed that through their philanthropy their names would be held up for praise in perpetuity and they were largely, though not completely, right. This was reputation laundering on a massive scale. They set the standard for the present-day super-rich to follow.

Here the focus is on Andrew Carnegie, the Scottish-born steel and rail magnate whose market manipulation, use of favourable government tariffs from his political friends and ruthless mergers and acquisitions took him to the top. Carnegie used violence to face down the trade unions and resisted government intrusion (except where it benefited him). He and his rivals took as their intellectual lodestar the English philosopher Herbert Spencer. His notions of genetic hierarchy and the survival of the fittest allowed them to develop their priorities of profit, low unit-labour costs and low taxation that continue to dominate the discourse among the twenty-first century's financial and political elite.

Yet one treatise more than any other has influenced the global super-rich. Carnegie was its author. His immodestly named *Gospel of Wealth*, an extended essay of barely twenty pages, sets out the nobility and obligations of men who make money. No regulation or meddling should stand in the way of the glorious task of acquiring wealth. Once this has been achieved, however, the fortune should be invested back into society, not by the state but by the successful and enlightened individual who earned it. The worst sin they can commit is to die rich. Inheritance is a dirty word.

Contemporary governments have followed the first part of this stricture, while passing over the second.

Andrew Carnegie's story epitomises the American Dream which drew so many immigrants to the United States in the late nineteenth and early twentieth centuries, and still forms such an important part of the American national identity. Born in a small weaver's house in the

Scottish town of Dunfermline in 1835, by the time he sold up and retired from business in 1901 he was hailed by his contemporary and fellow robber baron J.P. Morgan as 'the richest man in the world'.[1]

By 1835, the Industrial Revolution had transformed Britain. Carnegie's father, Will, was a handloom weaver whose huge machine took up most of the ground floor of the modest family home. But such skilled manual workers started to lose out when factory production took off. Dunfermline's first steam-powered textile mill opened when Andrew was a small boy; it soon had a devastating effect on his father's business and changed the family's life. In 1848, the Carnegies, like millions before and since, left for America in search of a better life.

Two of Carnegie's aunts had settled in Pittsburgh, and it was there that the family made their way. Pittsburgh was a rapidly industrialising city. Father and son were taken on at a textile factory, with the boy earning $1.20 a week. Will was not cut out for factory work and soon went back to selling his wares door to door, from which he never made more than a paltry sum.[2] The son blossomed in the factory, taking to the rapid advances with aplomb. It was the younger men who got on in the new world of technology, just as they would a century and a half later in Silicon Valley.

Carnegie's can-do attitude led to instant promotion, first to an administrative role in the factory. Soon he was taking night-classes in double-entry book-keeping; this knowledge enabled him to escape the shop floor, never to return. He was taken on as a messenger boy at the telegraph office. The boys worked on commission and scrapped for the right to deliver out-of-town messages, which were worth more. Carnegie arranged a system in which they shared the work and split the profits.[3] He was then hired as a telegraph operator for the Pennsylvania Railroad, putting him in on the ground floor of another emerging industry. He would be promoted to the rank of a regional superintendent in charge of a section of the line before becoming superintendent of the whole line in 1859, at the age of twenty-three.

To top up his salary, Carnegie began looking for modest investments that could deliver big returns. He had already acquired a taste for calculated risk. As the breadwinner of the family (his father had since died), he advised his mother to make an investment of $600 in ten shares of Adams Express stock. Such was her confidence in her son's ability (or such was her gullibility) that she mortgaged her home to do it. The moment when the first dividend was paid was indelibly etched on Carnegie's mind: 'I can see that first check of $10 dividend money,' he would reminisce on his retirement. 'It was something new to all of us, for none of us had ever received anything but from toil.'

That last word is vital to understand Carnegie and the many self-made men who became barons. Blood, sweat and toil were for people who had still to make it in life, or never would. Manual labour was for losers. Carnegie's aim was to make his money do the work for him.

His first significant return came from a firm that had devised a new concept of overnight accommodation in trains travelling long distance. The Woodruff Sleeping Car Company produced an annual dividend of $5000 within its first two years. Carnegie was on his way to wealth; he began to diversify his portfolio. With the Woodruff money, in 1861 he invested in the Columbia Oil Company. Four payments between June and October 1863 returned a staggering 25–50 per cent each.[4] By the mid-1860s, while drawing a salary of $2400 from the Pennsylvania Railroad, his actual annual income – counting his investments – was closer to $50,000.[5] Why, then, did he bother to keep his job on the Pennsylvania Railroad?

The Civil War was in full cry. Carnegie was a staunch abolitionist, seeing the institution of slavery as flying in the face of the equality of man. However, his commitment to the cause did not extend to putting himself in harm's way. He calculated that a job in this vital sector might save him from having to fight on the front line. The railways had become extremely important for moving troops and supplies, and for communication. Cities like Pittsburgh and Washington, held by the Union, were isolated and often served by a single line of track. In the war's first months, Confederate cavalry wreaked havoc by tearing up the tracks during raids. In his autobiography Carnegie told of how he had shed blood (actually this was due to a rogue metal spring catching his face) while helping to secure for the Union the crucial line into Washington. He was in Pittsburgh when Union troops repaired the track.[6]

By 1864, with Lincoln's army desperate for more troops, the draft became more pervasive. Initially Carnegie escaped because his boss wrote to the Secretary of War describing how his 'services were found to be indispensable to the railroad'. In March, in spite of all his efforts, his number was called. He then used a draft broker, a common (and legal) practice whereby a drafted man could pay another to join up in his place. An Irish immigrant volunteered and was given a tidy $850, while Carnegie bought himself out of the horrors of war.[7] He had mastered the art that is the preserve of the wealthy – paying the poor to do their dirty work.

The same year, with the war still raging, he left for a 'grand tour' of Europe with his friends Harry Phipps and John 'Vandy' Vandevort – 'the boys', as they called themselves. They took a walking trip around England and visited the spa towns of Bath and Leamington. In Italy they took in St Peter's in Rome and the Leaning Tower of Pisa. The boys noted that Carnegie would pay top dollar for everything, even items, Vandy noted, which 'could easily be bought for about fifty per cent less'.[8] The young American was flashing his cash in hotels, restaurants and shops. He wanted everyone to know that he was so wealthy he didn't need to scrimp as his parents had done. Money was, he assumed, buying respect.

The other advantage of Carnegie's salaried position on the railroad was the contacts it gave him in Pittsburgh society. He and his friends quickly saw the opportunities that the impending victory of the Union would present. The South and the West were opening up. American settlers were fulfilling the 'manifest destiny' of the country – to spread from shore to shining shore. Now the era of reconstruction promised even more business for young men such as Carnegie. The new towns would need building materials, livestock, telegraph lines and, most of all, railway tracks and rolling stock.

Carnegie's first self-made venture had already made significant profits. The Keystone Bridge Company produced iron railway bridges to replace wooden ones that caught fire and collapsed, jeopardising troop movements. With its importance to the Union Army, Keystone had been an instant success, and with it began Carnegie's favoured practice of mergers and acquisitions, creating economies of scale – larger companies that could buy in bulk and drive down costs. Recognising the importance of iron and steel in driving expansion, as Alfred Krupp was doing across the Atlantic in Germany, Carnegie resolved to secure a steady supply of metal. When the partners of an iron firm with whom he was acquainted fell out, he persuaded one of them, Tom Miller, to step down and be replaced by Carnegie's younger brother. In exchange, Miller and Carnegie set up another iron company together.[9] In May 1865 the two firms merged to form Union Iron Mills – named in honour of the Union's victory in the Civil War – with the Carnegie brothers as president and vice-president.

In the five years after the Civil War ended, 25,000 miles of railway track were laid in the United States, followed by another 50,000 in the next decade.[10] The pace of development was unlike anything that had gone before. The new lines constituted a tenth of the world's railway mileage. The exhilaration of technical progress – and the money to be made from that progress – dominated public discourse.

Carnegie was making a two-pronged profit as both manufacturer of the iron and steel needed in railroad construction and investor in the railroad companies themselves. Freight provided a large chunk of the income. The railroads would charge a tariff per ton of steel or even per head of cattle. For a producer, buying into a railroad company and using his influence to reduce tariffs for his own goods was a smart move. Carnegie owned slices of the companies, and helped set the fees. Equally important were the raw materials driving the expansion – iron and coal, as well as limestone, which was used to line the crucibles in the great steel factories. Next came the financing, the access to capital. The three legs of the process – railroads, raw materials and banks – became mutually dependent. The titans of each sector bought stakes in the others; and they developed cartels so that newcomers would fail to break through to challenge their hegemony. They created new markets and manipulated them. In place of competition came the cartels.

The key to a successful business, Carnegie believed, was to keep costs low. Just as in his investments, he tried to maximise his returns, so he squeezed the maximum production out of his workforce. 'Watch the costs,' he said, 'and the profits will take care of themselves.'[11] In his steel mills, the workers worked twelve-hour days, doing a whole twenty-four hours on alternate Sundays, irrespective of the prospect of accidents – just so they would be allowed to take the following Sunday off. For Carnegie and his generation of investors and industrialists sitting in their plush offices, the money kept rolling in. The workers, just back from the front, had no other option but to take employment where they could find it.

In 1867 the writer and founder of *The Nation* magazine, E.L. Godkin, likened this new generation of businessmen to 'robber barons'. Godkin borrowed the term from feudal German lords who carved up territory between themselves and charged tolls (which were unauthorised by the Holy Roman Emperor) on anyone seeking to use the primitive roads crossing their lands, just as the Americans were overcharging rivals to use their new railroads.

In barely a decade, Carnegie had escaped the poverty of his roots in spectacular style. Most of his rivals, men who had done well out of the war, were of similar age and background, and they shared his fierce ambition. As a schoolboy, Rockefeller had declared: 'When I grow up I want to be worth $100,000. And I'm going to be too.'[12] This self-made route to great wealth became part of American folklore, and after the collapse of communism it was adopted by oligarchs in the former Soviet Union. The lowlier the beginnings, the tougher the journey, the greater became the later sense of entitlement to act as they pleased. They had barely disguised contempt for the slower, patrician form of capitalism that had preceded them.

Rockefeller got his first big break in 1862, buying into an Ohio oilfield for a return of $4000.[13] It took him a little longer, until the early 1870s, to consolidate his fortune, as he steadily acquired oil refineries, cut costs and saw off the competition. The Standard Oil Company would in subsequent decades turn Rockefeller into the world's first billionaire.

The most ostentatious of the group was Vanderbilt, who rose from small-time ferryboat operator on Staten Island to become the dominant figure in the US transportation system. He showed the way when he bought and then merged three railroads in New York State in 1867, voting himself a $26 million bonus in the process.[14] They all made money off the back of the Civil War. Young speculator J.P. Morgan was implicated in the sale of faulty weapons to the Union Army at six times their value. He also had a telegraph line installed in his Wall Street office so that he could buy and sell gold with the advantage of news from the front before anyone else had the information – an early example of insider trading. These are the roots of the contemporary bank's fortune.

Status was all. In the Gilded Age, the new industrialists were celebrities. Newspapers and magazines were growing rapidly, and a cover story about one of the titans of the age guaranteed increased sales. They knew how to secure good publicity. During this period, they sunned themselves in the affection of popular opinion.[15] Journalists working for newspapers owned by the barons were required to profile them indulgently.

Having made their fortunes, the task for the robber barons was to secure their place in society. A home in New York was essential. They applied their competitive fervour to designing plans for their great houses, vying to outdo each other with the lavishness of their personal real estate. Two Carnegie lieutenants, Charles Schwab and Henry Clay Frick, lived next door to each other, but saw neighbourly relations as a form of sport. Schwab deliberately built his mansion to overshadow that of his colleague. It contained ninety rooms, six lifts, a sixty-foot-long swimming pool and a garage that could hold twenty cars. A miniature coal-fired power station was built to provide electricity for the edifice. Schwab spent a staggering $8 million on his mansion, including a pipe organ costing $100,000; a world-class musician was paid a stipend of $10,000 a year to play it for the entertainment of guests.

Inside their palaces, the barons fraternised and partied. Within the gossipy elite, however, divisions had already emerged. Old money – even if it was just a few years older – derided the new. Society hostess Elizabeth Drexel Lehr ascribed the vulgarity to the new millionaires 'trying to forget with all possible speed the days when they had been poor and unknown'.[16] Most people didn't quibble about the source of the wealth, as long as they were invited to the right parties. The premier hosts of New York society were the newly moneyed Vanderbilts. Their parties were legendary; their fancy-dress ball of 26 March 1883 was one of the most famous of all. The inside of the family mansion was turned into a sumptuous garden:

> A delightful surprise greeted the guests upon the second floor, as they reached the head of the grand stairway. Grouped around the clustered columns which ornament either side of the stately hall were tall palms overtopping a dense mass of ferns and ornamental grasses, while suspended between the capitals of the columns were strings of variegated Japanese lanterns. Entered through this hall is the gymnasium, a spacious apartment, where supper was served on numerous small tables. But it had not the appearance of an apartment last night; it was like a garden in a tropical forest. The walls were nowhere to be seen, but in their places an impenetrable thicket of fern above fern and palm above palm, while from the branches of the palms hung a profusion of lovely orchids, displaying a rich variety of colour and an almost endless variation of fantastic forms.[17]

Many of the guests modelled themselves on works of art. Mrs Vanderbilt herself dressed as a Venetian princess. Others wore period costumes inspired by European aristocrats. Gauche? Vulgar? Yet, in an echo of the celebrity-obsessed modern era, the public were eager to see more. Such was the interest among New Yorkers lining the Vanderbilts' street that the police were called in to keep order.

Party hosts went in search of ever-greater flamboyance. Boredom and predictability were social sins. Mockery provided amusement and sport. Millionaire coal owners gave dinners with their servants dressed as miners. One event was themed the 'poverty social', where guests came dressed in rags and 'scraps of food were served on wooden plates. The diners sat about on broken soapboxes, buckets and coal hods. Newspapers, dust cloths and old skirts were used as napkins, and beer served in a rusty tin can.'[18] This report came from Thorsten Veblen, author of *The Theory of the Leisure Class*. Written in 1899, on the eve of President Theodore Roosevelt's 'trust-busting' campaign against the barons, it has become one of the most compelling texts of the era. The book was so popular at the turn of the century that it was dramatised and played to large audiences in theatres and concert halls.

Veblen, who coined the term 'conspicuous consumption', opens his dissection of the super-rich with the observation: 'The institution of a leisure class is found in its best development at the higher stages of the barbarian culture; as, for instance, in feudal Europe or feudal Japan.' The super-rich of the late nineteenth century, he noted, were so divorced from the rest of society that their only reference points were each other: 'The desire for wealth can scarcely be satiated in any individual instance, and evidently a satiation of the average or general desire for wealth is out of the question.' Veblen encapsulates public confusion that continues to this day: 'Public anger against the questionable means by which millionaires grasped their wealth continued to be coupled with avid interest in the Big Money men who lived Big Lives surrounded by lavishly uniformed servants, pure-bred racehorses, sleek yachts, and expensive wives in Big Houses along New York's Fifth Avenue, Big Cottages at Newport, and Big Estates in Tuxedo Park.'

Mark Twain's was another powerful voice of criticism. One of his most famous letters is that to Vanderbilt in 1869, lamenting his greed but also the public's idolisation of him. It was published in *Packard's Monthly*, 'an American magazine devoted to the interests, and adapted to the tastes, of the young men of the country', as it defined itself. The periodical wore its politics on its sleeve, declaring at its launch in 1868 its intention to fight 'the evils of the day, pursuing them as they are, without mitigation or remorse'. Twain wrote:

> How my heart goes out in sympathy to you! How I do pity you, Commodore Vanderbilt! Most men have at least a few friends, whose devotion is a comfort and solace to them, but you seem to be the idol of only a crawling swarm of small souls, who love to glorify your most flagrant unworthiness in print; or praise your vast possessions worshippingly; or sing of your unimportant private habits and sayings and doings, as if your millions gave them dignity; friends who applaud your superhuman stinginess with the same gusto that they do your most magnificent displays of commercial genius and daring, and likewise your most lawless violation of

commercial honour – for these infatuated worshippers of dollars not their own seem to make no distinctions, but swing their hats and shout hallelujah every time you do anything, no matter what it is. I do pity you.

Twain wondered out loud whether Vanderbilt had a soul or any form of human compassion. The tycoon was too busy fighting his way to the top of New York's rich list, and flaunting his wealth, to bother with such criticism.

Carnegie was less interested in these lavish parties, going along to them only if they served a business purpose. By this point the robber barons were looking for other ways to flaunt their wealth: an art collection was becoming a necessity. Morgan elbowed his way to become leader in this particular market. He enlisted agents in Antwerp, Vienna, Paris and Rome to scour Europe for anything that could remotely be considered a masterpiece. As Veblen notes, being good at business was no longer enough for them. They competed for the top spot in their social lives, their art and their public profiles: 'The new captain of industry in his turn now received "the deference of the common people", became the "keeper of the National Integrity" and with a becoming gravity offered himself as philosopher and friend to mankind, as "guide to literature and art, church and state, science and education, law and morals – the standard container of the civic virtue".'[19]

By the time he reached the age of fifty, with more money than he knew what to do with, Carnegie started to focus less on his companies. He confined his work to the mornings, often skipping board meetings. His operations were put under the control of his senior managers, the most important of whom was Frick.[20] The two men had met when Frick was on his honeymoon. They developed a close business relationship. Frick became chairman of the Carnegie Steel Company, assuming for himself day-to-day charge of operations. One of the most important of these was the Homestead mill, which had been acquired from a neighbour and rival in financial trouble, and would become synonymous with one of the most violent labour disputes of the era.

Carnegie did not start out as hostile to workers' organisations, as some of his contemporaries were. He described the right of workers to unionise as 'no less sacred than the right of the manufacturer to enter into associations and conferences with his fellows'.[21] He also argued against the practice of hiring 'scab' labour to break strikes. These articles, coming from Carnegie's brand of distant paternalism, and written at a time before strikes hit his companies, annoyed Frick. Yet was the self-proclaimed 'progressive' Carnegie any different from the proudly traditional Krupp in Germany? Whatever his early thoughts, they shifted under pressure to maximise the bottom line. In 1888 he decided, as part of his relentless drive to cut costs, to introduce a sliding scale of wages in his Edgar Thomson mill, tied directly to steel prices. This would guarantee profit for the company since, if prices fell, they still would not fall below the level of costs. When notice to this effect was posted at the factory, the workers walked out. Carnegie's response was to shut the mill and withdraw to his New York mansion, waiting for the workers to give in. The strike dragged on for five months until Carnegie had to reappear and, at a mass meeting of the workforce, convinced them to return to work.

Worse was to come. In the summer of 1889, when Carnegie was away in Scotland, a strike broke out over pay and working conditions at the Homestead mill. He instructed the company president, W.L. Abbott, 'to shut down and wait, as we did at ET [Edgar Thomson], until part of the men vote to work'.[22] Abbott, however, lost his nerve and brought in non-unionised labour from outside. They were beaten back by the increasingly powerful union, which forced the company to recognise its right to speak for the men. Tension grew as new contracts were negotiated. The process dragged on interminably, damaging productivity. An increasingly agitated Frick declared in March 1892 that the company was heading for bankruptcy unless 'industrial control' was wrested from the union.[23] On 2 June, the *Pittsburgh Post*, under the headline 'Carnegie Makes a Point', reported that the company had hired a thousand men with a no-strike clause.[24] A battle was looming, but as ever Carnegie had disappeared for the summer to his castle in the Scottish Highlands. The men walked out. Carnegie cabled Frick: 'All anxiety gone since you stand firm. Never employ one of these rioters. Let grass grow over the works.'[25] He encouraged Frick's intransigent stand, telling him: 'Of course, you will be asked to confer, and I know you will decline all conferences, as you have taken your stand and have nothing more to say. Of course you will win, and win easier than you suppose, owing to the present condition of markets.'[26]

In order to clear the union pickets, Frick brought in the Pinkerton National Detective Agency, a notorious private sector security firm. The atmosphere in the town was combustible. Townsfolk harassed those they suspected of giving information to management or operating under cover for Pinkerton. The Pinkertons arrived at Homestead, floating downriver towards the mill on a barge, in the early hours of 6 July. The workers and their families, who had been tipped off, attacked them with old Civil War blunderbusses, dynamite and explosives rolled down the hill to the river on a railway car. The Pinkertons fired back, killing nine workers and wounding more, before being overwhelmed and driven out of town. The workers' victory, however, was pyrrhic. Frick brought in four thousand Pennsylvania state soldiers to enforce order and secure the mill. The workers were gradually starved into submission. Those deemed not to have been troublemakers were allowed back in, as long as they accept new terms and conditions as well as no-strike clauses. After their humiliation, the Pinkertons were equally furious about their treatment. Some said they had been double-crossed; they had been ordered to guard property, not break a strike. Some complained they had been living only on crackers while holed up on their riverboat.[27] It is likely that, for all the vague allusions to 'your plans' in his telegrams to Frick, Carnegie knew more or less exactly what was going on. The local paper put it succinctly: 'It is believed the firm are trying to hasten a conflict with the men so they can appeal for state bayonets to protect the new employees [i.e. strike breakers].'[28]

Effigies of Carnegie and Frick were hung on telegraph poles throughout the town.[29] Carnegie's role in the lockout was lampooned in the national press, as he, not Frick, was the public face of his company. One cartoon depicted him as 'The Modern Baron with Ancient Methods' standing atop a castle-like steelworks ready to pour hot tar on invaders.[30] Frick was unrepentant, seeing the fury as a small price to pay for establishing flexible working. Unit-labour costs had been lowered by 20 per cent. He wrote to Carnegie, with no irony: 'It is hard to estimate what blessings will flow from our recent complete victory.'

Carnegie felt deeply ambivalent about the Homestead dispute, which would soon prick his conscience. He shifted the blame squarely on to his subordinate. He wrote to British Prime Minister William Gladstone: 'It was expecting too much of the poor men to stand idly by and see their work taken by others.'[31] The incident shattered Carnegie's reputation as a good employer. Two weeks later, a young Lithuanian anarchist, Alexander Berkman, burst into Frick's office and shot him twice before stabbing him. Remarkably, Frick survived and was back at work within a week. The incident boosted his reputation, even among those who disagreed with his methods; it made Carnegie, thousands of miles away, look like a wimp. One newspaper would later contrast Carnegie's philanthropy with a moral cowardice that had begun during the Civil War: 'Ten thousand Carnegie Public Libraries would not compensate the country for the direct and indirect evils resulting from the Homestead lockout.'[32]

The Homestead 'victory' encouraged employers across the country to drive wages further downwards. Industrial relations had been tense, as nascent trade unions became more radicalised. Much of America's expanding industrial working class had arrived as recent immigrants from Europe. They brought their political traditions of socialism, anarchism and trade unionism with them. As early as 1877, a huge strike had erupted on the Baltimore & Ohio Railroad, when the company cut its wages as a response to a dip in trade. This strike, known as the 'Great Upheaval', was suppressed only with the deployment of the National Guard, who killed dozens of workers. In 1886, a bomb was thrown at police during a labour protest in Haymarket Square, Chicago, after which they fired into the crowd. Eight officers and at least four workers were killed. Just after Homestead, in 1893, another railroad strike took place at the company of George Pullman, a sometime business partner of Carnegie, which led to more deaths. In late nineteenth-century America the rule of the robber barons did not go unchallenged. During this period, some 37,000 strikes were recorded.

The workers' grievances were founded in straightforward economics. Throughout the 1870s and 80s the US economy had been growing at a faster rate than at any time in its history – and yet industrial workers saw few rewards for their endeavours. The average annual income was less than \$400, a fraction of what was spent by the barons on any of their lavish parties. Most workers lived below the poverty line, scrimping and saving, and putting in as many hours as they could in often-dangerous conditions. During this period, 35,000 workers died each year in industrial accidents, an extraordinarily high figure, largely because of management's refusal to install safety devices or to shorten the hours of work. To do either would have eroded profitability.

Six years after an event that helped define the history of American industrial relations in that epoch, Carnegie returned to Homestead to dedicate one of his libraries. He struck a contrite tone: 'As it was by the labour of my hands that I first earned my living, my title to the name of workingman must pass unchallenged in any part of this world. Take, therefore, this building as the gift of one workingman to other work-ingmen.'[33] He would later express regret that he had grown too removed from his workforce. 'We assemble thousands of operatives in the factory, and in the mine, of whom the employer can know little or nothing, and to whom he is little better than a myth. All intercourse between them is at an end. Rigid castes are formed, and, as usual, mutual ignorance breeds mutual distrust.'[34] Yet he did not, and nor did any of the other barons, see anything but merit in the unregulated economy. As Veblen put it: 'The America of the post-Civil War era was a paradise for the entrepreneur, untrammelled and untaxed.'

The making of money, the harnessing of industrial labour, was of itself virtuous. Did the robber barons believe this, or did they hope that by endless repetition, across a pliant media and deferential public space, they would have others believe it? The answer must be a combination of the two. This peroration from the pulpit in a Sunday school address by Rockefeller epitomised the mindset: 'The American Beauty rose can be produced in the splendour and fragrance which brings cheer to its beholder only by sacrificing the early buds which grow up around it. This is not an evil tendency in business. It is merely the working-out of a law of nature and a law of God.'

In the space of two decades, a tiny group of industrialists had created their own self-justifying bubble. They had separated themselves off from the 99 per cent. How could they justify their enormous wealth sitting alongside so much poverty? How could they explain, historically and socially, what had happened? Some did not bother to try, as long as the money gushed in. But the more enquiring among their number were intrigued to find an explanation. Was it virtue? Was it genetic?

Charles Darwin's theory of evolution, *On the Origin of Species*, had been published in 1859. The thinker who adapted and applied evolutionary theory to sociology was Herbert Spencer. By the time his *Synthetic Philosophy* started appearing in serial form in 1864 (with the Civil War still raging), *Atlantic Monthly* was suggesting that Spencer had 'already influenced the silent life of a few thinking men'.[35] One phrase provided them with an easy answer, an easy soundbite to justify their sudden surge to the top of the pile. The rail magnate James Hill spoke for his generation: 'the fortunes of railroad companies are determined by the law of the survival of the fittest'.[36]

The American continent was the laboratory in which this vast experiment was taking place. Drawing in hard-working people from across the world, and expanding westwards through its seizure of Native American land, the population and productive capacity of the country were increasing at extraordinary rates. Spencer saw it as a crucible in which to form 'a finer type of man than had hitherto existed',[37] albeit one made exclusively from white Aryans. One of the most attractive aspects of his thinking for the robber barons was the link he made between moral and material progress. As they made the world (or at least themselves) richer, so they were improving the moral fibre of society.[38]

Carnegie was one of Spencer's most enthusiastic followers. He celebrated his mentor's embrace of man's self-improvement: 'Nor is there any conceivable end to his march to perfection. His face is turned to the light; he stands in the sun and looks upward,' he declared. The steel man longed to meet his intellectual hero. While in England in the summer of 1882, he heard that Spencer was to embark on a lecture tour of the United States. Carnegie procured himself a cabin on board the same ship to New York as Spencer and ensured they struck up a friendship. He had built up the philosopher in his mind as a superhuman figure and was surprised to see him engaged in an undignified argument with a waiter on board: 'Never did I dream of seeing him excited over the question of Cheshire or Cheddar cheese.'[39]

Wherever Spencer went he was mobbed. The problem was, the Englishman had few kind words for the places he visited. Of Pittsburgh, the city where so many of his disciples had made their fortunes, he said: 'Six months here would justify suicide.'[40] Publicly, he hid his ill-temper and praised American industrialism: 'The extent, wealth, and magnificence of your cities, have altogether astonished me.'[41] It seemed like his optimistic view of human progress was being borne out.

Hotel managers and railway agents competed for the privilege of serving him. At an event in Delmonico's restaurant in New York, the great and the good gathered to pay homage. Spencer was uneasy, asking his associates to hide him in an anteroom so he did not have to engage in niceties with strangers. The organisers were desperate to impress him. The feast of fine French food lasted two and a half hours, with a new course arriving every ten minutes. The after-dinner speeches were opened by former Secretary of State William Evarts, who proclaimed: 'As no room or city can hold all his [Spencer's] friends and admirers, it was necessary that a company should be made up by some method out of the mass, and what so good a method as natural selection?'[42]

This attempt at a joke betrayed not only Spencer's influence on the American super-rich, but also their view of themselves. They were indeed a self-selected elite. The *Social Register*, throughout the 1880s, published details of the few hundred families at the top of American society, whom it described as 'the socially elect' and 'naturally included in the best society'.[43] This was a curious mix of theological and Darwinian terminology of which Spencer's wealthy fans would have approved. Spencer, in his speech at Delmonico's, praised America's institutions but argued that its people had not yet evolved enough to be worthy of them. Looking around at the room of grey-haired tycoons ageing before their time, he feared that they were working themselves into the ground. 'I may say that we have had somewhat too much of "the gospel of work". It is time to preach "the gospel of relaxation".'[44] The barons, with one eye on how to spend their fortunes, were inclined to agree. Spencer continued this theme in his one newspaper interview. The American character, he said, was not yet fully refined, but would eventually achieve 'a finer type of man than has hitherto existed'. Americans might 'reasonably look forward to a time when they will have produced a civilisation grander than any the world has known'.

At the end of Spencer's trip, standing on the quayside in New York, he took the hands of Carnegie and Edward Youmans (a science writer who had organised the tour) and proclaimed: 'here are my two best American friends'.[45] He had known Carnegie for only three months. Carnegie's fawning, his eagerness to impress Spencer, continued long after. The following year, he heard that the philosopher was taking a trip to Australia. 'I wish I were your companion,' he wrote to him, signing his letter, 'to you, reverence'.[46] In his autobiography, Carnegie explained the influence Spencer's teachings had on him:

> Reaching the pages which explain how man has absorbed such mental foods as were favourable to him, retaining what was salutary, rejecting what was deleterious, I remember that light came as in a flood and all was clear. Not only had I got rid of theology and the supernatural, but I had found the truth of evolution. 'All is well since all grows better' became my motto, my true source of comfort. Man was not created with an instinct for his own degradation, but from the lower he had risen to the higher forms. Nor is there any conceivable end to his march to perfection.

He then posited the following thought: 'It would be no greater miracle to be born to a future life than to have been born to live in this present life. The one has been created, why not the other? Therefore there is reason to hope for immortality. Let us hope.'

Carnegie's more immediate desire was more prosaic: to lead a comfortable, quieter life. He was drawn, as new money so often is, to the rustic charms of British country life. Even before he had established himself as a member of the super-rich, he had written home to his cousin in Scotland, explaining his wish to live in the manner of a gentleman, 'to expand as my means do and ultimately own a noble place in the country, cultivate the rarest flowers, the best breeds of cattle, own a magnificent lot of horses and be distinguished for taking the deepest interest in all those about my place'. In 1887 he married Louise

Whitfield, the daughter of a New York merchant and twenty years his junior; they honeymooned on a steamship around the Scottish Highlands and Islands.

From that point on, Carnegie lived his winters in America and his summers in Scotland. Skibo Castle, in Sutherland near the northern tip of the country, had been built in the twelfth century. It had fallen into disrepair since the eighteenth century, but Carnegie was immediately enamoured of its beauty – and potential. He leased the dilapidated castle and its estate in 1897, taking up the option of buying it a year later. He substantially remodelled it, at a cost of £2 million, adding sculpted gardens, fairy-tale turrets and an eighteen-hole golf course. From its roof he flew a flag amalgamating the Union Flag and the Stars and Stripes, a testament to his transatlantic identity.[47] Skibo was not as expensive as his sixty-four-room mansion in New York. But it did enable him to live the genteel life he had wished for. The castle remained in the Carnegie family until 1982, after which it was turned into an exclusive private members' club, called the Carnegie Club, and venue for celebrity weddings, such as Madonna's to Guy Ritchie in 2000.

So quickly did Carnegie make money that he planned to retire at the age of thirty-five. His aim, he wrote to himself in a secret New Year's resolution at the end of 1868, was to quit so early so that he could 'settle in Oxford and get a thorough education making the acquaintance of literary men'. He would then move to London, 'taking part in public matters, especially those connected with education and improvement of the poorer classes'.[48] That was the year he made his first $50,000. He pledged that this figure would be his annual salary. Anything above that he would give away. He did neither of these things, not immediately anyway. His first philanthropic act would be a long time coming. He first donated funds in 1881, for a library to be built in Dunfermline. He always retained a soft spot for his hometown.

On his first visit back he was shocked by what he saw. One of his aunts listened to his stories of business exploits; she said she hoped his success would enable him one day to 'keep a shop on the high street'.[49] She could not imagine how rich his railroad investments were already making him, let alone what his fortune would amount to in the future.

How the new land of opportunity had overtaken the old country. How small the latter looked: 'Here was a city of the Lilliputians. I could almost touch the eaves of the house in which I was born.'

He tried to donate a library to Pittsburgh at the same time, but had to wait until state law was changed to allow taxes to be levied to maintain it; it finally opened in 1887. He regarded both of these towns as his home: the first had made him who he was; the second had made him his fortune. In Dunfermline, he bought one of the largest old estates, Pittencrief, where he had scrumped apples as a boy. He turned it into a public park for the city.[50]

Having made his money off the back of others' labours, it was time to practise compassion. In order to focus on his ambitious plans for philanthropy, Carnegie first needed to retire. A buyer had to be found for his business empire, one of the biggest in the world. First out of the starting blocks was J.P. Morgan. His motive was not any affection for Carnegie's achievements, but raw competition. He had long wanted to diversify from finance into steel and, in doing so, to 'eliminate Carnegie from the steel industry'.[51] His attempt to hoover up the conglomerate coincided with growing discontent from within at Carnegie's semi-detached style. The infighting had become destabilising. Since Homestead, Carnegie had been trying to buy Frick out of the company. Hearing that his boss was bad-mouthing him in private, Frick stormed into a board meeting (as usual, Carnegie was absent) and accused him of cowardice: 'Why was he not manly enough to say to my face what he said behind my back?' Frick went further, writing to Carnegie: 'For years I have been convinced that there is not an honest bone in your body. Now I know that you are a god-damned thief.'[52]

The two eventually settled, through gritted teeth. They reached a compromise valuation for Carnegie to buy out Frick's shares. Aside from vastly increasing Frick's fortune, Carnegie had broken an agreement about the sale price, leaving him vulnerable to outside investors. Morgan exploited the situation to push through his deal. To do so, he schmoozed Carnegie's most trusted lieutenant, Schwab, by inviting him to be guest speaker at a dinner he was giving for Vice-President Teddy Roosevelt. There, Morgan floated the idea of buying Carnegie's empire. Schwab seemed receptive, knowing of his boss's desire to retire. He took the news to Carnegie, who asked to be given a night to sleep on it. The next morning, Carnegie handed Schwab a piece of paper with a figure written on it: the amount he wanted. Schwab took it back to Morgan, who opened the paper to find the figure of $480 million. He agreed to pay it without negotiation.

The two barons met, briefly, to shake hands on the deal, and Morgan congratulated Carnegie on becoming 'the richest man in the world'. He wasn't wrong. The previous incumbent had been Vanderbilt. It is said that in 1876, the year before his death, his doctor prescribed him champagne to deal with a severe stomach pain. 'I can't afford champagne,' Vanderbilt is said to have replied. 'I guess sody water will do.' He was worth $110 million.

These numbers, stunning for their time, reveal just how much money was made in the Gilded Age. The *New York Tribune*, in an investigation to find the number of American millionaires in 1892, identified over four thousand.[53] The Carnegie–Morgan deal made a fair few more. It marked the moment of the transfer of power from one titan to another. As Carl Hovey wrote, in his life story of Morgan (written fawningly while his subject was still alive): 'It has been said that millionaires, when they are frightened, run to JPM like chickens to the mother hen. Something of the sort certainly took place upon this occasion.' The chronicler's tone might not have been the most objective, but he was not wrong.

The dinner to celebrate the founding of the new company, US Steel, was held, fittingly enough, in the East End of Pittsburgh at the Hotel Schenley in January 1901. It was attended by eighty-nine millionaires, many of them Carnegie's.[54] Some of these overnight new recruits to the super-rich club couldn't believe their luck, and celebrated with parties and gambling trips. Alexander Rolland Peacock, who had been vice-president of Carnegie Steel, woke up one morning and, without bothering to change out of his pyjamas, drove around the city in a $7000 car, paying off the debts of old friends and acquaintances.[55]

Carnegie demonstrated the sobriety befitting a man who by now was used to wealth. He had become old money. At the age of sixty-six, he could turn his attention full time to his philanthropic ambitions. First recipients of his largesse were the Carnegie libraries, donated to municipalities across the English-speaking world. More than three thousand were established in forty-seven US states before his death. Opening his Pittsburgh Museum in 1895, Carnegie said that he hoped it would give the labouring classes a taste of the world that he had seen. His optimism about the trajectory of mankind, despite the labour wars and factional fights he had engaged in to keep his empire running, remained undiminished: 'There is nothing we have done here that can possibly work evil; all must work good ... there is nothing here that can tend to pauperise, for there is neither trace nor taint of charity; nothing which will help any man who does not help himself; nothing here is given for nothing.'[56]

Museums in his name opened across the country, particularly in the Midwest, often with a focus on natural history. Education was at the heart of his projects. The Foundation for the Advancement of Teaching, which opened in 1905, continues to manage teachers' retirement funds today. Strangely, for an avowed secularist, Carnegie funded the restoration of seven hundred church organs throughout America. Public baths followed libraries, providing workers with more sanitary places to wash and rest. He set up the Hero Fund after a mining disaster in Pennsylvania, to provide money for the families of people who died saving others.

Ten years after the sale of his company to Morgan, Carnegie still had more than $150 million in wealth. Well into his seventies, he was tiring of the burden of philanthropic decision-making. On the advice of friends, he established a trust to which he could transfer the bulk of his remaining fortune as well as responsibility for distributing his wealth after his lifetime. The world's largest philanthropic organisation, the Carnegie Corporation of New York, was born. (Two years later Rockefeller copied him with one of his own.) The corporation's capital fund, originally worth about $135 million, had a market value of $1.5 billion a century later. By the time of his death, Carnegie had given away at least $350 million. A relatively meagre $10 million was to be split between his friends, relatives and colleagues.[57]

*

Andrew Carnegie's politics were a curious amalgam. The man who looked to maximise the bottom line in all his business activities then zealously sought to give his money away. The man who would not tolerate worker dissent yet had his roots in the Chartist movement of the 1840s, with its emphasis on modest moves towards political probity and democracy. Even before setting sail for the New World, he was convinced that all men were created equal. He ascribed his adopted country's rapid material progress to hard work and its political system. Everything that reformers had been struggling for in Britain, he thought, had been achieved in the United States, as enshrined in its great constitution. In 1853 he wrote home to a cousin in Scotland: 'We have the Charter for which you have been struggling for years.'[58] He despised the British royal family and aristocracy and fervently hoped that one day the country would adopt republicanism.

In the 1880s Carnegie was a high-profile recruit to the 'Nineteenth Century Club', a progressive but elitist debating society which was, in the words of its founder Courtlandt Palmer, 'a radical club, not too radical, but just radical enough'.[59] For his first public speaking engagement Carnegie spoke against the motion that the Gilded Age had created an 'aristocracy of the dollar' which had replaced old landowners with a new – and worse – tyranny. He passionately defended capitalism, declaring that America had demonstrated an 'aristocracy of intellect'. He was a staunch Atlanticist, a proponent of the superiority of the British–American 'race'. He even hoped for reunification of some kind between the two countries. 'Fortunately for the American people,' he wrote, 'they are essentially British'. Although he conceded that 'the small mixture of foreign races is a decided advantage to the new race, for even the British race is improved by a slight cross',[60] he identified non-English-speaking immigration to the United States as a threat, because groups arrived with their own traditions, unaware of the responsibilities which citizenship in a democracy conferred upon them.[61] He wanted to lift the masses out of ignorance so that they could fulfil their civic role, but this did not stop him from employing thousands of European immigrants and giving them precious little time off to study history or develop their English skills.

In Britain, Carnegie was an influential voice in the Liberal Party, contributing funds to its more radical MPs. In 1882, he was on the point of launching a syndicate of newspapers for English workers, trumpeting science and republicanism, but nothing came of the plans.[62] When he met Gladstone in the early 1880s, he took the opportunity to correct what he thought of as English misconceptions about America. Gladstone suggested someone should write a book on the subject, so Carnegie got to work. The result, *Triumphant Democracy*, appeared in 1886. It caused a stir with its carefully researched data on the pace of American industrial expansion, ascribing that to its superior political system. Popular with liberals and radicals, *Triumphant Democracy* was a huge commercial success, selling over thirty thousand copies in the US and forty thousand in Britain.[63] Conservative reviewers were less impressed: the *St James Gazette* pointed out that America's rise could be put down entirely to luck – to its huge reserves of raw materials.[64]

Three years later Carnegie produced his seminal work. Published in the *North American Review*, it was originally called *Wealth*; he was persuaded by Gladstone to expand the title for a British audience. *The Gospel of Wealth* is a manifesto to wealth creation that would have served all the protagonists of this history well. Carnegie's Chartist roots should have left him uncomfortable with the sharply rising inequality of the late nineteenth century (as with our contemporary times). His answer was his own variant of 'trickle-down': everyone will benefit from wealth creation, but inevitably and necessarily, some will benefit more than others.

> The contrast between the palace of the millionaire and the cottage of the labourer with us today measures the change, which has come with civilization. This change, however, is not to be deplored, but welcomed as highly beneficial. It is well, nay, essential, for the progress of the race that the houses of some should be homes for all that is highest and best in literature and the arts, and for all the refinements of civilization, rather than that none should be so. Much better this great irregularity than universal squalor.

He adds, with his newly acquired mix of Darwinism and determinism:

It is a law, as certain as any of the others named, that men possessed of this peculiar talent for affairs, under the free play of economic forces must, of necessity, soon be in receipt of more revenue than can be judiciously expended upon themselves, and this law is as beneficial for the race as the others.

His economic recipe would have made modern free-market proselytisers proud. Everyone, he argues, has a sacred right to property, savings, wealth and low taxation. He speaks of 'the right of the labourer to his hundred dollars in the savings bank, and equally the legal right of the millionaire to his millions. Every man must be allowed "to sit under his own vine and fig tree, with none to make afraid".' Low unit costs and flexible labour laws provided a one-way route to gentrification and upward mobility.

Carnegie was also one of the first to explain the advantages of globalisation:

Today the world obtains commodities of excellent quality at prices, which even the preceding generation would have deemed incredible. In the commercial world similar causes have produced similar results, and the race is benefited thereby. The poor enjoy what the rich could not before afford. What were the luxuries have become the necessaries of life. The labourer has now more comforts than the farmer had a few generations ago. The farmer has more luxuries than the landlord had, and is more richly clad and better housed. The landlord has books and pictures rarer and appointments more artistic than the King could then obtain.

The name Carnegie is now synonymous with the culture and practice of philanthropy. He talked, intriguingly for a man of his fortune, of 'surplus wealth' as 'the property of the many'. Yet the idea was not just to give money away – indeed, he abhorred such a notion, differentiating (as many modern-day politicians and business leaders do) between the 'deserving' and 'undeserving' poor. 'It were better for mankind that the millions of the rich were thrown into the sea than so spent as to encourage the slothful, the drunken, the unworthy,' he writes. Hand up, not hand out: 'In bestowing charity, the main consideration should be to help those who will help themselves.'

The *Gospel* has become the gospel for the twenty-first-century super-rich and their modern variant of philanthrocapitalism – the application of free-market business techniques to charity-giving. Long before the investor Warren Buffett pledged to give tens of billions of dollars of his fortune to the Gates Foundation, he gave Bill Gates a copy of Carnegie's text (see Chapter 13). Chuck Feeney, an Irish-American billionaire who made his money in airport duty-free stores, presented copies of the *Gospel* to his children to explain why he had decided to give away most of their inheritance.

Carnegie's foundations did not just divest money to their own causes; they sought to engineer societal change in their own image. His was a late nineteenth-century, anti-monarchist variant of *noblesse oblige*. Individual endeavour, he argues in the *Gospel*, will always be more effective than measures undertaken by the state. Leave it to the good men who have become rich. They have already demonstrated their superior credentials in the accumulation of wealth; from that point they can focus on the betterment of society.

Thus is the problem of rich and poor to be solved. The laws of accumulation will be left free, the laws of distribution free. Individualism will continue, but the millionaire will be but a trustee for the poor, intrusted for a season with a great part of the increased wealth of the community, but administering it for the community far better than it could or would have done for itself.

The duty of the man of wealth, he adds, is:

To set an example of modest, unostentatious living; to provide moderately for the legitimate wants of those dependent upon him; and, after doing so, to consider all surplus revenues which come to him simply as trust funds, which he is called upon to administer, and strictly bound as a matter of duty to administer in the manner which, in his judgment, is best calculated to produce the most beneficial results for the community – the man of wealth thus becoming the mere trustee and agent for his poorer brethren, bringing to their service his superior wisdom, experience, and ability to administer, doing for them better than they would or could do for themselves.

There are, Carnegie states, three ways of 'disposing' of wealth: 'It can be left to the families of the decedents, or it can be bequeathed for public purposes' or finally it can be 'administered by its possessors during their lives'. The first option 'is the most injudicious'. In monarchical countries (the system he despises), the estate is usually left to the first-born son: 'The condition of this class in Europe today teaches the failure of such hopes or ambitions.' This leaves individuals and societies lazy and feckless: 'It is no longer questionable that great sums bequeathed often work more for the injury than for the good of the recipients.' Carnegie becomes a strong advocate of death duties: 'Of all forms of taxation this seems the wisest.'

Option number two – making a legacy gift on death to an institution – is not much better than giving it to the family: 'Men who leave vast sums in this way may fairly be thought men who would not have left it at all had they been able to take it with them. The memories of such cannot be held in grateful remembrance, for there is no grace in their gift.' The industrialist, the banker, the trader should not have left it to the last minute to think of giving his money away. Carnegie encapsulated his sense of mission: 'The man who dies thus rich dies disgraced.'

Carnegie died in 1919, at the age of eighty-three, a man anything but disgraced. He had long since withdrawn from the cut and thrust of business, leaving the field open to a new generation as well as to old rivals such as Morgan. The banker who had bought him out had emerged as the first among equals. Lauded by business leaders and politicians back home, Morgan was fêted by kings abroad. Edward VII was keen to see him whenever he was in England. 'From the King down,' noted a court circular, 'all concentrated their attention on Mr Morgan, and their curiosity was not unmixed with awe.' The King 'received him as a personal guest at London, making it apparent to all who saw the two men upon this occasion that the King regarded Mr Morgan as the financial monarch of the world'. Kaiser Wilhelm II of

Germany also welcomed him, decorating him with the Order of the Red Eagle and sending Morgan a marble bust of himself. The banker responded to his advisers after meeting the Kaiser: 'he pleases me'. This marked the 'new aristocracy of money accepting and being accepted by the old aristocracy of blood'.

The new aristocracy was busy building monuments to its own vanity. The estate of Biltmore, constructed in the Blue Ridge Mountains of North Carolina in 1895 by George Vanderbilt II, grandson of the railway tycoon, stood as the great monument to the robber barons. Vanderbilt toured the chateaux of the Loire for the right model and employed a thousand labourers to recreate his dream. The 250-room palace came with an indoor swimming pool, bowling alley, lifts and intercom system at a time when the average American home had neither electricity nor indoor plumbing.

A decade earlier, Thomas Carnegie – Andrew's brother – had bought up almost all of one of the idyllic Sea Islands off the Georgia shoreline. Cumberland Island, a third larger than Manhattan, was a venue for solitude but also for parties. Thomas and his wife gave their nine offspring money to buy their own mansions or, to use their parlance, cottages. Just up the coast is Jekyll Island, where the Vanderbilts and Rockefellers built a club in 1886 to entertain their friends and business associates. They hunted in the winter and sailed in the summer, racing their state-of-the-art yachts in the harbour. They also talked big ideas, an early Davos by the sea, even testing out new technology: the first transatlantic phone call was made from the island. It was there, in 1910, that a group of bankers, including Rockefeller and Paul Warburg, meeting under the ruse of a duck-shooting excursion, quietly hatched the idea of creating the Federal Reserve. The founder of *Forbes* magazine, Bertie Charles Forbes, wrote later:

> Picture a party of the nation's greatest bankers stealing out of New York on a private railroad car under cover of darkness, stealthily riding hundreds of miles South, embarking on a mysterious launch, sneaking onto an island deserted by all but a few servants, living there a full week under such rigid secrecy that the names of not one of them was once mentioned, lest the servants learn

the identity and disclose to the world this strangest, most secret expedition in the history of American finance.

A visit to these islands helps in understanding how complete was the transformation of the robber barons. A new aristocracy was created, each generation acquiring grandeur and a sense of *noblesse oblige*.

Carnegie's autobiography, published in 1920, a year after his death, was the first significant memoir of an American capitalist. The book is no match for *The Gospel of Wealth*. This passage, however, is most instructive as an indication of one school of thought. It comes from Carnegie's editor, John C. Van Dyke:

> Nothing stranger ever came out of the Arabian Nights than the story of this poor Scotch boy who came to America and step by step, through many trials and triumphs, became the great steel master, built up a colossal industry, amassed an enormous fortune, and then deliberately and systematically gave away the whole of it for the enlightenment and betterment of mankind ... in the course of his career he became a nation-builder, a leader in thought, a writer, a speaker, the friend of workmen, schoolmen, and statesmen, the associate of both the lowly and the lofty.

The historiography of the robber baron period brings the story up to date. The assessment of their contribution and moral standing has ranged from the paid-for hagiographies of their time, through furious denunciations, to, more recently, revisionist praise. The appraisals have spanned the genres – from novel to economic treatise to history, from film to theatre, each one reflecting the political and economic priorities of its generation and often sparking heated debate. In his 1884 memoir, the financier Henry Clews talked of the 'Parisian, indeed almost Sybaritic, luxury and social splendour' of life in New York. Clews, who had been an economic adviser to President Ulysses Grant, wrote:

> Soon nothing remains for the wives of the Western millionaires but to purchase a brownstone mansion, and swing into the tide of

fashion with receptions, balls and kettledrums, elegant equipages with coachmen in bright-buttoned livery, footmen in top-boots, maid-servants and man-servants, including a butler, and all the other adjuncts of fashionable life in a great metropolis.

In the first decade of the twentieth century, writers such as Upton Sinclair, with *The Jungle*, and Frank Norris, with *The Octopus* and *The Pit*, focused on the relationship between poverty, greed and corruption. These works were written during one of those rare moments in American history when a president has taken on vested business interests. Theodore Roosevelt's anti-trust campaign was a direct assault on the monopoly practices that had so enriched the robber barons, a group he famously denounced as the 'malefactors of great wealth'. In 1911 Roosevelt broke up the Rockefeller oil empire, regulated the railroads and cut the feared J.P. Morgan down to size. Business overall was subjected to greater competitive pressure. The President was deeply impressed, and influenced, by the investigative journalism of Lincoln Steffens and Ida Tarbell, the so-called 'muckrakers'. Tarbell described Rockefeller's fortune as based on 'fraud, deceit, special privilege, gross illegality, bribery, coercion, corruption, intimidation, espionage or outright terror'.

Biographies of Andrew Mellon, Carnegie and Rockefeller were often laced with moral censure, warning of the threat they posed to democracy and their 'parasitism'. One book, more than any other, evokes the decadence and moral bankruptcy: F. Scott Fitzgerald's *The Great Gatsby*, written in 1925 in the midst of the Roaring Twenties and on the eve of the Great Crash. Fitzgerald's account was fictitious. This one was not:

Mansions and chateaux of French, Gothic, Italian, Barocco and Oriental style lined both sides of upper Fifth Avenue, while shingle and jigsaw villas of huge dimensions rose above the harbour of Newport. One would have a bedstead of carved oak and ebony, inlaid with gold, costing $200,000. Another would decorate his walls with enamel and gold at a cost of $65,000. And nearly all ransacked the art treasures of Europe, stripped medieval castles of their carvings and tapestries, ripped whole staircases and ceilings from their place of repose through the centuries to lay them anew amid setting of a synthetic age and simulated feudal grandeur.[65]

So wrote Matthew Josephson in his 1934 book, titled, appropriately enough, *The Robber Barons*. The author, like others before him and since, was both enthralled and horrified by the demonstrations of wealth. He emphasised the venality of politics, the concentration of wealth, the crudities of taste, and the struggle of the masses. But the importance of his work was to show – at a time when America was grinding to a halt and before the start of the New Deal – the extent to which the robber barons had not acquired their riches on merit, contrary to the myth they had built for themselves. These industrialists, he wrote, had demanded a free hand in the market place:

promising that while seeking to enrich themselves they would help 'build up the country' for the benefit of all the people. And when they had resorted to the methods of the plunderer and the conspirator, they had remained immune to the law, since our society imposed virtually no rules in this game, no ethics of business conduct ... This type of the successful baron of industry now presented itself as the high human product of the American climate, the flower of its own order of chivalry, much wondered at, envied or feared in foreign lands whose peers had arrived somewhat earlier at coronets, garlands and garters. How they overran all the existing institutions which buttress society; how they took possession of the political government (with its police, army, navy), of the School, the Press, the Church, and finally how they laid hands upon the world of fashionable and polite society. In short order the railroad presidents, the copper barons, the big dry-goods merchants and the steel masters became Senators, ruling in the highest councils of the national government, and sometimes scattered twenty-dollar gold pieces to newsboys of Washington. But they also became in even greater number lay readers of churches, trustees of universities, partners or owners of newspapers or press services and figures of fashionable, cultured society. And through all these channels they laboured to advance their policies and principles, sometimes directly, more often with skilful indirection.

This righteous indignation continued through the 1960s and beyond, but with the advent of Reagan and Thatcher and the new hegemony of free-market ideology, it was eclipsed by a cultural and intellectual reclamation of Gilded Age tycoonery. In the 1990s and 2000s a number of biographies were published, emphasising the brilliance of these men, their implacable will to succeed, their pioneering roles in strengthening the country's industrial base and their mastery of technology. Taken together, this literature might be said to constitute a new genre: the misunderstood robber baron. Things might not have been pretty, so the argument went, but at the end of the day they were a blessing that endowed America with wealth and power.[66]

The assessment of Andrew Carnegie and his generation is mixed and confused, reflecting our contemporary times. He, like those around him, used every form of financial skulduggery to reach the top, as Josephson rightly argues – carving up the railroads, the steel and oil industries and the banks among themselves, cutting deals to the exclusion of competitors. They threw money around until some of them became bored and looked for more productive ways to spend their fortunes. And on what moral basis did they earn the right to become the arbiters of social advancement in America and beyond?

Carnegie thought long and hard about the philosophical justification for his actions. He was convinced that laws, regulations and taxation were signs of a backward country, averse to business and enlightenment. He pursued philanthropy with the same tenacity he had shown in his profit-making ventures. His thinking set the trend that the modern breed of oligarchs, of Silicon Valley computer coders and bankers and hedge-funders would follow. As Thomas Carlyle put it in the 1840s, 'the history of the world is but the biography of great men'. Carnegie and his fellow robber barons believed they were imbued with such greatness.

CHAPTER 10

Mobutu Sese Seko –
The walking bank vault

I don't think wealth actually changes people.
Jeff Bezos

The Cold War notion of 'my enemy's enemy is my friend' produced some of the most colourful kleptocrats of all time. The middle part of the twentieth century supplied no shortage of examples. François 'Papa Doc' Duvalier of Haiti combined the expropriation of wealth by a small coterie with murder and torture. His actions led to a brain drain of the professional classes and the further impoverishment of his country. However, his desire to annoy Cuba's Fidel Castro won him the reluctant support of Washington. More reliable was General Anastasio Somoza García of Nicaragua: as President F.D. Roosevelt said of him, he may be a 'son of a bitch, but he's our son of a bitch'. Somoza presided over a traditional economically and socially conservative regime, combined with repression and extortion. Concessions granted to foreign (mainly US) companies, and kickbacks, helped him amass a fortune estimated at $400 million. Ferdinand Marcos and his wife Imelda proved similarly useful in the Philippines. She insisted her shopping trips around the world were a duty she was obliged to fulfil, to be 'some kind of light, a star to give guidelines to the poor'.

The most egregious example of the client head of state and member of the super-rich was Congo's Mobutu Sese Seko. He seized power in a coup in 1965, then, thanks to support from Washington and Western Europe, used his position to turn himself into one of the twentieth century's most ostentatiously wealthy figures. He was, as a French government minister called him, the 'walking bank vault with a leopard-skin cap'. He consolidated his control by allowing his friends to steal from state organisations and executing rivals in front of large audiences. The United States turned a blind eye to his state-sponsored violence, intimidation and theft (as did the French and the Belgians). In return for commodities contracts with Western companies and for helping to contain communism across the continent, Mobutu enjoyed access to US presidents from Eisenhower to George Bush Senior. His American sponsors dropped him late in the day, only when pro-democracy movements brought down Soviet rule.

Mobutu's vast property portfolio was legendary: from the French Riviera to his favourite palace, Gbadolite, his 'Versailles of the Jungle', a thousand kilometres from the capital Kinshasa. He convinced himself, and sought to convince his people, that his self-enrichment was a patriotic duty. The wealth and prestige of the chief, he argued, were the best barometers by which the fortune of a developing country could be measured.

This chapter is more than a study of excess. It highlights the links between wealth sequestration, criminality and larger geostrategic considerations. It is where personal self-enrichment and *realpolitik* reach their apotheoses.

As he sipped his favourite pink Laurent Perrier champagne of a late afternoon, President Mobutu could contemplate life's good fortune. Not many world leaders, illegitimate offspring of a chambermaid and a cook, have had the money and the gall to build themselves a marble palace deep in the jungle, replete with a runway large enough for Concorde to fly his wives and mistresses to their shopping trips in New York and Paris.

Few have embezzled and emasculated their country as completely as this one man – Mobutu Sese Seko Kuku Ngbendu Wa Za Banga; or, to give him his proper title and pay him due homage, 'the all-powerful warrior who goes from conquest to conquest, leaving fire in his wake'. He did it because he could. He took over a country teetering on the brink of anarchy soon after it had freed itself from colonial rule. He tortured and publicly executed his opponents. He enriched enough people to provide him with a buffer. And, as a reliable bulwark against insurgent communism across Africa, he enjoyed the essential patronage of the United States and much of the world almost until his dying days.

The Congo into which Joseph Désiré Mobutu was born in 1930 was a classic commodity-rich trading outpost – a vast land bigger than France, Germany, Italy, Spain and Britain combined. During the Scramble for Africa in the late nineteenth century, the regime of King Leopold II of Belgium was riven by corruption and brutality (as depicted in Joseph Conrad's 1902 novel *Heart of Darkness*). Millions died as a result of terrible working conditions, on top of the millions of lives lost in the Portuguese slave trade. The vast majority of the survivors were desperately poor, although the Belgians produced a small layer of 'native' society in their own image. This university-educated middle class became known as the *évolués*.

A bright but troublesome teenager, Mobutu was sent to work in the Force Publique, Belgium's paramilitary colonial police force, entirely commanded by a white officer class. This was not a place where a native, no matter how talented, could usually find career advancement. As a sergeant, he turned his hand to administrative tasks, becoming first a typist then a reporter entrusted with writing pro-Belgian puff pieces for army publications. He was earmarked for promotion, but only to a certain level, as the top jobs were out of bounds for Africans.[1] In 1956 Mobutu left the army to become a full-time journalist. It was at this time that he came across several of the young Congolese intellectuals who were agitating against colonial rule. One of those was Patrice Lumumba, a travelling beer salesman and political firebrand. In and out of jail, Lumumba helped found the Mouvement National Congolais (MNC), one of dozens of political parties that were springing up in this heady and fragile moment. Mobutu invited his new friend to lunch at his home with his wife. When news of another demonstration reached them, they jumped on to Mobutu's motorbike and rode together in the muggy afternoon air, talking loudly over the sputtering of the exhaust, intoxicated by the excitement of political change. Two years later, one of them would orchestrate the murder of the other.[2]

But that was in the future. In January 1960, Mobutu was sent to Brussels on a fellowship, a considerable achievement at a time when only sixteen black Congolese citizens had graduated from university. A round-table conference was taking place there between the colonial government and opposition groups, as Belgium began the process of navigating a very gradual retreat from empire. Mobutu inveigled himself into the diplomatic scene, coming to the attention of both sides. Lumumba, who had been in custody and facing trial for stoking more anti-government protests, was released just in time for the start of the talks. He asked Mobutu to run the ramshackle Brussels office of the MNC. What he didn't know was that his ambitious friend, and now aide, was already acting as an informer for the Belgians.[3] US officials, meanwhile, had noted his intelligence and 'great potential'.[4]

The talks resulted in a setback for the Belgians. Realising that neither the US nor the other colonial powers would help them hold on to the Congo, they agreed to bring forward the date of independence – to the summer of that year. Lumumba and Mobutu returned home as more riots were gathering pace. In the May elections nationalists swept the polls, with the MNC emerging as the largest party. As Lumumba prepared to assume the role of Prime Minister, under the moderate President Joseph Kasavubu, he appointed his loyal friend Mobutu as Army Chief of Staff.

The independence ceremony on 30 June was to be a carefully stage-managed affair. King Baudouin would represent the departing power, while Kasavubu would speak for the new nation. The tone would be a blend of paternalism from Baudouin and quiet respect from Kasavubu, and the Belgian King would depart the scene in a dignified manner, safe in the knowledge that his country's economic and military power still held sway in the nominally independent new state. Nobody counted on Lumumba, who had been excluded from the official bill, grabbing the microphone. He proceeded to give an extraordinary speech documenting the horrors of slavery and colonialism while Baudouin squirmed in his seat: 'Who will forget the rifle fire from which our brothers perished, or the jails into which were brutally thrown those who did not want to submit to a regime of injustice, oppression, and exploitation which were the means the colonists employed to dominate us?'[5]

The Belgians had assumed a slow withdrawal. Lumumba had other ideas. Days after independence, the Force Publique, still led by Belgian officers, mutinied after Lumumba told the soldiers of the radical changes he was planning. Bill Close, an American doctor to the Mobutu family, witnessed the moment that established Mobutu's reputation for fearlessness. Having driven to a mutinous military camp, Mobutu confronted the men:

> Standing at attention with his shoulders back and his fists clenched, he commanded: 'drop your weapons'. A low murmur came from the men. No one moved. Their weapons were levelled at the Colonel. I held my breath. Two men in the front row dropped the butts of their rifles, lowered the barrels, and the guns clattered to the ground. In seconds, the crashing of weapons echoed in the camp. The mutiny was over.[6]

This year of 1960 witnessed a stampede towards decolonisation. Some seventeen African countries gained independence, all struggling to establish a smooth transition. Nowhere was the process more chaotic than in the Congo. The country was quickly falling apart. The 'Congo crisis' dominated international news. Eleven days after the independence ceremony, the mineral–rich south–east province of Katanga declared itself a separate state, under the leadership of Moïse Tshombe. This move was backed clandestinely by the Belgians, the Americans and multinational mining companies, who were alarmed by Lumumba's plans to seize their profits. President Eisenhower's administration had already given up on Lumumba, describing him as 'Castro or worse'. Preparations were made to assassinate him for his supposed communist leanings.[7] It is possible that Eisenhower signed off on the plans, but the doctrine of plausible denial ensured that nothing was written down.[8] The contrast between this and the words of praise heaped on Mobutu later could not have been greater.

Rebuffed by the Americans, Lumumba flirted with the Kremlin for support, as the Cold War logic of the time dictated. This angered the

Americans further. It also alarmed Mobutu, who opposed Lumumba's relationship with Moscow from a nationalist point of view, seeing it as evidence of a second wave of colonialism – even though he judged his own close relationship with the CIA to be nothing of the sort.[9] In August 1960, Lumumba accepted an offer of Soviet help to bring the secessionist provinces to heel. This proved the last straw for President Kasavubu, the United States and Mobutu. A week after Lumumba's government was dissolved, Mobutu's troops arrested him. It was a coup in all but name, but Mobutu stopped short of a full military takeover. Kasavubu was to be given a second chance to salvage a civilian government. Mobutu and his paymasters were playing a waiting game. He thought it best to let the situation spiral into chaos before presenting himself and the army as saviours of the nation.

Placed under house arrest, Lumumba was removed from political life. In November, he attempted to escape and reach his supporters in the east of the country. He was captured by Mobutu's troops, who flew him to Katanga and turned him over to Tshombe. Lumumba was tortured and then killed by Tshombe's troops, with the full knowledge of Mobutu and in the presence of Belgian officers. His death was kept quiet for as long as possible. A decision was taken to dig up his body. Rumour had it that one of his hands was still sticking out of the ground, so the Belgian deputy chief of the local police force sawed his body into pieces and dissolved it in sulphuric acid. This gave rise to the apocryphal story that Mobutu scattered parts of Lumumba's body across the Congo from an aircraft, in order to stop his spirit reassembling. When news of his death finally became public, protests took place in dozens of world capitals. Lumumba became an instant hero of the anti-colonial movement, with the Soviets naming one of Moscow's universities after him.

The United Nations had nineteen thousand troops deployed in the country, but could not assert any control. They found themselves caught between the interests of Lumumba, Tshombe, Mobutu and the Americans and the Belgians. Initially the UN was keen to give Mobutu the benefit of the doubt. By now he had developed a reputation as a solid, moderate potential leader with which the West could do business (in both meanings of the term). The UN's Special Representative to the

Congo, Rajeshwar Dayal, described him as 'a rather diffident but patriotic man who felt powerless in the face of events that he could neither fully understand nor influence'.[10] It was suspected in chancelleries around the world that Mobutu was on the CIA payroll before he took over as President, although such thoughts were confined to discreet conversation. Dayal later recalled how operatives would bring Mobutu 'bulging briefcases containing thick brown paper packets which they obligingly deposited on his table. We could not tell what they contained, but could not help but guess.'[11]

Some of the best details of American policy during this period were revealed through State Department cables made available under Freedom of Information legislation in the early 1980s and published in a book called *The Congo Cables*. They showed the extent of American complicity and a willingness to turn a blind eye to Mobutu's human rights abuses and corruption as he established his regime as a bulwark against communism.

Mobutu's access to American presidents was unmatched by any other leader on the continent (with the exception of those who ruled apartheid South Africa). In May 1963, he took the first of many trips to the White House. During the customary photo op, President Kennedy fawned: 'General, if it hadn't been for you, the whole thing would have collapsed and the Communists would have taken over.'[12] Mobutu replied, with all the self-deprecation he could muster: 'I do what I am able to do.'[13] According to one cable, Mobutu said after a tour of US military installations that he was eager to send over a number of Congolese students for training. He also wanted to arrange six weeks of parachute training for himself and ten officers at Fort Benning. Kennedy said he would be 'delighted'.

Kennedy gave Mobutu a C-45 US military aircraft, although it would look quaint next to the chartered Concorde jets he would later use.[14] Presidents – Republican and Democrat – came and went, but the approach stayed the same. Richard Nixon praised his economic stewardship: 'You are a young man from a young nation,' he proclaimed. 'There is much we can learn from you.'[15] Under Jimmy Carter, Mobutu received nearly half of all US funding to Africa. When Ronald Reagan welcomed him to the White House a few years later, he described him as 'a voice of good sense and goodwill'. At each step of the way they were fully briefed on the extent of corruption and self-enrichment taking place in the Congo. Set against that were the higher priorities of anti-communist assistance and preferential treatment for Western companies in commodity exploitation.

One of the most important witnesses to the events was Larry Devlin, CIA station chief from 1960 to 1967, and self-styled mentor to the dictator. Early on he helped to establish the narrative of Mobutu the patriot: 'He was a courageous man and a strong but realistic nationalist when I dealt with him in the 1960s.'[16] Devlin and other Americans would continue to insist, long after Mobutu had left the stage, that they had no other choice but to support him. This, they argued, was a real war in the Congo; and if the Soviets had won, that would have changed the face of the African continent and the rest of the world. Public plaudits and support for leaders around the world similar to Mobutu were standard practice. The Americans sought to identify useful friends wherever they could, and irrespective of their commitment to human rights, democracy or financial probity. The Somoza dynasty, which ruled Nicaragua for forty years, was guaranteed a warm welcome at the White House. The first Somoza was so close to the Americans he was known at home as 'El Yanki'. His son, 'Tachito', attended Kennedy's inauguration, where he offered to help overthrow Fidel Castro.[17]

In 1965 any lingering hopes that the Congo might emerge from the turbulence with some form of constitutional or democratic government disappeared. In the parliamentary elections President Kasavubu outpolled Prime Minister Tshombe; the president attempted to have the prime minister removed. The impasse provided Mobutu with the opportunity he had been waiting for. The army moved in, replacing all the leading figures and imposing Mobutu as President. One of the first military takeovers in Africa, the coup could not have succeeded without American-financed mercenaries and other covert assistance being deployed to suppress rebellions in the regions. Mobutu immediately consolidated his power, ruling by decree and using a referendum that 'approved' a new constitution by 98 per cent. He was initially popular, playing on public frustrations with politicians, and adopting patriotic colours and symbols. He was declared 'the embodiment of the nation' and his decisions were placed 'outside the scope of the various articles of the Constitution that limit, to a certain degree, the powers of the President'. His aim, he told his people in one of his first addresses, was to 'save the nation, to put an end to chaos and anarchy'.[18] A master of populist touches and an adept orator, Mobutu would make unannounced visits to schools and hospitals, regularly going to the renovated Hospital Mama Yemo (which he had named after his mother). Mobutu 'persuaded' friendly businessmen to pay for television sets in all the wards, letting it be known that he would be pleased by their philanthropy.[19]

He clamped down on all forms of opposition. In one march, fifty students were shot dead, their bodies never to be returned to their families. Opposition leaders were disappeared into military camps and not seen again.[20] As the dictatorship indulged in ever greater brutality, Mobutu's style of governing brought no condemnation from the West. Faced with a series of uprisings, particularly in the east of the country, he used a mixture of punishment and reward that would serve him well for the next twenty-five years. Some rebels were given amnesties; others were killed. The choice of whom to woo and whom to punish was often arbitrary. Four cabinet ministers were publicly hanged. Pierre Mulele, an avowed Maoist who had led a rebellion in one province, had his eyes torn out and his genitals ripped off.[21]

Washington provided its puppet with information and logistics to combat any threats to his rule. In 1966, US intelligence tipped him off about a planned uprising by supporters of Tshombe. The 'Pentecost Plotters', as they became known, were found guilty after ten minutes in a military court and hanged.[22] The execution was botched and the victims took twenty minutes to die, watched by a large, silent crowd. Mobutu explained the reasoning behind the hangings to a Belgian journalist: 'The respect due a chief is something sacred and it was necessary to hit with an example. We were so used to secessions and rebellions in this country. It was necessary to cut all that short so that people could not start again. When a chief decides, he decides. That is that.'[23]

Yet the brutality was accompanied by stability and economic progress, of sorts. The first decade of Mobutu's thirty-two-year reign was a time of some hope. People had money in their pockets; television arrived; the bars stayed open late; hydroelectric power stations were built. By the end of 1967, the CIA reported: '[The Congo's] future looks brighter than at any time since independence.'[24] Some, however, were privately nervous. By the time Devlin returned to the country in 1974, after an assignment in Indo-China, he thought Mobutu was 'already round the bend'. He added: 'All I could think of were the stories I'd read about the court of Henry VIII or Louis XIV.'[25] Such misgivings did not stop the funnelling of money to Mobutu in the name of Cold War logic. He received, personally, up to $25 million from the CIA. By the 1990s, total US aid to his regime had reached $2 billion, much of it ending up in Mobutu's pocket.[26] The IMF and Western banks piled in with more.[27]

Mobutu had support from the Western powers; he had supreme control of his own country; he could steal its resources whenever he wanted. He needed an ideology and some political underpinning. In 1967 he created the Popular Movement for the Revolution (Mouvement Populaire de la Révolution – MPR). It promoted the doctrine of 'Mobutuism' – with no purpose beyond veneration of the leader, with no content beyond slogans such as 'practical revolution' and 'neither left, nor right, nor centre'.[28] The MPR was the only party in the Congo. Membership was obligatory. Five years after its founding, Mobutu's information minister announced: 'Today the fusion is complete: the MPR is the state.'[29] Perhaps he was aware of the quote attributed to Louis XIV: '*L'état, c'est moi.*' Perhaps he wasn't. In 1971, Mobutu embarked on a project he called 'authenticity', creating a new form of nationalism that drew from Congolese and other African traditions. The country was renamed the Republic of Zaire. The capital, Leopoldville, was renamed Kinshasa. Western names were rejected in favour of traditional ones; Zairians were required to call each other 'citizen'. Most foreign music was banned. Men had to wear abacosts (shorthand for '*à bas le costume*' or 'down with the suit'). These simple, Mao-style two-piece suits became the regime's haute couture. Mobutu himself dressed in his trademark leopard-skin cap and held an ebony walking stick, carved with the figure of an eagle on the top.

The economic corollary of authenticity was 'Zairianisation', launched two years later, which ordered that foreign-owned businesses be turned over to Zairian 'citizens' – for that read Mobutu's clique.

From one day to the next, Portuguese restaurant owners, Greek shop-keepers, Pakistani TV repairmen or Belgian coffee growers saw the work of a lifetime disappear. A theatre of the absurd was created. Generals were allowed to run fisheries, and diplomats soft-drink factories. Political cronies were given control of the timber industry.[30]

Initially, as few as three hundred close supporters of the regime directly benefited. They created a new caste, dubbed the *Grosses Légumes*. Overnight, Zaire became Africa's leading importer of luxury goods such as Mercedes cars and Rolex watches. Straddling the ever-blurring line between state and business, the Fat Vegetables made money in any way they could. Once ensconced in a government ministry or running a state-controlled firm, they would vote themselves pay increases and allowances. One official gave himself a bonus of $1000 a day every time he had to work away from the office; staying at home netted him millions.[31] In government ministries and the military, millions of dollars were lost to phantom civil servants who didn't exist, while the real ones often didn't get paid.[32]

Some of the absurdities fell into the category of human greed and corruption. At other times they were the result of desperate economic mismanagement. Zairian diplomats abroad often siphoned off money; other times they were trying simply to keep their missions going. Cleophas Kamitatu, an ambassador to Japan, sold off the embassy and his residence. He insisted later he had no choice, as he was not receiving any funds from central government. In Washington, the ambassador sold the embassy's cleaning equipment for the same reason.[33]

Mobutu, naturally, made sure he was the largest beneficiary of Zairianisation. But as he was fashioning an image for himself as the nation's paternalistic chief, he had to be seen to show concern about the probity of public officials. He took to denouncing corruption in rallies in a manner similar to the increasingly wealthy leaders of the Chinese Communist Party of today (see Chapter 12). In one speech to his ruling party, he proclaimed: 'Everything is for sale and everything can be bought in this country. And in this trade, the slightest access to power constitutes a veritable instrument of exchange.'[34] Mobutu was partly criticising the system, but a tone of pride can be detected in the comment too; he was, after all, responsible for it.

Mobutu's personal share of the Zairianisation smash-and-grab turned him, as a private individual, into the country's third-largest employer, with an agricultural business empire called Cultures et Élevages du Zaïre (CELZA) employing 25,000 people on 22 plantations.[35] CELZA produced 26 per cent of the nation's rubber, 23 per cent of its cocoa, and 13 per cent of its palm oil – all important export items – as well as cattle, tea and coffee. Overnight Mobutu had transformed himself into a wealthy farmer.[36] For as long as prices for Zaire's huge stocks of copper, cobalt, diamonds and zinc remained high, the President and his friends assumed all would be fine. The West had its client state. Mobutu had his cronies who were creaming off cash from that state. Other African leaders sought to emulate him.

It did not take long for the economy to unravel. The businesses taken over by the *Grosses Légumes* began to nosedive – either their Western parent companies took revenge by cutting off supplies, or the new local owners, who had no intention of running them as proper businesses, embarked on ostentatious asset-stripping. Shortages became chronic. One of the *Légumes*, Mobutu's uncle Litho, took control of the capital's most upmarket grocery store. Within weeks the stock on its shelves had been reduced to coarse soap and canned chicken. Everything else had been snatched.[37] Resentment grew as working conditions in the Zairianised businesses fell apart. One shop manager working for a *Légume* described the situation: 'Their firms have been given to you, our Zairian brothers, with the idea that we will be well treated. A Zairian treats his Zairian brother completely like a slave.'[38] Uncle Litho was later arrested at the Swiss border driving a Rolls-Royce stuffed with gold and foreign currency. Mobutu raised bail, securing his release.

A brief digression is in order here, to show that Mobutu was merely one of a group of Cold War kleptocrats who shared common characteristics. Ferdinand Marcos of the Philippines engaged in a similar programme of self-enrichment after his declaration of martial law in 1972. Companies were turned over wholesale to members of his clique. A college fraternity pal took a monopoly of the sugar industry, alongside joint control of the media alongside the President's brother-in-law. The car, shipping and airline industries were parcelled off to other friends and golf buddies.[39]

The global prize for ostentation could go to Imelda Marcos, First Lady and first grafter. She sought to emulate royalty, often sporting a diamond tiara and purple sash, to set off her $300,000 engagement ring and a fourteen-carat diamond gifted to her by Ferdinand as a silver-wedding present. She is best remembered for her wardrobe: her legendary 3000-plus pairs of shoes (the exact number remains uncertain), 15 mink coats, 1000 handbags (including five shelves of Guccis), 68 pairs of gloves and 105 racks of assorted designer clothes, most of which still bore their labels.[40] Then there was the small matter of a 175-piece art collection including paintings by Botticelli and Canaletto, as well as a fake Michelangelo. Filipinos had a fairly good inkling about her shopaholic tendencies, but the scale of her purchases came to full light only when the regime was overthrown in 1986. When her jewels were valued, one emerald brooch was found to be worth $750,000; a set of jewellery, including a bracelet and earrings, was valued at $1.5 million – a modern-day equivalent of Marie-Antoinette's necklace, which famously provoked the ire of French society on the eve of the 1789 revolution.[41] Department stores in fashion capitals around the world would open especially for Imelda and her entourage, staying open until whenever she was finished. The final two years of their rule saw the Marcos family spend an estimated $68 million, of which upwards of $11 million went on clothes and various household accoutrements.[42] All of this took place in a country where one-third of the population was earning a dollar a day.[43]

Just down the road was President Suharto, the Indonesian dictator who had come to power in 1965 with the active support of the United States. His wife, Ibu Tien, secured a tidy profit from the army's smuggling of luxury cars for the elite. She also used the army's muscle to cajole the business community into funding her pet project – Taman Mini Indonesia Indah, a theme park based on Disneyland.[44]

Across the world, leaders and their friends were indulging themselves in a similar manner. In Latin America, the effect of thirty-plus years of Somozas, Noriegas, Stroessners and Pinochets enriching themselves and their cliques on the general populations was devastating. The Gini

coefficient of inequality for the region soared from 0.48 in the 1970s to
0.52 in the 1990s.[45]

In 1974, with an economic crisis looming, Mobutu left Zaire for visits
to China and North Korea. The Americans were worried, but not
unduly so. Impressed by the 'revolutionary discipline' he witnessed on
his trip, Mobutu returned determined to bring order. He identified ten
'scourges' ravaging the country, assigning a cure to each. The remedy
for 'disrespect for authority' was 'fidelity to Mobutu'; in order to
combat the 'enrichment of a few individuals' he proposed to reinforce
import controls. To deal with 'social problems', the following decree
was issued: 'Abolition of the Ministry of Social Affairs; assignment of
all social functions to Mrs Mobutu.'[46]

Discipline was not the only thing that had impressed Mobutu about
revolutionary China. He invited the Chinese to build a *maison de la cul-*
ture in Kinshasa to replicate the Cultural Palace in Beijing; and he
ordered all bars closed until evening and created a committee to com-
pose a national, revolutionary and authentic ballet.[47] He then announced
a policy of 'radicalisation'. Businesses were to be nationalised after all.
The *Grosses Légumes* had to turn over their enterprises to the state and,
like the intellectuals in Mao's China, 'devote themselves to agricultural
activities'.[48] However, Mobutu quickly realised the dangers of alienat-
ing an elite that had profited from his rule. By depriving them of their
revenue streams, he risked losing their support. He quietly backtracked:
radicalisation was reduced to targeting foreign-owned businesses, or, as
Mobutu derided them, 'the new 300 Zairian families'.[49]

While he might have admired the grandiloquent and fiery gestures
of Mao, Mobutu knew where his geostrategic interests lay. From the
start of his rule, he allowed his huge country, which borders nine
African nations, to be used as a staging post for supporting Western-
backed anti-communist guerrilla movements. It was good diplomacy
and good business. He stashed away more than $1 million, earmarked
for Jonas Savimbi's UNITA movement in Angola's civil war, which was
funnelled through Zaire by the Americans. Up to five flights left
Kinshasa for Angola each week, overseen by the CIA and with the full
knowledge of Mobutu, who was paid for his trouble.[50] In return,

Mobutu was able to call on Western help whenever he needed to put down a rebellion in a restive province.

By the end of the 1970s, real wages had fallen to one-tenth of their level at independence. Schools, hospitals and other public services operated on a system of bribery. The breakdown of healthcare led to the re-emergence of diseases like measles and tuberculosis and even an outbreak of plague.[51] In 1976 Archbishop Eugène Kabanga of Lumumbashi launched a stinging attack on what the system meant for ordinary people:

> The thirst for money thus transforms men into assassins. Why is it that our courts of justice can only be obtained by fat bribes to the judge? Why are prisoners forgotten in jail? Why, at the opening of school, must parents go into debt to bribe the school principal? All means are good to obtain money, or humiliate the human being.[52]

So desperate were conditions that, even under a dictatorship as harsh as Mobutu's, protests and strikes began to take place again. The most dramatic dispute occurred at Zaire's national airline, where workers threatened to blow up jet aircraft if their paltry end-of-year bonuses were taken away to pay the state's debts. They won, but that was a very rare example.[53]

Mobutu's most effective way of keeping power was to ensure that nobody else was in a position to challenge him. He kept a tight inner circle around himself. Beyond this was a wider group, the 'reigning fraternity,' mostly drawn from the President's home province of Équateur. Entry into this club was denoted by the grant of a presidential gift, such as a Mercedes or a luxurious home. The new member would replicate this system with his own cronies, one rung below.[54] This was corruption, by trickle-down. It was a question of how long you could keep your hand in the till. Everything was sanctioned from the top, quite openly. Mobutu exhorted his supporters in a television interview: 'Go ahead and steal, so long as you don't take too much.'[55] Yet, at the same time, and seemingly unperturbed by the contradiction, he would declare the country could tolerate 'neither wealthy individuals who are too rich nor paupers who are too poor'.[56] He publicly acknowledged that the state had become 'one vast marketplace', while exempting himself from this description.[57]

Between 1965 and 1990, Zaire saw no fewer than fifty-one governments, an average of two per year. Ministers were allowed two cars – they usually opted for a Mercedes and a Jeep. Their deputies were entitled to one. After their quick tenure was over, their successors would find that the cars, along with the office furniture, had been taken, so the gifts had to be made all over again. The same applied to the military. In one year, Mobutu purged half of his generals.[58] Anyone promoted to a senior position knew they had little time to lose in lining their pockets.[59] Mobutu would spread rumours about ministers and businessmen to their peers, creating a climate in which everyone suspected everyone else. To satisfy his lust and to project his role as supreme leader, he would also pick and choose mistresses among the wives of his many political associates. A former cabinet minister acknowledged the deal: 'You get money or a Mercedes–Benz, and he takes your wife, and you work for him.'

Mobutu would punish and reward the same people. One example was Nguz Karl i-Bond, a vociferous opponent of the regime in the 1980s who was arrested and tortured. He then lived as a political exile, testifying about the savagery of the regime to a US congressional committee. He described how private chartered jets flew to Europe to sell cobalt and diamonds, the proceeds from which went straight into Mobutu's bank accounts.[60] He claimed that top European diplomats and politicians were bought off and that the wife of the French President wore diamonds that were a gift from Mobutu.[61] Within a few years, however, he had returned to Zaire and was made Prime Minister for a time, a career move sweetened with a payment of $10 million.[62]

While keeping the political class on its toes through a mixture of terror and expectation, Mobutu felt he needed something more solid to underpin his regime – a fully fledged public relations strategy, a cult of personality. That, he concluded, was the least a rich man like himself was entitled to. First of all, he made sure that the story of his birth and upbringing was turned into official folklore. This romanticised his relationship with his hometown of Lisala and the Congo River. The most famous story that was spun was the tale of the leopard. As a boy, Joseph was walking with his grandfather when a leopard sprang out of the undergrowth. Mobutu shrank back, and his grandfather castigated him for showing fear. Ashamed, the boy took a spear and killed the animal.[63] Mobutu relayed this tale to show how he had conquered fear early in life, and he took on the mantle of the leopard, which became a talisman for him, explaining the hats that became synonymous with him.

Mobutu was referred to as 'The Guide', 'The Father of the Nation', or, taking after Mao, 'The Helmsman'. The cult of personality contained a religious component. He was 'The Prophet' or 'Our Clairvoyant Leader'.[64] Every morning schoolchildren sang: 'One country, one father, one ruler: Mobutu, Mobutu, Mobutu!'[65] His face was omnipresent on television (including during weather forecasts) and billboards. Pilgrimages were set up at important locations from his early life.[66] Around the world, similar dictator-kleptocrats adopted a similar approach to self-veneration. In the Philippines, youth groups were given training programmes describing Ferdinand and Imelda Marcos as 'Father and Mother of the Nation'. Marcos had a fifty-foot monument of his own head erected gazing, Mount Rushmore-like, out onto a major park in Manila.[67]

The longer he ruled, the more worried Mobutu became about his legacy. He reached into history and tradition to glorify his rule. He may genuinely have thought that his actions expressed 'the will of the people' – a people 'freed' from colonialism. On her deathbed in 1971, Mobutu's mother warned him again and again: 'you must love your people'. Why, Mobutu asked, did she keep on repeating her plea?[68] He put it like this:

In our African tradition, there are never two chiefs. Can anyone tell me he has ever known a village with two chiefs? It belongs to the chief to live with his own decision, to evaluate it, and to accept its consequences. It is on this sole condition – because he will have weighed in advance the consequences and accepted alone all the risks of his option – that his decision will be honest, and therefore good for the people and, finally, authentically democratic.[69]

In the 1970s and 80s, Mobutu's control was so complete that he could, and did, take long trips abroad without fear of being toppled. While he was away, the youth wing of the MPR and its paramilitary organisation terrorised the streets.[70] Along with the riot police, they used torture as a method of choice against suspected dissidents. This included whipping with barbed wire and beating the soles of victims' feet with sticks.[71] Mobutu galvanised his young hoodlums to crush dissent, declaring during one rally in 1988: 'You are not going to wait for the gendarmes. You are not going to wait for the soldiers. You have shoes; kick them. I'll say it again; kick them. You have hands; hit them!'[72]

The MPR regime was classically totalitarian, taking over all aspects of Zairian life and removing the boundaries between government, politics and business. The party created a pyramid of thieving, down to village level. The civil service payroll numbered 600,000, eight times as many workers as the World Bank judged was necessary to keep the government going. By the mid-1980s, annual income had shrunk to less than $120 – little more than the price of a pair of good shoes in a Kinshasa designer store.[73] Zairianisation had blurred the lines between the public and private sectors and between business and politics. One company, Sozacom, was part of a network of organisations used by Mobutu to siphon off profits to his various bank accounts.[74] The state copper company, Gecamines, lost at least $240 million every year to corruption, money logged under the heading 'Exceptional Recovery Deficit'. This theft continued long after copper prices slumped in 1974, and annual unaccounted deficits of hundreds of millions of dollars in the company's accounts became the norm.

In the 1970s, 20 per cent of state revenue went directly to the President's office. By the 1980s, with nothing to stop him taking what he wanted, Mobutu's fortune in Swiss bank accounts topped $5 billion. He was, one should note, merely following in the footsteps of King Leopold II, who amassed a fortune of his own through graft and forced labour.

Larry Devlin, Mobutu's CIA minder, casts doubt on the extent of Mobutu's overall personal wealth: 'Mobutu was alleged to have had a personal fortune of five billion dollars. If true, I have often thought he must have received poor investment advice, because people writing about him used that unchanging figure for more than twenty years,' Devlin writes.

In complaining to me of allegations that his fortune amounted to five billion dollars, he once commented that he was probably worth not more than fifty million dollars. When he travelled in the interior, one of his aides usually carried a briefcase filled with bank notes for distribution to the village chiefs he encountered on his travels. The chiefs would expect their leader to do something for the village – a new roof for the local school, a new well, or some other good work – and, naturally, Mobutu expected the chief to insure [sic] that the village remained in lock-step with his government.[75]

The amount Mobutu actually stole will never be known. What is incontrovertible is that all institutions, not least the central bank, were treated as his wallet: in 1977 alone he withdrew $71 million for his own use. Bank accounts were set up around the world for the President's personal purposes. Powerful individuals and companies were 'encouraged' to turn over profits to him with no questions asked. Gecamines was ordered to deposit all of its $1.2 billion export revenue into a presidential account in 1978.[76] Export duties were a favourite source of income; foreign aid was a source of top-up revenue.

Mobutu's friends abroad were busy copying him. Ferdinand Marcos opened his first Swiss bank account in 1967. After the declaration of martial law in his country in 1972, he embarked on a similar spending spree. He and Imelda, using the names William Saunders and Jane Ryan, had $1 million in Swiss accounts by 1968, at a time when his official salary was barely $2000.[77] Ferdinand and Imelda set up a series of companies and foundations through which to launder their money, with almost comic transparency. In a letter to one, the Sandy Foundation, Marcos wrote: 'In the event we would wish to make withdrawals, we will send you a cable with the words "Happy Birthday" authenticating our message with the agreed-upon code.'[78] By the time of his overthrow in 1986, they had twenty-five Swiss and French bank accounts, holding hundreds of millions of dollars. In Indonesia, Suharto used a similar network of foundations, companies and accounts to store and move his fortune, which totalled half a billion dollars.[79]

Across his vast country Mobutu built, or simply took for himself, a dozen palaces in different provinces in case he was in the area and needed to stay. As he rarely travelled to some parts of Zaire, some of them were hardly used.[80] These countryside palaces were among Mobutu's most extravagant residences, including a $5.2-million villa near the estate that had belonged to King Leopold. His pride and joy was Gbadolite. In the late 1980s, Mobutu decided he needed a new palace to project his majesty, something to rival Versailles. He could not have chosen a more remote location, in one of the most inhospitable corners of the jungle. A large swathe was cleared to build his own Xanadu, with its giant swimming pool, collection of rare animals and ornate fountains and, of course, an international airport just for him. It sat somewhat oddly against the wattle huts of the old village nearby, which were untouched by any sort of government investment. Mobutu appeared to believe that the joy locals would feel at the sight of his marbled extravaganza would act as a spur. 'Let them build better houses when they want to. Maybe the palace will inspire them,' remarked one loyal official.[81]

The palace cost the tidy sum of $100 million to build and $15 million each year to keep it in a state of perpetual readiness for the great man to visit, even though initially he spent just a few days a year there. One visiting Western journalist described Mobutu's taste:

> The room was awash with Louis XVI furnishings, Gobelins tapestries, paintings by Renoir and Monet and, at the far end, a magnificent mahogany bar stocked with fine cognacs, calvados and assorted spirits. Each bottle was about the size of a Balthazar of champagne. Zaire is renowned for its exceptional sculpture, but nothing in the place resembled anything even remotely African. I've seen my share of dictators' digs but this one was over the top. There was something very twisted about Mobutu's taste. Nothing he owned even hinted at his African heritage. For all his bluster about the continent's rich history, having thrown off forever the yoke of colonialism, Mobutu made his hometown haven into a simple reflection of his greed. He was the Gordon Gekko of Africa and his bizarre proclivities confirmed it.[82]

In 1992, Gbadolite was used as the venue for the wedding of Mobutu's daughter Yaki to the Belgian businessman Pierre Janssen. The 2500 guests watched the bride in her $70,000 wedding dress before devouring 1000 bottles of wine and a four-metre-long wedding cake, which had been made in France and flown in especially at the cost of thousands of dollars.

The following year, a reporter from *Time* magazine visited Mobutu there, describing how men would arrive with designer suitcases bulging with $100 bills. Then:

> Like an amiable monarch amid courtiers, Mobutu bows gracefully to kiss a woman's hand and banters politely with a local Jesuit priest before herding everyone across an immense terrace toward a buffet laden with lobster and thick steaks. In the 100 degrees heat, a wave of satisfaction seems to envelop the presidential party, a sense that all is still well in this remote hinterland far from the chaos afflicting the rest of the country. Exquisite flower gardens and vast plantations of pineapple imbue Gbadolite with an air of bucolic tranquility.[83]*

---

* The Gbadolite complex was only one of many vanity projects. Mobutu's Kinshasa mansion contained a private zoo in its grounds, setting a trend for future dictators to follow. Ramzan Kadyrov, the present-day leader of Chechnya, has filled his personal zoo with panthers, leopards and bears. A short walk away in his heavily fortified compound, he has a lake where he can practise jet-skiing as well as his own race-course.

The construction of personal follies appears part of the terms and conditions of loyal allies of the Kremlin. After the February 2014 uprising in Ukraine, the extent of the opulence of the deposed President, Viktor Yanukovych, was discovered. His gaudy assemblage included the ubiquitous pool and private cinema, alongside a collection of icons and vintage cars. His *pièce de résistance* was a replica of the white Steinway piano John Lennon gave Yoko Ono for her birthday in 1971, and at which he was filmed singing 'Imagine'. What Yanukovych thought of the line 'imagine no possessions' is not yet known.

Perhaps the closest successor to Mobutu in terms of imaginative spending was Muammar Gaddafi. When he was toppled in 2011, there were fears for the lives of the nine lions he personally owned in a zoo next to his Bab al-Aiziya complex. When his Michael Jackson-style Neverland lair was ransacked, impoverished Libyans could see the billions he had spent on himself. The most striking part of his estate was a fairground, with a children's roundabout on which adults could sit in teapots and teacups.

In Nsele, north of Kinshasa, Mobutu built a replica Chinese village containing a pavilion and gushing fountains. He decided the capital needed a place where the nation's rich could mingle with the international community. Construction of the Hotel Intercontinental began on his instructions. Guests could conclude a black-market deal with Lebanese diamond traders while enjoying the finest views of the Congo River and tucking into a meal. Foreign pilots, employed as part of the CIA-backed scheme to break the UN arms embargo to Angola, would enjoy a drink while waiting for their latest mission. The hotel's staff kept Mobutu informed about the comings and goings.[84]

The President's property empire was international.[85] Across Belgium, the Mercedes and BMWs of his henchmen became common sights.[86] Luxury residences were purchased in Spain, Venice and Paris. He couldn't bear not to have a place on the French Riviera. So he acquired the Villa del Mare, perched between the village of Roquebrune-Cap-Martin and the scenic peninsula of Cap Ferrat (and a mere twenty minutes' drive from the Villa des Cèdres, which a century earlier had been occupied by Leopold II). The twentieth-century variant of the rapacious ruler ensured that his pink-and-white-marble-colonnaded chateau was kitted out with indoor and outdoor swimming pools, gold-fitted bathrooms and a heliport. When buying the estate for $5.2 million, Mobutu asked, as an afterthought, whether the price was in US dollars or Belgian francs. The fact that one currency was worth thirty-nine times more than the other at the time was of little consequence.[87] One of the most extravagant was the estate at Lausanne in Switzerland. He liked the doctors and would fly there on his private jet whenever he needed a health check.

For all his palaces, Mobutu preferred to spend time on his luxury yachts, cruising the river to which he attached so much importance for the wellbeing of his country. Adorned with expensive, silk-upholstered furniture and carrying selected guests, these vessels would take the President to villages where he would meet and greet the locals. 'His charm,' recalled his doctor Bill Close, 'could disarm an angry man, who might even come out from the interview with a smile on his face.'[88] That he was equally at ease in the company of villagers and world leaders was one of Mobutu's enduring strengths.

Tellingly, Mobutu kept a copy of Machiavelli's *The Prince* by his bed. He had mastered the art of manipulation and ingratiation. He bestrode the world stage with panache, an instantly recognisable figure in his leopard-skin toque. Global dignitaries loved to visit his country. When, in 1974, he presided over the great world-heavyweight boxing match – the 'rumble in the jungle' – between Muhammad Ali and George Foreman, hundreds of millions of people around the world watched. A sense of black African pride was palpable, and Mobutu reaped the benefit. Yet almost none of the global audience had any notion of what was really going on in the country.

Even as Zaire descended into deeper trouble, Mobutu continued to receive foreign aid unabated. Erwin Blumenthal, an IMF banker, tried to rein in the systemic corruption. Mobutu's usual practice when they met was to agree to Blumenthal's demands, send him away, and carry on regardless. He would give his visitors his word as a soldier. He agreed to place his uncle on a banking blacklist; it made no difference. IMF economists discovered gaping holes in Zaire's national finances at a time when the country was supposed to be adhering to its 'structural adjustment' programme of austerity. Kim Jaycox, the IMF's vice-president, met Mobutu on board his favourite yacht, the *Kamanyola*. 'Occasionally,' Jaycox recalled, 'he would threaten to throw me to the crocodiles, in a joking way.'[89] It was not as if warnings were not sounded. In 1984 a CIA official, John Stockwell, noted: 'In the Congo today, 25 per cent of the people are starving, while Joe Mobutu has a personal fortune of about $4.5 billion.' He added, sarcastically: 'That is the result of what the CIA considers a successful covert action.'[90] The World Bank finally stopped lending Mobutu money in 1991, only because he had stopped paying interest on the loans.

Even as late as 1989, Mobutu had been described as 'one of our most valued friends' by President Bush during a visit to the White House.[91] The following year, holding the rotating chair of the UN Security Council, Zaire helped push through the resolution supporting the US-led invasion of Kuwait against Saddam Hussein. Bush publicly expressed his gratitude, but behind the scenes the alliance with the ageing kleptocrat had already become an embarrassment.

As the Cold War came to an end and the geopolitical logic dramatically shifted, the pressure for change became impossible for even Mobutu to resist. One of the most shocking events for him was the execution on Christmas Day 1989 of his friend Nicolae Ceauşescu of Romania, which he watched on television.

In April 1990, six months after the fall of the Berlin Wall, Mobutu announced the creation of a new 'Sovereign National Congress' that would pave the way for multi-party elections. Opposition leaders returned from exile. But the skilled political operator managed to play the dozens of new political parties in the new system off against each other as craftily as he had done with individuals in the old one. Barely two weeks after his declaration, commandos went on the rampage on the campus of the University of Lubumbashi, a provincial stronghold of political activism. Estimates put the number of dead at up to a hundred. Protests against Mobutu's rule were growing on all sides. Underpaid soldiers mutinied. In September 1991 three weeks of marauding by the national army laid waste to several major cities. Hundreds were killed, including the French Ambassador. A few months later, dozens more died when soldiers opened fire on a march demanding higher living standards.[92] The country was on the brink of civil war. Proclaiming himself the saviour, Mobutu suspended his fledgling Congress.

The embarrassment was getting too much for the Americans. The Clinton administration revoked Mobutu's travel visa and imposed sanctions. As his grip on power began to wane, the country descended further into chaos. Inflation was running at more than 16,000 per cent, caused largely by a scam in which senior regime figures would print thousands of notes every day and immediately exchange them for dollars or francs, making a vast profit before the international markets cottoned on. So bad was the run on the local currency, called the Zaire, that a 500,000-Zaire note had to be issued. This gained the nickname 'the prostate', after Mobutu's cancerous organ. In 1993, a private German printing company halted shipments to Kinshasa of thousands of tons of the Zairian currency, claiming it had not been paid for. Most of the population could afford to eat only once a day. Unemployment was estimated at 80 per cent. Access to clean water was disappearing; the communications system had all but ceased to function.[93] In 1996

The Economist summed up the chaos: 'They call it a country. In fact it is just a Zaire-shaped hole in the middle of Africa.'[94]

The system had become a monster that even Mobutu could no longer control. Public services, always chaotic, collapsed completely. Hospitals employed armed guards to stop patients sneaking out during visiting hours without paying their bills. The fees could be settled with TVs, radios or watches if the patients had no money.[95] Fields were overgrown, roads were pot-holed, taxis and buses rusted and barely held together.[96] With the formal economy destroyed, the poor did anything they could to survive. Streets and restaurants were full of people selling clothes, radios, sandals, fake designer perfume, and anything in between. Post Office staff joined the action, stealing international newspapers sent through the post and employing boys to sell them on the streets.[97]

The President's advisers were busy running their own businesses. One took $9 million worth of diamonds to Belgium and sold them, asking for a receipt for only $6 million.[98] Thus Mobutu was cheated out of $3 million in profit. Janssen, his Belgian son-in-law, claimed that when one of Mobutu's own sons was sent to America to buy a fleet of armoured Cadillacs he lost $600,000 in a mugging. He received replacement money from the President, no questions asked.[99] People were becoming less fearful of the Leopard. Or perhaps Mobutu had so much money that he simply did not notice, or chose not to notice, the losses. Sitting on top of a hollowed-out state, Mobutu retreated to Gbadolite.

So detached did he become from real life that he started acting out comparisons to Caligula and other decadent rulers of ancient times. Some stories had it that he, like them, engaged in incest. One member of his entourage related how Mobutu was called in front of his family in their village to account for his behaviour. When accused, he shouted, 'Don't you know that you are talking to a marshal?' An old mama of the family is said to have replied: 'In Kinshasa you are a marshal. Here you are Mobutu; you are a child of the village, our child.' Another family elder piped up: 'Mobutu is damned. There is nothing more we can do.' The Leopard himself remained uncharacteristically silent.[100]

Mobutu relied increasingly on foreign fighters to help him out of his predicament. He was not picky, opting for mercenaries from international private companies or for gangs of armed men from rebel groups based in neighbouring countries. This behaviour, which during the Cold War might have been accepted as part of the proxy conflict, was now seen as dangerous. Among the groups receiving Mobutu's favour were the Angolan UNITA, as well as the genocidal Hutu units of the Rwandan Army that sought refuge after they were toppled from power in 1995.[101]

The Rwandan genocide and the subsequent shift of political power in that country dealt a fatal blow to Mobutu's regime. An alliance of anti-Mobutu rebel groups headed by Laurent Kabila was able to come together finally to topple the dictator. In 1996, while Mobutu was in Europe for prostate surgery, they invaded the country from the east. Initially dismissing Kabila as a 'petty smuggler', Mobutu did not anticipate the speed with which his state would crumble.

Mobutu and Kabila met for talks on a boat off the coast of Zaire on 4 May 1997, brokered by South African President Nelson Mandela. Kabila reportedly refused to look Mobutu in the eyes, fearing he would be cursed if he did so.[102] Although Mobutu remained intransigent, it became clear that even his closest generals and advisers were turning against him. After a seven-month rebellion, his troops were ordered not to put up a fight against Kabila's forces. Mobutu fled the country from his palace in Gbadolite. As a testament to three decades of larceny, not all of his luggage could fit on the Boeing 747 that was waiting to take him away. France, one of his closest allies until it became no longer fashionable, refused him asylum. He landed in Togo, only to be turfed out after a few days. This was a humiliating end for a man who had been fêted across the West as a bulwark against communism.

A few months after finally relinquishing power, Mobutu died of cancer in exile in Morocco, one of the few countries prepared to house him. He did not live to see the subsequent war that engulfed the new Democratic Republic of the Congo and, through disease and combat, claimed several million lives between 1998 and 2003 – a war caused largely by the fractured state Mobutu had left behind.

*

The despot had pledged to die on native soil. He may have been delusional, but he believed all the way through that he was a patriot serving his country well. He certainly shared the view of the US that he was better than the (Soviet-backed) alternative. Any amount of embezzlement, thievery and torture was excusable as long as the nation survived. Mobutu's own view of his rule is encapsulated in a line in a speech from the 1970s: 'the houses continue to belong to their owners even if they were built with stolen money, for by building them they were building up Zaire'.[103] As late as 1994, apparently with a straight face, he told the nation: 'I must complete my task. I cannot leave this type of inheritance to posterity. Completing my task means leaving this country something worthwhile.'[104]

What he left was chaos and empty coffers. One of Kabila's ministers, on the day he took up his job, found only $2000 in the central bank's vaults.[105] Even now, more than half the population lives on less than the World Bank's poverty threshold of $1.25 a day.

It has always been possible for rich rulers to justify their behaviour as being for the benefit of their people or as a necessary evil. Among Cold War populist dictators this tendency was even more prevalent. Ferdinand Marcos said in a TV interview shortly after his overthrow: 'I have committed many sins in my life, but stealing is not one of them.' Eva Perón, the ostentatious First Lady of Argentina, wrote in her will: 'My jewels do not belong to me. The greater part were gifts from my people. I do not want them to fall into the hands of the oligarchy, and therefore, I will that they constitute in the museum of Peronism a permanent value which may only be used in direct benefit of the people.'[106] Perhaps she did not see herself as part of 'the oligarchy', just as Mobutu saw himself as sitting above, and separate from, 'the politicians'. They made a show, when it suited them, of standing against other elite interests in society. Indonesia's Suharto argued that public servants could more or less take what they wanted as long as they were generally acting in the 'public good'.[107] These contradictions allowed kleptocrats like him and Mobutu to make speeches criticising corruption when they were the biggest culprits of all.

When you are the state and the law supports you, psychologically it is perhaps only natural that you assume that the wealth of the nation is yours.

The kleptocrats' money-laundering operations were so mind-boggling that it was impossible to reclaim all the money stolen. Even after the Swiss banks cooperated with the government of the Philippines to find Marcos's cash, for example, they returned only a few hundred million of a fortune as high as $10 billion. In 2013 the body in charge of recovering the money called off the hunt, claiming the costs of the exercise had created a 'law of diminishing returns'.[108] The Commission on Good Government was able to take back a ruby and diamond tiara from the vault of one of the Swiss banks, but the $8 million it was expected to fetch would be small change compared to the money ploughed into real estate and businesses, never to be seen again.[109]

As for Mobutu, the Swiss banks found in their vaults only $3 million of the $8 billion fortune Kabila's government claimed he had. A Swiss politician blasted his country's banks for their 'grotesque behaviour', noting: 'This is a financial empire and it is here in Switzerland.'[110] Many of the Mobutu millions had perhaps already disappeared into investments, bribes, kickbacks and rewards for loyal henchmen by the time Kabila took power.[111]

One explanation for Mobutu's longevity, beyond rule by fear, is the self-interest of Zaire's educated middle class. A critical mass of people accepted the system for what it was, and quite literally bought into it. Kabila, after taking power, put it like this: 'Who has not been a Mobutuist in this country? Three-quarters of this country became part of it. We saw you all dancing in the glory of the monster.'[112] Another is *realpolitik*. As Mobutu's CIA minder Larry Devlin put it, 'We needed him and he needed us.' That is, until they no longer needed him. After all the years of mutual favours, his American backers summarily dropped him in the early 1990s. He complained, with a certain justification: 'I am the latest victim of the Cold War. The lesson is that my support for American policy counts for nothing.' The end of the Cold War led the Americans to abandon their dictator-kleptocrats (the Russians had no choice, as their influence had already waned), but a number of them survived.

Recent estimates of the fortune stolen by Egypt's Hosni Mubarak coalesce around the figure of $40 billion, which would have made him one of the world's richest men.[113] He was toppled only in 2011. It remains unclear how much he is still secretly hoarding.

Mobutu the supposed monster may have had the last laugh. In October 2013, amid stirrings of nostalgia for the long-serving ruler, it was announced that his body was being flown home and would be re-interred. Not quite posthumous rehabilitation, but it seems that even the most violent profiteers, with their palaces and Concordes, have their admirers. Some Congolese argue that, for all his personal enrichment, he brought electricity and jobs, at least at the beginning. As the Gbadolite palace complex remains abandoned and overgrown, as millions struggle to overcome civil war and trauma, his reputation continues to haunt a nation whose wealth he stole.[114]

PART TWO

Now

CHAPTER 11

The sheikhs

It is great wealth to a soul to live frugally with
a contented mind.

Lucretius

Akhenaten did it. Louis XIV did it. When you have more money than
you have time to spend it, why not create for yourself a dream city?
That is what, at the turn of the twenty-first century, three leaders in the
Persian Gulf have done.

Dubai, Abu Dhabi and Qatar have raced to global attention. They
have become leaders in finance, transport and tourism, and through
acquisitions around the world have become the pre-eminent purchasers
and sponsors of sport and art. They have also become essential players
in matters of diplomacy and warfare – that's not bad progress for three
strips of land in the desert.

In the 2000s Dubai became the epicentre of gaudy wealth. From
celebrities to financiers, from footballers to mere tourists, the giant construction project in the sand welcomed them all. Private artificial islands
rose from the sea; luxury high-rise blocks played host to the global elite
sheltered from the rest. Each new building, each new seven-star hotel,
vied to become the brashest and the tallest. The whole project is the
brainchild of Sheikh Mohammed bin Rashid al-Maktoum, affectionately known as Sheikh Mo. As the flow of oil began to slow down, he

created a business model based on property, tourism, shipping and finance. Until the 2008 financial crash, the wealth kept on pouring in. When the bubble burst, some indebted foreigners fled. Mo went cap in hand to his cousin, Sheikh Khalifa, the ruler of the oil-rich and only slightly more demure neighbouring emirate, Abu Dhabi. After that blip, Dubai resumed its perpetual upward curve towards riches and expansion.

Khalifa's ambitions have been similarly grandiose, but his focus lies elsewhere. His plan has been to turn Abu Dhabi into a global centre for art and architecture to rival London, Paris and New York. Saadiyat (meaning Happiness) Island is one of the world's most ambitious cultural projects, creating opulent homes for new branches of the Louvre and the Guggenheim as well as galleries of Arabic art.

The third ruler in this triumvirate was Sheikh Hamad bin Khalifa al-Thani, the Emir of Qatar, who put his similarly tiny state on the global map by establishing the al-Jazeera television network and winning the right to host the 2022 FIFA World Cup. More than the other two, Qatar became a key player in Middle East diplomacy, not least the civil war in Syria.

These leaders learned from the failures of the Saudi royal family and their model of instant wealth of the 1970s. Europe, and London in particular, became the playground for sheikhs and their hangers-on. A decade or so of conspicuous consumption (out of sight and seemingly out of mind of Islamic law) did not lead to economic transformation. The wealth was squandered. For Sheikhs Khalifa, Mo and Hamad, money was never going to be enough. They were born into it; their families have more than they could possibly know what to do with. Their ambition was to carve out a permanent legacy, for themselves and their aspiring nations. Their states have become symbols of the triumph of globalised wealth.

When the al-Maktoum family took over in 1833, Dubai was a small fishing and pearling community. Sheikh Maktoum bin Butti, the founding father of Dubai's ruling dynasty, and his heirs, saw the sheikhdom survive rebellions, gain independence from its larger neighbours in the Gulf, and come under the 'protection' of the British Empire. By the early twentieth century, Dubai had become the busiest trading post and a major entry point to the Persian Gulf. In the pre-oil era, foreign trade and the re-export business formed the cornerstone of the economy. The Great Depression, loss of trading networks during the Second World War and the decline of Britain as a global power relegated Dubai and the other emirates into backwaters.

As with the rest of the region, the great glut of oil was Dubai's immediate salvation. In the late 1960s, Sheikh Rashid bin Saeed al-Maktoum exploited the young emirate's new resource wealth to great effect. He established the Dubai Petroleum Company and opened it to foreign investment. In so doing he created a clever system of economic interdependence, with Western powers keen on the continuation of al-Maktoum rule.

The Dubai of then bore virtually no resemblance to the emirate of the present day. Few buildings made inroads into the vista of desert stretching to the horizon. Dubai's first hotel opened in 1960, with just thirty-five rooms. The local airline, Gulf Air, was not much of an advertisement for the country. Unless you were involved in the oil trade, why would anyone need to go there? But the oil was gushing in. By 1991, production peaked. Rashid was keen to exploit the newfound wealth, but was wary of change. He sought to inculcate in his children a link with their roots, the importance of social conservatism and the transience of wealth. He famously said: 'My grandfather rode a camel, my father rode a camel, I drive a Mercedes, my son drives a Land Rover, his son will drive a Land Rover, but his son will ride a camel.'[1]

This was the family into which the third of four sons, Mohammed bin Rashid al-Maktoum, was born in 1949. He and his brothers grew up in a compound with no electricity or running water (or so it is said in official accounts) and they were encouraged to be hardened horsemen and hunters. Mohammed was sent to England at the age of seventeen, enrolling in the Bell School of Languages in Cambridge. While the official biography talks of a prestigious European liberal arts education, the Cambridge connection was purely geographical. While in the UK, he developed an early love of horseracing, a sport that would ease his passage to the top of the British establishment.

When Mohammed was twenty-two, his father oversaw Dubai's

independence. It aligned with Abu Dhabi and five other emirates to form the United Arab Emirates. Sheikh Rashid had always been conscious of the finite stocks of oil, and wary of over-reliance on the natural resource that would be the scourge of many a developing nation. He used the oil wealth to diversify the economy and invest in new roads and buildings, seeing the potential for Dubai to become a hub in a region of instability. Regional tensions, which had flared in the early 1970s, served as a warning sign. Marriage proved a useful diplomatic tool. Sheikh Rashid gave away his daughter to the Emir of Qatar in return for a wedding gift of $700 million, which was used to finance the building of a port.

Few around the world were paying much attention to Dubai. When the words 'Arab' and 'oil' were put together, the spotlight fell elsewhere: Saudi Arabia. In a precursor to the Russian invasion of the mid- to late 1990s, London's most expensive real estate, restaurants and nightclubs became the preserve of a small group of super-rich Saudis. Sometimes they were instantly recognisable in their dishdashes, the whiteness of their traditional outfits contrasting with the grey city skies. Much of the time they would dress less obtrusively in Western clothing. Almost always, when it came to having a good time, it was men who were seen. The women were hidden away, usually at home in Riyadh or Jeddah, as the men gambled and cavorted their money away in London or the south of France. Wads of notes were carried in briefcases and doled out as if confetti.

As with the oligarchs today, London proved adept at prostration. Everything was done to make the Arab super-rich feel welcome, including turning a blind eye to behaviour that would have got them in serious trouble at home. The late King Fahd, while still a prince, lost a reported $6 million one night at the tables in Monte Carlo. Another member of the ruling family was said to have lost £2 million in three nights at Ladbrokes, but apparently undeterred, he tipped the waitresses with £100 chips. One of the biggest names was Adnan Khashoggi, playboy arms dealer and reputedly the world's wealthiest private individual at the time. In the early 1980s his fortune was estimated at up to $40 billion, with homes around the world. His estate in the Spanish resort of Marbella hosted parties that he hoped were as extravagant as anything seen since America's Gilded Age. It was said that champagne was kept in cooled trailers parked around the estate.[2]

Saudi oil production peaked in 1977. For several years before and several years after, the country displayed its financial and political might. Meetings of OPEC – the Organisation of the Petroleum Exporting Countries – became political dramas, with Saudi Arabia's all-powerful Oil Minister, Sheikh Yamani, at the centre. The untold riches were, however, doing little to improve Saudi society. The country remained as fiercely conservative as ever, closed to outside influences. The American historian and Middle East expert Daniel Pipes wrote in 1982 of 'the curse of oil wealth'. The trouble with booms, he said, is that they usually don't bring either sustained economic growth or cultural improvements: the riches they create are spent 'with abandon, disrupting normal behaviour, fomenting unrealistic expectations and inspiring envy'.

Pipes cited the story of Shakhbut ibn Sultan, the ruler of Abu Dhabi for four decades until he was overthrown in 1966 (with the help of British officers who politely ushered him on to a plane). Abu Dhabi had first struck gold back in 1959 – some twenty years after Saudi Arabia and Kuwait – but instead of galvanising the hapless Sultan, the onset of money overwhelmed him. Hoping to prevent oil revenues from reaching his subjects and upsetting their way of life, he literally hid the cash from the oil companies under his bed. When mice ate some of it, he put the rest in the bank. But he still refused to spend it, saying: 'I am a Bedou. All my people are Bedou. We are accustomed to living with a camel or a goat in the desert. If we spend the money, it is going to ruin my people, and they are not going to like it.' Pipes was correct in his analysis of the present, but wrong about the future. The next generation of leaders in the UAE were far more strategic, and successful, in their use of new-found money.

Sheikh Mohammed was forty-two on his father's death in 1990. After serving as head of the Dubai police, he had been appointed Minister for Defence for the UAE at the age of twenty-eight. He also showed early credentials as a businessman. His eldest brother, Sheikh Maktoum bin Rashid al-Maktoum, assumed the throne, but within five years of the succession he issued a decree naming Sheikh Mo as Crown Prince. Sheikh Mo had in a short space of time improved his reputation (and increased his personal wealth) within both Dubai and the UAE. His high-profile business successes, victories in international endurance horse races and popular traditional Arabic poetry allowed the elite Emirati families to enjoy their new-found ultra-wealth, as they were reassured by his emphasis on traditional values. From his office on the top floor of the taller of the two Emirates Towers, Sheikh Mo presided over the expansion of the emirate and his personal authority. By the time Maktoum died of a heart attack in 2006, power had effectively long been transferred.

The last decade of his life saw an economic transformation remarkable for any time in history. Dubai grew from a provincial city of 600,000 people to a global hub of over two million. In the 1980s and early 1990s, its economy depended on international oil consumption and a tight group of foreign companies. Then production began to decline steadily; Dubai was losing out to its neighbour. By 2008, Abu Dhabi accounted for about 90 per cent of the UAE's oil exports; and its oil reserves stood at an extraordinary $17 million per citizen – eleven times that for Dubai. Sheikh Mo refused to let Abu Dhabi's superior oil wealth cast a shadow over Dubai: 'We want to be number one. The second place . . . nobody knows.'[3] Dubai – less well endowed with natural resources – had to diversify, to use its resources more creatively.

Sheikh Mo began the process of constructing a new model state, a global city-corporation. Nothing would be allowed to stand in the way of progress. Dubai was turned into a giant construction site. Land was reclaimed and desert receded as word went out to aim high and build high. In 1994 construction began on the Burj Al Arab. It was to be the world's tallest hotel. The marketing material proclaimed that it would be 'taller than the Eiffel Tower'. It would be the world's first self-styled 'seven-star' hotel (an accolade that, even though meaningless, would be adopted by rival new hotels). With its shard of steel and glass, built in the shape of a traditional dhow, the Burj became Dubai's symbol of nationhood. Sports stars were invited to parade their wares, not in the lobby, but up top – on the helipad on the roof. Tiger Woods teed off from there (into the sea); Roger Federer knocked up in a game of singles with Andre Agassi, while David Coulthard performed some doughnuts in his Formula One car. The celebrity endorsement was perfect.

Galvanised by the publicity that Dubai's mega-structure was drawing, Abu Dhabi's ruler, Sheikh Khalifa, wanted something even more eye-catching for his emirate. The result was the Emirates Palace, a monument to garishness. It opened in 2005. More palace than hotel, this marble and granite structure stretches more than a kilometre from end to end (guests are provided with golf buggies to transport them to their rooms). It contains 6000 square metres of gold leaf and has 7000 doors, 12,000 signs and 1002 chandeliers made with Swarovski crystals. The centre of the palace is dominated by a grand atrium, the biggest in the world. Its gold-gilded dome outstrips the one in St Paul's Cathedral in size (if not taste). The public lounge is the size of two football pitches. VIPs have the choice of arriving by helicopter or being driven through a fake Arc de Triomphe, leaving lesser visitors to make do with an orgy of fountains. Where else in the world would you see a vending machine dispensing gold bars? Mansa Musa's Mali had been dusted down for our contemporary times.

Next up in the lurid stakes in Dubai were a couple of artificial archipelagos – the Palm and the World. These became favoured holiday homes for footballing multi-millionaires and celebrities from the world of film and fashion. So keen was Dubai to advertise their names that many were given subsidies to buy their luxury properties. Dubai turned itself into the global hub of greed. Each symbol of luxury had to be outdone by the next. The most dramatic was the Burj Khalifa. Construction of this giant office tower-cum-hotel-cum-exclusive apartment complex began in 2004, under its original name Burj Dubai. It overtook Taipei 101 to become the world's tallest building.

These gravity-defying, sea-defying, desert-defying buildings were central to Sheikh Mo's business plan for his city-corporation. He recalled some of the early urban design discussions: 'A group of people brought me the drawing of a small shopping mall and a few buildings around it. I just said two words, "Think Big." After talking and discussing for three days, this is what it has become. Dubai Mall is the biggest mall in the world and Burj Khalifa is the tallest tower in the world.'[4]

Sheikh Mo and his planners upended the conventions of architecture by announcing his grandiose ideas long before the plans were drawn up. The hype – the 'I want a slice of the pie' mentality – was essential to feed the speculation that fed Dubai's rapid economic growth. It was not essential for the property to succeed financially, or even for the project to come to fruition. In terms of advertising, in terms of inward investment, Brand Dubai seemed impregnable.

Glamour and gigantism were necessary but insufficient ingredients for success. Equally important were the tax regime and the infrastructure. Specialist deregulated 'free zones' were established, allowing international businesses to operate without paying either corporation or income tax. Initially, foreign nationals were not allowed to buy property. Once ownership rules were relaxed a steady influx became a flood. Everyone wanted a slice of the action, without the inconvenience of having to give anything back. Sheikh Mo led from the front – his holdings were exempt from tax.

Dubai was a tax-free safe haven in a troubled region. It was easy to live in and increasingly easy to get to. Infrastructure did not accompany growth; it was the catalyst for that growth (unlike many Western nations, where transport links are often an afterthought). It took Emirates only twenty years to become one of the top ten airlines in the world. By 2020, it is expected to be the biggest international long-haul carrier. The airport contributes nearly a third of total GDP and provides 20 per cent of the employment in the emirate.[5] The growth in the ports and road system is similarly impressive. In the 1990s, Abu Dhabi and Dubai banded together to build a 150-mile road linking the two emirates. Desert once separated them; one might have seen the odd Bedouin walking on the sand. Over time, all that has disappeared. Now the cities are connected by marble and concrete, stretching as far as the eye can see.

The boom could not have been delivered without Dubai's largest population group – an invisible underclass of construction workers from the Indian subcontinent. From the early 2000s, civil society organisations sought to draw attention to their plight. In 2006, Human Rights Watch reported: 'one of the world's largest construction booms is feeding off workers in Dubai who are treated as less than human'.[6]

Labourers were recruited from poor shanties by recruitment agencies based in their home countries, offering to pay their flights out to Dubai (where the streets would be paved with gold) and to provide work, adequate living conditions and a subsistence wage. The workers would be required to surrender their passports on arrival, and to pay back the money loaned for their flights. Newspaper reports suggested that more than twenty thousand filed complaints with the government about the non-payment of wages and labour camp conditions. They were in modern-day bondage, and had no choice but to continue to work in the searing heat in order to pay back their debts. Charity workers and journalists who tried to investigate their plight were often not welcomed back to Dubai.

This was not the narrative that the public relations teams hired by the Dubai government wanted the world to hear. Nor was it something the wealthy inhabitants wanted to notice, as they sped past construction sites in their air-conditioned cars. The sad truth is that very few people care – not the expat employees of property or financial service companies; not the thousands who descend upon the UAE on package holidays in five-star (or seven-star) luxury: cheap weekend breaks; cheap labour.

One of the ingenuities of Sheikhs Mohammed, Khalifa and Hamad was that they kept two entirely different demographics comfortable and catered for. Foreigners were indispensable to making the country work and in Dubai they comprised 80 per cent of the population. They had entirely separate needs and cultural reference points from those of the locals. Both sets passed by each other in designer shops and expensive restaurants, but had little interaction beyond that. Western hedonism was tolerated, as long as it remained behind closed doors. Expats, visiting businessmen and tourists could lounge in their hotels or villas, play tennis and drink copious amounts of alcohol. Problems arose only when they were picked up for drunkenness or kissing (or worse) in public.

Shopping malls and other forms of safe entertainment were built for everyone's retail pleasure. Locals and foreigners were united in the common goals of making and spending money. The first shopping festival was established in 1996, generating $1 billion in revenue in its first year. Dubai became home to high-profile sports events. Its international film festival has drawn in Hollywood A-listers such as Orlando Bloom, George Clooney and Tom Cruise, as well as big draws from across the Arab world. Elton John, Iron Maiden, Jennifer Lopez and Justin Bieber have all headlined rock concerts. Their fees are small change for Sheikh Mo. In 2008, Kylie Minogue was paid a reported $1.5 million for appearing at the launch of the Atlantis, a pink monstrosity of a hotel.[7] Some two thousand celebrity guests were flown in for a feast of lobsters and a fireworks display the organisers heralded as 'seven times grander' than the one that had just marked the opening of the Beijing Olympics. As ever, scale is what mattered.[8]

By the end of the first decade of the twenty-first century, Dubai's GDP per capita stood at more than $40,000 – placing it among the richest nations in the world.[9] If expatriates were taken out of the equation, the figure for the local population would probably rise into the hundreds of thousands. Property and patronage have made many of them very rich and – as long as they do not criticise the regime – will keep them rich. Public criticism is in short supply. The media are strictly controlled. Public opinion is gauged through regional *majaalis*, or forums for discussion, with the findings reported back to Sheikh Mo's personal court.

At the heart of the system is 'rentier' wealth – the distribution of money from on high to less wealthy Emiratis. From the 1970s, with oil wealth flowing in, Sheikh Rashid offered free housing to his poorer subjects. This continues today, alongside free education and healthcare. The state also offers employment assistance, such as free office space and financial assistance for start-ups. Families given property during the early growth years maximised their profit by selling or renting it out to property developers or expatriates. As the economy boomed, so rents soared, but nobody seemed to mind. The expats had their costs paid by their companies, and the government was happy because the more the local landlords received, the less it needed to provide in subsidies.

Behind the glittering globalised façade are ethnocentric policies aimed at preserving a national elite and preventing a blurring of the line between foreigners and nationals. The Sheikh Zayed Marriage Fund was established in 1992, providing payments of around $19,000 every year to each of 3000 national couples struggling to meet the cost of dowries. It also explicitly aims to 'encourage marriages between UAE nationals'.[10] The financial carrot is accompanied by a legislative stick. Local women who marry expatriate men have their citizenship and that of their children taken away. Foreigners who bring themselves to the attention of the authorities run the risk of being refused extensions to their residency permits, or even being told to leave early – the financial penalties of such punishments are too severe for them to contemplate. Everyone has an incentive to conform.

Dubai's pact with its citizens and expats is carefully calibrated, modelled largely on Singapore. It is an enticing proposition for those who place wealth creation and private freedoms (notably the freedom to consume) above public freedoms (free expression, free elections). The philosophy is to build the 'consumer citizen', anaesthetised by wealth and luxuriating in authoritarian capitalism. Although he would hardly use those terms himself, Sheikh Mo is proud and open about the trade-off. His benevolent paternalism and material wellbeing are presented as more than adequate substitutes for democratic rights for his 'consumer citizens'. Instead of political rights, nationals are offered an economic stake in the prosperity of the emirates; and the deal is much the same for expats and international businesses. As the Emirati academic Abdul Khaleq Abdulla puts it: in Dubai 'politics are inconceivable'.[11]

In January 2008, Sheikh Mo summed up his philosophy:

We don't see politics as our thing; we don't want it, we don't think this is the right thing to do. We are engaged in a different type of war that's really worth fighting – fighting to alleviate poverty, generating better education, creating economic opportunity for people, and teaching people everywhere how to be entrepreneurs, to believe in themselves. I always ask: How can I help? What can I do for people? How can I improve people's lives? That's part of my value system. It's too late for me to change that system, but it isn't too early for me to say to the world that the Dubai narrative is all about changing people's lives for the better through smart capitalism, willpower and positive energy.[12]

Instead of politics, he advocates an almost messianic humanitarian capitalism. Despite styling himself as CEO of his city-corporation, he is keen to present his vision of Dubai as driven by more than just the maximisation of his profit margin:

> To term our emirate 'Dubai Inc.', as some do, suggests that commerce, more than anything else, is our leitmotif. It is true, of course, that Dubai has been a trading port and a commercial hub for several centuries. But the ethos of Dubai was, and is, all about building bridges to the outside world; it was, and is, about creating connections with different cultures. I learned my capitalism in the bazaars and boardwalks of Dubai. And perhaps the fundamental question that I learned to always ask was: how can we serve as agents of positive change? That's why I prefer to call Dubai 'Catalyst Inc.'[13]

Sheikh Mohammed's vision of Dubai as a global city is inextricably linked to the business interests of the wider al-Maktoum family. They pay no tax and own majority stakes in all the large holding companies and Sovereign Wealth Funds. Sheikh Mo holds a 99.7 per cent share in Dubai Holding and a majority share in Dubai World, two of the three major companies that manage much of the emirate's wealth. A portfolio of subsidiary companies is responsible for most of the extravagant building projects. Much of Dubai's land belongs to the al-Maktoum family, giving them free rein to maximise the opportunities provided by real estate, tourism, shopping and free-trade zones. These corporations are headed by individuals from loyal families of the elite: they are marketed as ultra-modern brands, yet they are run according to patrimonial networks stretching back generations, composed of the descendants of tribes and merchant families. The same families staff the emirate's administration and fill its senior roles. In an effort to introduce a modicum of modern governance, Sheikh Mo created the Dubai Executive Council. Meeting in the taller of the two Emirates Towers, the DEC effectively directs the business of the emirate. It might be an improvement on the past, but its transparency and accountability are highly circumscribed. The DEC is answerable to one man.

Andrew Carnegie, arguably the best known of the United States of America's 'robber barons': key to any understanding of global wealth and power through the ages

The cover of *Harper's Weekly* magazine, showing the Pinkertons' surrender during the Homestead lock-out. Management of the steel company had brought the detective agency in to clear union pickets after workers went out on strike against Carnegie's changes to pay and conditions

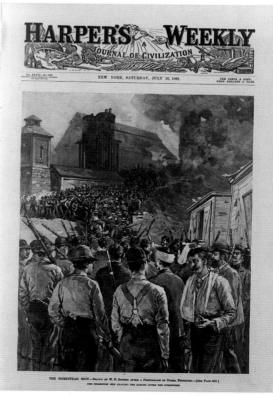

President of Zaire Mobutu Sese Seko meeting Prime Minister
Margaret Thatcher in 1981

(Gamma Keystone via Getty Images)

Mobutu's ruined palace at Gbadolite: hubris and corruption come home to roost

(Getty Images)

Monarch of Dubai
Sheikh Mohammed bin
Rashid al–Makhtoum
with George W. Bush
(Pablo Martinez Monsivais / AP / Press
Association Images)

Sister of the Emir of
Qatar, Sheikha al Mayassa
bint Hamad bin Khalifa
al–Thani with Prince
Charles at Mathaf, Doha's
Museum of Modern Art
(Getty Images)

Russian oligarch Alisher Usmanov holds up a Dynamo FC jersey, marking his company's
sponsorship deal. Usmanov also holds a large stake in Arsenal FC

(UIG via Getty Images)

A local derby? Usmanov and Roman Abramovich watch their football clubs, Arsenal and
Chelsea, go head to head in 2009

(REUTERS / Eddie Keogh)

Oligarchs Boris Berezovsky and Abramovich talk tough at the
Russian Duma in June 2000

Wang Jianlin, chairman of Dalian Wanda Group (left), and Jack Ma, chairman of Alibaba, at CCTV's China Economic Person of the Year Award, December 2013

(Getty Images)

King of the geeks: founder of Facebook, Mark Zuckerberg

(REX/Sipa Press)

A long friendship and even longer rivalry: Steve Jobs and Bill Gates in 1991

Google founders Larry Page
and Sergey Brin

A fallen titan: chairman and CEO of Lehman Brothers Dick Fuld is sworn in during hearings on the collapse of the bank in 2008

(Getty Images)

Happier times: RBS chief executive Fred Goodwin opens the bank's new £350-million Edinburgh headquarters with Queen Elizabeth II in September 2005

(Getty Images)

To help soften the hyper-capitalism image and to manage his reputation, Sheikh Mo has appropriated an idealised imagery of Dubai's heritage and Bedouin identity. Following on from the examples of Mansa Musa (see Chapter 3) and later Muslim rulers, such as the Ottoman leader Suleiman the Magnificent, charitable donations and gestures of piety are presented as personal acts of the leader. Dubai's international aid budget constitutes 3.5 per cent of its GDP, four times the Western state average, and well above the UN-required level. Sheikh Mo also made one of the largest gifts in history when he donated $10 billion to a new Arab education trust – the Mohammed bin Rashid al-Maktoum Foundation.[14] Dubai and the wider UAE have used such philanthropy and humanitarian task forces to demonstrate a depoliticised support for the Arab cause. The al-Maktoum Foundation and the Mohammed bin Rashid Charitable and Humanitarian Establishment are vehicles through which the Sheikh supports a wide range of projects in Palestine – including schools, orphanages and hospitals. In 1995, he extended aid to non-Arab Muslims in Bosnia and Kosovo, funding airlifts of wounded Bosnians to hospitals in Dubai as well as raising $15 million for the building of new mosques in Kosovo, a sum that Sheikh Mo publicly doubled with his own money.

The flexibility that allows Brits to go on drinking binges (as long as they stay out of the path of the police) while respecting Islamic norms is writ even larger on the diplomatic stage. Thanks to its economic wealth and stability in the middle of a turbulent region, Dubai has become the destination of choice for all sides. Iranians have been able to trade through the port, evading US sanctions, as long as they do so discreetly. Much has been written about key al-Qaeda figures owning property in the emirate. Everyone can go there to relax, no questions asked, as long as they refrain from their other activities while on Dubai soil. In the meantime, it is not just Western corporations that have built up a significant presence; security agencies from all sides use Dubai as a useful listening post.

The lifestyle pact is no coincidence. It is synonymous with Sheikh Mo himself, and was inculcated by his father. The tension between cultural conservatism and Western-oriented economic liberalism runs through his family life. He married his first wife, Sheikha Hind bint Maktoum bin Juma al-Maktoum, in 1979. Of his twenty-three official children, he has had twelve with Sheikha Hind, who lives in Jameel Palace and is not photographed in public. His second wife, Princess Haya, is the Oxford-educated daughter of the late King Hussein of Jordan, and half-sister of the current King, Abdullah. They married in 2004, just before Sheikh Mohammed officially assumed power in Dubai. She is a public figure, and is frequently pictured wearing Western clothing and engaging in charity work. As a former Olympic showjumper, Princess Haya shares her husband's love of horses and she accompanies him on trips to his stables in the UK, America, Japan, Australia and Ireland.

Sheikh Mo's image portrays him as a visionary leader, poet, horse-man and philanthropist, a simple soul who has been entrusted with the onerous task of doing good: 'I need little from my world. My prayer mat and water bottle are in my car wherever I go, together with my work documents and my vision.' From time to time, the modesty PR takes a back seat. In 2006 he planned to have a verse of his own poetry written into a cluster of man-made islands in the Persian Gulf. The main theme of the poem is his prowess as a horseman. The Arabic script would have read:

> Take wisdom from the wise
> It takes a man of vision to write on water
> Not everyone who rides a horse is a jockey
> Great men rise to greater challenges.

These lines, extolling Sheikh Mo's personal entrepreneurial ideology, were to be visible from space. This was one of the few grand schemes that didn't come to pass. It was probably one act of veneration too many.[15]

Large portraits of the ruler are to be found around Dubai, often depicting him in traditional clothing on a white horse. Traditional and modern are seamlessly interwoven. Sheikh Mo uses Facebook and Twitter to connect with his subjects as well as the face-to-face recep-tion of residents in his *diwan*, his princely court. He breeds camels (a nod to the Middle East) while being seen in his morning suit at Ascot rubbing shoulders with the British horseracing elite.

As with the rest of his population, he is keen on retail therapy. His global shopping sprees on behalf of the state have seen him purchase: the New York department store Barneys; a share of Standard Chartered Bank; half of the Las Vegas strip; and stud farms in the UAE, Britain, Ireland and Australia. He briefly acquired the *QE2* luxury liner, with plans for it to be turned into a luxury hotel, only to conclude it wasn't glitzy enough, and offload it on to the Chinese.

Having augmented his fortune largely through real estate in Dubai, he expanded his portfolio of luxury properties across the world. These include several mansions and estates in the UK, including the £45-million Dalham Hall in Suffolk and the £55-million, 800-acre Turnberry golf course in Scotland. He outdid himself in 2010 when he bought a $308-million penthouse in Monaco as a 'safe investment' in rocky economic times. The garage of his palace is said to contain more than a hundred cars, including a smattering of Rolls-Royces, Lamborghinis, Ferraris and Mercedes. At one time, he owned the world's largest yacht: the *Dubai* came in at 162 metres long, with 8 decks and luxury accommodation for 115 guests and 80 crew. It was rumoured to have cost over $300 million, only to be overtaken for size by Roman Abramovich's *Eclipse* (see Chapter 12). To the chagrin of the Russian oligarch, he in turn was knocked off the super-yacht perch by Sheikh Khalifa, whose cruiser-plaything, the *Azzam*, comes in at just under two hundred metres long.

In 2008, *Forbes* estimated Sheikh Mo's personal wealth at $18 billion. That was before Dubai came down with a crash. Rather than oil, it was debt that financed Dubai's boom. This model was highly successful, but it was sustainable only while Dubai was in the middle of a speculative bubble. When property prices plummeted in late 2008, the emirate was no longer able to convince potential investors it could pay back its debts and the loans dried up.

The oil price collapsed to $50 a barrel, a third of its peak value. The stock market plunged. Dubai World, one of the investment conglomerates, defaulted on its loan repayments, sending the markets into disarray. After all, which organisation, or individual, in Dubai had not borrowed heavily, on a wing and a prayer to Sheikh Mo? Half of all the region's construction projects were put on hold or cancelled, leaving a trail of half-built towers on the outskirts of Dubai stretching into the sand. Desperate sellers sent property prices plunging by 60 per cent. The expatriate community panicked. Thousands of foreigners lost their jobs and their work visas, and under the law were required to leave the country within a month. Others were in an even worse state, getting into negative equity and debt. Falling into arrears is punishable by jail. Airport car parks filled with hire-purchase Porsches left abandoned, keys in the ignition and notes from panicked owners taped to windscreens apologising for defaulting on their repayments.

Unprecedented criticism of Dubai followed in the international press. As the crisis unfolded, Sheikh Mo attempted to reassure international investors, but he became increasingly irritated by the media – telling press critics to 'shut up'.[16] By 2009, a PR department had been established in Dubai to 'preserve and promote the image of the emirate by providing timely and accurate information to the local and international media'.[17] Unofficially dubbed 'Brand Dubai', it was presented as an attempt to improve transparency for investors. In reality, it formalised the intensive reputation management Sheikh Mo had practised ever since taking power.

He had to go cap in hand to his older cousin, Sheikh Khalifa, who handed out $10 billion to help Dubai stave off the threat of default. Its 2010 debt was rescheduled. But it was a close-run thing. Abu Dhabi itself had taken a risk, a calculated one, confident that the billions stashed away in its Sovereign Wealth Funds would act as collateral on the loan. As a gesture of thanks, Sheikh Mo renamed the Burj Dubai, the grandest of all the emirate's skyscrapers, the Burj Khalifa on the day of its inauguration – the most expensive naming rights the world has yet seen. For all the positive gloss of brotherliness, this was a humbling experience. The supreme confidence of this one man had been punctured. That was more than an issue of hubris. Sheikh Mohammed's image was the business of Dubai, which he personally marketed. The bailout made clear to the world where the power – and the money – really lay.

*

Dubai and Abu Dhabi are by far the two most important of the seven emirates that form the UAE. As the largest contributor, Abu Dhabi holds the presidency of the federation by right. The stereotype has it that Dubai is the merchant of bling, while Abu Dhabi is more cautious and studious, focusing less on tacky homes for footballers and more on building art galleries and universities. Yet this difference in emphasis is overstated. Khalifa is also partial to super yachts, seven-star hotels and football clubs – as the 2008 purchase of the English Premier League team Manchester City by his half-brother and Deputy Prime Minister Mansour bin Zayed bin Sultan al-Nahyan attests.

Abu Dhabi, like Dubai, has grown out of all proportion in recent years. Much the quieter, and more conservative, of the two emirates, it is nevertheless barely recognisable from the city of a decade ago. Construction work is frenetic. The Sheikh's dream project is Saadiyat Island, just off the coast of downtown Abu Dhabi – the most ambitious cultural project the modern world has ever seen. Some £20 billion is being spent on constructing five museums and galleries, to rival anything in the West. The Louvre Abu Dhabi will be in the shape of a flying saucer. This will house the ruling family's growing collection of art, along with loans from the Paris Louvre, the Musée d'Orsay and the Pompidou Centre. Alongside will be a new Guggenheim, twelve times the size of the original in New York. The brains behind Saadiyat believe it will attract whatever shows it wants.

Among the project's 'starchitects' are Jean Nouvel (for the Louvre) and Frank Gehry (Guggenheim), while the Performing Arts Centre and Zayed National Museum come courtesy of Zaha Hadid and Norman Foster respectively. Money talks, just as it has done to attract some of the global university brands to the Gulf. Gehry – after completing his Guggenheim contract – proceeded to attack the project in his customary fruity language. 'It's like a group grope,' he complained, not about the individual buildings, but about their clustering in one spot across a road bridge alongside the ubiquitous luxury hotels and golf courses. 'One building by me, one by Norman Foster, one by Zaha, one by Jean Nouvel, one by Daniel Libeskind. It becomes a cabinet of horrors.'[18]

Some artists have threatened to boycott Abu Dhabi in protest at curbs on freedom of expression. Yet the criticism tends to be rhetorical, and temporary. The plight of manual labourers working on Saadiyat has, belatedly, caught the attention of the international media, as it has done in Dubai and Qatar (where public criticism of conditions for workers building stadiums for the 2022 World Cup has caused acute embarrassment). Yet the overriding impulse of the many Westerners who are enjoying the wealth of the region is not to ask questions.

The third member of the Gulf's super-rich leaders' club is the one on whom attention has been least focused. But it is catching up fast and may even have outstripped the other two in strategic importance. Qatar, led until mid-2013 by Sheikh Hamad, is buying its way to global pre-eminence. Thanks to its huge natural-gas reserves, it became the world's richest country in terms of per capita income in 2010 (overtaking Luxembourg). Its 250,000 citizens earn an average of $100,000 each a year; 10 per cent of them are dollar millionaires; and nobody pays income tax. Sheikh Hamad's dynasty may be worth tens of billions, but far more remarkable is the fact that virtually all of Qatar's citizens could count themselves as rich by international standards. Even in Mansa Musa's Mali the poor still existed.

So what to do with all the money? The emirate's shopping list comprises, in no particular order: hosting the World Cup; Paris Saint-Germain Football Club; and sponsorship of the best team in the world, Barcelona. The sports bill stands at £10 billion and rising. In property and finance, acquisitions in London alone include the Shard skyscraper, the Mayfair compound that has housed the US Embassy, a large part of the Olympic Village, Chelsea Barracks and Harrods department store, along with stakes in Barclays Bank, Credit Suisse, Santander, the London Stock Exchange, Volkswagen and Porsche. Among the universities lured to set up campuses in the Gulf state are University College London and Washington's Georgetown.

Sheikh Hamad's ventures into the arts were spectacular. Under him, Qatar became by far the biggest player in the global art market. The Qatar Museums Authority spends almost £1 billion a year on acquisitions, and it is an ever-present player at Christie's, Sotheby's and other global auction houses. Some of the twentieth-century greats snapped up for pocket money are Mark Rothko, Francis Bacon, Jeff Koons, Roy

Lichtenstein and Andy Warhol. Damien Hirst's *Pill Cabinet* went for
£12.5 million. But it was the record-breaking acquisition of Paul
Cézanne's *Card Players* in early 2012 – for a staggering £160 million –
that most caught the eye. The great Western institutions, even with the
help of private philanthropy or government support, cannot come
close.

A woman is at the heart of this acquisitions programme – Sheikha
al Mayassa bint Hamad bin Khalifa al-Thani, the head of the QMA and
sister of the new Emir, Sheikh Tamim Bin Hamad Al-Thani, who took
over in June 2013. Her brief encompasses purchases, sponsorships and
the creation of new palaces of culture. The Museum of Islamic Art
which she opened in Doha, the Qatari capital, in 2008 is – like Abu
Dhabi's Saadiyat Island – just the start of a grand plan that includes Rem
Koolhaas's National Library and a National Museum designed by Jean
Nouvel. They need to be filled with works, hence the giant hoover-
ing up of items of value.

The finest art collections, eye-catching modern architecture and
some of the world's biggest sports teams and competitions might be
enough for many a world leader. For Sheikh Hamad and his son, and
for Sheikhs Khalifa and Mohammed, such prizes are necessary but
insufficient. Their dream is to turn their individual emirates and the
Gulf in general into the centre of the world.

Part of that comes down to transport and infrastructure. Qatar
Airways and Abu Dhabi's Etihad are giving Dubai's Emirates a run for
its money. All three are soaring ahead of their Western competitors.
From travel stopovers to business conventions, people are flocking to
the Gulf because of the ease and convenience. The same is beginning
to apply to international diplomacy. Qatar has positioned itself as a
player and a go-between, welcoming Iranians and Israelis, and assert-
ing itself more forcefully in conflicts from Libya to Syria. The
Americans rarely take decisions in the Middle East without first having
quiet words with the Qataris and the rest of the UAE.

The process of opening up to all comers and becoming a global
power is not without risk. It exposes such states to scrutiny that the
ruling families are deeply uncomfortable with. In Abu Dhabi, the
arrival of the English-language newspaper the *National* marked an

attempt to demonstrate a certain amount of free speech, although after
a while it toned down its reporting of the UAE. Al-Jazeera provides
outspoken news, in Arabic and English, but it too knows when to soft-
pedal, as and when required by the Qatari government.

When Dubai was hit by the financial crisis there was much crowing in
the West: the upstarts in the desert were getting their comeuppance.
The *Schadenfreude* was short-lived. Dubai stayed in the doldrums for
only a few years. In October 2010, Dubai World reached agreement
with its creditors to reschedule its $25 billion debt. The property
market was still shaky. But with infrastructure spending continuing
apace, Dubai gradually restored investor confidence.

Then came the Arab spring – the revolutions that toppled the old
guard in Tunisia, Egypt, Libya and Yemen – and sent autocrats across
the region scurrying for cover. City-states such as Bahrain, which had
been seen as oases of calm, were engulfed in demonstrations.
Entrepreneurs from those countries, and from elsewhere in the region,
wanted somewhere secure to conduct their businesses. Investors sought
a safe haven for their money. As these so-called springs turned into winters, with coups and massacres in Egypt and elsewhere, most of the
international corporations that still had a presence in the 'old' Arab
world bailed out and moved to the Gulf. Economists estimate that $30
billion – all tax free, naturally – flowed into Dubai in the three years
after the first uprising in Tunis.

Dubai has bounced back. Giant schemes that were on hold have
been reactivated. Even though the city-state remains heavily indebted,
it is as if nothing ever happened. Property prices have recovered most
of their pre-crash values. In 2013 Dubai was the strongest residential
market in the world. The stock market has surged.

Mega-projects are back in vogue. Sheikh Mo has approved the plans
for Mohammed bin Rashid City, a city within the city, named after the
one and only. This will include a hundred hotels, a Universal Studios
theme park, and – as if they didn't have enough already – the world's
largest shopping mall, naturally called 'The Mall of the World'. This will
eventually dwarf the Dubai Mall, which in 2012 was visited by sixty-five
million people, making it the most popular tourism destination on the

globe. Half a dozen other theme parks are planned. One will feature a model of the Taj Mahal, four times bigger than the real thing. The original Tourism Vision 2020 – outlined in the boom years, of doubling the number of visitors to twenty million by 2020 – was back on track.[19] A new five-runway airport, Maktoum International, will triple air capacity. It is part of an even larger project, Dubai World Centre, which is billed as an 'aerotropolis' that will integrate air services, manufacturing, commercial and residential developments with Jebel Ali, the busiest shipping hub between Singapore and Europe. The sobriety was short-lived; the resilience has been astonishing.

There was one more challenge for Sheikh Mo to face, and this time it was intensely personal, going to the heart of his intricate reputation management. In April 2013, the British Horseracing Authority disclosed that eleven horses in the charge of Mahmood al-Zarooni, his favoured trainer, had tested positive for anabolic steroids. All eleven were banned from racing and al-Zarooni faced disciplinary charges. The horses belonged to the famous Godolphin thoroughbred stable, which is the Maktoum family's private property. The horses were wintered in Dubai and then sent to Newmarket for the European flat-racing season. Sheikh Mo declared he was 'appalled and angered' and would 'lock down' the stables in the wake of Al-Zarooni being charged. The incident, which was described as 'the biggest doping scandal in racing history', was acutely embarrassing for the owner, who immediately sought to put distance between him and his stable's practices: 'I have many trainers and if one of them does the wrong things, you know – they [the horseracing authorities] gave him eight years, and I gave him lifetime. Finished.'

The scandal struck at the heart of everything Sheikh Mohammed had sought to do. He had taken on the work of his father, building a city from the desert into a global hub for finance, property and aviation. He had placed Dubai on the world map, making it famous for building projects that are ludicrous and awe-inspiring in equal measure, as well as for its decadence and fast money. But he needed more than that – something that money could bring closer but not guarantee. He craved international respectability, and he was ever alert to anything that threatened that goal.

The rulers of Dubai, Abu Dhabi and Qatar have never had to make money. They have inherited oil wealth, but they have used it as a route to the top of the world's financial, social, cultural and political networks. For all the financial drama Dubai has faced, it has proved that the rich can outlast an initial boom by diversifying their assets and their businesses. For all the delays to the new artistic superstructure in Abu Dhabi, and the problems with the football extravaganza in Qatar, their two leaders have already achieved their goal of turning their city-states into global players.

The Emirati academic Abdul Khaleq Abdulla encapsulates their projects: 'The state as brand and the city as brand, just as with the branded commodity and the branded corporation, is a natural phenomenon. There is no difference in the age of globalisation between the commodity, the state, merchandising, the city, cultures, and services. The surface, in this day and age, is as important as the content itself.'[20] Like others in history, these sheikhs have constructed seats of power in their own image. Their corporate-government empires may be on a new scale, but they borrow from a familiar template.

CHAPTER 12

The oligarchs

As a philosopher I can observe how people
bow and scrape before him. It is a contortion
of the spine, which the finest acrobat would
find difficult to imitate.

Heinrich Heine on
Baron James de Rothschild

The word 'oligarch' was first used to describe Greek aristocrats who
worked to overthrow Athenian democracy, which they equated with
mob rule. They feared that the populace, if empowered, would undermine the state through their low education and lack of respect for
culture and the law. In early 1990s Russia, the inverse was true. The
modern-day oligarch was synonymous with lawlessness and the subjugation of old values to the altar of new money.

In the ensuing twenty years, vulgarity has given way to a more
sophisticated form of ostentation – if that is not an oxymoron. The
origin of the oligarchs' wealth remains the same: the carving-up of the
natural resources of a former superpower between a small number of
influential individuals. Oil and gas provided a route to instant riches, as
did steel, aluminium and other metals. Resentment of this helped to
pave the way for Vladimir Putin in 2000 and his promise to restore
order. Putin tore up the previous sweetheart deals with the oligarchs,
making clear that in order to thrive, indeed survive, they must show

obeisance to him and refrain from venturing into politics. The klep-
tocracy of the Yeltsin years was re-nationalised, brought back under the
wing of the state. The security elite and the economic elite became
one.

In China, the deals were more open. Public expressions of loyalty to
the Communist Party were essential for anyone serious about making
money, and even then it was important to garner the right allies at the
right time. Personal fortunes were dependent in large part on political
sponsors.

London became the playground, and sometimes the battleground,
for Russia's elite. China's first generation of super-rich appeared more
at home in the United States, while snapping up assets or putting away
their cash in Singapore and Dubai.

The key priority for most oligarchs now, alongside wealth preservation, is reputation management. Top international lawyers, public
relations executives and advisers are employed to produce better media
coverage and introduce the oligarchs to the elite of Western society,
particularly the aristocracy. Along with property and business interests –
many of which are safely invested in the West – the oligarchs have
acquired art galleries, football teams, foundations and other charities.
They build libraries and swimming pools for the private boarding
schools that their children attend.

These figures crave for themselves and their families acceptance by
the old establishment. So, are they any different from the robber barons
who made their money through a mixture of violence and intimidation, but also through entrepreneurship and smart business skills, and
who were seen as pillars of society by subsequent generations? Are the
Carnegies and the Rockefellers of the nineteenth century merely the
precursors of the Usmanovs and Wangs of the present day?

It was a muggy day at the end of July. Russia's elite decamps from
Moscow for as much of the summer as it can – to the opulent dachas
that line the outskirts of the capital or, as was increasingly in vogue, to
the south of France or the Seychelles. This was no ordinary business
meeting. Two dozen of the country's richest men had been summoned
to the Kremlin by the recently installed president. Vladimir Putin had

taken over at the start of the year, after the sudden resignation of the ageing and alcoholic Boris Yeltsin. The former KGB chief was moving quickly to consolidate his power. First in his sights were the oligarchs, the small group who in the early and mid-1990s had amassed huge wealth by taking over the natural resources of the former Soviet state.

In 1994, bankers and administration officials had come up with a plan to help Yeltsin and his administration raise cash and create new private sector companies. The scheme was called 'loans for shares'. At the heart of it was the President's inner circle – the 'family', as it was dubbed – comprising his daughter Tatyana, her husband and a few friends. Chief among them was Boris Berezovsky, nicknamed the 'grey cardinal' and described by the *New York Times* as 'the chief lobbyist for the new elite'. Alongside Berezovsky were Mikhail Khodorkovsky, Roman Abramovich and Vladimir Gusinsky. In the raw capitalism of early post-communist Russia, everything – and everyone – was up for sale, as long as you had the right connections.

The hegemony of this first generation of oligarchs reached its peak in 1996. Yeltsin's popularity had plunged; in a number of the regions the state had been stripped of cash and public sector workers were not being paid. The increasingly impoverished many resented the dissolute and corrupt few. But the business world and the West needed Yeltsin: the slim possibility of a re-emergence of the Communist Party at the impending general election spooked them. At the World Economic Forum at the start of that year Berezovsky and the rest of the clan agreed to bankroll Yeltsin's re-election campaign. They spent up to fifty times the legal limit on advertising and marketing. Television was the key medium: Berezovsky owned the main channel, ORT, and made sure that it put objectivity to one side in order to produce the 'right' result.

Two years later, the financial crash that hit emerging markets badly stung many of Russia's new super-rich. The oligarchs retrenched. They were becoming increasingly perturbed by Yeltsin's erratic behaviour and his health. Russia, they agreed, needed a strongman to succeed him, but one whom they could control. Various figures had been tried out initially as Prime Minister, only to be hastily removed. By 1999, they believed they had alighted on a suitable candidate: Vladimir Putin. Berezovsky took it upon himself to talk to him discreetly, while he holidayed in the French resort of Biarritz. He was impressed with the modesty of the condominium Putin was renting – a far cry from the lobster, champagne and private-jet lifestyle to which he and his associates had become accustomed. After a day of discussion on the veranda, Putin told him, 'All right – I'll give it a shot', as long as it was Yeltsin who put the formal offer. That was done, and after a brief test as Prime Minister, Putin took on the main job on millennium night.

The super-rich men who gave him his opportunity never believed for a moment that he would turn against them. Within weeks he had. While campaigning for the presidential election of March 2000 – a foregone conclusion that confirmed him in office – Putin vowed to 'rid Russia of the oligarchs as a class'. Resentment of the rich played well with a population that deeply resented what had come to be known as *prikhvatizatsiya* – a play on the word 'privatisation' denoting theft. George Soros had tried doing deals in Russia but gave up, describing it as 'robber capitalism'. A World Bank report around the same time showed that thirty individuals controlled 40 per cent of the $225 billion output of the Russian economy, and almost all of its most important sector – natural resources. Precious little of that money ever made it into the exchequer.

From the collapse of the Soviet Union in 1991 until the end of Yeltsin's rule, the state had effectively absented itself from the policing of society. Distinctions between legality and illegality, morality and immorality, barely existed. There were no firm definitions of organised crime, money laundering or extortion; by implication, all commercial transactions were illegal and legal at the same time. *The Russia We Lost*, a popular film in the 1990s by the renowned director Stanislav Govorukhin, depicted a country that had been taken over by a gold-digging elite and a criminal underworld. Boris Nemtsov, Finance Minister at the start of the decade when Western-inspired 'shock therapy' was all the rage, later lamented: 'The country is built as a freakish, oligarchic capitalist state. Its characteristics are the concentration of property in the hands of a narrow group of financiers, the oligarchs. Many of them operate inefficiently, having a parasitic relationship to the industries they control. They don't pay taxes and they don't pay the workers.'

IT WAS A TIME WHEN MILLIONS STARVED, THE HEALTH SYSTEM AND ECONOMY COLLAPSED. MILLIONS DIED OF BASIC ILLNESSES LIKE TB.

The oligarchs   309

Yet, for all the faults of the Yeltsin years, it was a time when Russians could speak out and try their hand at new business or cultural ventures. It was a time of hope and *tusovki* – parties among actors, musicians, writers and students no longer watching out for the censor.[*]

Within weeks of his re-election, Putin started to make good on his promise to rout the oligarchs. The first blow fell on Gusinsky (see Prologue). A man who had tried his hand at theatre directing, he quickly realised that serious money could be made in business, and commodities in particular. For Putin, that was not the problem. What irked him was that Gusinsky was also trying to become a political force in his own right. His holding company, Media-Most, included a new television station called MTV and a newspaper called *Sevodnya* (Today), which were the first of their kind in Russia – outspoken and investigative. The Kremlin did not appreciate their reports about the war in the separatist republic of Chechnya or about other difficult issues. Gusinsky was arrested and thrown in jail on charges of corruption. He was released after only a few days and fled the country. He now divides his time between Israel and New York. Repeated attempts by the Kremlin to have him arrested and extradited have been seen off.

Several other businessmen suddenly found themselves and their companies under investigation for their roles in the sell-offs of the early 1990s. The problem was not where to start, but where not? Pretty much everyone who had got rich had something to hide. In his State of the Union address in July 2000, Putin set out his stall: 'We have a category of people who have become billionaires, as we say, overnight,' he said. 'The state appointed them as billionaires. It simply gave out a huge

---

[*] I remember writing in 1991 of one such party, in which I was surprised to see so many expensively dressed people (in the USSR – which it still was – wealth was seen as the preserve of Westerners). The event was taking place in the courtyard at the back of the Theatre of the Lenin Komsomol, the Lenkom. Despite its name, the theatre had become one of the more fashionable, and daring, venues in town. As I arrived, a charity auction was taking place to raise money for a monument to dead children 'from Hiroshima to Chernobyl'. The memorial was never built, but the hundreds of guests had a good time. I had stumbled upon the New Russians at play for the first time. That was the year when *homo sovieticus* met money. The money accumulated in the hands of a few; the atmosphere soured. As the wealth gap increased, as infrastructure worsened, Putin was a popular choice.

amount of property, practically for free. They got the impression that the gods themselves slept on their heads and that everything is permitted to them.'

Addressing the oligarchs a few weeks later, like a head teacher admonishing errant children, Putin warned them that he was not talking about isolated cases; he was coming after them all, as a group. 'You built this state yourselves, to a great degree,' he began, 'through the political or semi-political structures under your control, so there is no point in blaming the reflection in the mirror.' A man of clipped language, he did not need to spell out the deal he was offering the oligarchs. They could carry on their business dealings inside and outside Russia as long as they did not meddle with politics and looked after the financial interests of the *siloviki* – the political/security establishment.

[handwritten margin note: ALL JEWS]

One of those present was Khodorkovsky, chairman and CEO of Yukos, the biggest of the Russian energy giants, and at the time the richest man in the country and sixteenth-richest in the world (a few other Russians had made it into the top hundred). Khodorkovsky had already riled Putin by funding opposition groups ahead of elections to parliament, the Duma, and by clashing with him publicly over the ultra-sensitive issue of corruption. Khodorkovsky, like the others, had used the chaos of the early to mid-90s to buy up assets at knockdown prices. Having studied at a prestigious chemistry institute, he ran a computer import business under the wing of the Communist Party's youth movement in the 1980s during the Gorbachev era of perestroika (economic reform). He had set up what became one of the first private banks, Menatep. He could not have done any of that without, to use an old Soviet term, *blat i svyazi* (influence and connections): 'juice', as the Americans call it. After acquiring a fertiliser firm in 1994, his big breakthrough was buying Yukos, at a state auction, for the absurdly low price of $350 million. As the firm made inroads across the energy sector, Khodorkovsky convinced himself he could run a business independently of the Kremlin and that his position insulated him from danger. He was by no means alone in allowing hubris to get the better of him. Even after his business associate, Platon Lebedev, was arrested in July 2003, Khodorkovsky continued to believe Putin would not come after him. That summer he arranged the takeover of a rival oil firm, Sibneft, with Abramovich, turning Yukos into a global giant. (Abramovich's earlier purchase of Sibneft in 2001, from Berezovsky, would be the subject of bitter legal battles in London with his erstwhile friend.)

For Putin, this was the final straw. He could not allow the most powerful force of political opposition to become Russia's most powerful businessman. Khodorkovsky's downfall that autumn was dramatic. Heavily armed commandos in balaclavas stormed his private jet in the Siberian city of Novosibirsk as he was embarking on the latest leg of a tour of the country to garner support. He was hauled off the plane and charged with theft. Conviction was a foregone conclusion – judges do not gainsay their political masters in Russia – and his jail term increased later on further charges of tax evasion and embezzlement. After spending ten years in jail, Khodorkovsky was released by Putin in December 2013, on the eve of the Sochi Olympic Games. He was spirited out of the country to Berlin. Such is the fear of retribution engendered by the Kremlin that it seems unlikely he will cause major trouble from exile.

Of the other members of the original clan, Berezovsky fled to Britain before Putin could get him, then mounted a one-man campaign of denunciation from his gilded cage in Surrey. The Godfather of the Yeltsin regime, he became quickly isolated, fending off a succession of trials *in absentia*. He condemned Putin at every turn, describing Russia as a 'banana republic', talking of assassination plots and surrounding himself with heavy security. No matter how vituperative he may have been, his latter-day conversion to the rule of law was unconvincing. In March 2013 he was found dead at his home in Ascot. The postmortem suggested he had hanged himself, but such was the frequency of targeted assassinations of troublemakers, those who knew Berezovsky in Russia and Britain didn't rule out the possibility of a more sinister end.

While a small number of the super-rich failed to survive the transition from Yeltsin to Putin, many emerged unscathed. The survival technique was straightforward: keep your head down; keep out of politics; spirit most of your money, and possibly your family, out of the country; and give a stake of your company and its profits to those with power and influence. As long as the business set abided by these strictures, there was little standing in the way of them becoming extremely wealthy.

Indeed, most were delighted by Putin's intention to reimpose his version of order. As long as everyone with money knew the rules, nothing would stand in the way of profits. Barely months into the new President's tenure, Pyotr Aven, the president of Alfa, Russia's most successful private bank, suggested that Putin should model his regime on that of Chile's Augusto Pinochet, combining Reaganomics with authoritarian control. 'The only way ahead is for fast liberal reforms, building public support for that path but also using totalitarian force to achieve that. Russia has no other choice,' he said. 'I'm a supporter of Pinochet, not as a person but as a politician who produced results for his country. He was not corrupt. He supported his team of economists for 10 years. You need strength for that. I see that parallel here. There are similarities in the situation.'[1] He was speaking for many in Russia's financial and business community.

By the early 2000s, the Russian super-rich had established themselves as a visible global presence. Switzerland was a favoured destination for their money. Its banks were as secret and helpful as ever until international pressure was exerted on them to impose greater regulation. From that point more relaxed destinations – such as the Caribbean, Cyprus, Lithuania and Singapore – came into vogue. France was the chosen destination for rest and relaxation, with the finest chateaux on the Côte d'Azur (the likes of which King Leopold and President Mobutu used to frequent) snapped up. The ski resort of Courchevel turned itself into a Russian enclave of fur coats and helipads, where diners would feast on oysters and foie gras, washed down with vodka and Chateau Pétrus. (The price tag of thousands or the tens of thousands per bottle depended on the year.) Sometimes vintage wine and vodka were mixed in the same glass.

The epicentre of the new wave was London, which acquired the nickname 'Londongrad'. From the early 2000s, a service industry established itself to cater to the oligarchs' every requirement. One of the most important was the massaging of their reputations. Men who had made money in the Wild East of the early 1990s were keen to have inconvenient stories about their past – the cartels and acquisitions of state industries at absurdly low prices – expunged from the records. Former British government ministers queued up to represent them in the House of Lords. Spin-doctors did their PR, tasking juniors in the office to 'improve' their clients' Wikipedia entries – the internet made it easier to launder reputations, but also easier to be found out. The term used by professionals for this broad service was 'reframing narratives'. Several law firms helped Russians to use Britain's hideously indulgent defamation culture to slap suits on enquiring journalists at the first sign of trouble. London became known as 'the town called sue'. So pervasive was 'libel tourism' that the US Congress enacted a law to protect Americans from English courts. By 2013, the English law on defamation was improved, marginally.

As for the Russians' financial affairs, tax advisers ensured they paid as little as possible on their earnings and on the lavish properties they bought through offshore shell companies. (The practice was not confined to Russians; anyone could do it as long as they had the money to spirit away.) Corporate law firms helped Russians settle historic scores with each other, racking up huge fees for determining who had double-crossed or threatened whom to buy or sell lucrative assets. Russian slang terms such as *krysha*, which roughly translates as 'protection money', are now common parlance in English courts. Some of the major law firms estimate that more than half of their commercial work is now done on behalf of Russian and other East European clients.

In March 2002, the *London Evening Standard* ran an article on the top fifty residents of London's richest borough, Kensington and Chelsea. Not a single Russian featured in it. Khodorkovsky's conviction the following year changed that, convincing his peers that nobody was safe. They needed to get their money out and their families out. Super-rich Russians began to dominate the London property market, on the lookout for the most prestigious homes in the best-known locations as safe havens and investments. Although prices dropped slightly straight after the global banking crash of 2008, the slip was minimal and temporary. Since then, the value of homes with an asking price of more than £10 million has soared by a total of 30 per cent, unlike anything else in the UK or in Europe. The more ostentatious the home, the better: One

Hyde Park, a luxury block next to the department store of choice, Harrods, became a convenient central London bolt hole. In 2011, shortly after it opened, one owner spent a record £136 million on two flats, and another £60 million adapting them. The owner was Rinat Akhmetov, Ukraine's richest man. Given that his assets were estimated at well over £10 billion, this was pocket money.

The main UK residence for most oligarchs was usually in the countryside. The most exclusive estate agents were put on permanent alert for properties coming on the market in the Home Counties. They were in search of luxury (they had enough of that in their many urban dwellings), but also authenticity. They wanted bucolic splendour and to play the *Downton Abbey* squire. Traditional English upper-class pastimes such as polo became popular, as did annual appearances at Royal Ascot and the Henley Regatta. They latched on to celebrities and minor royals, seeing in them a route to respectability. Private boarding schools welcomed their children, and their chequebooks.

Russian oligarchs have generally found it easier to establish a financial – and social and reputational – foothold in Britain than in the United States. Apart from the weather, what is there not to like? So great was the exodus to London in the early 2000s that the community fed on itself and grew, aided by Britons eager to seize on the opportunities brought by the flood of new money. Shops and companies catering purely to Russian needs opened their doors, whether in fine wines, private jets or speedboats.

One of the reasons why Russians chose Britain was that the American authorities had an annoying habit of asking intrusive questions, and sometimes refusing entry on the grounds of financial irregularity. Britain has had no such qualms. In the search for the super-rich, this was competitive tendering and Britain ensured it came in with the most attractive bids. The Labour governments of Tony Blair and Gordon Brown were particularly indulgent, turning a blind eye to the cash being laundered, and refusing to tighten regulations on tax avoidance. After a campaign of sustained pressure, in 2008 Brown's administration finally imposed an annual levy of £30,000 on non-domiciled residence, a risible amount for these so-called 'non-doms'. 'All money is good money' was the mantra. In the same year, the IMF put London in the less than salubrious company of Bermuda, the Cayman Islands and Switzerland as 'an offshore financial centre'.

The welcoming tone was set early on by Peter Mandelson, who as Trade and Industry Secretary famously stated in 1998: 'We are intensely relaxed about people getting filthy rich.' He hastened to add: 'As long as they pay their taxes.' Later ennobled and serving as the EU's Trade Commissioner, Mandelson found himself embroiled in controversy over his links with Oleg Deripaska, 'the king of aluminium'. On one trip he went with Deripaska and the banking scion Nat Rothschild on Deripaska's Gulfstream jet to Siberia. Rothschild later revealed in court (where he was trying to sue a British newspaper) that the three had toured one of Deripaska's smelting plants, played five-a-side football and had a floodlit game of ice hockey. The group then enjoyed a traditional Russian sauna, a *banya*, and were entertained at their host's chalet by a Cossack band. The story came to light only in the midst of a furious political row when Mandelson and Rothschild were joined on Deripaska's super yacht, the *Queen K*, off Corfu in 2008, by George Osborne, the Conservative Party's shadow finance spokesman, who in 2010 would go on to become Chancellor of the Exchequer. For readers, this was intriguing evidence of Russian new money at the heart of the British political establishment.[2] The public reaction was the usual mix of disdain and envy.

A favoured saying among New Russians went: 'There are three words that begin with the letter C in the English language: Courchevel, Cartier and Chelsea.' One purchase, above all others, propelled Roman Abramovich on to the global stage: Chelsea Football Club. No acquisition before that had enjoyed such publicity, and arguably none has since. The quintessential self-made man, Abramovich began as a street trader in the late 1980s, selling anything from rubber ducks, to dolls, to retreaded car tyres. It was his friendship with Berezovsky, whom he met in 1992, which provided the opening on to the bigger stage. Three years later the two had bought a controlling stake in the oil firm Sibneft under Yeltsin's original 'loans for shares' scheme.

From 2000, as soon as the tide turned, Abramovich ceased all contact with Berezovsky and what was left of the Yeltsin 'family'. He volunteered to become governor of Chukotka, spending more than

£100 million on the remote, impoverished province in the Russian Far East. His message to Putin – 'You see, we oligarchs can be loyal' – was as clear as the President's warning had been to them. By 2004, a few months after transforming himself into the face of European football, Abramovich had shot from nowhere to the number-one spot in the *Sunday Times'* Rich List, the Bible of London's transnational wealthy, who check their status every year.

As he took on companies and grew them, so he amassed a portfolio of properties, jets and yachts. For all his ostentation, Abramovich shunned the limelight, almost never speaking in public and shielding himself with a large team of bodyguards and advisers. After divorcing his first wife, a one-time Aeroflot stewardess, with the assistance of a highly paid British legal team, he branched into art with his new, younger partner, Dasha Zhukova, the daughter of another oligarch. Her forays into the art world began with the Garage Centre for Contemporary Culture, housed in a Soviet Constructivist-era bus depot on the northern outskirts of Moscow. She then moved and expanded the project into Gorky Park, in the centre of the capital, handing the Dutch starchitect Rem Koolhaas the task of creating the city's premier modern art gallery. Her next move will be into the former imperial capital – a nineteen-acre island and former naval yard in the heart of St Petersburg that she is calling New Holland, which she hopes will be part of an international arts chain linking MoMA in New York with London's Tate Modern and the Pompidou Centre in Paris.[3]*

Other Russians have gradually caught up with Abramovich, and several have overtaken him. Most of the Russian super-rich (those valued at less than $1 billion are considered small fry) did not make their money through great inventions or originality. For all the exhortations, Russia's economy has not diversified under Putin and the country has very few of the technological whizz-kids of India or China, not to mention the United States. The key to wealth in the post-communist

---

* As with the sheikhs, as with the super-rich of previous eras, the oligarchs see art as a demonstration of power and place, putting them at the forefront of the global cultural and social establishment. Money, it seems, is no object in Abramovich's quest. His purchase in 2008 of Francis Bacon's *Triptych, 1976* for more than £50 million made it the most expensive piece of post-war art.

era was access to natural resources. Some of them are figures connected with the Soviet era, or their descendants. Others are self-made, spotting an opportunity in the 1990s and making sure the right contacts were kept sweet. Almost all are men between forty-five and sixty-five, and few would be considered charismatic.

ALL
NEW
BOYS

Two of the most prominent oil men, Mikhail Fridman and Leonid (Len) Blavatnik, were important figures in a highly lucrative but acrimonious joint venture with Britain's BP, TNK–BP – the largest private transaction in Russian history. Fridman had started off scalping theatre tickets and washing windows for money. Ukrainian-born Viktor Vekselberg, another key player in the deal, made his money in aluminium and oil. He thrust himself on to the global scene with a somewhat more refined purchase – that of Fabergé eggs. He has since become the world's largest collector, at a cost of more than $100 million. Vekselberg also became chairman of the Skolkovo Foundation, a pet project of Dmitry Medvedev (the Russian President for a few years, but always Putin's underling) to produce its own version of Silicon Valley. This too has struggled to get off the ground. These three men – Vekselberg, Fridman and Blavatnik – have been at or close to the top of *Forbes*'s Russian Rich List since it was created in 2003.

More recently the man bestriding the top of that hit parade has been Alisher Usmanov. Like the others, he made his fortune in metals, but quickly assumed the other two roles of the successful Russian oligarch – he became a big name in global sports and arts sponsorship, and he kept on the right side of the Kremlin. Usmanov's first major foray into public philanthropy took place in 2007. An art collection owned by the late exiled musician Mstislav Rostropovich was about to be auctioned in London by Sotheby's, much to the chagrin of the Russian state (even though Rostropovich had fled the Soviet Union). Suddenly the auction was cancelled; it transpired that an anonymous billionaire had purchased the works – which included paintings by Grigoriev and Roerich and porcelain and glass once owned by Catherine the Great – at well above the highest estimated price. The name of the white knight was revealed to be Usmanov, who subsequently announced that it would go on permanent display at the Konstantin Palace near St Petersburg.

A few weeks earlier he had followed in Abramovich's footsteps by entering the English football scene and becoming one of the main shareholders at Arsenal, gradually increasing his stake in the club to close to 30 per cent. (He ensured he had the biggest corporate box in the stadium, bigger than those of the other directors, by knocking two into one.) His other sporting passion is fencing, which he took up at the age of thirteen and went on to become Uzbek junior champion. He is now president of the International Fencing Federation. His arts sponsorship has included paying for an exhibition of Tate Gallery Turner oils and watercolours in Moscow, and for an exhibition of Russian art at London's Royal Academy.

As he diversified his holdings from commodities to technology and media, Usmanov bought up Russia's second-largest mobile phone company, MegaFon, and acquired shares in Silicon Valley start-ups. One of his companies, mail.ru, bought a 10 per cent stake in Facebook in 2009, at the height of the global financial crisis. Under the terms of the deal with Mark Zuckerberg, brokered by Goldman Sachs, Usmanov agreed that he would receive no voting rights or seats on the board. It was an unconventional but highly lucrative deal for Usmanov, who netted several billion after Facebook floated in 2012.

That single success made Usmanov into Britain's richest man that year, with his wealth estimated at £13.3 billion, knocking India's most prominent steel magnate, Lakshmi Mittal, off the top spot. By 2013, three of the top five positions on the *Sunday Times'* list were held by Russians (the other two were Blavatnik and Fridman), but it was Usmanov who was leading the way. He bought a Grade I-listed Tudor mansion, following in the footsteps of other super-rich owners of the house, including John Paul Getty. It is said that he prefers his home in leafy Hampstead, for which he paid £50 million in 2008. Since then he has sought to build a bathing complex in the garden, modelled on the leisure facilities enjoyed by Roman emperors. His neighbours have been less than thrilled with the plans. As for getting about, he has availed himself of the ubiquitous oligarchic mega-yacht, moored off Sardinia's Costa Smeralda, while his fleet of planes includes a Boeing 737 and an Airbus A340 reputed to be Europe's largest private jet –

although such is the competition that these accolades of 'biggest ever' come and go with alarming regularity.

Usmanov's achievement is not bad for a man whose first business venture was plastic bags. He did what all successful businessmen do: he spotted a market opportunity. In Soviet times, even in the late 1980s, Russians would traipse around with their string bags on the off-chance of finding something to buy, until Usmanov's plastic bags appeared in the shops. But this is not the classic rags-to-riches tale. The son of a public prosecutor, Usmanov was sent to a prestigious Moscow school. From there he won a place at the famous Moscow State Institute of International Relations, MGIMO. Both of these institutions provided fertile networking opportunities. Like Abramovich, but unlike Berezovsky and Khodorkovsky, he has fastidiously kept on the right side of the Kremlin. One episode reflects this perfectly. In 2006 he bought the weekly newspaper *Kommersant*, previously owned by Berezovsky. The paper was regarded as a serious business and political publication, which did not easily self-censor. That was until 2011, when Usmanov sacked the editor and the head of the publisher's holding company after they ran an unflattering issue on Putin's election victory, entitled 'Victory of United Ballot Stuffers' – a play on the name of the President's party, United Russia. Usmanov apologised for the 'ethical breach' and said the article had 'bordered on petty hooliganism' – a catch-all phrase used to denounce all forms of unwanted criticism.

For Usmanov, as for the other oligarchs, reputation is central to everything he does. The House of Lords has been a happy hunting ground for Russia's super-rich, with a number of peers taking on roles as advisers or directors of their companies. Usmanov has had a decade-long association with Lord (David) Owen, a former Foreign Secretary, and in November 2012 he persuaded a former City Minister, Lord (Paul) Myners, to join the board of MegaFon shortly before its flotation on the London stock market, to soothe investor concerns about the company's governance.

One chapter in particular causes Usmanov reputational headaches. In August 1980 he was sentenced to an eight-year prison term in Uzbekistan for fraud, theft of state or civil property and conspiracy to receive bribes. He has always insisted that the jailing was politically motivated and a reflection of the chaos and corruption of late Soviet times, pointing out that in 2000 the Uzbek Supreme Court overturned the judgement. Usmanov's decision to buy Arsenal shares shot him to global prominence and with that the enquiring eyes of the media. A number of British and other journalists began looking into his past. On 19 November 2007, the *Guardian* newspaper published a piece entitled 'The Colourful Life of Football's Latest Oligarch', including a detailed email exchange with Usmanov involving thirty-seven questions. The paper wrote:

> The first time many journalists heard Usmanov's name was when Schillings, a firm of libel law specialists which prides itself on a reputation for ruthlessness, fired off a letter to every major media organisation in Britain, announcing that their client had purchased his first tranche of Arsenal shares and warning against any 'defamatory statements or invasions of his privacy'. Schillings were concerned about what they described as 'a matter of historical record'. Their client had been 'imprisoned for various offences under the old Soviet regime', they wrote. 'Our client did not commit any of the offences of which he was charged. Our client was fully pardoned after President Mikhail Gorbachev took office. All references to these matters have now been expunged from police records.'

In the exchange, Usmanov repeatedly complained of 'misinformation' and described the charges as 'trumped up'. He also denied that his businesses had benefited from any relationship with Uzbekistan's long-standing leader, Islam Karimov, or his daughter Gulnara.[4]

The more established he became in British public life, the more Usmanov's public relations team succeeded in shifting media attention away from his past and towards his new roles as global businessman and philanthropist. Those entrusted with looking after his interests were leaving nothing to chance. In November 2012, at the time of the MegaFon flotation, one of Britain's public relations firms, Finsbury, was forced to apologise after *The Times* revealed it had made a number of changes and deletions to his Wikipedia entry.

Some oligarchs have established reputations in the UK and elsewhere that have sought to develop an image that goes beyond mega-yachts, mansions and football teams. One who has tried harder than most is Yuri Milner. A son of intellectuals and a physicist by training, in 1990 he became the first Russian non-émigré to receive an MBA at a US university. He spent the first half of the 1990s at the World Bank in Washington, watching in frustration as his peers carved up the spoils of Russian privatisation. He later described this period as his 'lost years'. He quickly caught up, however, working with Khodorkovsky at Yukos and then tying up the Facebook deal with Usmanov. He has been Russia's global face of internet venture capital, investing heavily in a number of global technology giants – from Twitter, to Spotify, to China's Alibaba.

Yet the temptation to spend ostentatiously seems impossible to resist. To keep up with the Silicon Valley Joneses, Milner paid $100 million for a mansion in Los Altos Hills, an ersatz eighteenth-century French chateau overlooking San Francisco Bay. The home, with fourteen bed-rooms, a ballroom, home theatre, library, gym and staff quarters, exchanged hands at twice its market value – but that did not trouble him unduly, even if it left others in the Valley quietly scoffing. The other side of Milner, the scientist, is the one he prefers to project. In 2012 he established the Fundamental Physics Prize, with its award of $3 million far outstripping the Nobel Prize.

Identifying the biggest beneficiaries of the Great Russian Sell-Off of the 1990s remains difficult and often dangerous. In 2004, hired killers gunned down the launch editor of the Russian edition of *Forbes*, Paul Klebnikov, as he left his Moscow office. Klebnikov, an American of Russian origin, had acquired a reputation for digging into the murky dealings of Russia's rich and corrupt. *Forbes* continued to publish its list of the country's wealthiest people – alongside Bloomberg, the *Sunday Times* and others around the world.

The full picture of the Russian elite remains incomplete, and their (usually British) libel lawyers remain as voracious as ever to deter the prying eyes of the media. The more colourful names may not even be the wealthiest. More curious still is the position of the President him-self. In disclosures required by the electoral authorities, in 2012 Putin claimed that his annual official income was $187,000, with assets confined to a small apartment and three cheap cars. His actual wealth is a matter of speculation, from parlour games to Wikileaks cables putting the total into the tens of billions. One of the claims made by a whistleblower, Sergei Kolesnikov, who left the country in 2010 and is now believed to be in hiding in Western Europe, is of a 'palace' on the Black Sea for which official funds were diverted. Russian newspapers provided further information, all of which has been denied by the Kremlin.[5] What is not in dispute is that a number of figures close to Putin from his early St Petersburg days are in senior economic positions. These include Yuri Kovalchuk, whose formerly small St Petersburg bank went on to control a number of subsidiaries of the energy giant Gazprom, and Gennady Timchenko, who runs a private trading company, Gunvor, which trades a considerable amount of Rosneft's oil internationally. In cables released by Wikileaks, US diplomats describe Gunvor as 'of special note' in a broader system of opaque dealings. A 2009 cable said the company is 'rumoured to be one of Putin's sources of undisclosed wealth'. Gunvor insists that Putin 'is not a beneficiary' of the company or its activities.[6]

Other, more high-profile figures who took part in a dacha cooperative called Ozero, or Lake, with Putin back in the 1990s are now key figures in major corporations. Igor Sechin, perhaps the President's closest confidant, was put in charge of Rosneft, which took over Yukos after Khodorkovsky's demise. President-cum-Prime Minister-cum-right-hand man Dmitry Medvedev was also chair of Gazprom. Vladimir Yakunin, who was given responsibility for the railway network, said Ozero 'was not the reason for certain people's appointments, but the fact that we were all from Leningrad, that we knew each other, that everyone had experience behind them … I also choose my deputies on their experience, knowledge, my personal impression of a person. It's natural.'

Putin's genius, or cunning, was to denounce the first generation of oligarchs, and to create a second that was much more in his own image. Under his long rule, the *siloviki*, the security and political establishment, has merged with business. The historian and essayist Perry Anderson encapsulated his achievement in 2007:

Putin has turned the tables on them. Under his system, a more organic symbiosis between the two has been achieved, this time under the dominance of politics. Today, two deputy prime ministers are chairmen, respectively, of Gazprom and Russian Railways; four deputy chiefs of staff in the Kremlin occupy the same positions in the second largest oil company, a nuclear fuel giant, an energy transport enterprise and Aeroflot. The minister of industry is chairman of the oil pipeline monopoly; the finance minister, not only of the diamond monopoly, but of the second largest state bank in the country; the telecoms minister, of the biggest mobile phone operator. A uniquely Russian form of *cumul des mandats* [holding more than one office at the same time] blankets the scene.[7]

The notion of 'clean' or 'dirty' money is irrelevant in Russia. Such is the brutality of public life that nobody is sure where the boundaries lie or whether they are safe. Yet the oligarchs have done what they can to insure themselves by taking as much money out of the country as possible and avoiding crossing Putin or those close to him.

Kremlin Inc. is not a registered company; it has no directors and no shareholders. For a tiny number of Russians it has provided unimaginable winnings. While relations were comparatively warm, the Americans and the West turned a blind eye (some of their own were, in any case, in on the act). But after Russia's annexation of Crimea and the violence in other parts of Ukraine in early 2014, the US and the EU not only imposed sanctions, but they also made public some of the links between Putin and the wealth snatchers. For the first time the information was out in the open. And yet there appeared little sign that it would make any difference. The power structures were too wealthy, and too entrenched, to be challenged.[8]

Nobody can pinpoint the time or place when Deng Xiaoping said: 'To get rich is glorious.' Indeed, he almost certainly didn't use the phrase, but history has willed him to do so. The man credited with unleashing capitalism on communist China from the early 1980s had a somewhat different priority. He wanted to safeguard the position of the

Chinese Communist Party. The best, perhaps the only, way to do it at a time when the state ideology was imploding across the world was to embrace its economic nemesis.

Like the New Russians, who came a decade before them, the first generation of Chinese tycoons have clung limpet-style to political power. Unlike Russia, the nexus between the ruling party and the business elite has come about not as a result of threats and deal-making, but through a highly visible official policy. Theoretically and rhetorically, the wealth of the big companies and their bosses belongs to the state. Deng's embrace of capitalism made clear that the state would retain the commanding heights of industry, finance and all sectors of the economy. Many entrepreneurs deny that their company is *siying*, or privately run, preferring the term *minying*, which roughly translates as 'run by the people'. It is a verbal conceit that, of course, very few believe. But it is a useful formula that helps publicly to define the power relationship and the terms of engagement.

Attempts to discern the wealth of senior party figures and their offspring, the so-called princelings, have proven extremely difficult. When news organisations try to produce details – such as the *New York Times'* revelations about the family of former Premier Wen Jiabao in October 2012 or Bloomberg's report in June that year about the financial dealings of the relatives of the current leader, Xi Jinping – they face immediate reprisals. These have included the blocking of websites (in Chinese and English), the rejection of visas for staff and the cancellation of all-important business contracts. The *New York Times* alleged that, as a result, Bloomberg executives had decided to hold back on investigations into the wealth and assets of prominent Chinese figures and not to publish other articles inside China that are deemed sensitive.[9] Undeterred, in January 2014 an international group of media organisations, including Britain's *Guardian*, published the most comprehensive details yet of the use of offshore financial havens by China's elite. The report – by the International Consortium of Investigative Journalists – disclosed that more than a dozen relatives of political and military leaders, including Xi's brother-in-law, Wen's son and son-in-law, and the daughter of another former premier, Li Peng, had used companies based in the British Virgin Islands. Leading international banks and accountancy firms had helped them come to these arrangements. Just as the Russians could always rely on good service from Western companies for their discreet needs, so the same seemingly applies to the Chinese.

Such allegations are deeply inconvenient for the leadership. Since coming to power in 2012, Xi has made rooting out corruption a top priority, so much so that his attacks on illicit money-making were seen as contributing to the drop in China's growth rate in the first half of 2013. But who should be targeted and who should be left well alone? The goal posts are kept deliberately vague. Revelations about the corruption of some officials are deemed acceptable, patriotic even; but anyone who puts into the public domain inconvenient facts about the wealth of a politician or official who is in favour may find themselves serving long prison sentences for 'rumour mongering'.

The National People's Congress is by far the wealthiest legislature of any country; it may be the wealthiest in human history. According to some estimates, its seventy richest members make more than the total net worth of all members of all three branches of the US state.[10] The top sixty had an average net worth of just under $1.5 billion in 2011. At first glance, this might seem a classic case of politicians creaming off the wealth, and in some respects it is. Most of the time, however, the direction of travel is the opposite: the state has co-opted those who have made money into its various parliamentary (or rubber-stamping) bodies. Nobody with money-making ambition would be foolish enough to turn down an invitation to take part. All aspiring billionaires are reminded to look over their shoulders. Financial success is virtually impossible for anyone who attempts to operate outside the political system.

From the days of the Tang and Ming dynasties, China's elite has been careful to hide its wealth behind high walls. Sales of luxury items are rampant among the top 1 per cent, but where possible the acquisitions — or the identities of the purchasers — are kept out of sight. Limousines invariably come with blacked-out windows; fine wines are drunk in restaurants hidden away in secure compounds.

In the Bric nations — Brazil, Russia, India and China — and in other emerging economic powers, the newly affluent understand that their wealth is unprotected. Property rights are only nominally guaranteed by the constitution; the judiciary is a long way from being independent. An entire stratum of Chinese has followed the Russians in sending their families abroad, partly to give the next generation of princelings a Western education or cleaner air. One of the favoured destinations for these so-called 'naked businessmen' is the United States, which has an allocation of residency permits for the global wealthy. In 2011, Chinese accounted for two-thirds of the five thousand investment immigration visas issued by the American authorities.

Hundreds of billions of dollars have been stashed away offshore, just in case, much of it put into properties in the US, the UK, Singapore, Hong Kong and Dubai. Secret bank accounts in Singapore and Switzerland are bulging with Chinese money. One recent study found that half of China's super-rich now have investments abroad. According to the National Association of Realtors, Chinese buyers spent more than $8 billion on residential real estate in the US in 2012–13. Money has also gone into gold, pearls, diamonds and wine. In November 2013, the world's most expensive case of wine – a 1978 Burgundy, Romanée-Conti – sold at Christie's in Hong Kong for $476,000, to a Chinese bidder.

As late as July 2001, Jiang Zemin's decision to allow entrepreneurs officially to join the Party stirred a rare public split among the leadership and deep disquiet in the conservative rank and file. Deng, and Jiang after him, grasped what many of their conservative opponents never did – that the party had much in common with private entrepreneurs, who disliked democratic politics and independent unions as much as they did. The party's distrust of the private sector was not about money, nor the flagrant contradiction between individual wealth and the official Marxist and Maoist pantheons. The real issue was the threat that the foreign and local private sector might become a political rival.[11]

According to *Forbes*, in 2012 there were 421 billionaires in America, 96 in Russia, 95 in China and 48 in India. The rate of growth in China is outstripping the rest. Between 2005 and 2010 the number of billionaires in China grew from 2 to 64. In a report looking at 216 countries, Credit Suisse noted that 6 per cent of the world's total of 'Ultra High Net Worth Individuals' – those with more than $50 million in disposable income – came from China. That is second only to the US, albeit still with half the total. Of the 'merely rich' – the top

1 per cent – four-fifths of this group is under forty-five years old in China, a proportion vastly greater than anywhere else.

Whereas Russian fortunes were made suddenly and often violently in the early to mid-1990s through the privatisation of natural resources, China's first generation of super-rich made money from a wide range of enterprises – from cheap consumer durables to finance. But the key to unlocking wealth in China is land. It is the currency on which all else depends.

Wang Jianlin's route to financial stardom epitomises the opportunities and risks of communist–capitalist China. The son of a Red Army hero who fought for Mao during the Long March, he spent seventeen years in the People's Liberation Army. He uses that experience to advertise his credentials as an ordinary man who knows all there is to know about hardship and thrift. 'In the early days we really had to scramble to eat,' he remarked. When food was available, he used to half-fill his rice bowl on his first time through the canteen queue so that he could eat it quickly enough to go back for seconds before the food ran out. 'That experience helped shape my character, taught me never to give up and never bow your head to hardship.'

Man-of-the-people meets loyal communist meets entrepreneur: the script could not be better written. He was decommissioned in the mid-1980s as the armed forces were slimmed down: 'My dream at first was to be a soldier, but I was among the million who were disarmed, so I went into business.' He took a job in the coastal city of Dalian in his native Sichuan Province. He turned around an unglamorous and failing municipal property business that nobody wanted. His success allowed him to branch out into other parts of the country, a move that was rare at the time. He snapped up housing developments and built commercial properties before diversifying into culture and entertainment, creating China's largest cinema chain. His company, Dalian Wanda (*wanda* means 'many successes'), rose to become the biggest commercial real estate developer, catering to the aspirational dreams of China's rapidly expanding middle class. The Dalian Wanda Group now counts dozens of five-star hotels, numerous karaoke bars and more than seventy 'Wanda Plaza' shopping malls as part of its $50 billion portfolio of assets. Wang runs his company with a military rigour he learned in the army: 'In our company if I make a decision and you do not carry it out immediately, you need to pay a fine. The basic principle is I command and my employees carry it out immediately.'[12] Alfred Krupp would have been proud.

By 2010 Wang had eased his way to the number-one slot on China's rich list and he was fast becoming a global player, thanks in large part to the buying opportunities that came with the global financial crash, particularly in the United States. His 'war chest' for potential acquisitions around the world was said to contain £20 billion. Top of his shopping list were hotels, cinema chains and television stations. His first major foray was his purchase in 2012 of AMC, America's second-largest cinema chain, turning his merged company into the largest in the world, with six thousand screens across Asia and the United States. Europe was next; he would, he declared, own a fifth of all the world's cinemas by 2020. There is no reason to doubt that he will succeed in his ambition.

A few months after buying AMC, he indulged himself in one of his hobbies by purchasing the British niche yacht-maker, Sunseeker, for £300 million. The firm's powerboats have featured in James Bond films, and it is now increasingly focused on markets such as Russia, Brazil, Mexico and, inevitably, China, whose clients have apparently requested mah-jong tables and karaoke rooms to be fitted out. 'We wanted to buy 30 Sunseeker yachts because we are planning to build three marinas here in China,' Wang said with methodical logic. 'So then we thought it would be a better deal if we just bought the company.' Alongside the essential private jet, Wang has a Sunseeker super yacht, which is often moored in Shanghai. 'I was one of the first in China to buy one,' he told one interviewer, before bringing himself back into check. 'I am not a person who pursues luxury. I am not like those people who, once they have money, compulsively squander it or show it off. Just don't show off, don't flaunt your wealth because nowadays China's wealth gap is relatively big.'

At first glance, such an observation from a man of Wang's wealth and power might seem improbable. But the fear of *luan*, or chaos, is never far from the surface, and the yawning wealth gap contributes to that insecurity. Policy-makers and the business community talk about it openly, but the impulse to make money and to spend it is hard to resist.

Wang followed up the Sunseeker acquisition with a much larger project. In a deal worth $1.1 billion, Dalian announced in June 2013 that it was building Europe's tallest residential tower in London, at a prime location close to Battersea Power Station. This would also house the first branded Wanda five-star hotel outside China. Wang was joining the Russians in the spotlight, with all the trappings of a senior member of the global super-rich. The wealthier he has become, the more he has enjoyed the limelight. In September 2013 he invited celebrities such as Leonardo DiCaprio, Nicole Kidman and John Travolta to help open his Chinese version of Hollywood in Qingdao, to mark his $5 billion investment in the Chinese film industry. Yet everywhere he goes he makes sure that officialdom is on his side. Speaking at the World Economic Forum's 'Summer Davos' in September 2013 – held, inevitably, in Dalian – Wang was candid about the role of business: 'China is a government-oriented economy. No one can say he can run his business entirely without government connections. Anybody who says he or she can do things alone without any connection with the government in China is a hypocrite.' According to the *New York Times*, one of the investigations Bloomberg decided not to publish was into Wang 'and his financial ties to the families of party leaders'.[13]

Earlier in 2013, Wang had a close shave. His association with one individual almost got him into terrible trouble. The dramatic fall from grace of Bo Xilai, the ambitious Communist Party chief of Chongqing, a municipality of some thirty million people, could have rebounded directly on to Wang's business prospects. Several senior Dalian businessmen were questioned about their association with a man who was about to be imprisoned and denounced as a corrupt enemy of the state. Wang managed to extricate himself from the affiliation, insisting that he had gone no further than was necessary to conduct business: 'I know Bo Xilai well. But our relationship was based on our work, we didn't have a personal relationship.'[14] Others were not so lucky. What clinched it for Wang was not his status – after all, Bo had been one of the most powerful men in China – but his previous loyal relationship with the party and his strong connections with those in favour in Beijing. Around the time of Bo's arrest Wang's company announced that he was receiving an award at the central Chinese leadership compound in the capital – a rare honour.

The Bo case was a salutary reminder of what can happen when your patron falls. As late as 2008, the top of the Chinese rich list remained a dangerous place. The wealthiest man in China at the time, Huang Guangyu, who was head of a national home-appliances chain-store network, Gome, with an estimated fortune of $6.3 billion, was detained for alleged insider trading. He was sentenced to fourteen years.[15] The first reaction to the arrest of people like Huang is not 'What did he do wrong?' but 'Who did he offend?'

In December 2012, two generations of Chinese entrepreneurs played out their different visions for wealth, live on state television. Picking up an award for 'economic figure of the year', Wang found himself on stage with Jack Ma, president of e-commerce giant Alibaba, and a fast-rising star. Ma told the audience that a revolution was taking place that would sweep away the offline world of bricks and mortar: shop fronts, he declared, would soon be a thing of the past. An increasingly annoyed Wang bet Ma 100 million renminbi (around $16 million) that online spending would not exceed 50 per cent of total retail spend by 2022. Ma declined the wager (betting is technically illegal in China), but the challenge was on.[16]

Ma relishes the role that has been assigned to him as the ultra-modern face of Chinese business. The *Financial Times*' 'person of the year' for 2013, he likens himself to Silicon Valley stars such as Mark Zuckerberg and Jeff Bezos, rather than the likes of Wang, whom he would regard as too old school. Born in the south-eastern city of Hangzhou, he is the son of performers of 'ping tan', a traditional musical storytelling technique that was banned during the Cultural Revolution. An unimpressive student, he preferred to hang around a local hotel, befriending foreign tourists to improve his English. After twice failing the national university entrance exam, he was admitted to a teaching institute. In 1994, with China gradually opening up, he started a translation business that allowed him to travel to the United States. There he came into contact for the first time with the early internet pioneers. Back in Hangzhou he set up China Yellow Pages, an online business directory, at a time when state-controlled media were not even allowed to mention the internet. He sold that business and worked briefly for the Ministry of Foreign Trade, an experience that allowed him to build up his government network. The most important contact came to him by chance when he was assigned to take an American guest on a tour of the Great Wall. That visitor was Jerry Yang, co-founder of Yahoo; the two struck up an instant friendship.

In early 1999 Ma pooled $60,000 with a group of friends at his flat to found Alibaba. He had come up with a simple but compelling business model: he would enable small Chinese companies to look for global buyers online, opening up markets that had until then been confined to trade shows. After struggling to make a profit in its first few years, his start-up finally took off. From there, he launched Taobao (Search for Treasure), an online shopping service. Ma made what seemed a ludicrous claim that he was going to war with eBay. He declared: 'Ebay may be a shark in the ocean but I am a crocodile in the Yangtze River. If we fight in the ocean we lose but if we fight in the river we win.' Within a few years, eBay's share of the Chinese market had collapsed from virtual dominance to less than 10 per cent; soon after, it quit altogether. Ma had become the king of Chinese e-commerce.

Two years earlier, he had struck a deal with his old chum Yang. Yahoo took a 40 per cent stake in Alibaba at a cost of $1 billion; under the deal, Ma would run the joint venture. It didn't take long for him to outwit the Americans. By then, Yahoo was mired in controversy after it had handed over to the authorities private email information that led to at least two Chinese journalists and activists being convicted of subversion.

By 2012, Alibaba's share of the world's fastest-growing domestic market was so great that just two of its portals exceeded the global sales of eBay and Amazon combined; alone, it accounted for 2 per cent of China's gross domestic product. Ma had become so powerful that few dared to criticise him publicly for a management style that adapted the neo-religious conformism of Silicon Valley to a Chinese setting. The twenty thousand workers are called Aliren (Ali people). One former employee, Hao Wu, described the corporate ethic:

Every business group was assigned a dedicated HR liaison, known as its 'political commissar' (I kid you not), who monitored employees' performances. Every quarter, performance reviews were mandated, with 50 percent based on their adherence to the company's values. Those with bad value scores, even top performers, got fired.

Those who survived these reviews were treated like family. Everyone was given a nickname, their unique and exclusive Alibaba identity, after a character in martial arts fantasy novels – which Jack loved. Alirens were encouraged to treat each other as brothers and sisters, and Jack periodically officiated at group weddings.[17]

Hao likened Ma's approach to that of a certain Chinese ruler: 'For a brief moment, I thought I understood why so many before me had followed Mao Zedong, the great helmsman, in the Communist revolution,' he wrote. 'Sometimes I wondered whether Alibaba truly resembled the idealised legend of the Red Army, where cadres and soldiers formed a close surrogate family and together ushered in a new era by sacrificing everything personal for the collective.'

With 600 million registered users (of whom around 100 million shop on its sites on any given day), Alibaba is now conceivably the most powerful private organisation in China. While Ma relishes the fight with other entrepreneurs, he always keeps on the right side of the Communist Party. He is quite happy to hand over data from his customers if the authorities require it. 'We create value for the shareholders and the shareholders don't want us to oppose the government and go bankrupt,' he has said. Whatever government officials ask for, 'we'll do it'.

Therein lies the secret of the success of China's first generation of post-communism super-rich – loyalty to the Communist Party. In the 1990s, seeing the direction of travel, a number of Hong Kong tycoons lined up against the political reforms belatedly introduced by the outgoing British governor, Lord Patten. The very public expectation of Western leaders that a growing middle class in Russia and China would give rise to greater yearning for democracy has proved misplaced.

Whether they have made their money in the 'old industries' – such as Zong Qinghou, a one-time factory worker who sold soda and popsicles and for many years held the top spot on China's rich list – or on the internet – such as Baidu's Robin Li or Ma Huateng of Tencent –

the wealthy have made sure that they do not rock the boat politically and they choose their allies carefully. They know only too well that just three decades ago the Party denounced entrepreneurs as 'self-employed traders and pedlars who cheat, embezzle, bribe and evade taxation'. Old perceptions, they fear, die hard.

Of all the various indices over which the participants secretly fret, one in particular at the end of 2013 provided a fitting symbol for the shift in power. Wang Jianlin marked his ascent to the global establishment by topping the annual *Estates Gazette* Rich List, which denotes the wealth of the big players on the London property scene, knocking the Duke of Westminster off his perch. The previous year Wang hadn't even made the top 250. Around the same time, he made his first splash on to the global art market, snapping up a Picasso, *Claude et Paloma*, at auction in New York for $28 million – more than twice the expected price. He personally made the bid by phone.

Contemporary China and Russia present the same extreme opportunities to make very large sums of money very quickly as existed in the Roman Republic, Renaissance Italy and the United States after the Civil War. The greater the risk, the greater the rewards: the lack of a transparent civil society has favoured a particular type of businessman, one with a highly developed nose for survival and a flexible approach to ethics.

The same could be said to apply to the Westerners who have done deals with them, and service their needs. A reverse scramble is taking place. Whereas, from the late Middle Ages to the end of the Second World War, Europeans flocked to new lands to extract and exploit their wealth, now politicians from once-rich countries are behaving as supplicants. The sight of a British prime minister and other leaders kow-towing on trips to Moscow and Beijing – begging for inward investment entirely on their hosts' terms – has become increasingly familiar. The shift is about more than geography and power. It marks the resurgence of a tooth-and-claw authoritarian way of doing business.

The submissiveness of Western governments to the oligarchs was put under the spotlight during the protests in Ukraine in early 2014 that toppled its pro-Kremlin President, Viktor Yanukovych, and the

UKRAINIAN POLITICS IS JUST A GAME OF MUSICAL CHAIRS BY A SUCCESSION OF COMPETING THIEVING OLIGARCHS TIMOSHENKO / YANUKOVYCH / POROSHENKO.

subsequent Russian takeover of Crimea. For some observers, particularly in Britain, the reluctance of the UK government to do anything that might jeopardise London's position as the no-questions-asked bolt-hole for Russian (and any other global) wealth came as a shock. It shouldn't have done. The practice had been established a long time before and will be hard to undo.

For the moment, the top of the global rich lists is still dominated by Americans, with Bill Gates regaining the top spot from Mexico's Carlos Slim in 2014. Two Indians, Mukesh Ambani and Lakshmi Mittal, feature in the top twenty, as does the veteran Hong Kong industrialist Li Ka-Shing. It is only a matter of time before the army of Russians and the likes of Wang and Ma ease past them. The direction of travel points one way.

CHAPTER 13

The geeks

It is better to live rich than to die rich.
Samuel Johnson

Few people can claim to have become a billionaire by the age of thirty – and to have changed the world to boot. A cluster of geeks either side of the millennium falls into this exclusive category. From kids in their garages, to university fraternities commenting on girls' appearances, to school dropouts, the super-rich who made Silicon Valley carved out a distinctive path to wealth and fame. Geniuses in their specific fields of engineering and computer science, they brought the internet into the lives of billions of people, first on their unwieldy computers, then with their smartphones, in hardware, software and social networks. In so doing they changed the way people communicated and shopped, transforming access to information for all individuals – and about all individuals.

In order to develop and make money from their inventions, they depended on the expertise of the Wall Street establishment. Venture capitalists put the likes of Mark Zuckerberg, Larry Page and Sergei Brin, and Steve Jobs on to the road to riches. Facebook, Google and Apple became mega-brands. But they are more than that – they have become part of the fabric of ordinary life for billions of people.

Having made their fortunes, and grown a little older, these one-time loners in front of their screens became the new aristocracy. The Californian Camelot had access to American presidents and world leaders whenever they wanted, sometimes inviting them into their lavish homes. They ensured they shaped policy not just in their field but far beyond, too.

The early years of the computer revolution gave rise to a hacker culture among hardware and software developers, from which later entrepreneurs would spring. The hacker ethos was based on the idea that computer programming was an activity that was changing the world. Partly influenced by the music, drugs and hippy counterculture of the 1960s, it cultivated a mystique around the relationship between the geeks and their computers.[1] These pioneers saw themselves like the craftsmen-turned-industrialists of the nineteenth century – they believed that only they held the key to the advancement of society. Socially and economically liberal, they believed that they – the Arthurian knights of their age – were better equipped than governments to solve some of the globe's most intractable problems.

In the way they made and spent their money, the technology giants combined the free market thinking of America's East Coast with the more rebellious goal of creating an open internet. As they produced ever more outlandish and innovative products, they believed they could change the course of communication and human behaviour. The T-shirts and sandals were the public accoutrements to a fierce free-market ethic. They saw the state as, at best, interference; at worst, a malign force. Eventually as they became ever larger, these companies – Microsoft, Google, Apple, Amazon – became financial monoliths, accused of deploying the monopolistic and anti-competitive practices of the steel and railroad magnates of the nineteenth century.

They also emulated the strongly anti-union and low-tax culture of their antecedents. The use of tax havens and other devices to minimise payments led to a fierce backlash in a number of countries. Company executives had previously calculated that the attractiveness of their super-brands would not suffer as a result. They also believed that their model of philanthropy, based on centuries of tradition but repackaged for the modern age, would be seen to more than compensate for the niggling problems of politicians objecting to tax-avoidance. Just as their predecessors had done, across the ages and across the continents, they assumed that their membership of the political, economic and cultural elites would ensure their dominance.

Bill Gates was the master of ceremonies, the poster boy for Western prosperity, at the turn of the third millennium. He had made more money than anyone else in the world, and was accruing it at a faster pace than he knew how to spend it. He had featured more often than he could count on the covers of magazines. His riches kept on coming. He topped the *Forbes* Rich List each year from 1995 to 2007, and once more in 2009 and 2014. (Either Carlos Slim or Warren Buffett has knocked him off the perch, but he always remained in the top three.) He is currently worth around $70 billion, or the equivalent to the GDP of a medium-sized country, such as Kenya, Guatemala or Lithuania. It is said it makes no sense for him to pick up a $100 bill left by a stranger on the ground. He might as well stand motionless, as the interest on his wealth accrues at more than that amount every second – and all that, despite the fact that he spends billions on worthy causes.

Gates owns islands, private jets, an assortment of fast cars and paintings. Yet, in his choice of clothes and haircut, he tries hard to display the demeanour of the everyman. In November 1994, fairly early on in his career, he spent $30.8 million at auction, a record price for a book, on Leonardo da Vinci's *Codex Leicester*, making it the most expensive manuscript ever sold. Rather than a single document, it is a mishmash of Leonardo's thoughts on everything from the moon to the movement of water. The meandering nature of his scribbles would have intrigued Gates – a man who sees himself as well equipped to take on the world's problems. 'Of course he designed all sorts of flying machines, like helicopters, way before you could actually build something like that,' Gates said of the document, displaying a boyish fascination. 'So every one of these notebooks are amazing documents – they're kind of his rough-draft notes of texts that he eventually wanted to put together.' It is easy to see the attraction of this for the man who began writing computer code by hand and ended up presiding over rapid technological development. As for the money side: 'I remember going home one night and telling my wife Melinda that I was going to buy a notebook; she didn't think that was a very big deal. I said, no, this is a pretty special notebook.'[2] This use of studied understatement is fashionable among some of the contemporary super-rich. A sign of having *really* made it is not to have to try too hard. That, in itself, takes some effort.

Gates's ultra-modern mansion near Microsoft's corporate head-quarters in Seattle, Washington, is carved into the side of a hill that overlooks Lake Washington. Nicknamed Xanadu 2.0, it is built from seven types of stone. Along with the Olympic-sized swimming pool and underwater music system, it has a twenty-seat Art Deco cinema (perhaps the twenty-first-century equivalent of the Renaissance private chapel) and a large private library with a domed roof. Unsurprisingly, it is big on technological gadgets. The lights are computer-controlled, while speakers are hidden beneath the wallpaper to allow music to follow you from room to room. Portable touchpads control everything from the TV sets, to the temperature, to the lights, which brighten or dim to fit the occasion or to match the outdoor light. Guests are surveyed in advance. On arrival, they are given a special pin to wear, which connects them to the home's electronic services, automatically adapting to their taste in music, art, temperature and lighting.[3]

Gates was born into a wealthy Seattle family in 1955; his mother and maternal grandfather were bankers and the family ethos was one of high achievement. At the age of seventeen he developed his first business venture, attempting to market Traf-O-Data, a computerised device designed to improve the collection of data on road traffic. The following year he went to Harvard, but he dropped out before finishing his degree to concentrate on programming. He and his friend Paul Allen were already in the process of writing code for the Altair – a pioneering microcomputer that was the precursor of today's PCs. They flew to Albuquerque, New Mexico, to show their progress to MITS, a tech company. They found a scene that would greet many visitors to many a Californian start-up office in later years: a chaotic jumble of people working at all hours of the day, seven days a week, for the love of computing. They had no doubt that their technological tinkering had world-changing potential. 'It was a grand and glorious crusade,' one MITS executive recalled.[4]

The programming language Gates and Allen wrote for – and sold to – MITS was soon copied and altered by many techies. This was part of the hacker mentality of 'open sourcing' and sharing. But it didn't impress Gates and Allen. In an 'open letter' to the community, Gates argued that software should be paid for, just as hardware was. 'Who can afford to do professional work for nothing?' he asked. 'Most directly, the thing you do is theft.'[5]

In 1976, at the age of twenty-one, he incorporated Micro-Soft (it would later lose the hyphen). For the first five years, he personally reviewed every line of code written by his developers. At a time when there were only around a hundred PCs in the world, Gates proclaimed he wanted 'a computer on every desk and in every home running Microsoft software'.[6] This was not hyperbole. He was convinced his ambition was rooted in hard facts: he had identified a market opportunity and was hell bent on securing it. As with Alfred Krupp and steel, as with Henry Ford and cars, Gates looked at the early computers and imagined a global product.[7] He had the technical know-how; he had determination in spades. All he needed was some luck.

Microsoft's big break came at the beginning of the 1980s, when it signed a deal to provide the operating system for IBM's computers. Soon they were developing their own systems; the first commercial version of Windows – the product that would turn Microsoft into a global behemoth – was released in 1985. Gates had moved from the rarefied world of West Coast computing and on to the world stage. He was named one of *Good Housekeeping*'s '50 Most Eligible Bachelors'. He made it on to the cover of *Time* magazine (but to his chagrin, only after Steve Jobs). In 1986 the company went public. Gates was initially reluctant to do so, but he had offered initial employees stock options (a model which was to be copied by future companies like Facebook), and all those working for him were convinced they were sitting on a fortune.[8] They were right. With Microsoft's initial public share offering, Gates became the world's youngest self-made billionaire at the age of thirty-one.

As he entered the 1990s, with new companies coming on to the market, Gates's strategy was clear: he was determined to put Windows in an unassailable position. The end of Microsoft's agreement with IBM left him free to do that. Gates had, since the early days, talked of 'monopolising' the software industry, although the company's lawyers advised him to avoid the word.[9] His drive to lock down the software market at the expense of competitors brought him into collision with the US government. Microsoft had been making its internet browser, Internet Explorer, the default on all computers that ran Windows, a practice which its critics complained had unfairly seen off an older competitor, Netscape's Navigator. The government was compelled to act, but the only piece of legislation it could cite was the century-old Sherman Antitrust Act, the same legislation which had been passed in 1890 in a vain attempt to fetter the robber barons' monopolistic bullying.

The authorities' interest in possible monopolistic practices began as early as 1991 with an inquiry by the Federal Trade Commission. That was then taken up by the Department of Justice, resulting in a settlement in 1994. Four years later, Microsoft was taken to court, accused of violating that deal and for other anti-competitive practices. The *New York Times*' report from the courtroom described Gates's performance as 'evasive and uninformed, pedantic and taciturn – a world apart from his reputation as a brilliant business strategist, guiding every step in the Microsoft Corporation's rise to dominance in computing'. It noted that in two hours of videotaped questioning selected by Justice Department lawyers from their twenty-hour deposition of the witness, he 'professed ignorance of key meetings and strategies that lie at the heart of charges in the government's antitrust suit against his company. These included purported plans to bully competitors like Apple Computer Inc. and the Netscape Communications Corporation into abandoning Internet software markets that Microsoft sought to dominate.' The paper added that in some cases the answers were so uncooperative that the District Court judge hearing the case 'chuckled and shook his head'.

Gates did not enjoy the experience. Microsoft vigorously argued that the accusations levelled against it were motivated by rival companies' jealousy. Some free-market economists, such as the guru of Reaganism and Thatcherism, Milton Friedman, denounced anti-trust measures as un-American: 'You will rue the day when you called in the government,' he declared. 'From now on the computer industry, which has been very fortunate in that it has been relatively free of government intrusion, will experience a continuous increase in government regulation.'[10] Nevertheless, Microsoft was found in violation of the Sherman Act and in June 2000 an order was served to hive off production of Internet Explorer to a separate company. The following year, the government and Microsoft reached a settlement that required the company to share some of its technology with others. Given the punishments it could have faced, and for all the criticism, the final terms were little more than a slap on the wrist. Was this recognition of where the real power now lay?

Microsoft's legal battles were by no means over. In the 2000s, the European Commission repeatedly fined the company for anti-competitive behaviour. By this point Gates was removing himself from the corporate front line to devote himself to what he called his second career – as a philanthropist. In January 2000, he stepped down as chief executive, taking a one-day-a-week chairmanship, leaving the helm of a company he had co-founded in 1975. He was only forty-four years old. Like Andrew Carnegie, having ruthlessly made money, Bill Gates wanted single-mindedly to give it away. In 1997, he had given an initial $94 million to set up a charitable trust, renaming it two years later as the Bill and Melinda Gates Foundation. Its coffers have grown over the years to $2 billion, with the focus on development and health programmes, particularly tackling AIDS, tuberculosis and malaria.

The more Gates's personal wealth rose through Microsoft's share valuation, the more he sought to give away. [*Bullshit*] His current pledge is to divest himself of $4 billion every year. In a keynote commencement address at his alma mater, he spoke of the privileged upbringing he had had: 'I left Harvard with no real awareness of the awful inequities in the world and the appalling disparities of health, and wealth, and opportunity that condemn millions of people to lives of despair.'[11] An expensive Ivy League education, it seems, had failed to teach Gates the basics of the world beyond his high-achieving and privileged milieu. He was not alone in that. Nor would he be the first entrepreneur to discover the horrors of poverty only after he had made his fortune and could afford to relax.

[Handwritten annotation: THIS IS A SCAM. GATES CLAIMS TO HAVE GIVEN AWAY 90% OF HIS MONEY. BUT THE NEXT YEAR HE HAS 70 BILLION, $80 BILLION THE YEAR AFTER THAT, $90 BILLION THE YEAR AFTER THAT, ETC.]

Ever the computer scientist, Gates enumerated the value of life: 'No-one funds things for that other three billion. Someone estimated that the cost of saving a life in the US is $5 million or $6 million – that is how much our society is willing to spend. You can save a life outside of the US for less than $100. But how many people want to make *that* investment?'[12] He told a meeting of the World Health Assembly in 2005 that he and Melinda 'couldn't escape the brutal conclusion that in our world today some lives are seen as worth saving and others are not'. Yet, unlike other Silicon Valley billionaires, Gates does not see the internet, in itself, as the key to solving the world's most intractable problems. His is a more traditional view, perhaps in keeping with his generation: 'Take this malaria vaccine, this weird thing that I'm think-ing of. Hmm, which is more important, connectivity or malaria vaccine? If you think connectivity is the key thing, that's great. I don't.'[13]

Even in its early days, the Gates Foundation had a larger annual global health budget than the World Health Organisation. In 2006 it received a further $1.5 billion from Warren Buffett – number two behind Gates on the *Forbes* Rich List at the time – with a promise to increase that over the remainder of his lifetime to $31 billion. The friendship between computer pioneer and financial mogul, separated by twenty-five years in age, dated back to 1991, when Gates was persuaded by his mother to attend a meeting where Buffett and Katharine Graham, then publisher of the *Washington Post*, were present. Gates was reluctant to go, but the two hit it off immediately. Gates credits Buffett with encouraging him to read a copy of the *World Development Report*, an analysis of poverty levels around the world by the World Bank.

One story, three years later, testifies to the kinds of bonds established by the super-rich in their hermetically sealed worlds. In 1993, Gates secretly had the pilot divert his private jet to Omaha, Nebraska, where Buffett was waiting on the tarmac. He then drove Bill and Melinda to his local jewellery store, Borsheims, to advise them on an engagement ring. 'Look, Bill, this is none of your business, but when I got married, I spent 6 per cent of my net worth on the ring,' Buffett said to Gates. 'I don't know how much you love Melinda.'[14] For men who have everything, such moments assume a special importance. Buffett had bought a stake in the venerable shop and wanted to show it off. Gates wanted his wife-to-be to see the man close up.

The more successful Gates became, the more he became convinced that he and other members of the super-rich were imbued with special talents. He was not alone. A sense of superiority and hypercharged ego was deemed to be an integral part of the character of the internet billionaire, as they mixed with their own as well as with bankers, hedge-funders, venture capitalists and private equity moguls. They came to assume that their talents were transferable to anything they chose to apply their minds to. The phenomenal success of the geeks in their field has led them to pursue a turbocharged version of philanthropy which takes as its starting point the attitude of Carnegie and his 'gospel of wealth', but goes far beyond it in its ambition and influence. Gates has acknowledged his debt to what he called 'the first generation of big philanthropists', including Carnegie, Rockefeller and Henry Ford.[15]

They coined the terms 'philanthrocapitalism' and 'creative capitalism' – the use of business practices to serve broader societal needs. In a January 2008 speech to the World Economic Forum, Gates spelled out the ideological path he had chosen. He began by professing, as Carnegie had, his faith in human progress: 'In significant and far-reaching ways, the world is a better place to live than it has ever been.' But the improvements brought about by technology were not, he said, reaching enough people quickly enough. 'We have to find a way to make the aspects of capitalism that serve wealthier people serve poorer people as well,' he said, hailing an approach in which governments, businesses and non-profit organisations would harness the power of markets to effect positive social change. The language is borrowed from the private sector. Buzzwords include: 'market conscious', ' impact oriented' and 'maximising leverage'. This market-led vision comes from scepticism about the capacity of governments to solve big social problems. 'The closer you get to it and see how the sausage is made, the more you go, oh my God! These guys don't even actually know the budget,' Gates declared. 'It makes you think: can complex, technocratically deep things – like running a healthcare system properly in the US in terms of impact and cost – can that get done? It hangs in the balance.' He even casts doubt on the ability of voters to decide what are the important issues that need to be tackled:

> It isn't just governments that may be unequal to the task. On this analysis, the democratic process in most countries is also straining to cope with the problems thrown up by the modern world, placing responsibilities on voters that they can hardly be expected to fulfil. The idea that all these people are going to vote and have an opinion about subjects that are increasingly complex – where what seems, you might think . . . the easy answer [is] not the real answer. It's a very interesting problem. Do democracies faced with these current problems do these things well?[16]

In the early 2000s, Gates was persuaded to meet rock star Bono: 'I have to admit, I did not make it a priority. And then there was a Davos [meeting] that was in New York after 9/11, so Bono, Bill Clinton and I met, and I was kind of amazed that he actually knew what he was talking about and had a real commitment to making things happen. It was phenomenal. Ever since then we've been big partners in crime.'[17]

He cited Bono's 'RED campaign' – whereby consumers would pay a small premium on certain products in order to donate to causes they cared about – as one of the best examples of creative capitalism.[18]

Gates and Buffett have had a number of chats thrashing out their ideas on philanthropy. In one discussion, Buffett made a proposal which illuminates the thought processes of many of the self-made billionaires in modern America and, indeed, around the world. If governments were not to be trusted to solve social problems, he argued, surely corporate America was best placed to step in? He proposed that a certain percentage of corporation tax be set aside and 'administered by some representatives of corporate America to be used in intelligent ways for the long-term benefit of society. This group, who think they can run things better than any government, could tackle education, health, etcetera, or other activities in which government has a large role.'[19]

In 2010 Gates, Buffett and Facebook founder Mark Zuckerberg signed a 'Giving Pledge' which committed them to give away at least half of their wealth. By the start of 2014, 122 of the richest people on the planet had signed up. The billionaire media magnate Michael Bloomberg linked his decision directly to the question of reputation that dogged Carnegie and other robber barons: 'Giving also allows you to leave a legacy that many others will remember. Rockefeller, Carnegie, Frick, Vanderbilt, Stanford, Duke – we remember them more for the long-term effects of their philanthropy than for the companies they founded, or for their descendants.'[20] Bloomberg is a rare example in the United States of a wealthy businessman going directly into electoral politics, rather than seeking to influence it more discreetly, or being rewarded by a president with a prestige appointment. The closest equivalent in career trajectory would be Silvio Berlusconi, TV mogul turned Italian Prime Minister, but not in their behaviour or tastes. On finishing his third term as Mayor of New York, he too styles himself foremost as a philanthropist.

Buffett became the model of the good billionaire. He inveighed against unfair taxation, declaring in a speech at Stanford in 2007 that he had just paid 17.7 per cent tax on his $46 million earnings, whereas his assistant had paid 30 per cent on her $60,000. The Obama administration tried later to bring into law what was called the Buffett Rule – no household making more than $1 million each year should pay a smaller share of its income in taxes than is paid by a middle-class family. The wording was kept deliberately vague so as not to offend against American notions of 'hard work', but even so it failed to get through Congress.

'The truth is I have never given a penny away that had any utility for me,' Buffett told a summit on philanthropy in 2013. He promised he would give his children 'enough so they feel they could do anything, but not so much that they could do nothing'. Have the contemporary super-rich learned the lessons of the decadence and fossilisation that allowed previous dynasties to die out? The ability to 'do anything' is still far beyond the comprehension of ordinary mortals, but it was an important pointer, following in the footsteps of Carnegie and his disdain for pampered offspring. Gates has pledged to give more than double the lifetime total (in contemporary value) given away by Carnegie and Rockefeller combined. That would be some feat. The combined wealth of Gates and Buffett is almost the same amount as owned by the bottom 40 per cent of the US population.

The Gates Foundation has pledged to give away all of its funds not more than twenty years after Bill and Melinda's deaths, having successfully identified the world's most urgent problems. To this end, most of the foundation's work has been geared towards the eradication of polio. This would be only the second time in history that a disease could be declared totally eradicated (after smallpox in 1980); a suitably grand aim.[21] For Gates, his success with Microsoft is directly applicable to the work of the foundation. 'Both of us,' he says of himself and his wife, 'worked at Microsoft and saw that if you take innovation and smart people, the ability to measure what's working, that you can pull together some pretty dramatic things.'[22]

No matter how laudable are the goals of Gates and Buffett, it is troubling that the fates of hundreds of millions of people, in effect, hang on the charity of a small number of private citizens.

For all the glamorous conferences and pledges, according to the *World Wealth Report*, only 11 per cent of the global rich, and only half of the richest thirty people, are active philanthropists. Prestige awaits those who are. Along with the geeks and the bankers, two other groups have joined the ranks of the philanthrocapitalists – celebrities and politicians who see themselves as celebrities. A latecomer to the party is Tony Blair. The former British Prime Minister – whose consultancies for various controversial governments, such as Kazakhstan, have made him wealthy (although not in Gates's or Buffett's league) – told a Global Philanthropy Forum attended by Bill and Melinda, Bill Clinton and Google's Larry Page and Sergei Brin that philanthropy was about 'strategic investing'. It was, he said, 'not just about giving money but giving leadership. The best philanthropists bring the gifts that made them successful – the drive, the determination, the refusal to accept something can't be done if it needs to be – into their philanthropy. It is creative not passive; it seeks to disrupt not follow conventional thinking.'

Modern-day philanthropy, as embodied by the Giving Pledge, is an elite club. It is 'specifically focused on billionaires and those who would be billionaires if not for their giving'. It is a gentleman's agreement, a 'moral commitment to give, not a legal contract'. By the turn of the twenty-first century, in America alone there were 45,000 charitable foundations, most run as businesses and taking advantage of considerable tax incentives offered to philanthropic organisations. The savvy use of tax differentials is regarded as a bonus in the dispensing of money, but it is even more helpful in the making of money. The members of the philanthropists' club play by the same rules they set themselves when they were getting rich. And those rules, while legally entirely sound, are morally not to everyone's taste.

The issue of tax-avoidance schemes applied by the major tech companies has only in recent years become an issue of hot debate. The practice of offshoring has merely been borrowed from the financial services, commodities and other sectors. In September 2012, an inquiry by the Senate Committee on Investigations highlighted practices by Microsoft and Hewlett-Packard (but it could have been referring to any of a dozen other tech multinationals). In one example, it wrote: 'From 2009 to 2011, by transferring certain rights to its intellectual property to a Puerto Rican subsidiary, Microsoft was able to shift offshore nearly $21 billion, or almost half of its US retail sales net revenue, saving up to $4.5 billion in taxes on goods sold in the United States, or just over $4 million in US taxes each day.'

According to Senator Carl Levin, a committee member: 'Major US corporations are increasingly earning their profits here but shipping them overseas to avoid paying the taxes they owe. At a time when we face such difficult budget choices, and when American families are facing a tax increase and cuts in critical programmes from education to health care to food inspections to national defence, these offshore schemes are unacceptable.'

Meanwhile, Microsoft paid no corporation tax on online software sales of $1.7 billion in Britain in 2011, as the relevant office handling the sales was situated in Luxembourg.[23]

When asked about his company's tax, Gates falls back on the three pro forma justifications deployed by tech chiefs: their practices are entirely legal; it is for governments, not companies, to make tax law; and companies abide by whatever the law and the tax rate of any jurisdiction they are operating in. 'If people want taxes at certain levels, great, set them at those levels,' he argues. 'But it's not incumbent on those companies to take shareholder money and pay huge sums that aren't required.'[24] Since the economic crash and the collapse in living standards for many, the more brash philosophical argument is deployed less – that they, the kings of the internet, know better than governments how to spend the cash, and therefore the more money they keep in their hands, the better in the long run it is for society.

Gates's reputation is now firmly lodged in the work of the foundation, which is just as he would like it. Microsoft, with all its legal controversies, now appears almost in parentheses in profiles of the mogul. He was, however, a pioneer, part of the first generation. His successors operated in a much more crowded field. Jeff Bezos, who by his own admission knew next to nothing about books, would found Amazon and become an overnight success, as would Pierre Omidyar, who saw the potential of peer-to-peer trading and set up the phenomenally popular auction website eBay. The rise to billionaire status was staggering in its speed. Steve Jobs, at the time of his early death in 2011, had amassed a comparatively modest fortune of up to $11 billion. Omidyar's fortune is similar, while Bezos has around $35 billion to his name. Ten years later, the development of social networks online would produce a new wave of billionaires, as sites such as MySpace and Facebook battled for a share of the market. In 2008 Mark Zuckerberg would become the world's youngest self-made billionaire at the age of twenty-three; it had taken Bill Gates eight years longer to reach that milestone.[25] By 2013 Zuckerberg was worth $19 billion.

These men took compulsive competitiveness to new heights. At every step of the way they were determined to create something special, to corner the market, and for their product to take over the world. The line between success and failure was thin – a sharp elbow from a former mate or the idea just not being quite good enough. For all the T-shirts, shorts and sandals, for all the shared spliffs, egalitarianism had no place in Silicon Valley. Second-best was for losers.

Steve Jobs took a bumpier path to wealth and recognition than his contemporary Gates. His company, Apple, was founded in the same year as Microsoft, and initially sold circuit boards as a two-man operation out of his family home in California. It was a quick success, going public in 1981 and making millions for its founders. But whereas Gates retained an iron grip, Jobs found himself fired by the company he founded. He created his own team to work on his baby project, the Macintosh computer, even flying a skull-and-crossbones flag from the building and proclaiming, 'It's better to be a pirate than to be in the Navy.' In 1985 Apple unceremoniously dumped him. Some of his detractors cited as a reason his 'wild and petulant emotional swings', but such character traits were hardly unusual for the geeks.[26]

Jobs set out on his own, establishing a new company – NeXT – thanks in no small part to its main investor, the venture capitalist and sometime presidential candidate Ross Perot. He also bought the animation company Pixar, which teamed up with Disney to produce the highly successful movie *Toy Story*, on which Jobs was credited as an executive producer. In 1996, in an act of humble pie and corporate pragmatism, Apple bought NeXT, and Jobs was rapidly promoted to save a company that was hovering on the brink of bankruptcy. By 2000 he was CEO, on a nominal $1 annual salary, mostly being paid through shares in the company that rose to be worth in excess of $2 billion.

Jobs had always been closer to the hacker culture than Gates. Hailing from California, he was more influenced by the counter-culture and in the 1970s he was known for turning up to hacker events shoeless or in sandals, just as Zuckerberg would later do in the Facebook offices. Having travelled to India, he was interested in Buddhism; he also sported a Fidel Castro beard and embraced vegetarianism.[27] In the 1990s one satirical commentator described him as 'the most dangerous man in Silicon Valley because, it is said, he wasn't in it for the money'. He added: 'Gates sees the personal computer as a tool for transferring every stray dollar, deutsche mark, and kopeck in the world into his pocket. Gates doesn't really give a damn how people interact with their computers as long as they pay up. Jobs gives a damn. He wants to tell the world how to compute, to set the style for computing. Bill Gates has no style; Steve Jobs has nothing but style.'[28] The comparison may stray wildly into caricature, but it is not totally unfounded.

Jobs kept on winning the reputation game against Gates: the Silicon Valley free spirit versus the hard-nosed boss; the innovative craftsman set against the monopolistic capitalist.[29] An obsessive designer and technologist, Jobs turned each Apple invention and product launch into a ceremony of worship. From the earliest Apple Macs, through to the iPods, iPhones and iPads, he would have young aficionados queuing round the block outside Apple stores in cities around the world. His products became the ultimate style statements in a globalised culture united in the veneration of brands.

To him, that was enough. He didn't need to do more to prove his worth or his legacy beyond making sure that the next product would engender similar hysteria. He was far less concerned with charity. On his return to the company as CEO he closed Apple's corporate philanthropy programmes to save money, not reinstating them when profits reached into the tens of billions. He had set up his own charitable foundation in the 1980s, as he felt he ought to, but wound it down because, according to his biographer, he disliked the showy world of professional philanthropy. He did not take the Giving Pledge. Even before his untimely death in 2011, aged fifty-six, Jobs did not see the need to offer an explanation, but as the two men grew older he and Gates developed a mutual respect. 'I think the world's a better place because Bill has realised that his goal isn't to be the richest guy in the cemetery,' Jobs said shortly before he died. Bono was one who argued that Jobs's technological contribution was just as important as any financial one.[30]

Pierre Omidyar marks the second generation of geeks – those who began to profit from the business potential of the internet as its number of users grew exponentially throughout the 1990s. Unlike most of the others, he actually completed college, graduating from Tufts University with a computer science degree in 1988. After a couple of early attempts to set up online shops, one of which was bought by Microsoft, he became less interested in selling to people and more in enabling people to sell to each other. On Labour Day 1995 he launched a website called Auction Web, for which he had written the code himself. This would become eBay, which by mid-1997, even at a time when the internet was still a minority sport, was seeing 800,000 transactions every day. The idea was simple: people would bid for each other's goods; users would be responsible for packaging and shipping them; and eBay would take a cut of each transaction. It was a phenomenally successful formula that transformed Omidyar into a billionaire after the company's initial public stock offering in 1998.

In 2004, Omidyar and his wife Pamela launched the Omidyar Network. Like the Gates Foundation, it sees markets as key to solving social problems; it invests in both for-profit companies and social enterprises. But unlike traditional foundation-based models, the network sees itself as an active investor, particularly in social enterprise and other companies in the developing world.[31]

A signatory to the Giving Pledge, Omidyar has embraced the freedom-of-expression agenda of many of the original cyber-utopians. For many of those earlier pioneers in the 1980s and 90s, the internet was going to be a rules-free place, a break with the hierarchical and vertical structures that dominated the offline world. It was all about 'horizontal' relationships and breaking down old barriers. This vision of geek paradise increasingly clashed not just with the money-making ambitions of the start-ups that became corporations but with governments' realisation that they needed to reassert control. In a short space of time, piggybacking on the same technologies and in some cases developing their own, governments overtook the tech companies in their ability to monitor the habits of citizens. This was the conclusion to be drawn from the leaks provided by the whistle-blower Edward Snowden in 2013. The extent of the surveillance of all forms of communication by the US National Security Agency, and its British sister organisation GCHQ, took many by surprise. The reaction among the new internet elite was mixed. A few companies were clearly profiting from close relationships with the spy agencies. Others were meekly providing what they demanded, while claiming to be upset about it. Some were genuinely outraged.

One of those was Omidyar. He had previously sunk money into a small investigative journalism website in Hawaii. At the height of the Snowden furore, he announced a much bigger venture: he was putting $250 million into an online global investigative news portal called First Look Media. One of its key figures would be Glenn Greenwald, an American journalist who had become the main conduit for Snowden, providing a succession of sensational revelations for the *Guardian* newspaper.[32] By funding a project seen to be directly challenging US power,

Omidyar was showing perhaps a more rebellious streak than his fellow geeks. Ideological warrior for free speech, or business pioneer for new media? Either way, Omidyar was enjoying his reputation as a revolutionary: 'News organisations that have been around a while have a lot of traditions and ways of doing things that may have served them for many years but perhaps make them less flexible in the digital era. As an entrepreneur, it just makes more sense to start something new.'[33] He had in his sights one of his rivals, Jeff Bezos, who demonstrated a commitment to traditional media by making an altogether different acquisition.

As a toddler, Bezos showed an early aptitude for the do-it-yourself problem-solving that is a hallmark of Silicon Valley: he was found trying to dismantle his playpen with a screwdriver. As a teenager he enjoyed fixing broken farm equipment at his grandfather's ranch in Texas. His grandfather worked for the Defense Advanced Research Projects Agency, an arm of the US Department of Defense tasked with producing technological innovations in the Cold War for use against the Soviets. Robots and unmanned vehicles were among its early projects, and in 1969 it established ARPAnet – the precursor to the internet. A committed 'Trekkie', Bezos's obsession with space travel was piqued at an early age by his grandfather's work.

Like Gates, Bezos tried his hand at running his own business from an early age. At seventeen, he set up summer school classes, charging $150 for a two-week science camp called the Dream Institute, which included reading *Gulliver's Travels* and studying black holes. At Princeton he came to the unhappy conclusion that he wasn't going to make it as a scientist, so he switched majors from physics to computer programming. After various jobs, he jacked in a potentially prestigious placement at a Wall Street firm to head west, where the internet action was happening.[34] He was mesmerised less by talk of a brave new online world, more by its commercial potential after realising the importance of a court ruling about sales tax. He was going to sell online, but he couldn't decide what. He honed twenty areas down to five – CDs, computer hardware, software, videos and books. He chose books as his product of choice not because of any passion for them, but because he realised someone was going to make a fortune from selling them in this new way, so it might as well be him. They were a familiar product, easy to catalogue, store and ship, and therefore the potential online market for them was huge.[35]

A few months after setting up shop in his garage, in July 1995, his fledgling company sold its first book. Its title was *Fluid Concepts & Creative Analogies: Computer Models of the Fundamental Mechanisms of Thought*. Bezos named his firm Amazon, after the world's largest river, to indicate his ambition for it, and also because it would appear first in alphabetical listings of online retailers. He chose Seattle, the home of Microsoft, as his base, because he assumed that was where the best people were to be found. In the early days, the small number of customers would phone Bezos's office (or rather home) and give their bank card details to make purchases.[36]

Amazon's first break came when Jerry Yang of Yahoo offered to put the site on his 'What's Cool?' listings; that week Amazon took thousands of orders and Bezos and his fellow 'managers' had to stay up all night packaging the books, because they hadn't yet hired anyone else to do it.[37] This conjures up an image (or a carefully cultivated myth) of the Victorian industrialist doing his bit on the factory floor, desperate to get his invention and his company up and running. Bezos had bought 10.2 million shares in his company for a tenth of a cent each. By the time of Amazon's initial public share offering in 1997 they floated at $18 apiece, netting the thirty-three-year-old $184 million overnight.[38] Still, by Silicon Valley standards, that was a relatively slow start.

He had a similar acquisitive and hoarding approach to Gates. His business model was rapid expansion to corner the market and achieve an unassailable position before anyone else caught on. Market share was what mattered. Profits would come later. It eventually worked, phenomenally, but at the start it was tough going. Early on, Bezos took great pleasure in claiming to have a million titles 'in store'. In fact, they were in the warehouses of his major distributors. He extolled the virtues of the online shop against its traditional rivals, even hiring mobile billboards to drive past Barnes & Noble bookstores with the slogan 'Can't find that book you wanted?' The war with Barnes & Noble was to be won by providing as speedy and easy a way of shopping as possible. Amazon developed a 'one-click' system that allowed customers to add products to their virtual shopping cart with minimum effort. This was patented – despite concerns that the terms of the patent were far too broad – and when Barnes & Noble put its own one-click 'express lane' option on its website in 1999, Amazon filed a suit that was settled out of court. This recourse to litigation was something that finds an echo in the industrial revolution with the nineteenth-century robber barons jockeying for position in their market.[39]

When the dotcom bubble burst at the end of the 1990s, Amazon's losses were staggering. In 2000 alone the company posted a loss of $720 million.[40] Bezos went from *Time* magazine's 'person of the year' in 1999 to the boss of 'amazon.con'. Furious at the treatment he received, he resolved to make sure Amazon became a vast retail empire, crushing any rival in its path. Some of his original comrades in arms had wanted to be at a quirky online bookseller. Bezos had other ideas. Now a multi-billion-dollar monolith, Amazon is known for its uncompromising (to put it mildly) approach. Recent media investigations have been highly critical of how it treats its workers, who were reported to be working hard for pitifully low wages in cavernous warehouses.[41] Its low unit-labour costs and economies of scale allow it to undercut bookstores and online rivals. The firm is also known for a culture of intense corporate secrecy. It succeeds, spectacularly, as a retail convenience that has millions of people clicking every day to buy not just books, but household and other goods too. Bezos's achievement has been unmatched in retail; but to find glamour, he has had to look beyond the day job.

Back in 2000 he created a private aerospace company called Blue Origin, with the aim of making space travel more affordable.[42] He had once promised to build 'space hotels and colonies for two to three million people in orbit', and was reportedly in discussions with Richard Branson about joint commercial space ventures.[43] In the summer of 2013 he took the media world completely unawares by announcing that he had bought the *Washington Post*. The paper of Woodward and Bernstein, in family hands for several generations, had just been sold to a man who had done for thousands of bookstores. Yet the paper had fallen on hard times and was in a downward spiral. For a mere snip at $250 million, Bezos had entrusted to himself the task of revamping one of the world's great symbols of 'old media'.[44] He began the careful process of investment, particularly in its digital output.

The *Post* was not the only newspaper in trouble. The *New York Times* did not stand in the way of Carlos Slim making a large investment in 2008 (see Conclusion), but it did baulk when an eccentric Chinese oligarch came knocking at the door in 2013. Chen Guangbiao, a recycling tycoon said to have made it into the top four hundred on China's rich list, is reported to have a business card advertising his wares as 'China Moral Leader', 'Earthquake Rescue Hero' and 'Most Well-known and Beloved Chinese Role Model'. He promised he could improve the paper and 'reform' its coverage of his country. His offer was not taken up.

The prize for the greatest double act in Silicon Valley is beyond contention. Larry Page and Sergei Brin, sons of academics, one an immigrant from the Soviet Union, came upon the idea of organising the internet while students at Stanford. They alighted on an old-fashioned solution to a very modern problem. It was one thing to search the internet, hard though that was at the time; it was quite another to provide an order to it. They borrowed the academic idea of citation, or peer review, producing algorithms that would change access to instant information for ever. They needed a name for their plan. They originally came up with 'backrub', but that wouldn't do. Just as any über-nerd mathematician might, they liked the idea of 'googol' – the number one followed by a hundred zeros – but they misspelled it when buying the domain name. Their challenge was to work out how their brilliant new idea could make money. Initially they were wary of allowing advertising, but once they were persuaded of the merits of a separate paid-for block on each page, the model was found. The rest, as they say, is history – the fastest growth of any company in US corporate history.

Google is now worth more than $100 billion – more than the *New York Times*, *Washington Post*, Disney, Dow Jones, Amazon and General Motors combined. It runs more than a million servers in data centres around the world, processing over a billion search requests every day. It has devoured everything in its way – YouTube (for video sharing), the phone company Motorola (which it later sold on), map companies, anything that might provide the kernel of a new idea or might remotely pose a threat. Its latest obsession is robotics and the potential for artificial intelligence. With an army of technicians and inventors the world over, Google is constantly on the lookout for the great new idea – driverless cars, glasses displaying real-time information – that will make money and, more importantly, keep the corporate brand feeling as revolutionary and enticing as when they started out. The nightmare vision is of a new kid on the block that will steal the company's thunder, turning young internet users elsewhere.

Just as Sheikhs Mo and Khalifa cannot stop themselves from building bigger and higher, Google's corporate ethic is to be the best at everything. Such is its wealth, power and kudos that it attracts the smartest engineers and computer scientists, lawyers and lobbyists. It snaps up ambitious political advisers, providing a useful revolving door into the offices of presidents and prime ministers. Everyone is moulded to fit into a corporate brand that demands strong performance and even stronger loyalty. (Jack Ma of Alibaba modelled his approach on this.) With lavish restaurants, hang-out and chill-out areas, massage on tap and gyms, the young employees are encouraged to spend as much of the day as possible in this warm embrace. Google is extremely generous with its funding of online start-ups and organisations and ventures that promote an open internet. Its embrace of free expression is robust, while also important for its business model. Its credentials with respect to the protection of privacy are less convincing.

Yet in the course of 2013, it found itself in the US, across Europe and particularly in the UK in the eye of a storm over tax avoidance. The company was doing only what others were doing, assigning the more profitable sides of its business to jurisdictions with low tax regimes – tax jurisdiction shopping, to use the jargon. The routing of profits from Ireland (its European headquarters) to Bermuda via the Netherlands was hardly designed to endear. In spite of several warnings it failed to anticipate the barrage of criticism it would receive. Or perhaps it was impervious. Page and Brin, and the others brought up with the Californian libertarian mindset, were taken aback by the opprobrium heaped on their firm with the mantra 'don't be evil'. They could see no logic in handing money over to a state that would use it less efficiently and inventively than they would.

*

The third-generation geek has been immortalised in film. Facebook is widely acclaimed to have changed the way people interact with each other, not just on a personal level but socially, with its impact on popular movements and politics. And it all started in the dorm room of an awkward undergraduate who didn't quite know how to talk to girls. Mark Zuckerberg applied to Harvard in 2001 with an impressive list of high school awards to his name and the ability to write in ancient Greek and Latin. His real passion, though, like Gates before him, was coding. He began as a hacker, breaking rules to create a computer program. He stole photos of Harvard students from the books kept in the halls of residence, known colloquially as 'facebooks', and set up a website where students could rate each other's looks. It was an inauspicious start, leading to a ticking off from the college and accusations of sexism from women's groups on campus.[45]

Undeterred, Zuckerberg continued to work on programming projects based on the idea of a 'social network' like the recently launched MySpace and Friendster sites. The strength of The Facebook, as it was originally called, was that it allowed users to post updates and arrange real-life events while controlling their privacy settings. It soon spread across Ivy League colleges, eclipsing local rivals that were also in the early stages of development. By the summer of 2004, growth had been so spectacular that advertisers were lining up to buy space on the site. Facebook was beginning to turn a profit. Zuckerberg and his roommates, who had helped him on the project, hired a house in Palo Alto for the summer. There he met Sean Parker, co-founder of the music-sharing site Napster, who, four years into his venture, was deemed a Silicon Valley veteran. Parker was committed to the sort of peer-to-peer vision of the internet that Zuckerberg was pushing; he was impressed with the student's ambition, noting that he showed 'imperial tendencies'.[46] Parker's job was to act as the company's *de facto* president, using his links with investors to find money. He had a second, equally important, role – to buy the alcohol for Facebook's house parties, as nobody else was over twenty-one.[47]

In among the alcohol and the pool parties, Facebook's early years were punctuated by bitter internecine rivalry. One moment this was a venture in a college dorm, the next it was a multi-billion-dollar gold mine. Eduardo Saverin, a fraternity buddy of Zuckerberg, had been cut in for a third of Facebook in its early days, when it was still just a Harvard network. His job was to oversee the business side. His stake in the company was reduced when Parker arrived, and he felt like Zuckerberg was trying to push him out. After a bitter dispute and subsequent lawsuits, Saverin and Facebook settled out of court, and he still holds about 5 per cent of the company.

Zuckerberg was embroiled in controversies, not least with the Winkelvoss twins, two Olympic rowers and one-time comrades, who accused him of stealing their intellectual property. Almost immediately after the company's launch, they claimed Zuckerberg owed them damages for freezing them out, a claim he dismissed out of hand: 'I try to shrug it off as a minor annoyance, that whenever I do something successful, every capitalist out there wants a piece of the action.'[48] This, too, was settled out of court.

The early company culture was dominated by one individual whose 'vision' everyone at Facebook was required to subscribe to, just as everyone at Microsoft had under Gates and everyone at Amazon under Bezos. Employees who lived within a mile of the office were given a monthly $600 bonus in exchange for being 'on call' to come in when they were needed.[49] For all the boyishness, the juvenile office jokes and the management wandering around with no shoes on, this was a tightly controlled enterprise. Zuckerberg's own business card was testament to this: 'I'm CEO, bitch.'[50] Despite the bluster about changing the world, argues one former employee, 'the company's entire human resources architecture was constructed on the reactionary model of an office from the 1950s'.[51]

Zuckerberg's was a mix of pranks, sharp elbows but also messianic vision. Like Jobs, Page and Brin, he set out to change the world. Boasts that might have been dismissed as the hubris of youth turned out to be entirely accurate. From his early days of breaking college rules to create the Facemash page, Zuckerberg exhibited a psychology in line with the hacker ethic – a willingness to buck the system and a mistrust of authority; a desire to push things further to see what would happen.[52] He was a strong proponent – and hammered this home in speech after speech at staff meetings – of the idea that all information should be free and shared. He insisted he had never set out to run a company; a company was merely the means by which his project could be achieved. The earliest external bid for Facebook had come just two months after it was launched, back in 2004. An investor offered the then twenty-year-old Zuckerberg $10 million. He could have become a multi-millionaire overnight. But he didn't even consider it.[53] He made sure Facebook followed the path of earlier insurgent companies by resisting multiple buyout offers from established media companies, in order to keep himself in control. In doing so, as is the way of Silicon Valley, a company of anti-establishment hackers became a financial behemoth.[54]

As well as signing the Giving Pledge (along with his old college roommate and Facebook co-founder Dustin Moskowitz, the only two signatories under the age of thirty-five), Zuckerberg has also given to the Silicon Valley Community Foundation. Its chief executive has acknowledged the contradiction that much of the area's hardship is blamed on the tech companies themselves, their well-paid employees pushing up rents and eviction rates in surrounding neighbourhoods.

At the end of 2013 local activists began to blockade the private shuttle buses run by Facebook, Twitter, Apple, Google and their like taking employees from San Francisco to their corporate HQs in Menlo Park, Palo Alto and Mountain View. At least one bus had its windows smashed. The companies have reinforced security, ever increasing a sense of socio-economic gulf with the less 'wired' world around them. For young employees, inculcated into a corporate culture of 'cool' success, it has been a disorienting experience, but coupled with the public rows over privacy and tax, they are seeing their companies' moral standing being challenged at every turn. The vast majority of employees are very comfortably rewarded for their efforts, but they do not fall into the category of super-rich or even rich. Yet their bosses do, and are increasingly flaunting it.

One such occasion was the wedding in August 2013 of Sean Parker, Napster co-founder, former Facebook president and long-time buddy of Zuckerberg. The 'ridiculously lavish affair', as the *Los Angeles Times* described it, was themed on *The Lord of the Rings*. Each of the 364 guests had a custom-made costume. The venue was a campground in Big Sur, with *faux* bridges, a ruined stone castle, two broken Roman columns and a pen of bunnies 'for anyone who needed a cuddle'. Other details showed guests were treated to a feast that included pigs roasting on spits and a lounge area with ornate beds draped with what appeared to be bearskin blankets. Having failed to get permission for his architectural flourishes, Parker dealt with the problem by paying a $2.5 million fine. He then wrote a long blog post lambasting the media coverage: 'The reactions were so extreme, so maniacal, so deeply drenched in expletives, they seemed wasted on us; this was the sort of angry invective normally reserved for genocidal dictators.'[55] Perhaps he had in mind Zaire's President Mobutu, his marble folly at Gbadolite and his runway for chartered Concordes.

Zuckerberg had sent his regrets. One of the reasons why Parker's nuptials aroused such bemusement and ire is that the internet billionaires are usually more tasteful in their spending of money. Their mansions are not colonnaded but sleek and modernist, used more for corporate entertaining than for lavish partying. Two of the new generation of female leaders in Silicon Valley, Yahoo's Marissa Mayer and Facebook's Sheryl Sandberg, have used their homes to host fundraisers for Barack Obama. Rather than Porsches or Rolls-Royces, they prefer to drive expensive but eco-friendly vehicles: hybrids such as the Prius or the fully electric Tesla. That is the message they wish to give out: 'This is northern California – entrepreneurial, serious and socially aware. This is not brash New Jersey.'

It's been a long time since any of the internet billionaires has worked from a garage. Their corporations are among the most powerful in the world. When they want to see presidents and prime ministers, audiences are granted. Their views carry weight, and not just in the tech sector. Yet the T-shirts, the primary-colour offices and other forms of informality are a veneer. The message is strictly controlled; their lawyers are on call 24/7 for the latest battle with governments and for the latest takeover. The sight of Google, with its claims to a higher ethic, in the British parliamentary dock alongside Starbucks and Amazon was a reputational turning point. At least as damaging for Apple were revelations of the terrible employment practices in China's Foxconn factories, which make iPhone components. Yet there is little sign of consumers ditching their products, because they are attractive, indispensable and still market leaders.

For all the problems, there is something about this breed that sets them apart from those who have made their money by other means – through inheritance, expropriation or financial transfers. The geeks made their money in a similar way: they built their companies around one brilliant idea and joined the ranks of the super-rich overnight with the initial public share offering. Their eccentric revolutionary zeal is reminiscent of some of the adventurers who took to the high seas in search of new lands. With billions of people in developing countries only beginning to get connected, there is much more money to be made by the next college kid coming up with the next big thing. The first-generation geeks in their garages may have become global magnates, but the romanticism of the internet start-up remains intact.

The internet titans share the basic belief that they and their technologies have changed the world, perhaps even saved it. They are also convinced that their success in one area makes them qualified to use their vast wealth in others. This is why some have moved away from the companies that made them their fortunes and on to other things. Bill Gates's name will be more associated with philanthropy than personal computers in future decades, just as Andrew Carnegie's is more familiar when talking about libraries than about steel. Few care to remember the monopolistic practices that helped achieve their success. They have managed their reputations to perfection. They have then, to differing degrees, spent their lives hungering after the next project, whether it is eradicating polio or building a spaceship. Why not? they reason. After all, they have more money than they could possibly spend. Having conquered the world in one field, they are convinced they can do so in any other.

CHAPTER 14

The bankers

Let me issue and control a nation's money and
I care not who writes the laws.
Mayer Amschel Rothschild

Few of today's super-rich are as reviled as the bankers. Since the economic crash of 2008, these masters of the universe have been held almost universally responsible for bringing the Western economy to the brink of destruction. Others may have been gaudier (the sheikhs), wealthier (the geeks) and shadier (the oligarchs), yet it is the bankers who have become synonymous with the growing inequality and injustice of our times. Is their whipping-boy status the result of the decisions they made, their character traits, or bad luck?

With their private jets, sumptuous homes and sense of impunity and self-pity, bankers have cocooned themselves in isolation from lesser mortals. They have taken as many liberties as have been offered to them by politicians and regulators. Yet their behaviour throughout the ages has tended to reflect broader attitudes of society. At times of rapid growth and acquisition of wealth – such as the Florence of the early Renaissance, Europe of the early New World, and the United States straight after the Civil War – risk-taking was condoned, recklessness ignored. In the period between the end of the Second World War and the stock market 'Big Bang' of the mid-1980s restraint was seen as a virtue. That lasted until the deregulation of the Thatcher and Reagan governments, and the arrival of globalisation and new technologies. From that point, the great divergence of wealth within countries, and between countries, grew.

Since the days of the Medici, the banking profession has been integral to the development of capitalism. The great financial dynasties have followed in the footsteps of their Italian antecedents, mixing money with power politics. The Fugger family in Germany were their spiritual heirs, developing a vast fortune in the fifteenth and sixteenth centuries, bankrolling Charles V's bid to become Holy Roman Emperor and ensuring they were the go-to bank for Europe's elite. Jakob Fugger found a client in the Pope and in so doing drew the ire of religious reformers like Martin Luther.

Although their bank was founded in England, the Rothschilds became creditors to most of mainland Europe's major powers during the Napoleonic Wars of the early nineteenth century. Nathan Mayer Rothschild's favourite business was the issuing of loans to governments; banks and politicians have always profited from a close relationship with one another.

Nor is the cycle of boom and bust, or the trading in dodgy financial packages, anything new. Back in 1720, the South Sea Company – a corporation like Clive's East India Company – fell victim to a speculative bubble brought on by its own hubris. The collapse was startlingly similar to that of 2008: a massive liquidity crisis was brought about by companies and banks holding much more debt than they held in assets, and it even involved the practice of 'short selling' shares and buying them back as the price slid down, in order to make a healthy profit. The South Sea Bubble resulted in a wave of bankruptcies that could be tackled through massive government bailouts – and public fury.[1] Parliament was forced to consider a resolution calling on the guilty parties to be tied up in sacks and thrown into the Thames.[2]

Yet then, as now, once the initial anger had dissipated, business returned to normal. Parliaments pass laws establishing greater regulation. Bankers promise to act more responsibly. But the changes to their working practices are slight. The changes to their behaviour are superficial. Pay packets stay in the stratosphere. Contrition is thin on the ground.

They crashed the world and they think they are good people who have been hard done by.

Jimmy Cayne would leave Bear Stearns on Thursdays and take his private helicopter to the New Jersey coast for long golfing weekends.[3] He assumed that the firm was in safe hands. Nearly half of his employees were shareholders, so they had a double interest in the bank's success. Cayne liked to think he was building a firm in an atmosphere of consensus and cooperation, a team that could weather any storm and was in it for the long haul. 'There is no instant gratification here,' he said. Cayne's remuneration packages for his executives were so generous that one analyst compared the company's pay and bonus schemes to the miracle of loaves and fishes.[4]

A college dropout, Cayne had been a cab driver, photocopier salesman and scrap-iron dealer in the Midwest before moving to the East Coast in his thirties. He was determined to make a fortune at bridge tournaments (a passion, incidentally, he shares with Bill Gates and Warren Buffett). In 1969, at the age of thirty-five, he met Bear Sterns's future CEO, Alan 'Ace' Greenberg, who hired him over a tournament card table. Cayne quickly caught the eye of the board, running a brokerage division that catered to the wealthy. He coveted the lifestyles of his clients and resolved to become richer than they were. He enhanced his reputation further among his bosses by profiting from the near municipal bankruptcy of New York City in 1975, when he bought up city bonds and sold them on at high margins.[5] In 1993 he replaced Greenberg as CEO and, under his leadership, Bear Stearns gained a reputation as a tightly run ship. The bank came through the early 2000s recession in the US – brought about by the collapse of Enron and the bursting of the dotcom bubble – making record profits. In 2003 Cayne told a reporter: 'We are hitting on all 99 cylinders, so you have to ask yourself, what can we do better? And I just can't decide what that might be.'[6] Bear Sterns proclaimed itself the best financial firm to work for on Wall Street and Cayne ensured he was duly rewarded as the best-paid boss in town.

In 2006 Cayne was the first banker to reach a milestone that all had cherished and fought hard to get to – he was the first Wall Street chief to own a company stake worth $1 billion.[7] By that time a bank with a long-held reputation for respectability had become ever more involved in the purchase of dubious financial products. Neither the senior management nor the board raised concerns. One executive who raised out loud the risks was shown the door.[8]

With so much personally invested in the bank, Cayne couldn't imagine what could possibly go wrong.[9] By now a Grand Life Master, he famously stayed at a bridge tournament for ten days in the summer of 2007, with only sporadic access to a phone and email, while his bank lost $1.6 billion in bad hedge-fund investments.[10] Under Cayne, the firm's share price had risen tenfold in fifteen years, largely off the back of risky investments. Irresponsible lending had led its 'leverage ratio' – the proportion of assets to equity – to exceed 35:1. The regulators seemed intensely relaxed. On 11 March 2008, Christopher Cox, chairman of the Securities and Exchange Commission, the chief regulator for the US financial sector, said he was comfortable with the amount of capital that Bear Stearns and the other investment banks had on hand. Days later, as investors suddenly saw that the bank could not meet its obligations, Bear Stearns collapsed.

The Bush administration scrambled for a response. With any thought of nationalisation heretical to American politicians (unlike, as had just transpired in the UK, with the takeover of Northern Rock), Bear was encouraged to seek a merger with J.P. Morgan Chase. It was more a case of takeover by humiliation. J.P. Morgan offered to buy Bear's shares for $2 each; the board had no choice but to accept. Cayne's response was a mix of paralysis and denial: 'I felt nothing. You got a bad grade on your test. That's it. No appeal.' Only later did he add: 'I felt sad for me and for my Bear Stearns family.'[11] The price was eventually bumped up to $10, but still an august financial institution had been valued at little more than the real estate price of its New York head office.[12] A bank had been saved, but for voters there was a sting in the tail. Some $29 billion of public money had to be injected into Bears to provide liquidity, merely to enable the takeover. This set the pattern for the crisis.

Six months later, on Monday, 15 September 2008, television news bulletins captured what would become the iconic pictures of the era. Confused-looking young men and women, who had thought they were on a one-way path to success, walked out of their New York office, carrying cardboard boxes in search of yellow cabs. Lehman Brothers, one of the great names of Wall Street for a century and a half, had just filed for Chapter 11 – the largest bankruptcy in US history.

This collapse set off a far deeper wave of panic in the market. Politicians, bankers and regulators embarked on a frantic series of phone calls and meetings to come up with plans to rescue the big institutions – and save the global economy. Unlike companies in the 'real economy', the banks were deemed to be 'too big to fail', a phrase coined not in this time of panic, but by an official in 1984, at the height of the free-market Reagan years.[13]

Except for one bank: Lehmans. Like its competitors, it believed it was accident proof. The psychology of perpetual profits had become so embedded in financial institutions, and among political leaders, regulators and most economists, that to gainsay would be to show weakness. This was the 'smile or die' attitude present in many aspects of American life in the 2000s, including in the Bush White House during both the Iraq War and the financial crash. Many in corporate America were convinced of the notion of the 'law of attraction' – you can change the world by sending out positive thoughts.[14] Negative thinking was discouraged and ignored. Raghuram Rajan, an IMF economist, presented a paper to a meeting of international bankers at Jackson's Hole, Wyoming, in 2005, arguing that banks had exposed themselves to potential trouble by selling on their riskier debt packages. Conventional wisdom had it that they lessened risk by spreading it. Rajan later wrote: 'I exaggerate only a bit when I say I felt like an early Christian who had wandered into a convention of half-starved lions.'[15]

With hindsight, the source of the collapse is easy to spot. For years, US home values had been soaring, fuelled by ultra-low interest rates and excess credit from overseas. In a classic case of a market working by its own unarguable logic to catastrophic ends, newly emerging economies in the Middle East and Asia were keen to offload their budget surpluses, while the US deficit continued to grow – even in boom times. Much of the spare capital on offer was invested in a series of ever more complex financial instruments, which were packaged together and sold on repeatedly. Wall Street investors developed an enormous appetite for bonds backed by the mortgages of everyday folk. Firms like Lehmans would buy thousands of mortgages, bundling them together into securities, or what were known as 'collateralised debt obligations' (CDOs). They would then sell the cash flow from the mortgage payments to investors, including pension funds and hedge funds. These were deemed to be as safe as US Treasuries, but they carried a higher interest rate. The demand from hungry investors and homeowners was so great that eventually mortgage lenders loosened the underwriting criteria, doling out loans to people with poor credit ratings, people who would struggle to pay them back. These were sub-prime.

When the housing market turned down in 2007 and homeowners began to default on their loans, the system crumbled. The banks had massively over-leveraged themselves – their debts were growing much more quickly than their assets. This meant they would not be able to meet their obligations when the credit markets dried up. In order to mask their huge leverage ratios, and continue to make loans without needing to prove they had the capital to back them up, the banks set up a shadow system of arm's-length companies known as conduits or structured investment vehicles. This notionally legal manoeuvre allowed transactions worth billions of dollars to stay off the banks' balance sheets. Almost every bank and financial institution bought, repackaged and traded in these toxic instruments. Yet nobody was prepared for the extent of the sub-prime rot. When the problem first appeared, Ben Bernanke, chairman of the Federal Reserve, predicted that its effects 'would likely be limited'.

Lehmans had overexposed itself to the sub-prime market, with a debt to asset ratio similar to Bear's. The bank had been managing the books by classifying short-term loans as asset sales, making it look like the company had more cash and less debt. It did this just before announcing quarterly profits, thereby giving a false impression to shareholders and investors.[16] The man in charge was Dick Fuld, the longest-serving CEO on Wall Street. After flirting with a military career – he took part in a programme to join the Reserve Officers' Training Corps – he joined Lehmans as a trader at the age of twenty-three. His rise up the ranks was swift and effortless. His skill in banking trades was seemingly more sophisticated than his knowledge of the world. In 1986 he was brought to London to oversee the purchase of L. Messel, a brokerage firm in the City. When Messel staff told Fuld that they needed to open an office in Frankfurt to compete better in Europe, he replied: 'No way. We're never going behind the Iron Curtain.'[17]

Fuld took over Lehman Brothers in 1994 and presided over fourteen straight years of profit. He was dubbed 'the Gorilla'. He revelled in the nickname, keeping a stuffed gorilla in his office.[18] He took as his economic (and, if it ever entered his head, his ethical) reference point the approach of rival bankers. He was possessed with envy towards Goldman Sachs and its boss, Lloyd Blankfein; he was desperate to continue his quest for continuous expansion.[19] He became a parody of the narcissistic, go-getting banker, and yet in the 1990s and 2000s these character traits were seen as virtues. Giving the 2006 commencement address at his alma mater, the University of Colorado, he told students who were about to enter the workplace:

> Don't be afraid to compete. Don't be afraid to make a decision. And whatever you do, don't be a bystander. Whatever it is – try. If you lose, pick yourself up, try again and move on. When a reporter asked Thomas Edison: *'How did it feel to fail 10,000 times?'*, Edison replied: *'I didn't fail 10,000 times. The light bulb was an invention with 10,000 steps.'* Whatever you do, believe in yourself and don't give up.

He loved giving pep talks, and his audiences loved him for them. In an internal video to staff, he said of short-sellers (but he could have been referring to anyone who got in his way), using a mix of controlled menace and self-mockery that was standard fare in corporate circles: 'I am soft, I'm lovable but what I really want to do is reach in, rip out their heart and eat it before they die.'

In the year of the crash, Fuld earned $40 million.[20] As events unfolded, and Lehmans' exposure to toxic instruments was even more acute than its rivals', he went into denial. He refused several possible deals involving capital injections or mergers, insisting in each case that the suitor was undervaluing the bank. 'As long as I am alive, this firm will never be sold,' he declared. 'And if it is sold after I die, I will reach back from the grave and prevent it.'[21]

He was incensed that the Bush administration and the regulators had saved Bear Stearns but allowed his bank to go under, and his name to be trashed. He reserved particular ire for Henry 'Hank' Paulson, the former CEO of Goldman Sachs who was now Bush's Treasury Secretary and the man in charge of dealing with the financial crisis. His grievance was not entirely misplaced. His bank had behaved in largely the same way as others that were bailed out before and after; an embarrassing number of America's most prestigious institutions ended up insolvent. The cost of rescuing the banks in the United States was $700 billion. Trillions were wiped off the stock market. In the months and years to come, as Main Street suffered from the excesses of Wall Street, US unemployment rose to 10 per cent – a figure Americans hadn't seen since the Great Depression of the 1930s.

TRUE FIGURE: $23,700 BILLION.

These were privatised profits and socialised losses. When the times were good, bankers were fêted as entrepreneurial heroes, leaders of society, benefactors of great cultural institutions and friends of presidents and Congress. They were cushioned by ultra-low corporation and income tax and the use of offshore havens to bury their loot. Noninterference was a religion. When it all went wrong, the state came charging in (with the exception of Lehmans) to help them out. Intervention was briefly in fashion – for friends.

Yet, in spite of everything that was done to help the bankers and the legal exoneration they received (none of the main players faced prosecution), they continue to display a unique aptitude for self-pity. A year into the first administration of Barack Obama, who introduced a very tentative tightening of regulation, a certain hedge-fund manager called Dan Loeb wrote an email that became a classic. The subject heading was: 'Battered Wives'. 'Dear Friends/battered wives,' he wrote to a group of fellow hedgies: 'I am sure, if we are really nice and stay quiet, everything will be alright and the President will become more centrist and that all his tough talk is just words; I mean he really loves us and when he beats us, he doesn't mean it; he just gets a little angry.'

Another super-rich scribe opted for hyperbole over irony. In January 2014, Tom Perkins, a prominent venture capitalist who specialised in the tech sector, wrote to the *Wall Street Journal* to express his outrage at all the criticism: 'I would call attention to the parallels of fascist Nazi Germany to its war on its "one per cent", namely its Jews, to the progressive war on the American one per cent, namely the "rich",' he wrote. Lambasting the 'demonization' of his sort at the hands of the Occupy movement, he noted a 'rising tide of hatred of the successful' and a 'very dangerous drift in our American thinking'. He concluded his letter with the following rhetorical question: '*Kristallnacht* was unthinkable in 1930; is its descendant "progressive" radicalism unthinkable now?'[22]

Perkins was criticised in the media for his choice of comparison, but he was making a point that others would have loved to make. His fury alluded to a sense of persecution that most in the financial services industries feel about their treatment since the crash. It is ingrained because for thirty years they had enjoyed hegemony and adulation. None of their actions – the overexposure to risky debt, the development of financial products so complex that few understood them, the creative book-keeping, the resultant crisis – could have happened if the bankers had not first won a political argument. That argument was simple: we are crucial to your economy, we know best how to manage our affairs, so leave us alone to get on with it. The debate took some years to win, but it resulted in the rapid march of deregulation for the financial sector.

Banking had always been subject to laws and codes of practice. In previous centuries, banks could be established only if they demonstrated a minimum amount of capital and received permission from the powers that be. In the years following the Great Depression, with its bank failures and the wiping-out of the savings of small deposit-holders, stronger regulation was introduced. This political trajectory increased after the Second World War, with the state assuming an ever-greater role in the conduct, and ownership, of the economy. Prevailing wisdom was that the needs of financial institutions were subservient to the national interest. Post-war, the Bretton Woods system introduced fairly strict capital controls and fixed exchange rates. It also established the International Monetary Fund to regulate lending.[23] The US economist Arthur Bloomfield summed up the new mood of responsibility:

> It is now highly respectable doctrine, in academic and banking circles alike, that a substantial measure of direct control over private capital movements, especially of the so-called hot money varieties, will be desirable for most countries not only in the years immediately ahead but also in the long run as well. The doctrinal volte face represents a widespread disillusionment resulting from the destructive behaviour of these movements in the interwar years.[24]

In post-war, pre-deregulation America, the retail bank manager was seen as a sturdy pillar of local life. Usually an older man, he might be a member of the Rotary, perhaps a Freemason; he could be relied upon not to play fast and loose with citizens' spare change. Investment banks, even in that more stoical half-century period, always attracted the young and ambitious – people who were either smart or had been told they were smart. In the 1950s, the firms were known as 'white shoe' banks after the loafers worn by the Ivy League graduates they recruited.[25] But they were rarely public figures, engaged as they were in arcane activity that rarely impinged on people's lives. By the late 1960s, the banks were complaining that they were being strangled by red tape. They were suffering from interest rate controls, unable to compete or to increase capital and market share. Retail banks were reduced to offering new customers toasters. Something had to give.

The election victories of Margaret Thatcher in 1979 and Ronald Reagan in 1980 ushered in an era of rapid deregulation. The boundaries between the activities of different financial institutions became more blurred. The key moment in the UK came with passage of the Financial Services Act. The 'Big Bang' took place on 27 October 1986, when the London Stock Exchange changed its rules, abolishing middlemen in stock transactions and allowing computer-based trading. Stocks could now be bought and sold, and fortunes made, in the blink of an eye. Yet even its most ardent free-market proponents did not fully appreciate the changes that were being unleashed. In the US, the banking fraternity urged a loosening of the Glass–Steagall Act, a Depression-era law that, among other things, had separated investment banks from high street banks. Banks were now allowed to spend 5 per cent of their turnover on speculative activities. That was a considerable change, but it seems quaint compared to what happened next. By 1996 Alan Greenspan, the chairman of the Fed and lauded for more than a decade as one of the world's great economic figures, had raised this ceiling to 25 per cent.

The Big Bang and deregulation gave rise to a new breed of trader. The Thatcher and Reagan governments slashed their highest rates of income tax. In the US it fell from 70 to 28 per cent. Incredible opportunities opened up overnight for new players. The British financial sector had, in the words of one veteran of the industry, previously been dominated by the 'three pillars of conservative England: the public school, the gentleman's club and the country house'.[26] A gentleman trader could be taken at his word because of his background. As one said: 'good Etonian standards means a total trust – if you say you'll do something, you'll do it'.[27] Most kept normal office hours and left work by 5.30 p.m. Even in the mid-1980s, as some London banks moved from the Georgian buildings of the City to the brash new Docklands, the men who ran them insisted on furnishing their offices to replicate the wood-panelled studies of their schools and colleges.

The culture was changing before their eyes with the rise of the 'jobbers' – the traders and brokers from more humble backgrounds who were out to make their fortunes. These men were caricatured as 'wide boys' from Essex (England) or New Jersey (America) who arrived hideously early and stayed extremely late: they worked hard and played hard. The new traders despised the old investment bankers for what they saw as their aristocratic elitism. They were immortalised in Oliver Stone's 1987 movie *Wall Street*, with its hero or anti-hero Gordon Gekko, a fictional stockbroker modelled partly on the junk-bond king Michael Milken. Milken was jailed in 1989 for fraud and racketeering, but the exceptional salience of the film and the character was the nebulous line between legality and illegality. There was less ambiguity in

Gekko's moral compass. Greed, he famously declared, is good. In 2013, Hollywood produced another blockbuster portraying the same era, *The Wolf of Wall Street*, Martin Scorsese's pastiche of a cocaine- and sex-fuelled trader from the late 1980s.

This was the era when most of today's crop of leading bankers spent the formative years of their careers.

Bankers became socialised into a high-risk, high-reward environment, driven by Spencerian notions of superiority.[28] Unlike the Carnegies and Rockefellers, however, they did not bother to justify themselves intellectually. They just assumed everyone was fine with what they were doing, as long as everyone was getting richer (or at least everyone they knew). Successful bankers felt they'd done it the hard way, surviving their early years as juniors, working upwards of a hundred hours a week. They knew that it would be worth the slog because, as they were told on their first day of induction, they would soon be making 'more money than you ever dreamed possible'.[29] From the moment they were interviewed as Ivy League undergraduates, they were told that to work in this industry was to work alongside the best minds in the world. In the 2000s, investment banking was seen as the career of choice for bright young things. By way of example, some 40 per cent of Princeton's graduated classes in those years went into financial services. Goldman Sachs held weekly, and at some times of the year, daily recruitment events for Harvard students.[30] One Goldman investment banker, lamenting the lack of drive at other workplaces, where people arrived at nine and left at five, said: 'It is just a pain in the ass to get anything done in the real world.'[31] The internet giants were also on the prowl for the brightest and the best, but the kind of risk-taking they were looking for required a different mindset – an emphasis on ingenuity and innovation rather than the ruthlessness demanded by the banking treadmill.

Banks were one of the chief beneficiaries of the gospel of privatisation in the 1980s and 90s and the neo-liberal experiments that took hold in Europe and the Americas. The collapse of communism and the Soviet Union saw a huge expansion in the privatisation market. Deregulated currency markets were another source of profit: a staggering \$3.2 trillion was being traded daily by the 2000s. As for the derivatives market, by 2007 its value was eighteen times that of the global 'real' economy.[32] The deregulation juggernaut gathered pace. In 1999 legislation signed by President Clinton removed the last remaining Glass–Steagall restrictions. Lines demarcating which sorts of financial activity banks and other financial institutions could engage in became blurred to the point of non-existence. In theory, this allowed them to spread risk. The financial sector spent hundreds of millions of dollars lobbying Congress.[33] This might seem a large amount, but it was money well spent, opening the geysers to instant riches. In 2004 the SEC, nominally playing the role of regulator, relaxed rules governing the amount of debt banks could take on. The sector had effectively become self-regulating on the basis of nods and winks.

Even where there was supposed to be oversight from the public authorities, lines were blurred thanks to the revolving door. Bank chiefs became senior figures in US administrations, and politicians moved to banks when their time was up. One bank had special access – the leader of the pack, Goldman Sachs. The most visible case was Hank Paulson. In 2004, while he was CEO, Goldman wrote to the SEC to argue in favour of loosening the constraints on how much investment banks could leverage their capital. The subsequent rule change was a key to why so many investment banks failed, or nearly did, in 2008.[34] Paulson, together with Ben Bernanke, engaged in what one writer has termed a 'blitzkrieg offence' to try to steer a bailout package through Congress with as few conditions as possible placed on the bankers.[35] The Democrats were equally experienced in the trade. Long-time Goldman employee Robert Rubin was Treasury Secretary under Bill Clinton in the 1990s.[36] Other alumni from the bank who went on to government jobs were William Dudley, who served as CEO of the New York Federal Reserve, and Josh Bolten, who became chief of staff to George Bush.

When they weren't exchanging jobs, bankers were funding parties. As many have supported Democrats as Republicans. Some spread their largesse irrespective of political allegiance. John Mack of Morgan Stanley donated to George W. Bush's presidential campaign but in 2008 switched allegiance to Hillary Clinton.[37] This is known as 'having juice' on Capitol Hill and in the White House.

Goldman Sachs is possibly the most lucrative money machine that global capitalism has ever produced. It has always attracted the cleverest in the pack, and has always found a way of surviving or thriving, no matter what is thrown in its way. It brushes off criticism as the bleating of the envious. Of the many denunciations it has received, particularly in light of its role in the pre-crash years, none was more colourful than an article in the rock magazine *Rolling Stone* in April 2010, entitled 'The Great American Bubble Machine'. A witty and discursive essay, detailing the many sharp practices at the bank, it begins: 'The first thing you need to know about Goldman Sachs is that it's everywhere. The world's most powerful investment bank is a great vampire squid relentlessly jabbing its blood funnel into anything that smells like money.' Goldman's response was to point out that vampire squids are harmless to humans.

The vampire squid in chief was a squat, balding man from a humble home. The son of a postal worker and a receptionist, Lloyd Blankfein was born in 1954 in the South Bronx. His parents moved to a housing project in a rough Brooklyn neighbourhood. He started his working life selling soda at Yankees games, aged thirteen. Blankfein trades on this difficult upbringing: 'A soft drink was 25 cents and I think you got a 10 or 11 per cent commission. I'm thinking this tray is unbelievably heavy, and I'm going to walk all the way up there for 2 and three quarter cents? Guess what? I walked way up there for 2 and three quarter cents.'[38] He was tough and smart, the first in his family to go to college. And it wasn't just any old college, but the finishing school for the ultra-confident and ultra-networked. He went through Harvard on a scholarship, settling at a law company while unsuccessfully applying for banking jobs. Eventually, he was handed a break in 1981 by a commodities trading firm, J. Aron. In one of those CVs in which good fortune appears meticulously planned, Goldman bought J. Aron. Blankfein found himself employed by a company that had initially rejected him. By 2002 he was in charge of the whole trading floor. In 2006 he became CEO when Paulson went to the Treasury.

The more ruthless the bank's activities became, the more careful Blankfein was to guard his reputation. In 2004, in one of the more brazen naming-right appropriations of modern times, he donated to his alma mater Harvard a history chair, the Lloyd C. Blankfein Professor of History. The choice of subject was telling. This was not business or management or other modern schools. Blankfein was promoting ever-lasting values and erudition. Three years after his generous gesture, it was revealed that Harvard had found itself on the wrong side of a CDO bet with Goldman, losing at least $100 million in the process. According to a report in the *Boston Globe* in February 2007, a Goldman executive wrote to colleagues: 'That is good for us position-wise, bad for accounts who wrote that protection.'

Blankfein's first few years in charge of the bank went perfectly. In 2007 it made record profits of nearly $12 billion. His bonus was signed off at $68 million. Goldman was top of the tree, but not alone. That year, the total bonus pool for employees of the five largest US investment banks was $36 billion.[39] Later, when the term 'performance bonus' bore no resemblance to performance – when bankers paid themselves silly money for getting their institution and the global economy into trouble – they simply renamed corporate largesse the 'retention bonus'.

The Goldman Sachs business model is ingenious. It trades securities for large companies and pension funds, while at the same time acting as adviser to many of the companies whose securities it trades, giving it a perfect view of the market. Although it insists it erects strict 'Chinese walls' between its various functions, its activities have been likened to the croupier in the casino. In an early example in 1998, Goldman made tens of millions of dollars in fees when advising on the merger of the Daimler and Chrysler car companies. Within two years the merger had proved to be a disaster for the car industry. Goldman won another fee by advising the private equity firm which bought out Chrysler a decade later.[40]

In the period just before the crash, the bank packaged and sold mortgage securities that appeared designed to fail, and then shorted the bonds, making a killing for the firm while customers lost money. It was sued by the SEC over one such deal, and settled with a fine of $550 million, without admitting wrongdoing. This was a standard 'compromise' among chums in the banks, the regulators and politics. The

slap on the wrist was duly administered and everyone moved on, enjoying each other's company all the while in the Hamptons or on the ski
slopes of Vail.

During the fevered months around the time of the crash, one of
Goldman's ploys to protect its wealth was to take out billions of dollars
of swap positions with the insurance giant AIG, guarding itself against
default on complex derivatives. When the credit crunch hit, Goldman
made collateral calls against AIG and was blamed as a key player in the
collapse of the insurance empire, which required $180 billion of bailout
money from US taxpayers. The Treasury's decision to meet AIG's com-
mitments played into criticism of Goldman's influence; in the space of
a single week at the height of the crisis, phone records showed that
Blankfein spoke to the US Treasury Secretary twenty-four times. One
of the lines the bank used for *post hoc* self-justification was to praise its
decision to hedge many of its positions. But that approach just about
worked only because, time and again, taxpayers came to the rescue of
the counter-parties.

Another to help Goldman at the time was Warren Buffett. Famously
reluctant to put money into Wall Street, Buffett injected $5 billion into
the bank early on in the crisis, providing not just much needed cash,
but market confidence. After all, if the world's most successful investor
was risking his money, then surely the bank had emerged unscathed.
Buffett has a long history with Goldman. His father took him at the age
of ten to meet Sidney Weinberg, who led the firm for forty years and
saved it from bankruptcy during the Great Depression. Thanks to
Buffett's money, Goldman was able to inject at least as much again on
the market by selling stock. Blankfein said afterwards that he didn't
really need Buffett's assistance; he could have raised multiples of the
amount himself.

By 2009, hundreds of billions of dollars had been expended worldwide in bailing out the ailing system – most notably the $700-billion
Troubled Asset Relief Program (TARP), which poured in money to
recapitalise moribund banks. The world had entered what experts were
calling the Great Recession, and the debt crisis had knocked on to
engulf whole countries on the periphery of the Eurozone. Even in the
midst of the crash, so thoroughly had the free-market argument been

won that some on the political right denounced the very notion of state-sponsored bailouts. One Republican senator described TARP as 'financial socialism' and 'un-American'.[41]

No sooner were they back on their feet than the banks had begun to rewrite history. One former executive at Goldman Sachs who became an assistant treasury secretary heavily involved in the bailouts told the *New York Times*: 'Every single Wall Street firm, despite their protest today, every single one benefited from our actions. And when they get up there and say, "well, we didn't need it," that's bull.'[42]

In November 2009, after becoming the lightning rod for public anger at the banks, Blankfein began what he hoped would be a charm offensive. Previously Goldman's approach to public relations had been to harangue any journalist that stopped short of heaping praise on the company. The CEO was advised to give a small number of carefully controlled interviews. First he invited in the *Sunday Times* from London. He began with a few brief moments of self-flagellation, intended for effect: 'People are pissed off, mad, and bent out of shape. I know I could slit my wrists and people would cheer.' Then came the self-justification: 'We help companies to grow by helping them to raise capital. Companies that grow create wealth. This, in turn, allows people to have jobs that create more growth and more wealth. It's a virtuous cycle. We have a social purpose.' Challenged about the role of the sector as a whole in leading the financial world into the abyss, he replied: 'Everybody should be, frankly, happy. The financial system led us into the crisis and it will lead us out.'

By this point, the company was back making big money, and its employees had shed their momentary self-doubt. Average pay in 2009, a year of deep recession, for its 30,000 staff was a record $700,000. Total remuneration for the senior team was into the tens of millions. Asked about this, Blankfein posed a rhetorical question of his own: 'Is it possible to have too much ambition? Is it possible to be too successful?' As for his team: 'I don't want to put a cap on their ambition. It's hard for me to argue for a cap on their compensation.'

His great rhetorical flourish was still to come. Blankfein insisted he was merely a banker 'doing God's work'.[43] That quote went viral within minutes of publication. It seemed to epitomise everything that was wrong with the super-rich bankers of the twenty-first century. Blankfein insisted afterwards that he had been joking. Was this an example of insufferable arrogance or self-aware irony? In one sense, it was more the latter. For all his fast-talking brashness, Blankfein is less ostentatious than most of his peers. Rather than parade around on super yachts, he is more likely to be found at home reading a history book with his wife. Other bankers invoke God in a more plaintive manner. In the same month as Blankfein's ill-fated interview, the chief executive of Barclays, John Varley, told an audience at the church of St Martin-in-the-Fields in central London that banks were the backbone of the economy and that bonuses were necessary because 'talent is highly mobile'. Profit, he insisted, using a curious and colourful adjective, 'is not satanic'.

In 2010 Blankfein spearheaded a New Business Standards Committee, which was introduced to check the ethical underpinning of the banks' major trading decisions. For some who have seen its activities close up, such initiatives are nothing more than window dressing, designed to dupe politicians into believing that Goldman Sachs has changed and rediscovered its more sturdy roots. In March 2012, a senior executive sought to disabuse the gullible that any such rethink had happened. On the day he was leaving his post, a vice-president at the bank, Greg Smith, penned an opinion piece for the *New York Times*. Describing its approach as toxic and destructive, he wrote: 'I truly believe that this decline in the firm's moral fibre represents the single most serious threat to its long-run survival.' Smith's criticisms were headline news, fuelling speculation that the wounded Blankfein would be eased out, to allow the bank to refresh its reputation. That was to underestimate the man.

At least in the United States the authorities made attempts at regulation and scrutiny. Oversight in Britain, including over money laundering, was even more relaxed (see Chapter 12). Ever since its years in the wilderness in the 1980s, when Margaret Thatcher seemed to capture the mood with her sale of council homes, popular share-holding and 'loadsamoney' spirit, the Labour Party concluded it must project an uncritically pro-business approach if it were to be electable again. When Tony Blair came to power in 1997 he, as Clinton's Democrats had done in the US, continued the process of deregulation and celebrating wealth. He famously said, when asked about the super-wealthy: 'I didn't come into politics in order to make David Beckham pay more tax.' For high-earning footballers, also read bankers.

In 2004, halfway through Blair's second term in office, the writer and observer of social trends Anthony Sampson wrote: 'The centre of this Establishment has moved away from parliament and cabinet towards corporate boardrooms. The new members show the ability which characterizes any successful establishment, the ability to look after their own.'[44] He noted that for this group failure did not lead to punishment but a large pay-off and a new job elsewhere. Andrew Adonis, a former Labour cabinet minister and one of the party's leading thinkers, wrote in his book *The Myth of the Classless Society*:

> The Super Class, like the medieval clergy and the Victorian factory owners, has come not just to defend but to believe in the justice of its new wealth and status. Buttressed by a revamped official ideology (which even New Labour dares not question) lauding financial rewards as the hallmark of success and economic growth, and rejecting post-war notions of social cohesion, by the late 1980s the professional and managerial elite was unapologetic about the explosion of income differentials and prepared to concede few if any social disadvantages in the process.

He noted that Labour had fought shy of implementing a series of recommendations that aimed to tighten up boardroom remuneration and promote competition across financial services.

> In the UK under the Blair and Brown governments, bankers were feted by the political elite. In a national economy increasingly driven by the financial sector and the need to keep London as the pre-eminent financial centre of Europe, the ever-expanding, booming banks appeared to be a British success story, in contrast to the continued decline of big manufacturing companies. The City of London thrived on its reputation as the engine of the national economy.

It was a relationship of dependency, which increased when Gordon Brown succeeded Blair. He lavished praise on the banks, not least Lehman Brothers, as he opened their European headquarters in London's Canary Wharf in April 2004:

I would like to pay tribute to the contribution you and your company make to the prosperity of Britain. During its 150-year history, Lehman Brothers has always been an innovator, financing new ideas and inventions before many others even began to realise their potential. And it is part of the greatness not just of Lehman Brothers but of the City of London that, as the world economy has opened up, you have succeeded not by sheltering your share of a small protected national market but always by striving for a greater and greater share of the growing global market.[45]

Brown placed several senior bankers on government commissions. He counted several of these figure as his friends. He saw Alan Greenspan as a mentor, and any tax revenues from the banks as a boon that could help improve public services. Most ludicrously of all, he convinced himself that in his genius he had unlocked the secret of the everlasting bull market. The days of boom-and-bust, he famously said, were over.

A fellow Scotsman, and one British bank in particular, epitomised all that went wrong. In 2004 Fred Goodwin was knighted for 'services to banking'. In the first months of the new millennium, the Royal Bank of Scotland had taken the financial world by storm, making a swoop for its larger rival, NatWest. RBS had suddenly become Europe's second-largest bank and the fifth-largest in the world by market capitalisation. Goodwin had only moved into banking, from management consultancy, a few years before. At the age of forty-two, he was now one of the most powerful bankers in the world. In 2003, *Forbes* magazine made him its global businessman of the year, putting him on the cover and running a gushing interview with him. Harvard Business School was equally fawning in a report it produced the following year.

Goodwin's ego went into orbit. Like Blankfein and others with whom he competed, he enjoyed his reputation as a hard man. He chuckled at his nickname – Fred the Shred – which he earned for the way he cut costs and jobs in order to increase profits. When it came to self-promotion, he stopped at nothing. He ordered that a new head-quarters be built, conveniently close to Edinburgh airport and his private jet. He spent hours on the architectural plans, focusing on the idea of a large fountain and an external reflection pool. He was obsessed with the executive car fleet. The colour of each car had to be a par-ticular blue – Pantone 281. Everyone wanted a slice of him. The royal family – courted by bankers, oligarchs and anyone wealthy – also became admirers. Goodwin was a big name behind the Prince's Trust, and was later appointed to the Queen's Silver Jubilee Trust. Buckingham Palace swiftly accepted an invitation for Her Majesty to open his egotistical folly near the airport.

Goodwin went on the prowl for the next takeover. The hapless board waved through each project. Neither the non-executive directors nor the chief executive himself understood much about the collateral debt obligations, credit default swaps or over-leveraging against US sub-prime mortgages that underpinned the bank's balance sheet. In 2007, just as the holes in its finances were growing into a chasm, Goodwin's takeover of the Dutch bank ABN Amro – which had also overexposed itself on the US mortgage market – tipped RBS over the edge.[46]

To his credit, Brown moved quickly to stave off the collapse of the entire sector. Two months after Lehmans went bust in New York, the British government was forced to take a 58 per cent share in RBS, at a cost to taxpayers of £15 billion. RBS was not the only British bank to fail: Northern Rock had been nationalised after a run on its deposits, while HBOS was rescued thanks to a government-funded merger with Lloyds Group.[47]

Goodwin became public enemy number one, pilloried by a media that had once praised him and shunned by business colleagues who had queued up to see him. He now spends his time tending to his fleet of classic cars (the blow somewhat softened by his investments and his annual £340,000 pension, which he had agreed to reduce by 200,000). If the government hadn't prevented RBS from going bankrupt, his pen-sion would have been paid out of the pension-protection fund and been £28,000 a year.

Goodwin's home was attacked by vandals in 2010. What really hurt him was the extremely rare decision by the government, taken in the Queen's name, to strip him of his knighthood.

The sins of the many were being visited on one man. The scapegoating of Goodwin was selective. In the US, the UK and elsewhere (some German and Swiss banks were similarly reckless), none of the executives or non-executives have been prosecuted. The criminal test is extremely narrow and arduous. Only the very careless, such as Nick Leeson of Barings fame in the 1990s, and the ponzi fraudster Bernard Madoff, have ever found themselves behind bars.[48]

In February 2009, *Time* magazine listed '25 people to blame for the financial crisis'. The roll-call of shame included Cayne, Fuld and Goodwin (although, inevitably, not Blankfein), alongside Presidents Bush and Clinton, administration officials, central bank chiefs and regulators such as Cox, Paulson and Greenspan. Another on the list was 'the American consumer', for enjoying the good times a little too much, and for following the societal example of the bankers, or perhaps for setting it for them. 'We enjoyed living beyond our means – no wonder we wanted to believe it would never end.'

Most of the villains of the piece have quietly retired from public view. Dick Fuld rarely gives interviews and he is seldom seen in Manhattan, despite opening his own consultancy which is headquartered there. On one of the rare occasions when he stepped out in public, at a financier's party in Sun Valley, Idaho, he introduced himself as 'the most hated man in America'. His wife stepped down from the board of New York's Museum of Modern Art. He and his wife sold their 6000-square-foot Park Avenue apartment for $26 million. They offloaded, via Christie's, sixteen rare drawings, netting $20 million. Much of the money was required to fight lawsuits from furious investors. Yet they continue to own a nine-bedroom mansion in Greenwich, Connecticut, along with a forty-acre ranch in Sun Valley and a third residence on Jupiter Island, a ritzy barrier island in Florida, home to the likes of Tiger Woods.[49] He defended his $480-million personal fortune in Congress, saying he had earned it before things went wrong. In any case, the fact that his shares in Lehmans had declined to

$65 million (from as much as $1 billion) was surely, he insisted, punishment enough.[50]

Once, when tracked down by a reporter in 2009 to his country
hideaway in Idaho, Fuld snapped:

> You know what, people are saying all sorts of crap and it's a shame
> that they don't know the truth, but they're not going to get it
> from me. I've been pummelled, I've been dumped on, and it's all
> going to happen again. I can handle it. You know what, let them
> line up. You know what, my mother loves me. And you know
> what, my family loves me and I've got a few close friends who
> understand what happened and that's all I need.[51]

A loss of more than 90 per cent in assets would cause consternation for
anyone. Fuld remained, by the standards of normal mortals, an
extremely rich man, but compared to the company he kept it was a terrible fall from grace, or a terrible spot of bad luck – depending on your
point of view.

The bridge-playing Cayne also put his Park Avenue apartment up for
sale, for $14 million. The five-bedroom, five-bathroom, luxury prop-
erty apparently hadn't been used for years.[52] Cayne has quit banking to
concentrate on his real passion, hosting card games on the internet,
switching his fierce competitive instinct to another test of mathemat-
ics and bravado.[53]

As for the other players in the drama, Paulson now concentrates on
analysing US–China relations in his think-tank, the Paulson Institute,
and on giving money to environmental, conservational causes.[54] Cox,
in spite of his myopia at the time of the crash, now runs a lucrative
company that advises banks and other companies on how to navigate
the new regulatory landscape spawned by the crash. Greenspan rushed
out his memoir on the crash, which topped the *New York Times'* best-
seller list. He belongs to the same speakers' agency that represents Bush,
Blair and other politicians and celebrities. The demand for motivational
speakers from among this group is seemingly as strong as ever.

Among the many to emerge unscathed, the most important was
Blankfein. In April 2010, he was forced to listen to President Obama

harangue the bankers: 'some on Wall Street forgot that behind every dollar traded or leveraged, there is a family looking to buy a house, pay for an education, open a business or save for retirement'. The bank boss hurried out without a word, but he let it be known he wasn't pleased. Earlier, in 2009, barely months after the crash, *Vanity Fair* had awarded him the coveted number-one spot in its annual New Establishment list, ahead of the likes of Steve Jobs, Larry Page and Sergei Brin. He didn't like being chastised in public. Goldman hadn't just survived the crash, it had benefited from it, taking advantage of the easy money that had come from government and from a field that had narrowed with the demise of Lehman Brothers and the emasculation of Bear Stearns. The bank's assets had increased to $1 trillion. Blankfein was the highest-paid financial CEO in 2012, his earnings that year of $21 million adding to his $256 million fortune in Goldman shares. He was back dispensing wisdom – from advice for those seeking summer internships ('be a complete person')[55] to what he likes to do at weekends (lie on the couch).[56] Instead of being admonished by presidents, he was being invited back into the White House for cosy chats.

What unites winners and losers in this tale is an inability to account properly for their actions. Blankfein offered a vague apology in 2009, admitting that his bank had 'participated in things that were clearly wrong'.[57] He was apologising more for how the bank failed to manage its reputation, to get its message across, than for anything it had actually done: 'Post-crisis, I wish I had gotten a little quicker off the mark in describing who we were and what we did as a firm and how we looked to the world before everybody defined us for us.'[58] 'What could I have done differently?' Fuld asked. For him, it was a genuine question. Cayne admitted he had failed to 'rein in the leverage', but stopped short of an apology.[59] He was convinced that his bank was brought down by a conspiracy of hedge funds that stood to gain from Bear Stearns' death. In his departing speech to his executives he said he hoped the authorities would deal with the people responsible for the bank's collapse. He did not mean himself. The language of the *faux* apology is designed to suggest that these problems were nobody's fault, a natural occurrence in which everyone was equally involved and so no one can be blamed.

The same people who were convinced they had sorted the economy out for good have been quick to blame external problems since the crash.

Several of the key players were hauled before congressional committees. The most instructive exchange took place early on, in October 2008. 'Those of us who have looked to the self-interest of lending institutions to protect shareholders' equity, myself included, are in a state of shocked disbelief,' Alan Greenspan told the House Committee on Oversight and Government Reform. 'I made a mistake. Something which looked to be a very solid edifice, and indeed a critical pillar to market competition and free markets, did break down. And I think that, as I said, shocked me.' The man who had dismissed those drawing attention to growing bank debt as 'alarmists' and who, for his pains, had been awarded the Presidential Medal of Freedom in 2005, was asked: 'You had the authority to prevent irresponsible lending practices that led to the sub-prime mortgage crisis. You were advised to do so by many others. Do you feel that your ideology pushed you to make decisions that you wish you had not made?' Greenspan conceded: 'Yes, I've found a flaw. I don't know how significant or permanent it is. But I've been very distressed by that fact.'[60]

In parliamentary and congressional inquiries in the UK and the US, the language at the hearings was often fruity. Bank chiefs were summoned, in front of live television, for ritual dressing-downs. In June 2010, Carl Levin, chairman of the Senate Permanent Subcommittee on Investigations, attacked a Goldman Sachs executive for 'shitty deals', a phrase he used a dozen times to the evident delight of his audience. What they may not have known at the time was that all but one of the committee's ten senators had together received more than $500,000 in campaign contributions from the bank's political action committee and individual employees.[61]

The economist Joseph Stiglitz summed up what lay behind the politicians' play-acting: 'Virtually all US senators, and most of the Representatives in the House, are members of the top 1 per cent when they arrive, are kept in office by money from the top 1 per cent, and know that if they serve the top 1 per cent well they will be rewarded by the top 1 per cent when they leave office.'

The revolving door, he noted, was not a side-effect of the problem; it went to the very heart of the cause of the crisis and its aftermath: 'Much of today's inequality is due to manipulation of the financial system, enabled by changes in the rules that have been bought and paid for by the financial industry itself.'[62]

Behind the scenes, business was returning to normal. Lobbyists for the banks ensured planned curbs on derivatives, instruments once labelled by Buffett as 'financial weapons of mass destruction', would be watered down. The rules of the Dodd–Frank Act, American lawmakers' response to the crisis, were worn away to apply to as little as 20 per cent of financial markets.[63]

The bankers did not intend to smash a system in which they believed with religious fervour, and which had provided them with status and a constant source of personal riches. Yet it was that very same unshakeable belief that nothing could go wrong that led them to suspend their normal critical faculties. They fell for their own propaganda. They convinced themselves that they had rewritten the laws of finance and human nature. In the face of all historical understanding, they believed that bank crises were things of the past.

This was not a victimless crime. Across the world, small businesses went under and hundreds of millions of people lost their jobs and their hopes for a decent future. In Britain, it took more than five years for living standards to creep back to pre-2008 levels, and even then the improvement was extremely patchy. The bankers were also responsible for a series of specific scandals. It transpired that for up to two decades the major bankers had been rigging one of the key market instruments – the London Interbank Offered Rate (Libor) – and raking in fraudulent profits. Meanwhile, tens of thousands of ordinary workers lost money in mis-sold private pensions and a bogus insurance scheme called payment protection insurance (PPI). This was genuine hardship and suffering caused by individuals who knew what they were doing, who have not been punished and who bleat about their own treatment.

Back in the mid-2000s, the *Daily Mail* was already complaining about the bonuses that bankers were paying themselves. As the self-styled voice of the suburban middle class it identified a resentment that was growing, even when the going was good. On 5 February 2014, as yet more evidence emerged of criminal behaviour by the banks, the newspaper thundered in an editorial:

> For more than two decades, our leading financial institutions have been deliberately deceiving customers. But though the products mis-sold may have varied, one mystery endures. Why, after this long history of deception and grand larceny, has not a single senior banker been hauled before the courts? True, the banks have been ordered to pay enormous sums in compensation – some £20 billion over PPI alone. But show us the common crook who can expect to escape justice, simply by repaying the money he has stolen. Why should different rules apply to thieving bankers, whose only difference from petty conmen is the titanic scale of their crimes?

The paper concluded: 'This fraud won't cease until the guilty are behind bars.' That has not happened and almost certainly won't happen.

A similar sense of inchoate rage exists in the United States, particularly in those areas that have been ravaged by foreclosures, such as Detroit. In September 2013, in one county alone, more than eighteen thousand homes went under the auctioneer's hammer, at knock-down prices. As Crassus understood two thousand years ago, when misfortune strikes, there is always a killing to be made.

Alan Greenspan was right, if somewhat belatedly, when he admitted that he had found a flaw in the free-market laws that had driven his generation. But the flaw was as much psychological as it was economic. It resulted not only in the decisions that led to the crisis, but also in the inability of the likes of Cayne, Fuld, Goodwin and Blankfein to understand what drove them. Self-knowledge remains sorely lacking among bankers.

Yet they are desperate to move on, to draw a line, to try to forget about past misdeeds. Politicians are encouraging them to do just that. Timothy Geithner, Treasury Secretary in Obama's first administration and one of those familiar with the revolving door, spoke for many in government and in the banks in 2010: 'My basic view is that we did a pretty successful job of putting out a severe financial crisis and avoiding a Great Depression or Great Deflation type of thing,' he said. 'We saved the economy, but we kind of lost the public doing it.'[64]

The bankers dramatically failed in the reputation-management game, becoming individual and collective hate figures. That is not to indulge them in the sense of victimhood to which they now cleave, but to acknowledge the extent of the opprobrium heaped on them. They have come out by far the worst among the contemporary super-rich. The oligarchs engender a certain mystery. The geeks might have earned opprobrium through some of their policies, behaviour and tax avoidance, but that tends to be offset by the tangible and revolutionary changes they have made to people's lives. Bankers might provide liquidity, they might finance economic activity, but they don't produce 'things' that people rush out to buy.

And yet, as a group and as a self-sustaining cult, they have survived. At the start of 2014 the stock market was rising fast and some companies were reporting improved balance sheets. Some were not convinced. George Soros described the banking sector as 'acting as a parasite on the real economy', just as it did on the eve of the crash. Describing the profitability of the financial industry as excessive, he warned: 'the issue of "too big to fail" has not been solved at all'.[65] If Soros is whistling in the wind, what hope is there of learning the lessons? Visitors to sports events, theatres and art galleries cannot fail to see banks' logos on the walls. The old swagger is back. Who is to say that, as the crash recedes into history, the bankers will not recover their reputations? Think Carnegie, think Medici: is it impossible to believe that the same won't be true of their modern-day equivalents?

Conclusion

Well, whiles I am a beggar, I will rail,
And say there is not sin, but to be rich,
And, being rich, my virtue then shall be,
To say there is no vice, but beggary.
                    William Shakespeare, *King John*

In 1950, an immigrant father opened a bank account for his ten-year-old son. Half a century earlier, Khalil Slim had made his way from a Lebanese village to Mexico on his own at the age of fourteen, to escape the persecution of Maronite Christians and to establish a business. He did well in his adopted country, establishing a dry goods store and buying into real estate. He wanted his six children to do better than he and so he gave them a little money each to set them on their way.

Young Carlos was fifth in line. What he noticed about his new current account was how little a return he was getting on his deposit. He withdrew the money and began buying savings bonds. He discovered compound interest – and a root to instant wealth. At the age of twelve, Carlos Slim bought shares in a Mexican bank. Five years later he was working for his father's company, and after studying civil engineering at university, he started out as a trader, forming his own brokerage firm. In his early twenties, Slim's guiding light was none other than John Paul Getty and his musings, published first as a series of essays in *Playboy* magazine, called 'How to be Rich'. From the mid-1950s to the 1960s Getty was one of the world's richest men, with an estimated worth of $1.2 billion. That corresponds to $8.7 billion now, and while a sizeable chunk of money, it would not put him in the top 150 on today's global rich list, showing how far the super-rich have come over the past five

decades. Getty was not particularly interested in philanthropy, preferring to spend a smattering of his excess cash on collecting art (a legacy
which culminated in the opening of the museum that bears his name
at his Malibu 'villa' in 2006).

Slim heeded the teachings of his mentor and became rich many
times over. Acquisitions were to be his business, starting with a wedding gift from his mother (by this point his father had died) on account
of his marriage to Soumaya, a young woman from the Lebanese dias-
pora. The twenty-something couple were given enough money for a
decent-sized house, but Carlos had other ideas. He and his new wife
built a twelve-floor condo block, moved into a single floor, and rented
out the rest. They preferred the income to the luxury.

With money in the bank from his father's firm, Slim saw opportunities in Mexico's ailing economy. Any company in distress
corresponded to a potential purchase. Slim moved into construction,
real estate, mining, tobacco, food production and hotels. There was
barely a sector that he did not scour. The collapse of the peso in 1982
played into his hands. His biggest break came at the end of that decade
and the start of the 1990s. As we have seen, with the collapse of communism and the planned economy, privatisations afforded huge returns
for those with nous and the contacts.

In 1990 the Mexican government put the national telephone company, Telmex, up for sale. Most state-owned operators in those days
were poor, with customers waiting days for repairs or even for a fixed
line phone. In Mexico, the service was particularly bad. Large parts of
the country were unconnected. The economy was stagnant and overwhelmed by foreign debt, desperate for investment, especially in its
communications infrastructure. Slim submitted the highest bid for the
company and won the tender. For years after, the sale was dogged by
rumours of favours in return for his friendship with the President,
Carlos Salinas de Gortari. Both denied this, naturally. What mattered
was that one man had a licence covering the whole country. Telmex
became the cash cow for the rest of Slim's activities. According to a
report in 2012 by the Organisation for Economic Cooperation and
Development, Mexico has by far the largest market share of telecom-
munications of any major country in the hands of one company.

Mobile usage fees are the third-highest in the world and those for fixed lines the fourth-highest – and that for a country ranked sixty-eighth in the world in terms of per capita income.

The scale of Slim's domination of one country's economy has perhaps no contemporary equivalent. Telmex (in which he retains a 49 per cent share) controls nine-tenths of Mexico's landlines. His mobile operator, América Móvil, is the third-largest company in Latin America. In the late 1990s, worried about such overweening control, the Mexican government sought to increase its regulatory regime. The problem was that the salaries of the regulator's employees were a fraction of what was on offer in the private sector. It was desperately hard to keep tabs or exert any meaningful influence.

Slim and his six children (all of whom work for him) control more than two hundred companies, accounting for 40 per cent of the value of Mexico's main stock market index. His portfolio contains Inbursa, one of Mexico's most prominent banks; Volaris, an airline; a mining company; the Mexican branch of the retail chain Sears, five hotels; a bottling company; a cigarette manufacturer; a large stake in construction; insurance and financial groups; and valuable real estate – not to mention the phone companies.

In a country where average per capita income struggles to reach $15,000 per year, and where around two-fifths of the population live in either moderate or extreme poverty, Slim's economic dominance goes unchallenged. His wealth is equivalent to 5 per cent of Mexico's total annual economic output. In 2007 an opinion piece in the *New York Times* likened him to the robber barons: 'It takes about nine of the captains of industry and finance of the nineteenth and early twentieth centuries to replicate the footprint that Mr Slim has left on Mexico,' wrote Eduardo Porter, a member of the newspaper's editorial board. 'Like many a robber baron – or Russian oligarch, or Enron executive – Mr Slim calls to mind the words of Honoré de Balzac: "Behind every great fortune there is a crime." Mr Slim's sin, if not technically criminal, is like that of Rockefeller, the sin of the monopolist.'[1]

Slim cannot have been amused by such a portrayal and ensured he had the last laugh. In September 2008 he took a 6.4 per cent stake in the paper for $127 million – pocket money to assert a reputation, and certain authority, over the Grey Lady. In 2011 he increased his holdings.

Slim was the richest man in the world for several years (although Bill Gates has recently reclaimed the top spot). In many ways he conforms to the stereotype of the very rich man who does not need to try too hard. He lives in a large but not ostentatious home in Mexico City, preferring to watch sports on television (he is a baseball addict) than schmooze or show off. Like his competitors, he is developing a taste for philanthropy. His foundations sponsor anti-poverty and city-regeneration projects, providing computers, pairs of glasses and bicycles to schoolchildren. He owns a number of local football teams. His single most impressive contribution is perhaps the Museo Soumaya, an art gallery in Mexico City, which already has the largest collection of Rodin statues outside France, alongside works by Leonardo da Vinci, Picasso, Renoir, and the largest Dalí collection in Latin America.

What makes Slim stand out is not how he made his money (Carnegie and Gates, among others, had to shrug off accusations of monopoly practices), nor how he spends it (standard fare), but the question of geography. He is not based in the United States, which still provides by far the largest number of billionaires; nor does he fit into the categories of Gulf sheikhs, Russian or Chinese oligarchs, Silicon Valley whizz-kids or Wall Street or City of London bankers. He hails not from the developed world, but from the next generation of countries where money is being made fast. The Goldman Sachs economist Jim O'Neill, who coined the term 'Brics', now likes to speak of the Mints – Mexico, Indonesia, Nigeria and Turkey.

Watch for the next batch of super-rich from countries such as these and others. There is ample cash to spare for a tiny few in South Africa, Ghana and Angola, in Chile and Colombia, not to mention the burgeoning Asian economies, from Thailand to the Philippines to Vietnam. The Singaporean economist and diplomat Kishore Mahbubani has long argued that diplomatic and political institutions fail to take account of the growing wealth of Asia and other emerging economies. He claims that countries such as these, with their greater focus on collectivism and the role of government, have learned from the many mistakes of the Anglo-Saxon model. 'The first error was to regard capitalism as an ideological good, not as a pragmatic instrument to improve human welfare,' he wrote.[2] If so, there appears scant evidence to suggest that the super-rich of, say, China, Russia or India have heeded this message. Indeed, a game of catch-up is being played; the sense of entitlement of one group is simply being transferred to another.

Nor is there evidence that the new destinations for wealth are any more enlightened in its use. In the 1950s, the economist Simon Kuznets put forward the theory that industrialisation led initially to greater inequality in societies, but that this started to decrease after per capita income reached a certain level. Thus the beneficial changes that took place in America during the New Deal and in Europe after the end of the Second World War will, by this logic, necessarily take place in China, Russia and India. For that to happen, however, requires concerted intervention – something politicians have shown themselves unable or unwilling to do. Some economists and political scientists are beginning to posit the theory that, far from a rising tide lifting all boats, contemporary market capitalism relies on entrenched and increased inequality as its lifeblood. The French economist Thomas Piketty cites only two possible brakes on this natural and inevitable tendency – population growth and intervention. The problem is that governments have been well and truly co-opted, and even if they showed a determination to act, they would be unable, in any sensible or meaningful way, to tackle the root of imbalances such as unrestricted capital flows or tax havens. Concerted action is a chimera. The prospects for change are therefore minimal.

The 1 per cent and the 0.1 per cent are now truly international. They can, and do, come from across the globe, but they end up in the same places. They converge on familiar haunts. They alight on London, Singapore and Zurich for the 'no questions asked' philosophy of their governments and banks and the indulgent approach to tax. They buy properties in Paris and New York, and moor their yachts on the coastline between St Tropez and Portofino. They share mutually reinforcing lifestyles and values; they speak each other's language.

Do the examples of Carlos Slim, Nigeria's cement billionaire Aliko Dangote and Li Ka-Shing in Hong Kong show that anyone, anywhere, can join the ranks of the super-rich? In theory, yes, but in practice, the local environment counts for a considerable amount. The Nobel laureate Herbert Simon estimated that social capital is responsible for at least 90 per cent of what people earn in wealthy societies like those of the United States and north-west Europe. By 'social capital' he meant natural resources, infrastructure, technology, the rule of law and good government. These are the foundations on which the rich can begin their work. As early as 1995, Warren Buffett, the man on whom we can always rely for a sage remark about wealth, pinpointed the crucial advantage he had enjoyed on his way to untold riches: 'Society is responsible for a very significant percentage of what I've earned,' he remarked. 'If you stick me down in the middle of Bangladesh or Peru, you'll find out how much this talent is going to produce in the wrong kind of soil.'

At the heart of social capital is access to good education. This is where inheritance and tax return to the fray. According to a strict reading of the Buffett and Carnegie mantras, everyone should be entitled to the same start in life and money should not be passed down from generation to generation. Such egalitarianism and altruism are easier to preach than to practise because, even if their children had started with nothing more than the basics (which was not the case), they would have had an inbuilt network and social and academic support structure that puts them at an advantage. The more urgent task of the super-rich is to ensure that their offspring do not allow comforts to dull their senses and to squander the family fortune. The more self-made is the first-generation wealthy, the more determined he is to consolidate his children's place in the social and cultural hierarchy. New money becomes old money. Dodgy reputation becomes pillar of the establishment.

In virtually every aspect of their behaviour, the present-day ultra-wealthy have taken on the attributes of their predecessors from Crassus' time, through the Renaissance, to colonialism and industrialisation. The instinct to make and accumulate money goes to the core of human behaviour. That much is fixed. The variable in the equation is society's requirement to tax and regulate that activity. With the exception of the period between 1945 and 1979 or 1986 (the rise to power of Margaret Thatcher or the opening up of stock markets in the Big Bang), societies have indulged the super-rich. In earlier times access to information, or the lack of it, might have prevented a challenge, but the acquiescence of modern times is more curious.

Some, such as the Occupy movement, have adopted a more belligerent approach to the super-rich, but – even after the financial crash and the culpability of the bankers, and for all the resentment of a well-educated but under-employed young middle class – they have failed to make much political headway. The most persuasive voice for change emerged in 2013 with Pope Francis's encyclicals about poverty and 'unbridled capitalism'. In a message to the rich and powerful attending the 2014 World Economic Forum in Davos, he urged: 'I ask you to ensure that humanity is served by wealth and not ruled by it.' His has become a powerful moral voice for change, but the more rational arguments for greater distribution of wealth fail to gain traction. Politicians have displayed little desire, or courage, to ask the important questions, even less so now as the West emerges tentatively out of recession.

Economists may speak at length of the inefficiency of having so many people struggling on or just above the poverty line, unable to participate in the basic economic activity of consumption. They may note the 'marginal utility' of extreme wealth – the fact that the more money an individual has, the less productively he will spend it. After all, even the very richest must eventually tire of super yachts and mega-mansions. But essentially very little has changed. The years following the crash have not produced the transformative new thinking that many expected or hoped for. Changes to corporate governance, banking secrecy, off-shore havens and financial regulation have amounted to little more than tinkering. The mainstream centre-left, with its slightly more critical stance, has failed to reap electoral benefit in most countries, while the groups widely deemed responsible for the failure of unbridled markets has emerged Scot free. In order to secure viable prosecutions, convincing evidence of intentional and systemic fraud would have been required. Greed and recklessness are far harder to pin down in the criminal code, particularly in countries such as the UK and the US where the authorities have shown little appetite for such pursuits.

The economic crash did not damage the super-rich; rather the reverse. Their share of the pie has increased, just as the middle and working classes have been forced to retrench. Normal ideological serv-ice has resumed. The arguments have not changed: trickle-down and individual acts of philanthropy are, politicians proclaim, the best routes to a healthy society.

The voting public, meanwhile, is confused about wealth. When is it excessive and when is it deserving? It admires footballers who earn hundreds of thousands each week and film stars on the red carpet at the Oscars; so much, so understandable. It also devours gossip about B- and C-list celebrities and their lavish lifestyles, no matter how lacking they may be in talent. On one level, it appears able to differentiate between billionaires who have created products or services that have affected their lives – from Google and Facebook to Virgin and Top Shop – and the banks, hedge funds and private equity sharks who claim, wanly, that they are contributing to the public good by providing capital and liq-uidity. And even where people can agree on 'deserving' and 'undeserving' routes to wealth, there appears little consensus on what constitutes excessive wealth. Or, to render this into a more tangible conundrum: at what point does taxation start to be punitive and a dis-incentive to genuine entrepreneurship? The lack of clarity on these questions reinforces the status quo.

The promises made in 2007 and 2008, at the height of the crash – to learn lessons and introduce fundamental change – now seem quaint. It is too easy for political malcontents to blame media concentrations and the influence over politicians of business leaders and their armies of lobbyists. Of course, they have played an important role in diluting the appetite for change, but people will get away with whatever they can. Think of a crowd of teenagers at a fashionable high-street clothes store. Some (by no means all) will be tempted to smuggle a T-shirt or two into their bag, hoping that nobody will see. It is only the burly security guard and the electronic detector that stand in their way. Then think of the present-day oligarchs and bankers, and the robber barons, and Crassus and Medici. They got away with it because they could.

It is therefore less to the wealthy, but more to ourselves that we should look for answers. Why is it, amid all the talk of 'injustice', that voters cleave towards lowering or abolishing inheritance tax (the oppo-site of what Andrew Carnegie called for), while pressing their noses into the shop fronts of estate agents advertising multi-million-pound properties in London's swankiest neighbourhoods? The desire to do well, or greed – two sides of the same coin, depending on one's point of view – is as entrenched now as it has ever been. The hegemony of low-tax and deregulated markets around the world, coupled with ever more sophisticated mobile technology, has enabled many to get in on the act. Only a tiny few will get there, by fair means or foul. They will have pliant governments, parliaments, regulators and central banks to thank. As they have always done.

The victory of the super-rich in the twenty-first century is a product of two thousand years of history.

Acknowledgements

I feel I have lived and breathed the super-rich for eighteen months – not literally, I hasten to add. Indeed, most of my subjects are long dead. There has been no shortage of books recently about the mores of the modern-day wealthy. For me, the fascination in this project lay in the history, and its links to our contemporary times.

The primary location for the early stages of my research was the British Library, under the excellent leadership of Roly Keating. Later, I travelled to a number of locations and on each occasion I received friendly cooperation from academics and other experts. In London and Florence, Dr Serena Ferente, lecturer in European Medieval History at King's College London, provided great insights into the Medici dynasty. In the Dutch town of Hoorn, I spent invaluable time with Ad Geerdink, director of the Westfries Museum, arranged by the Dutch Embassy in London. I also received very useful input from Jur van Goor, the biographer of Jan Pieterszoon Coen, and from Dr Jan-Emmanuel de Neve, of the LSE and University College London.

In Versailles, senior curator Bertrand Rondot treated me to a fascinating behind-the-scenes tour of the lavish world of Louis XIV. At the Villa Hügel, Essen, I spent a very fruitful day in the Krupp historical archive, where the director, Professor Ralf Stremmel, and Dr Heinfried Voss were friendly and forensic hosts. Thanks also to Agnes Widmann for making the arrangements. At York University I received assistance from Dr Sethina Watson in my research into Alan Rufus and the Normans. Thanks go to the university's Nik Miller for organising my visit. In nearby Richmond local historian Marion Moverley was very kind in taking me around the castle. My final trip was to Trujillo, the delightful small town in Extremadura from where Francisco Pizarro and other *conquistadores* set off. In the region I had good meetings with Hernando de Orellana Pizarro, José Antonio Ramos Rubio and Josiane Polart Plisnier. My biggest thanks there go to Nuria Agullo for accompanying me and arranging a great stay.

Dr Henrik Mouritsen, Professor of Roman History at King's, gave me copious amounts of his time in my work on Marcus Licinius Crassus and the Roman Republic. Caroline Daniel, of the *Financial Times*, was an assiduous adviser overall on the modern section. John Arlidge, from the *Sunday Times*, was a cheerful and informative guide on the UAE and the rest of the contemporary chapters, while Luke Harding, of the *Guardian*, was helpful on the Russian oligarchs and Mali. Author and Africa aficionado Michela Wrong provided invaluable expertise on the Congo and Mobutu. For China, I am indebted to Jonathan Fenby for his advice, alongside Jamil Anderlini, the *FT*'s bureau chief in Beijing, and Rupert Hoogewerf of the Hurun Report in Shanghai. For general thoughts on the wealthy, who better to turn to than Philip Beresford, veteran compiler of the *Sunday Times'* Rich List?

Three friends and specialists gave up generous chunks of Christmas and New Year 2013 to read an early draft of the entire text – the business journalist David Wighton (formerly of the *FT* and *The Times*), Professor Conor Gearty from the London School of Economics and Mark Easton, Home Editor at the BBC. Their thoughts and suggestions were invaluable. They read later versions, too. I'm extremely grateful to them.

This book would not have been possible without the endeavours of my two researchers. Elly Robson contributed great work over the first year, and biggest thanks of all go to Edd Mustill, who was deeply involved in the project from start to finish, always on hand and ever vigilant for accuracy and new angles. I cannot recommend his work more highly.

More than a decade after publication of *Blair's Wars* it was a great pleasure to team up again with Andrew Gordon. My former editor at Simon & Schuster is now my agent at David Higham Associates, and it feels like we picked up where we left off. Andrew's biggest contribution this time was to team me up with Little, Brown, and its publishing director, Richard Beswick. Richard has been an inspirational editor, applying encouragement and improvements in equal measure as the work progressed.

Last but not least, thanks, as ever, go to my family for their forbearance and good cheer, particularly during the latter stages of the writing when I assumed all the attributes of a hermit. My wife Lucy also read a number of drafts, providing fresh thinking and wise counsel throughout. So, to Lucy, and my two daughters Constance and Alex, this is for you.

Notes

Chapter 1: Marcus Licinius Crassus

1 Plutarch, *Parallel Lives*, vol. 3, p. 317.
2 Plutarch, *Parallel Lives*, vol. 3, p. 315.
3 Allen Mason Ward, *Marcus Crassus and the Late Roman Republic*, p. 1.
4 Allen Mason Ward, *Marcus Crassus and the Late Roman Republic*, p. 1.
5 Plutarch, *Parallel Lives*, vol. 3, p. 329.
6 As cited by Tom Holland, *Rubicon*, p. 91.
7 William Stearns Davis, 'The Influence of Wealth in Imperial Rome'.
8 Plutarch, *Parallel Lives*, vol. 3.
9 F.E. Adcock, *Marcus Crassus, Millionaire*, p. 15; Gareth C. Sampson, *The Defeat of Rome*.
10 Plutarch, *Parallel Lives*, vol. 3, p. 318.
11 Sallust, as quoted by Keith Roberts, *The Origins of Business, Money and Markets*, p. 161.
12 William Stearns Davis, 'The Influence of Wealth in Imperial Rome'.
13 Plutarch, *Parallel Lives*, vol. 3, p. 319.
14 F.E. Adcock, *Marcus Crassus, Millionaire*, p. 11.
15 Plutarch, *Parallel Lives*, vol. 3, p. 336.
16 Plutarch, *Parallel Lives*, vol. 3, p. 320.
17 Appian, *The Roman History*, p. 221.
18 Plutarch, *Parallel Lives*, vol. 3.
19 Branko Milanovic, Peter Lindert and Jeffrey Williamson, *Pre-industrial Equality*.
20 Walter Scheidel and Steven J. Friesen, 'The Size of the Economy and the Distribution of Income in the Roman Empire', pp. 61–91.
21 Henrik Mouritsen, *Plebs and Politics in the Late Roman Republic*.
22 F.E. Adcock, *Marcus Crassus, Millionaire*, p. 18.
23 Plutarch, *Parallel Lives*, vol. 3, p. 335.
24 Plutarch, *Parallel Lives*, vol. 3, p. 357.
25 Cassius Dio, *Roman History*, vol. 3, p. 422.
26 Plutarch, *Parallel Lives*, vol. 3, p. 360.
27 Plutarch, *Parallel Lives*, vol. 3, p. 364.
28 Plutarch, *Parallel Lives*, vol. 3, p. 365.
29 Plutarch, *Parallel Lives*, vol. 3, pp. 367–8.

30 Gareth C. Sampson, *The Defeat of Rome*, p. 103.
31 Plutarch, *Parallel Lives*, vol. 3, p. 376.
32 Plutarch, *Parallel Lives*, vol. 3, p. 380.
33 Cassius Dio, *Roman History*, vol. 3, p. 447.
34 Plutarch, *Parallel Lives*, vol. 3, p. 419.
35 Plutarch, *Parallel Lives*, vol. 3, p. 255.
36 http://www.washingtonpost.com/blogs/wonkblog/wp/2014/02/19/who-was-the-richest-man-in-all-of-history/
37 Plutarch, *Parallel Lives*, vol. 3, p. 403.

Chapter 2: Alain Le Roux

1 See introduction to P. Beresford and W.D. Rubinstein, *The Richest of the Rich*.
2 E.M.C. van Houts, *The Gesta Normannorum Ducum of William of Jumiéges, Orderic Vitalis, and Robert of Torigni*, p. 161.
3 R.H.C. Davis and M. Chibnall (eds), *The Gesta Guillelmi of William of Poitiers*, pp. 107–9.
4 E.M.C van Houts, *The Gesta Normannorum Ducum of William of Jumiéges, Orderic Vitalis, and Robert of Torigni*, p. 163.
5 M. Swanton (ed.), *The Anglo-Saxon Chronicle*, pp. 199–200.
6 S. Baxter, 'Lordship and Labour', p. 108.
7 S. Baxter, 'Lordship and Labour', pp. 104–5.
8 M. Chibnall, *Anglo-Norman England 1066–1166*, p. 30.
9 M. Chibnall, *Anglo-Norman England 1066–1166*, p. 23.
10 William of Malmesbury, *A History of the Norman Kings*, p. 23.
11 B. Golding, *Conquest and Colonisation*, p. 61.
12 P. McGurk, *The Chronicle of John of Worcester*, vol. 3, p. 5.
13 B. Golding, *Conquest and Colonisation*, p. 35.
14 P. McGurk, *The Chronicle of John of Worcester*, vol. 3, p. 9.
15 W.E. Kapelle, *The Norman Conquest of the North*, p. 106.
16 P. McGurk, *The Chronicle of John of Worcester*, vol. 3, p. 11.
17 W.E. Kapelle, *The Norman Conquest of the North*, p. 3.
18 W.E. Kapelle, *The Norman Conquest of the North*, p. 118.
19 P. McGurk, *The Chronicle of John of Worcester*, vol. 3, p. 11.
20 W.E. Kapelle, *The Norman Conquest of the North*, p. 119.
21 M. Chibnall, *Anglo-Norman England*, p. 18.
22 P. Dalton, *Conquest, Anarchy, and Lordship*, p. 24.
23 William of Malmesbury, *A History of the Norman Kings*, p. 24.
24 William of Malmesbury, *A History of the Norman Kings*, p. 25.
25 P. McGurk, *The Chronicle of John of Worcester*, vol. 3, p. 13.
26 P. McGurk, *The Chronicle of John of Worcester*, vol. 3, p. 17.
27 R. Fleming, *Kings and Lords in Conquest England*, p. 114.
28 William of Malmesbury, *A History of the Norman Kings*, pp. 22–3.
29 P. McGurk, *The Chronicle of John of Worcester*, vol. 3, pp. 27–9.
30 M Swanton (ed.), *The Anglo-Saxon Chronicle*, p. 212.
31 D. Henson, *The English Elite in 1066*, p. 77.
32 W.E. Kapelle, *The Norman Conquest of the North*, p. 145.
33 J.A. Green, *The Aristocracy of Norman England*, p. 166.
34 M. Swanton (ed.), *The Anglo-Saxon Chronicle*, p. 200.

35 P. Dalton, *Conquest, Anarchy and Lordship*, p. 197.

36 See Alan Rufus's entry in the *Oxford Dictionary of National Biography*.

37 J.A. Green, *The Aristocracy of Norman England*, pp. 186–7.

38 M. Chibnall, *The Debate on the Norman Conquest*, p. 144.

39 J.C. Holt, *Colonial England*, p. 7.

40 B. O'Brien, 'Authority and Community', p. 81.

41 R. Fleming, *Kings and Lords in Conquest England*, p. 129.

42 See Alan Rufus's entry in the *Oxford Dictionary of National Biography*.

43 R. Fleming, 'Land and People', p. 35.

44 N. Davies, *The Isles*, p. 279.

45 D. Henson, *The English Elite in 1066*, p. 212.

46 S. Baxter, 'Lordship and Labour', p. 104.

47 M. Chibnall, *Anglo-Norman England 1066–1166*, pp. 37–8.

48 B. Golding, *Conquest and Colonisation*, p. 78.

49 See Alan Rufus's entry in the *Oxford Dictionary of National Biography*.

50 R. Fleming, *Kings and Lords in Conquest England*, p. 113.

51 P. Dalton, *Conquest, Anarchy, and Lordship*, p. 300.

52 J. Crick and E. van Houts (eds), *A Social History of England 900–1200*, p. 3.

53 D. Henson, *The English Elite in 1066*, pp. 74–5.

54 See C. Warren Hollister, 'The Greater Domesday Tenants-in-Chief', in J.C. Holt (ed.), *Domesday Studies* (Boydell, 1987), pp. 225–7.

55 P. Dalton, *Conquest, Anarchy, and Lordship*, p. 298.

56 P. Dalton, *Conquest, Anarchy and Lordship*, p. 43.

57 P. Dalton, *Conquest, Anarchy and Lordship*, p. 67.

58 R. Fleming, *Kings and Lords in Conquest England*, pp. 220–2.

59 M. Chibnall, *Anglo-Norman England*, p. 24.

60 B. Golding, *Conquest and Colonisation*, pp. 82–3.

61 P. Dalton, *Conquest, Anarchy, and Lordship*, p. 102.

62 P. Dalton, *Conquest, Anarchy, and Lordship*, p. 137.

63 P. Dalton, *Conquest, Anarchy, and Lordship*, pp. 166–7.

64 M. Swinton (ed.), *The Anglo-Saxon Chronicle*, p. 212.

65 B. Golding, *Conquest and Colonisation*, p. 179.

66 D.M. Hadley, 'Ethnicity and Acculturation', p. 240.

67 H.M. Thomas, *The English and the Normans*, pp. 134–5.

68 D. Crouch, *The Birth of Nobility*, pp. 157–8.

69 C. Warren Hollister, *The Greater Domesday Tenants-in-Chief*, p. 234.

70 R. Fleming, 'Land and People', p. 29.

71 R. Fleming, 'Land and People', pp. 32–3.

72 D. Crouch, *The Birth of Nobility*, p. 283.

73 D. Crouch, *The Birth of Nobility*, p. 265.

74 Based on the UK Gross National Income of £2.3 trillion in 2012.

Chapter 3: Mansa Musa

1 See John William Johnson, 'The Dichotomy of Power and Authority in Mande Society and in the Epic of Sunjata', in Ralph A. Austen (ed.), *In Search of Sunjata: The Mande Oral Epic as History, Literature, and Performance* (Indiana University Press, 1999).

2 E.W. Bovill, *The Golden Trade of the Moors*, p. 87.

3 P.L. Bernstein, *The Power of Gold*, p. 8.
4 P.L. Bernstein, *The Power of Gold*, p. 42.
5 T.F. Garrard, *African Gold*, p. 33.
6 A.J. Boye and J.O. Hunwick, *The Hidden Treasures of Timbuktu*, p. 45.
7 A.J. Boye and J.O. Hunwick, *The Hidden Treasures of Timbuktu*, p. 50.
8 J.O. Hunwick, 'The Mid-fourteenth Century Capital of Mali', p. 197.
9 T.F. Garrard, *African Gold*, p. 34.
10 C. Crossen, *The Rich and How They Got That Way*, p. 57.
11 A.J. Boye and J.O. Hunwick, *The Hidden Treasures of Timbuktu*, p. 33.
12 J.F. Ade Ajayi and M. Crowder, *A History of West Africa*, p. 27.
13 E.W. Bovill, *The Golden Trade of the Moors*, p. 90.
14 B.D. Singleton, 'African Bibliophiles', p. 3.
15 B.D. Singleton, 'African Bibliophiles', p. 4.
16 D. Chu and E. Skinner, *A Glorious Age in Africa*, p. 89.
17 J.F. Ade Ajayi and M. Crowder, *A History of West Africa*, p. 32.
18 Quoted in C. Crossen, *The Rich and How They Got That Way*, p. 52.
19 See P.R. McNaughton, 'Malian Antiquities and Contemporary Desire', pp. 22–8.

Chapter 4: Cosimo de' Medici

1 Cited in Tim Parks, *Medici Money*, p. 62.
2 Niccolò Machiavelli, *History of Florence*, Book IV, chapter 4.
3 Tim Parks, *Medici Money*.
4 Christopher Hibbert, *The House of Medici*.
5 Niccolò Machiavelli, *History of Florence*, Book VII, chapter 1.
6 Raymond de Roover, *The Rise and Decline of the Medici Bank 1397–1494*.
7 Niccolò Machiavelli, *History of Florence*, Book IV, chapter 6.
8 Vespasiano da Bisticci, *The Vespasiano Memoirs*, p. 213.
9 Paul Strathern, *The Medici*, p. 54.
10 Christopher Hibbert, *The House of Medici*.
11 Cited in Paul Strathern, *The Medici*, p. 61.
12 Rinaldo de' Albizzi reportedly expressed these fears to Bernardo Guadagni, the new *gon-faloniere*: Niccolò Machiavelli, *History of Florence*, Book IV, chapter 6.
13 Niccolò da Uzzano on being asked to support Rinaldo de' Albizzi's plans to expel Cosimo during the war with Lucca: Niccolò Machiavelli, *History of Florence*, Book IV, chapter VI.
14 Niccolò Machiavelli, *History of Florence*, Book IV, chapter 6.
15 Christopher Hibbert, *The House of Medici*, p. 55.
16 Vespasiano da Bisticci, *The Vespasiano Memoirs*, p. 216.
17 Niccolò Machiavelli, *History of Florence*, Book IV, chapter 7.
18 Machiavelli cited in Paul Strathern, *The Medici*, p. 76.
19 Christopher Hibbert, *The House of Medici*, p. 58.
20 Niccolò Machiavelli, *History of Florence*, Book V, chapter 6.
21 Christopher Hibbert, *The House of Medici*.
22 As cited by Paul Strathern, *The Medici*, p. 77.
23 Niccolò Machiavelli, *History of Florence*, Book VII, chapter 1.
24 Tim Parks, *Medici Money*, p. 43.
25 Raymond de Roover, *The Rise and Decline of the Medici Bank 1397–1494*, p. 32.
26 John McCabe, *Crises in the History of the Papacy*, pp. 234–5.

27 Cited in John McCabe, *Crises in the History of the Papacy*, p. 237.
28 Raymond de Roover, *The Rise and Decline of the Medici Bank 1397–1494*, p. 198.
29 Tim Parks, *Medici Money*, pp. 13–14.
30 Tim Parks, *Medici Money*, p. 10.
31 Tim Parks, *Medici Money*, p. 10.
32 Raymond de Roover, *The Rise and Decline of the Medici Bank 1397–1494*, pp. 199, 202.
33 Raymond de Roover, *The Rise and Decline of the Medici Bank 1397–1494*, pp. 205–6.
34 Compared to the subsequent ten years where profits averaged 6200 cameral florins. See Raymond de Roover, *The Rise and Decline of the Medici Bank 1397–1494*, p. 217.
35 Quoted in Paul Strathern, *The Medici*, p. 114.
36 Vespasiano da Bisticci, *The Vespasiano Memoirs*, p. 234.
37 Cited in Christopher Hibbert, *The House of Medici*.
38 Sarah Blake McHam, 'Donatello's Bronze "David" and "Judith" as Metaphors of Medici Rule in Florence', p. 32.
39 Christopher Hibbert, *The House of Medici*, pp. 73–4.
40 Tim Parks, *Medici Money*, p. 106.
41 Niccolò Machiavelli, *History of Florence*, Book VII, chapter 1.
42 Vespasiano da Bisticci, *The Vespasiano Memoirs*, p. 208.
43 Paul Strathern, *The Medici*, p. 125.
44 Paul Strathern, *The Medici*, p. 124.
45 Niccolò Machiavelli, *History of Florence*, Book VII, chapter 1.
46 As cited in Christopher Hibbert, *The House of Medici*, p. 60.
47 Niccolò Machiavelli, *History of Florence*, Book VII, chapter 1.

Chapter 5: Francisco Pizarro

 1 W.S. Maltby, *The Rise and Fall of the Spanish Empire*, pp. 22–4.
 2 R. Varon Gabai, *Francisco Pizarro and his Brothers*, p. 144.
 3 J. Lockhart, *The Men of Cajamarca*, p. 136.
 4 H. Thomas, *Rivers of Gold*, pp. 292–3.
 5 J. Lockhart, *The Men of Cajamarca*, p. 145.
 6 J. Lockhart, *The Men of Cajamarca*, p. 20.
 7 W.S. Maltby, *The Rise and Fall of the Spanish Empire*, pp. 26–7.
 8 H. Thomas, *Rivers of Gold*, p. 309.
 9 J. Hemming, *The Conquest of the Incas*, p. 36.
10 A.W. Crosby Jr, *The Columbian Exchange*, p. 11.
11 W. S. Maltby, *The Rise and Fall of the Spanish Empire*, p. 63.
12 H. Thomas, *The Golden Age*, p. 242.
13 J. Hemming, *The Conquest of the Incas*, pp. 47–8.
14 J. Hemming, *The Conquest of the Incas*, p. 73.
15 J. Lockhart, *The Men of Cajamarca*, pp. 96–7.
16 J. Hemming, *The Conquest of the Incas*, p. 74.
17 J. Lockhart, *The Men of Cajamarca*, p. 70.
18 W.S. Maltby, *The Rise and Fall of the Spanish Empire* p. 58.
19 J. Hemming, *The Conquest of the Incas*, p. 135.
20 R. Varon Gabai and A.P. Jacobs, 'Peruvian Wealth and Spanish Investments', p. 665.
21 J. Hemming, *The Conquest of the Incas*, p. 149.
22 J. Hemming, *The Conquest of the Incas*, p. 145.

23 J.G. Williamson, 'History without Evidence', p. 31.

24 H. Thomas, *Rivers of Gold*, p. 233.

25 H. Thomas, *Rivers of Gold*, p. 255.

26 J. Lockhart, *The Men of Cajamarca*, p. 32.

27 J. Hemming, *The Conquest of the Incas*, p. 146.

28 W.S. Maltby, *The Rise and Fall of the Spanish Empire*, pp. 67–9.

29 H. Thomas, *Rivers of Gold*, p. 222.

30 R. Varon Gabai and A.P. Jacobs, 'Peruvian Wealth and Spanish Investments', p. 661.

31 J. Hemming, *The Conquest of the Incas*, p. 376.

32 J. Lockhart, *The Men of Cajamarca*, pp. 47–53.

33 J. Lockhart, *The Men of Cajamarca*, p. 148.

34 H. Thomas, *Rivers of Gold*, pp. 264–5.

35 H. Thomas, *Rivers of Gold*, p. 259.

36 R. Varon Gabai, *Francisco Pizarro and his Brothers*, pp. 147–8.

37 N.D. Cook, *Born to Die*, p. 64.

38 H. Thomas, *Rivers of Gold*, p. 268.

39 N.D. Cook, *Born to Die*, p. 77.

40 A.W. Crosby Jr, *The Columbian Exchange*, pp. 52–5.

41 J. Hemming, *The Conquest of the Incas*, pp. 352–3.

42 P. Bakewell, *Miners of the Red Mountain*, p. 22.

43 R. Varon Gabai and A.P. Jacobs, 'Peruvian Wealth and Spanish Investments', p. 662.

44 R. Varon Gabai, *Francisco Pizarro and his Brothers*, pp. 192–3.

45 R. Varon Gabai, *Francisco Pizarro and his Brothers*, p. 257.

46 J. Hemming, *The Conquest of the Incas*, p. 369.

47 W.S. Maltby, *The Rise and Fall of the Spanish Empire*, p. 67.

48 J. Hemming, *The Conquest of the Incas*, p. 349.

49 J. Lockhart, *The Men of Cajamarca*, p. 162.

50 J. Lockhart, *The Men of Cajamarca*, p. 151.

51 R. Varon Gabai, *Francisco Pizarro and his Brothers*, pp. 91–3.

52 M. Drelichman, 'All that Glitters', pp. 320–5.

53 J. Lockhart, *Spanish Peru 1532–60*, p. 5.

54 J. Lockhart, *Spanish Peru 1532–60*, pp. 41–2.

55 H. Thomas, *The Golden Age*, p. 325.

56 H. Thomas, *The Golden Age*, p. 226.

57 H. Thomas, *The Golden Age*, p. 516.

58 H. Thomas, *The Golden Age*, p. 365.

59 H. Thomas, *The Golden Age*, p. 286.

60 R. Varon Gabai, *Francisco Pizarro and his Brothers*, pp. 113–14.

61 R. Varon Gabai, *Francisco Pizarro and his Brothers*, p. 122.

62 H. Thomas, *The Golden Age*, p. 336.

63 R. Varon Gabai and A.P. Jacobs, 'Peruvian Wealth and Spanish Investments', p. 672.

64 R. Varon Gabai, *Francisco Pizarro and his Brothers*, p. 295.

Chapter 6: Louis XIV and Akhenaten

1 Cited by Timothy C.W. Blanning, *The Culture of Power and the Power of Culture*, p. 16.

2 Timothy C.W. Blanning, *The Culture of Power and the Power of Culture*, p. 16.

3 Timothy C.W. Blanning, *The Culture of Power and the Power of Culture*, p. 40.

4   Peter Burke, *The Fabrication of Louis XIV*, p. 50.
5   Timothy C.W. Blanning, *The Culture of Power and the Power of Culture*, p. 47.
6   Timothy C.W. Blanning, *The Culture of Power and the Power of Culture*, p. 53.
7   Duc de Saint-Simon, *The Memoirs of Louis XIV and his Court and of the Regency*, vol. 5, chapter 36.
8   Duc de Saint-Simon, *The Memoirs of Louis XIV and his Court and of the Regency*, vol. 6, chapter 44.
9   Duc de Saint-Simon, *The Memoirs of Louis XIV and his Court and of the Regency*, vol. 8, chapter 74.
10 Peter Burke, *The Fabrication of Louis XIV*, p. 68.
11 Timothy C.W. Blanning, *The Culture of Power and the Power of Culture*, p. 35.
12 http://www.uni-mannheim.de/mateo/camenaref/cmh/cmh501.html#001
13 Duc de Saint-Simon, *The Memoirs of Louis XIV and his Court and of the Regency*, vol. 10, chapter 73.
14 Cited by Timothy C.W. Blanning, *The Culture of Power and the Power of Culture*, p. 40.
15 Cited by Timothy C.W. Blanning, *The Culture of Power and the Power of Culture*, p. 41.
16 Duc de Saint-Simon, *The Memoirs of Louis XIV and his Court and of the Regency*, vol. 2, chapter 11.
17 Duc de Saint-Simon, *The Memoirs of Louis XIV and his Court and of the Regency*, vol. 11, chapter 84.
18 Duc de Saint-Simon, *The Memoirs of Louis XIV and his Court and of the Regency*, vol. 10, chapter 74.
19 Duc de Saint-Simon, *The Memoirs of Louis XIV and his Court and of the Regency*, vol. 6, chapter 44.
20 Duc de Saint-Simon, *The Memoirs of Louis XIV and his Court and of the Regency*, vol. 6, chapter 44.
21 Duc de Saint-Simon, *The Memoirs of Louis XIV and his Court and of the Regency*, vol. 5, chapter 36.
22 Duc de Saint-Simon, *The Memoirs of Louis XIV and his Court and of the Regency*, vol. 6, chapter 44.
23 Cited by Timothy C.W. Blanning, *The Culture of Power and the Power of Culture*, p. 32.
24 The Egyptian Empire seems to have constantly ebbed and flowed across the eighteenth dynasty. In the conquered cities of Syria and Palestine, the Pharaoh set up vassal rulers supported by native Egyptian garrisons. The children of the rulers were taken to Egypt, and they paid for their protection by an imposed annual tribute. By contrast Nubia was regarded as an Egyptian colony and exploited directly for its vast gold reserves by a brutal military administration. This provided Egypt with a virtual monopoly of trade over much of the Near East, and vast profits, slaves and status. Thutmose III and his successor Amenhotep II were largely responsible for this great plenty. See Nicholas Reeves, *Akhenaten*.
25 Timothy C.W. Blanning, *The Culture of Power and the Power of Culture*, p. 35.
26 Peter Lacovara, 'The City of Amarna', p. 62.
27 Barry J. Kemp, *Ancient Egypt*, p. 257.
28 Barry J. Kemp, *Ancient Egypt*, p. 287.
29 Sue H. D'Auria, 'Preparing for Eternity', p. 171.
30 See the 'Aten Scarab', in Nicholas Reeves, *Akhenaten*, p. 50.
31 L.J. Foster, 'The New Religion', p. 99
32 D.B. Redford, 'The Beginning of the Heresy'.
33 Erik Hornung, *Akhenaten and the Religion of Light*, p. 34.

34 J.L. Foster, 'The New Religion', p. 99.

35 J.L. Foster, 'The New Religion', p. 101.

36 Erik Hornung, *Akhenaten*, p. 49.

37 Erik Hornung, *Akhenaten*, pp. 49–51.

38 Cited in J.L. Foster, 'The New Religion', p. 105.

39 http://www.theparisreview.org/blog/2011/08/22/frida%E2%80%99s-corsets/.

40 W.M. Flinders Petrie, *History of Egypt*, p. 214: 'If this were a new religion, invented to sat-
    isfy our modern scientific conceptions, we could not find a flaw in the correctness of this
    view of the energy of the solar system . . . a position which we cannot logically improve
    upon at the present day.'

41 Jan Assmann, *Of God and Gods*; Nicholas Reeves, *Akhenaten*.

42 Peter Burke, *The Fabrication of Louis XIV*, p. 5.

Chapter 7: Jan Pieterszoon Coen and Robert Clive

 1 W. Bernstein, *A Splendid Exchange*, p. 218.

 2 R. Findlay and K.H. O'Rourke, *Power and Plenty*, p. 177.

 3 Simon Schama, *The Embarrassment of Riches*, p. 28.

 4 W. Bernstein, *A Splendid Exchange*, p. 228.

 5 K. Ward, *Networks of Empire*, p. 67.

 6 R. Findlay and K.H. O'Rourke, *Power and Plenty*, p. 179.

 7 J. Adams, 'Principles and Agents, Colonists and Company Men', p. 17.

 8 V.C. Loth, 'Armed Incidents and Unpaid Bills', p. 715.

 9 F.S. Gaastra, *The Dutch East India Company*, p. 121.

10 J.R. Bruijn, 'Between Batavia and the Cape', p. 257.

11 J.R. Bruijn, 'The Shipping Patterns of the Dutch East India Company', p. 252.

12 W. Bernstein, *A Splendid Exchange*, p. 237.

13 J.C. Riemersma, 'Government Influence on Company Organisation in Holland and
    England 1550–1650', p. 37.

14 W. Bernstein, *A Splendid Exchange*, pp. 222–3.

15 W. Bernstein, *A Splendid Exchange*, p. 236.

16 J. Lucassen, 'A Multinational and its Labour Force', p. 20.

17 J. Israel, *The Dutch Republic*, p. 323.

18 K. Ward, *Networks of Empire*, p. 19.

19 J. Israel, *The Dutch Republic*, p. 324.

20 V.C. Loth, 'Armed Incidents and Unpaid Bills', pp. 710–11.

21 W. Bernstein, *A Splendid Exchange*, p. 227.

22 V.C. Loth, 'Armed Incidents and Unpaid Bills', p. 721.

23 G. Milton, *Nathaniel's Nutmeg*, p. 248.

24 G. Milton, *Nathaniel's Nutmeg*, p. 302.

25 F.S. Gaastra, *The Dutch East India Company*, p. 40.

26 V.C. Loth, 'Armed Incidents and Unpaid Bills', p. 723.

27 F.S. Gaastra, *The Dutch East India Company*, p. 43.

28 V.C. Loth, 'Armed Incidents and Unpaid Bills', p. 730.

29 *The Spice Trail: Nutmeg and Cloves*, BBC2, 24 February 2011.

30 G. Milton, *Nathaniel's Nutmeg*, pp. 317–18.

31 K. Chancey, 'The Amboyna Massacre in English Politics 1624–32', p. 585.

32 K. Chancey, 'The Amboyna Massacre in English Politics 1624–32', p. 584.

33   Quoted in J. Adams, 'The Decay of Company Control in the Dutch East Indies', p. 12.

34   D. Landes, *The Wealth and Poverty of Nations*, pp. 145–6.

35   J. Adams, 'Principles and Agents, Colonists and Company Men', p. 21.

36   K. Unoki, *Mergers, Acquisitions and Global Empires*, p. 56.

37   G. Milton, *Nathaniel's Nutmeg*, p. 270.

38   J. Israel, *The Dutch Republic*, pp. 344–7.

39   J. Israel, *The Dutch Republic*, pp. 344–7.

40   J. Israel, *The Dutch Republic*, pp. 351–3.

41   J.B. Hochstrasser, *Still Life and Trade in the Dutch Golden Age*, pp. 267–9.

42   J. de Vries, 'Luxury in the Dutch Golden Age in Theory and Practice', pp. 41–3.

43   G.B. Malleson, *Lord Clive*, p. 10.

44   C. Brad Faught, *Clive: Founder of British India*, p. 3.

45   R. Harvey, *Clive: The Life and Death of a British Emperor*, p. 25.

46   C. Brad Faught, *Clive: Founder of British India*, p. 14.

47   B.D. Metcalf and T.R. Metcalf, *A Concise History of Modern India*, p. 31.

48   A. Webster, *The Twilight of the East India Company*, p. 21.

49   B.D. Metcalf and T.R. Metcalf, *A Concise History of Modern India*, p. 44.

50   J.P. Lawford, *Clive: Proconsul of India*, pp. 58–9.

51   R. Harvey, *Clive: The Life and Death of a British Emperor*, p. 63.

52   Mark Bence-Jones, *Clive of India*, p. 48.

53   J.P. Lawford, *Clive: Proconsul of India*, p. 149.

54   B. Lenman and P. Lawson, 'Robert Clive, the Black *Jagir* and British Politics', p. 806.

55   B. Lenman and P. Lawson, 'Robert Clive, the Black *Jagir* and British Politics', p. 808.

56   J. Dalley, *The Black Hole*, p. 199.

57   J. Dalley, *The Black Hole*, p. 208.

58   J. Dalley, *The Black Hole*, p. 178.

59   A. Saxena, *East India Company*, p. 7.

60   A. Edwardes, *The Rape of India*, pp. 222–3.

61   S. Bhattacharya, *The East India Company and the Economy of Bengal*, p. 101.

62   G.B. Malleson, *Lord Clive*, p. 107.

63   J. Dalley, *The Black Hole*, pp. 104–5.

64   J.P. Lawford, *Clive: Proconsul of India*, p. 267.

65   B. Lenman and P. Lawson, 'Robert Clive, the Black *Jagir* and British Politics', p. 812.

66   N.C. Chaudhuri, *Clive of India*, p. 318.

67   A. Saxena, *East India Company*, p. 1.

68   F.S. Gaastra, 'War, Competition and Collaboration', pp. 57–60.

69   J. Harrington, *Sir John Malcolm and the Making of British India*, p. 182.

70   C. Brad Faught, *Clive: Founder of British India*, p. 68.

71   G.B. Malleson, *Lord Clive*, p. 135.

72   J.P. Lawford, *Clive: Proconsul of India*, p. 273.

73   N.C. Chaudhuri, *Clive of India*, p. 319.

74   B. Lenman and P. Lawson, 'Robert Clive, the Black *Jagir* and British Politics', p. 813.

75   B. Lenman and P. Lawson, 'Robert Clive, the Black *Jagir* and British Politics', p. 819.

76   H.V. Bowen, 'Lord Clive and Speculation in East India Company Stock, 1766', p. 908.

77   H.V. Bowen, 'Lord Clive and Speculation in East India Company Stock, 1766', p. 910.

78   H.V. Bowen, 'Lord Clive and Speculation in East India Company Stock, 1766', p. 912.

79   H.V. Bowen, 'Lord Clive and Speculation in East India Company Stock, 1766', p. 917.

80   H.V. Bowen, 'Lord Clive and Speculation in East India Company Stock, 1766', p. 906.

81 R. Harvey, *Clive: The Life and Death of a British Emperor*, p. 319.

82 J. Osborn, 'India and the East India Company in the Public Sphere in 18th Century Britain', pp. 206–7.

83 C. Brad Faught, *Clive: Founder of British India*, p. 71.

84 R. Harvey, *Clive: The Life and Death of a British Emperor*, p. 6.

85 C. Brad Faight, *Clive: Founder of British India*, p. 95.

86 P. Lawson and J. Phillips, 'Our Execrable Banditti', p. 229.

87 P. Lawson and J. Phillips, 'Our Execrable Banditti', p. 234.

88 P. Lawson and J. Phillips, 'Our Execrable Banditti', p. 238.

89 C. Brad Faught, *Clive: Founder of British India*, p. 94.

90 G.B. Malleson, *Lord Clive*, p. 195.

91 N.C. Chaudhuri, *Clive of India*, p. 464.

92 N.C. Chaudhuri, *Clive of India*, p. 465.

93 G.B. Malleson, *Lord Clive*, pp. 198–9.

94 P. Lawson and J. Phillips, 'Our Execrable Banditti', p. 227.

95 J. Harrington, *Sir John Malcolm and the Making of British India*, p. 166.

96 P. Lawson and J. Phillips, 'Our Execrable Banditti', p. 239.

97 See J. Harrington, *Sir John Malcolm and the Making of British India*, pp. 166–73 for a fuller discussion of this historiographical debate.

98 G.B. Malleson, *Lord Clive*, p. 184.

99 A. Webster, *The Twilight of the East India Company*, p. 2.

Chapter 8: The Krupps

1 H. James, *Krupp*, p. 2.

2 W. Manchester, *The Arms of Krupp*, p. 3. Particularly ironic given that one of Krupp steel's greatest attributes was its softness and malleability.

3 H. James, *Krupp*, p. 14.

4 W. Manchester, *The Arms of Krupp*, p. 47.

5 W. Manchester, *The Arms of Krupp*, p. 49.

6 Kruppische Gustahlfabrik, *A Century's History of the Krupp Works*, pp. 57–8.

7 W. Manchester, *The Arms of Krupp*, p. 93.

8 H. James, *Krupp*, p. 20.

9 W. Manchester, *The Arms of Krupp*, p. 69.

10 B. Menne, *Blood and Steel*, p. 89.

11 H. James, *Krupp*, p. 79.

12 W. Manchester, *The Arms of Krupp*, p. 112.

13 H. James, *Krupp*, p. 39.

14 W. Manchester, *The Arms of Krupp*, p. 109.

15 E.C. McCreary, 'Social Welfare and Business', p. 30.

16 W. Manchester, *The Arms of Krupp*, p. 117.

17 B. Menne, *Blood and Steel*, p. 92.

18 W. Manchester, *The Arms of Krupp*, p. 139.

19 H. James, *Krupp*, p. 51.

20 B. Menne, *Blood and Steel*, p. 115.

21 W. Manchester, *The Arms of Krupp*, pp. 187–9.

22 W. Manchester, *The Arms of Krupp*, p. 212.

23 W. Manchester, *The Arms of Krupp*, p. 96.

24 Kruppische Gustahlfabrik, *A Century's History of the Krupp Works*, p. 251.

25 H. James, *Krupp*, p. 83.

26 H. James, *Krupp*, p. 80.

27 H. James, *Krupp*, p. 57.

28 W. Manchester, *The Arms of Krupp*, pp. 94–5.

29 H. James, *Krupp*, p. 70.

30 W. Manchester, *The Arms of Krupp*, p. 159.

31 W. Feldenkirchen, 'Banking and Economic Growth', p. 126.

32 H. James, *Krupp*, p. 43.

33 W. Manchester, *The Arms of Krupp*, p. 176.

34 Kruppische Gustahlfabrik, *A Century's History of the Krupp Works*, p. 165.

35 S.M. Lindsay, 'Social Work and the Krupp Foundries, Essen', p. 93.

36 S. Berger, *Social Democracy and the Working Class in Nineteenth and Twentieth Century Germany*, pp. 25–6.

37 S.M. Lindsay, 'Social Work and the Krupp Foundries, Essen', p. 74.

38 Kruppische Gustahlfabrik, *A Century's History of the Krupp Works*, p. 171.

39 S.M. Lindsay, 'Social Work and the Krupp Foundries, Essen', p. 77.

40 S.M. Lindsay, 'Social Work and the Krupp Foundries, Essen', p. 82.

41 S.M. Lindsay, 'Social Work and the Krupp Foundries, Essen', pp. 86–7.

42 W. Manchester, *The Arms of Krupp*, p. 233.

43 Kruppische Gustahlfabrik, *A Century's History of the Krupp Works*, p. 221.

44 Kruppische Gustahlfabrik, *A Century's History of the Krupp Works*, p. 168.

45 E.C. McCreary, 'Social Welfare and Business', p. 39.

46 E.C. McCreary, 'Social Welfare and Business', p. 42.

47 R. Blick, *Fascism in Germany*.

48 See http://www.thyssenkrupp-vdm.com/en/corporate-information/ideas-management/.

49 From T. Pierenkemper, 'Pre-1900 Industrial White Collar Employees at the Krupp Steel Casting Works', pp. 384–408.

50 H. James, *Krupp*, p. 73.

51 S. Berger, *Social Democracy and the Working Class in Nineteenth and Twentieth Century Germany*, p. 68.

52 E.C. McCreary, 'Social Welfare and Business', p. 47.

53 H. James, *Krupp*, p. 75.

54 W. Manchester, *The Arms of Krupp*, p. 169.

55 W. Manchester, *The Arms of Krupp*, p. 174.

56 W. Berdrow, *The Letters of Alfred Krupp 1826–87*, p. 349.

57 S. Berger, *Social Democracy and the Working Class in Nineteenth and Twentieth Century Germany*, pp. 62–3.

58 B. Menne, *Blood and Steel*, pp. 126–7.

59 W. Berdrow, *The Letters of Alfred Krupp 1826–87*, p. 408.

60 W. Manchester, *The Arms of Krupp*, p. 155.

61 H. James, *Krupp*, p. 60.

62 H. James, *Krupp*, p. 81.

63 W. Manchester, *The Arms of Krupp*, p. 204.

64 Kruppische Gustahlfabrik, *A Century's History of the Krupp Works*, p. 39.

65 Kruppische Gustahlfabrik, *A Century's History of the Krupp Works*, p. 213.

66 B. Menne, *Blood and Steel*, p. 104.

67 B. Menne, *Blood and Steel*, p. 206.

68 W. Manchester, *The Arms of Krupp*, p. 242.

69 W. Manchester, *The Arms of Krupp*, pp. 250–1.

70 W. Manchester, *The Arms of Krupp*, p. 254.

71 P. Batty, *The House of Krupp*, p. 130.

72 W. Manchester, *The Arms of Krupp*, p. 247.

73 See http://www.britishpathe.com/video/funeral-of-krupp-workers/query/Occupation.

74 *The Krupp Trial before French Court Martial*, p. 60.

75 P. Batty, *The House of Krupp*, p. 159.

76 W. Manchester, *The Arms of Krupp*, p. 506.

77 I. Warner, *Steel and Sovereignty*, p. 7.

78 I. Warner, *Steel and Sovereignty*, p. 206.

79 I. Warner, *Steel and Sovereignty*, p. 232.

80 See http://www.theguardian.com/world/2013/aug/14/berthold-beitz.

81 http://www.thyssenkrupp.com/en/presse/art_detail.html&eid=TKBase_1375275934775_
    1124336141.

Chapter 9: Andrew Carnegie

1 L.B. Edge, *Andrew Carnegie: Industrial Philanthropist*, p. 99.

2 L.B. Edge, *Andrew Carnegie: Industrial Philanthropist*, p. 19.

3 L.B. Edge, *Andrew Carnegie: Industrial Philanthropist*, p. 23.

4 D. Nasaw, *Andrew Carnegie*, p. 78.

5 L.B. Edge, *Andrew Carnegie: Industrial Philanthropist*, p. 51.

6 D. Nasaw, *Andrew Carnegie*, p. 72.

7 D. Nasaw, *Andrew Carnegie*, p. 84.

8 D. Nasaw, *Andrew Carnegie*, p. 93.

9 D. Nasaw, *Andrew Carnegie*, p. 87.

10 D. Nasaw, *Andrew Carnegie*, p. 99.

11 L.B. Edge, *Andrew Carnegie: Industrial Philanthropist*, p. 66.

12 M. Josephson, *The Robber Barons*, p. 48.

13 S.D. Cashman, *America in the Gilded Age*, p. 54.

14 S.D. Cashman, *America in the Gilded Age*, p. 36.

15 M. Josephson, *The Robber Barons*, chapter 4.

16 S.D. Cashman, *America in the Gilded Age*, p. 46.

17 *New York Times*, 27 March 1883.

18 M. Josephson, *The Robber Barons*, pp. 339–40.

19 M. Josephson, *The Robber Barons*, p. 316.

20 H.C. Livesay, *Andrew Carnegie and the Rise of Big Business*, p. 122.

21 L.B. Edge, *Andrew Carnegie: Industrial Philanthropist*, pp. 84–5.

22 H.C. Livesay, *Andrew Carnegie and the Rise of Big Business*, p. 154.

23 M. Josephson, *The Robber Barons*, p. 369.

24 D.P. Demarest Jr, *The River Ran Red*, p. 35.

25 H.C. Livesay, *Andrew Carnegie and the Rise of Big Business*, p. 157.

26 D.P. Demarest Jr, *The River Ran Red*, p. 26.

27 P. Krause, *The Battle for Homestead, 1880–1892*, p. 309.

28 P. Krause, *The Battle for Homestead, 1880–1892*, p. 312.

29 Q.R. Skrabec, *The Carnegie Boys*, p. 87.

30 D.P. Demarest Jr, *The River Ran Red*, p. 46.

31 H.C. Livesay, *Andrew Carnegie and the Rise of Big Business*, p. 159.

32 H.C. Livesay, *Andrew Carnegie and the Rise of Big Business*, p. 158.

33 P. Krause, *The Battle for Homestead, 1880–1892*, p. 360.

34 A. Carnegie, *The Autobiography of Andrew Carnegie and 'The Gospel of Wealth'*, p. 324.

35 R. Hofstadter, 'The Pervasive Influence of Social Darwinism', p. 35.

36 R. Hofstadter, 'The Pervasive Influence of Social Darwinism', p. 37.

37 R. Hofstadter, 'The Pervasive Influence of Social Darwinism', p. 38.

38 D. Nasaw, *Andrew Carnegie*, pp. 228–9.

39 B. Werth, *Banquet at Delmonico's*, p. 268.

40 H.C. Livesay, *Andrew Carnegie and the Rise of Big Business*, p. 139.

41 B. Werth, *Banquet at Delmonico's*, p. xxiii.

42 B. Werth, *Banquet at Delmonico's*, p. 277.

43 F. Inglis, *A Short History of Celebrity*, p. 116.

44 B. Werth, *Banquet at Delmonico's*, p. 281.

45 R. Hofstadter, 'The Pervasive Influence of Social Darwinism', p. 39.

46 D. Nasaw, *Andrew Carnegie*, p. 226.

47 L.B. Edge, *Andrew Carnegie: Industrial Philanthropist*, p. 93.

48 R.J. Gangewere, *Palace of Culture*, p. 4.

49 D. Nasaw, *Andrew Carnegie*, p. 81.

50 L.B. Edge, *Andrew Carnegie: Industrial Philanthropist*, p. 104.

51 C. Hovey, *The Life Story of J. Pierpont Morgan*, p. 202.

52 H.C. Livesay, *Andrew Carnegie and the Rise of Big Business*, pp. 195–9.

53 S.D. Cashman, *America in the Gilded Age*, p. 50.

54 Q.R. Skrabec, *The Carnegie Boys*, p. 104.

55 Q.R. Skrabec, *The Carnegie Boys*, p. 113.

56 R.J. Gangewere, *Palace of Culture*, p. 22.

57 L.B. Edge, *Andrew Carnegie: Industrial Philanthropist*, p. 110.

58 A.S. Eisenstadt, *Carnegie's Model Republic*, p. 5.

59 D. Nasaw, *Andrew Carnegie*, p. 221.

60 A. Carnegie, *Triumphant Democracy*, pp. 26–7.

61 R.J. Gangewere, *Palace of Culture*, p. 10.

62 B. Werth, *Banquet at Delmonico's*, p. 267.

63 L.B. Edge, *Andrew Carnegie: Industrial Philanthropist*, p. 77.

64 E.S. Eisenstadt, *Carnegie's Model Republic*, p. 81.

65 M. Josephson, *The Robber Barons*, p. 331.

66 Doug Chayka, 'The Misunderstood Robber Baron'.

Chapter 10: Mobutu Sese Seko

1 J.K. Stearns, *Dancing in the Glory of Monsters*, p. 7.

2 D. van Reybrouck, *Congo*, p. 247.

3 S. Kelly, *America's Tyrant*, p. 15.

4 M. Wrong, *In the Footsteps of Mr Kurtz*, p. 64.

5 W.T. Close, *Beyond the Storm*, p. 56.

6 W.T. Close, *Beyond the Storm*, pp. 106–7.

7 D.F. Schmitz, *The United States and Right Wing Dictatorships*, pp. 21–2.

8 S. Kelly, *America's Tyrant*, p. 57.

9   M. Wrong, *In the Footsteps of Mr Kurtz*, p. 67.

10 M.G. Kalb, *The Congo Cables*, p. 94.

11 M.G. Kalb, *The Congo Cables*, p. 97.

12 D.F. Schmitz, *The United States and Right Wing Dictatorships*, p. 26.

13 M.G. Kalb, *The Congo Cables*, pp. 371–2.

14 W.T. Close, *Beyond the Storm*, p. 202.

15 W.T. Close, *Beyond the Storm*, pp. 246–7.

16 L. Devlin, *Chief of Station, Congo*, p. 266.

17 G. Livingstone, *America's Back Yard*, p. 73.

18 J.M. Haskin, *The Tragic State of the Congo*, p. 39.

19 W.T. Close, *Beyond the Storm*, pp. 228–9.

20 P. Ikambana, *Mobutu's Totalitarian Political System*, pp. 56–7.

21 J.M. Haskin, *The Tragic State of the Congo*, p. 40.

22 S. Kelly, *America's Tyrant*, p. 176.

23 W.T. Close, *Beyond the Storm*, p. 195.

24 D.F. Schmitz, *The United States and Right Wing Dictatorships*, p. 31.

25 M. Wrong, *In the Footsteps of Mr Kurtz*, p. 82.

26 J.K. Stearns, *Dancing in the Glory of Monsters*, p. 114.

27 C. Young and T. Turner, *The Rise and Decline of the Zairian State*, p. 71.

28 C. Young and T. Turner, *The Rise and Decline of the Zairian State*, pp. 209–11.

29 S. Kelly, *America's Tyrant*, p. 195.

30 D. van Reybrouck, *Congo*, p. 357.

31 M. Wrong, *In the Footsteps of Mr Kurtz*, p. 111.

32 A. Wedeman, 'Looters, Rent-scrapers, and Dividend Collectors', p. 463.

33 D. Aronson, 'The Dead Help No One Living', p. 85.

34 M. Wrong, *In the Footsteps of Mr Kurtz*, p. 148.

35 M. Wrong, *In the Footsteps of Mr Kurtz*, pp. 92–3.

36 C. Young and T. Turner, *The Rise and Decline of the Zairian State*, pp. 180–1.

37 W.T. Close, *Beyond the Storm*, p. 283.

38 C. Young and T. Turner, *The Rise and Decline of the Zairian State*, p. 348.

39 B.A. Aquino, *The Transnational Dynamics of the Marcos Plunder*, pp. 10–11.

40 B.A. Aquino, *The Politics of Plunder*, p. 92.

41 R. Manapat, *Some are Smarter than Others*, p. 64.

42 R. Manapat, *Some are Smarter than Others*, p. 21.

43 R. Manapat, *Some are Smarter than Others*, p. 7.

44 R.E. Elson, *Suharto*, pp. 198–9.

45 G. Livingstone, *America's Backyard*, p. 195.

46 C. Young and T. Turner, *The Rise and Decline of the Zairian State*, p. 352.

47 K.L. Adelman, 'The Zairian Political Party as a Religious Surrogate', p. 51.

48 J.M. Haskin, *The Tragic State of the Congo*, p. 48.

49 J. Depelchin, 'Transformations of the State and the Petite Bourgeoisie in Zaire', p. 35.

50 S. Kelly, *America's Tyrant*, p. 5.

51 M.G. Schatzberg, *Mobutu or Chaos?*, pp. 39–41.

52 C. Young and T. Turner, *The Rise and Decline of the Zairian State*, p. 73.

53 C. Young and T. Turner, *The Rise and Decline of the Zairian State*, p. 131.

54 C. Young and T. Turner, *The Rise and Decline of the Zairian State*, p. 105.

55 M. Wrong, *In the Footsteps of Mr Kurtz*, p. 95.

56 S. Diallo, *Zaire Today*, p. 72.

57   C. Young and T. Turner, *The Rise and Decline of the Zairian State*, p. 183.
58   C. Young and T. Turner, *The Rise and Decline of the Zairian State*, p. 118.
59   M.G. Schatzberg, *The Dialectics of Oppression in Zaire*, p. 20.
60   C. Young and T. Turner, *The Rise and Decline of the Zairian State*, p. 181.
61   M. Wrong, *In the Footsteps of Mr Kurtz*, p. 193.
62   M. Wrong, *In the Footsteps of Mr Kurtz*, p. 101.
63   M. Wrong, *In the Footsteps of Mr Kurtz*, p. 68.
64   K.L. Adelman, 'The Zairian Political Party as a Religious Surrogate', p. 54.
65   J.K. Stearns, *Dancing in the Glory of Monsters*, p. 154.
66   M.G. Schatzberg, *Mobutu or Chaos?*, p. 35.
67   B.A. Aquino, *The Politics of Plunder*, pp. 88–9.
68   W.T. Close, *Beyond the Storm*, p. 258.
69   C. Young and T. Turner, *The Rise and Decline of the Zairian State*, p. 211.
70   J.M. Haskin, *The Tragic State of the Congo*, p. 56.
71   M.G. Schatzberg, *The Dialectics of Oppression in Zaire*, p. 2.
72   M.G. Schatzberg, *Mobutu or Chaos?*, p. 47.
73   M. Wrong, *In the Footsteps of Mr Kurtz*, p. 178.
74   M. Wrong, *In the Footsteps of Mr Kurtz*, p. 110.
75   L. Devlin, *Chief of Station, Congo*, pp. 265–6.
76   J.M. Haskin, *The Tragic State of the Congo*, p. 52.
77   B.A. Aquino, *The Transnational Dynamics of the Marcos Plunder*, pp. 6–7.
78   B.A. Aquino, *The Politics of Plunder*, p. 24.
79   R.E. Elson, *Suharto*, pp. 294–5.
80   M. Wrong, *In the Footsteps of Mr Kurtz*, pp. 6–7.
81   http://www.nytimes.com/1988/09/29/world/mobutu-s-village-basks-in-his-glory.html.
82   http://www.vice.com/en_uk/read/my-life-with-big-men-0000321-v19n8.
83   Adam Zagorin, 'Leaving Fire in His Wake'.
84   M. Wrong, *In the Footsteps of Mr Kurtz*, pp. 19–21.
85   M. Wrong, *In the Footsteps of Mr Kurtz*, p. 96.
86   M. Wrong, *In the Footsteps of Mr Kurtz*, p. 53.
87   M. Wrong, *In the Footsteps of Mr Kurtz*, p. 96.
88   W.T. Close, *Beyond the Storm*, p. 253.
89   M. Wrong, *In the Footsteps of Mr Kurtz*, p. 205.
90   M.G. Schatzberg, *Mobutu or Chaos?*, p. 4.
91   S. Kelly, *America's Tyrant*, p. 1.
92   P. Ikambana, *Mobutu's Totalitarian Political System*, p. 60.
93   J.M. Haskin, *The Tragic State of the Congo*, p. 69.
94   J.K. Stearns, *Dancing in the Glory of Monsters*, p. 113.
95   M. Wrong, *In the Footsteps of Mr Kurtz*, pp. 133–5.
96   D. Aronson, 'The Dead Help No One Living', pp. 82–3.
97   M. Wrong, *In the Footsteps of Mr Kurtz*, p. 149.
98   M. Wrong, *In the Footsteps of Mr Kurtz*, p. 120.
99   M. Wrong, *In the Footsteps of Mr Kurtz*, pp. 222–3.
100 W.T. Close, *Beyond the Storm*, pp. 309–10.
101 J.K. Stearns, *Dancing in the Glory of Monsters*, p. 51.
102 J.K. Stearns, *Dancing in the Glory of Monsters*, p. 159.
103 J. Depelchin, 'Transformations of the State and the Petite Bourgeoisie in Zaire', p. 36.
104 M. Wrong, *In the Footsteps of Mr Kurtz*, p. 104.

105 D. Aronson, 'The Dead Help No One Living', p. 84.
106 B.A. Aquino, *The Politics of Plunder*, p. 99.
107 R.E. Elson, *Suharto*, p. 195.
108 'Philippines Hunt for the Marcos Fortune Set to End', *The National*, 2 January 2013.
109 'What Happened to the Marcos Fortune?', BBC, 25 January 2013.
110 'Swiss Banks Find Only $3.4m in Mobutu Assets', CNN, 3 June 1997.
111 M. Wrong, 'The Mystery of Mobutu's Millions'.
112 J.K. Stearns, *Dancing in the Glory of Monsters*, p. 9.
113 http://www.ft.com/cms/s/0/ace18a4e-b478-11e1-bb88-00144feabcdc0. html#axzz361LRH69P.
114 'Mobutu Sese Seko's Body to Return to Congo, Says Kabila', BBC, 24 October 2013.

Chapter 11: The sheikhs

1 http://www.gluckman.com/DubaiBiz.html.
2 http://www.vanityfair.com/magazine/archive/1989/09/dunne198909.
3 http://www.sheikhmohammed.com/vgn-ext-templating/v/index.jsp?vgnextoid= e61f854e4878a310VgnVCM1000003f64a8c0RCRD&vgnextchannel=d32d8960a5a1131 0VgnVCM1000004d64a8c0RCRD&vgnextfmt=speech&date=1350923846680&media type=SPEECH.
4 http://www.sheikhmohammed.com/vgn-ext-templating/v/index.jsp?vgnextoid= e61f854e4878a310VgnVCM1000003f64a8c0RCRD&vgnextchannel=d32d8960a5a1131 0VgnVCM1000004d64a8c0RCRD&vgnextfmt=speech&date=1350923846680&medi- atype=SPEECH.
5 http://www.dubaiairport.com/en/media-centre/Documents/Dubai%20Airports% 20Brochure_front%20FINAL.pdf.
6 http://www.hrw.org/news/2006/03/28/uae-address-abuse-migrant-workers.
7 http://www.telegraph.co.uk/news/picturegalleries/celebritynews/3491517/Celebrities- at-the-launch-of-Dubai-resort-The-Atlantis.html.
8 http://www.theguardian.com/world/2008/nov/21/atlantis-palm-dubai-kylie-lohan.
9 According to the World Bank, it falls within the top twenty.
10 https://www.abudhabi.ae/egovPoolPortal_WAR/appmanager/ADeGP/Citizen?_nfpb =true&_pageLabel=p_citizen_departments&lang=en&did=14362.
11 Abdul Khaleq Abdulla, 'Dubai: The Journey of an Arab City from Localism to Cosmopolitanism', p. 14.
12 http://www.sheikhmohammed.com/vgn-ext-templating/v/index.jsp?vgnextoid= 48cdefcd33287110VgnVCM1000007064a8c0RCRD&vgnextchannel=1048499192b133 10VgnVCM1000004d64a8c0RCRD&vgnextfmt=article&date=1200083385187&medi- atype=ARTICLE.
13 http://www.sheikhmohammed.com/vgn-ext-templating/v/index.jsp?vgnextoid= 48cdefcd33287110VgnVCM1000007064a8c0RCRD&vgnextchannel=1048499192b133 10VgnVCM1000004d64a8c0RCRD&vgnextfmt=article&date=1200083385187&medi- atype=ARTICLE.
14 http://news.bbc.co.uk/1/hi/world/middle_east/6672923.stm.
15 http://www.theguardian.com/theobserver/2013/apr/28/sheikh-mohammed-horses- doping-scandal-profile.
16 http://www.huffingtonpost.com/2009/12/04/dubai-ruler-sheik-mohammed_n_ 379674.html.

17 http://m.gulfnews.com/brand-dubai-will-set-record-straight-1.71943.
18 http://www.thesundaytimes.co.uk/sto/style/fashion/trends/article236648.ece.
19 http://www.dubaitourism.ae/aggregator/sources/2.
20 Abdul Khaleq Abdulla, 'Dubai: The Journey of an Arab City from Localism to Cosmopolitanism', pp. 12–13.

Chapter 12: The oligarchs

 1 http://www.theguardian.com/world/2000/mar/31/russia.iantraynor.
 2 http://www.theguardian.com/politics/2012/feb/10/nat-rothschild-loses-libel-daily-mail.
 3 http://www.ft.com/cms/s/2/a71190e8-2934-11e2-9591-00144feabdc0.html#axzz2sRm5GtaN.
 4 http://www.theguardian.com/world/2007/nov/19/football.russia.
 5 http://en.novayagazeta.ru/politics/8779.html.
 6 http://www.nytimes.com/2012/03/02/world/europe/ties-to-vladimir-putin-generate-fabulous-wealth-for-a-select-few-in-russia.html?hp.
 7 http://www.lrb.co.uk/v29/n02/perry-anderson/russias-managed-democracy.
 8 http://www.treasury.gov/press-center/press-releases/pages/jl23331.aspx
 9 http://www.nytimes.com/2013/11/09/world/asia/bloomberg-news-is-said-to-curb-articles-that-might-anger-china.html?_r=0.
10 Chrystia Freeland, *Plutocrats*, p. XX.
11 Richard McGregor, *The Party*, p. 197.
12 http://www.telegraph.co.uk/news/worldnews/asia/china/10325019/The-rise-and-rise-of-Wang-Jianlin-Chinas-richest-man.html.
13 http://sinosphere.blogs.nytimes.com/2013/11/28/bloomberg-code-keeps-articles-from-chinese-eyes/.
14 http://www.ft.com/cms/s/0/2b2746c0-a663-11e1-9453-00144feabdc0.html#axzz2qMt5XXgx.
15 http://online.wsj.com/news/articles/SB10001424052748703315404575251271890222924?mg=reno64-wsj&url=http%3A%2F%2Fonline.wsj.com%2Farticle%2FSB1000142405274870331540457525127189022924.html.
16 http://www.theatlantic.com/international/archive/2013/01/a-16-million-bet-on-the-future-of-chinese-retail/266883/.
17 Hao Wu, 'Who's Afraid of the Big Bad Alibaba?', *New America Foundation's Weekly Wonk*. Available at: http://www.slate.com/articles/technology/future_tense/2013/11/alibaba_group_ipo_will_jack_ma_s_chinese_e_commerce_conglomerate_conquer.html.

Chapter 13: The Geeks

 1 S. Levy, *Hackers*, pp. 7–8.
 2 http://www.microsoft.com/en-us/news/exec/billg/speeches/2007/01-30uklaunch.aspx.
 3 http://money.usnews.com/money/business-economy/articles/1997/11/23/xanadu-20.
 4 S. Levy, *Hackers*, pp. 225–6.
 5 B. Gates, 'An Open Letter to Hobbyists', 1976.
 6 R.X. Cringely, *Accidental Empires*, p. 99.
 7 R.X. Cringely, *Accidental Empires*, pp. 101–2.
 8 R.X. Cringely, *Accidental Empires*, p. 259.
 9 R.X. Cringely, *Accidental Empires*, p. 296.

10 http://www.cato.org/sites/cato.org/files/serials/files/policy-report/1999/3/fried-man.html.

11 http://news.harvard.edu/gazette/story/2007/06/remarks-of-bill-gates-harvard-com-mencement-2007/.

12 As told to Tom Friedman, *The World is Flat*, p. 279.

13 R. Waters, 'An Exclusive Interview with Bill Gates'.

14 http://www.nytimes.com/2006/06/27/business/27friends.html.

15 'Bill Gates Inspired by Carnegie, Other Early Philanthropists', *The Fire Hose*, 16 July 2013.

16 R. Waters, 'An Exclusive Interview with Bill Gates'.

17 http://www.forbes.com/sites/randalllane/2013/11/17/bill-gates-and-bono-on-their-alliance-of-fortune-fame-and-giving/print/.

18 B. Gates, 'A New Approach to Capitalism', pp. 7–12.

19 'Bill Gates and Warren Buffett Discuss Creative Capitalism', in M. Kinsley (ed.), *Creative Capitalism*, p. 23.

20 See http://www.givingpledge.org.

21 R. Waters, 'An Exclusive Interview with Bill Gates'.

22 N. Tweedie, 'Bill Gates Interview'.

23 I. Birrell, 'Bill Gates Preaches the Aid Gospel, but is He Just a Hypocrite?'.

24 http://www.smh.com.au/technology/technology-news/gates-on-tax-giving-his-kids-only-10m—and-still-doing-the-dishes-20130528-2n9od.html.

25 D. Jones, 'Facebook CEO is Youngest Self-made Billionaire'.

26 H. Blodget, 'Apple Had No Choice but to Oust Steve Jobs'.

27 S. Levy, *Hackers*, pp. 252–3.

28 R.X. Cringely, *Accidental Empires*, pp. 182–3.

29 L. Kahney, 'Jobs vs Gates: Who's the Star?'.

30 P. Whoriskey, 'Record Thin on Steve Jobs' Philanthropy'.

31 'The Omidyar Way of Giving', *The Economist*, 26 October 2013.

32 M. Hosenball, 'Here's Who's Backing Glenn Greenwald's New Website', Reuters, 15 October 2013.

33 T. Walker, 'Pierre Omidyar'.

34 R.L. Brandt, *One Click*, p. 34.

35 R.L. Brandt, *One Click*, pp. 45–6.

36 R.L. Brandt, *One Click*, pp. 57–60.

37 R.L. Brandt, *One Click*, pp. 73–83.

38 R.L. Brandt, *One Click*, p. 61.

39 T. Wolverton, 'Amazon, Barnes & Noble Settle Patent Suit'.

40 R.L. Brandt, *One Click*, p. 124.

41 http://www.bbc.co.uk/news/business-25034598; http://www.salon.com/2014/02/23/worse_than_wal_mart_amazons_sick_brutality_and_secret_history_of_intimidating_workers; http://www.theguardian.com/technology/2013/dec/01/week-amazon-insider-feature-treatment-employees-work.

42 http://seattletimes.com/html/businesstechnology/2017883721_amazonbezos25.html.

43 M. Ververka, 'Richard Branson's Otherworldly Space Quest'.

44 P. Farhi, '*Washington Post* Closes Sale to Amazon Founder Jeff Bezos'.

45 D. Kirkpatrick, *The Facebook Effect*, pp. 23–5.

46 D. Kirkpatrick, *The Facebook Effect*, p. 47.

47 D. Kirkpatrick, *The Facebook Effect*, p. 55.

48 D. Kirkpatrick, *The Facebook Effect*, p. 83.

49   K. Losse, *The Boy Kings*, pp. 73–5.
50   K. Losse, *The Boy Kings*, p. 24.
51   K. Losse, *The Boy Kings*, p. 25.
52   S. Levy, *Hackers*, pp. 39–41.
53   D. Kirkpatrick, *The Facebook Effect*, p. 41.
54   D. Kirkpatrick, *The Facebook Effect*, pp. 11–12.
55   http://www.latimes.com/business/technology/la-fi-tn-sean-parker-wedding-photos-20130801,0,1319875.story#axzz2r23BzdyI.

Chapter 14: The bankers

1   R.S. Grossman, *Unsettled Account*, pp. 88–93.
2   'Tied up in a Sack of Snakes and Thrown into the Thames', *Herald*, 10 February 2009.
3   Center for Public Integrity, 'After the Meltdown: Ex-Wall Street Chieftains Living it Large in a Post-meltdown World'.
4   L. Thomas Jr, 'Distinct Culture at Bear Stearns Helps it Surmount a Grim Market'.
5   W.D. Cohan, 'The Rise and Fall of Jimmy Cayne'.
6   L. Thomas Jr, 'Distinct Culture at Bear Stearns Helps it Surmount a Grim Market'.
7   http://online.wsj.com/news/articles/SB119387369474078336?mod=home_whats_news_us&mg=reno64-wsj&url=http%3A%2F%2Fonline.wsj.com%2Farticle%2FSB119387369474078336.html%3Fmod%3Dhome_whats_news_us.
8   'The Fall of Bear Stearns: Bearing All', *The Economist*, 8 March 2009.
9   R. Frank, *Richistan*, p. 44.
10   P. Mason, *Meltdown*, p. 8.
11   W.D. Cohan, 'The Rise and Fall of Jimmy Cayne'.
12   Center for Public Integrity, 'After the Meltdown: Ex-Wall Street Chieftains Living it Large in a Post-meltdown World'.
13   R.S. Grossman, *Unsettled Account*, p. 87.
14   B. Ehrenreich, *Smile or Die*, p. 185.
15   R.G. Rajan, *Fault Lines*, p. 3.
16   Center for Public Integrity, 'After the Meltdown: Ex-Wall Street Chieftains Living it Large in a Post-meltdown World'.
17   H. Stewart and S. Goodley, 'Big Bang's Shockwaves Left us with Today's Big Bust'.
18   A.R. Sorkin, *Too Big to Fail*, p. 23.
19   J. Green, 'Where is Dick Fuld Now? Finding Lehman Brothers' Last CEO'.
20   A.R. Sorkin, *Too Big to Fail*, p. 28.
21   J. Green, 'Where is Dick Fuld Now? Finding Lehman Brothers' Last CEO'.
22   http://online.wsj.com/news/articles/SB10001424052702304549504579316913982034286.
23   R.S. Grossman, *Unsettled Account*, pp. 252–6.
24   In J.G. Ruggie (ed.), *Embedding Global Markets*, p. 65.
25   P. Mason, *Meltdown*, p. 61.
26   P. Augar, *The Death of Gentlemanly Capitalism*, p. 33.
27   P. Augar, *The Death of Gentlemanly Capitalism*, pp. 34–5.
28   See K. Ho, *Liquidated*, pp. 104–6.
29   K. Ho, *Liquidated*, pp. 75–6.
30   K. Ho, *Liquidated*, pp. 39–47.
31   K. Ho, *Liquidated*, p. 103.
32   P. Mason, *Meltdown*, pp. 64–6.

33 P. Mason, *Meltdown*, p. 57.

34 Center for Public Integrity, 'After the Meltdown: Ex-SEC Chief Now Helps Companies Navigate Post-meltdown Reforms'.

35 P. Mason, *Meltdown*, p. 35.

36 J. Arlidge, 'I'm Doing God's Work'.

37 P. Mason, *Meltdown*, p. 4.

38 J. Arlidge, 'I'm Doing God's Work'.

39 C.M. Reinhart and K.S. Rogoff, *This Time is Different*, p. 210.

40 K. Ho, *Liquidated*, pp. 154–5.

41 P. Mason, *Meltdown*, p. 23.

42 http://www.nytimes.com/2009/10/26/us/politics/26caucus.html?hpw&_r=0.

43 J. Arlidge, 'I'm Doing God's Work'.

44 Anthony Sampson, *Who Runs This Place?*, p. 322.

45 Lehman Bros press release, 5 April 2004: http://www.lehman.com/press/pdf/040504_BankSt.pdf.

46 I. Martin, *Making it Happen*, p. 105.

47 'We Know why HBOS Crashed, but not the Secrets of its Disastrous Rescue', *Observer*, 7 April 2013.

48 'Why Have so Few Bankers Gone to Jail?', *The Economist*, 13 May 2013.

49 J. Green, 'Where is Dick Fuld Now? Finding Lehman Brothers' Last CEO'.

50 A.R. Sorkin, *Too Big to Fail*, p. 506.

51 http://www.telegraph.co.uk/finance/financialcrisis/6158452/Dick-Fuld-of-collapsed-bank-Lehman-Brothers-says-his-mother-loves-him.html.

52 J. La Roche, 'Ex-Bear Stearns CEO is Selling His Apartment for $14.95m'.

53 Center for Public Integrity, 'After the Meltdown: Ex-Wall Street Chieftains Living it Large in a Post-meltdown World'.

54 Center for Public Integrity, 'After the Meltdown: Ex-SEC Chief Now Helps Companies Navigate Post-meltdown Reforms'.

55 J. La Roche, 'Lloyd Blankfein's Advice to Interns – Relax'.

56 J. La Roche, 'What Lloyd Blankfein Does All Weekend'.

57 Center for Public Integrity, 'After the Meltdown: Ex-SEC Chief Now Helps Companies Navigate Post-meltdown Reforms'.

58 N. Goodway, 'My Regrets, by Goldman Sachs Boss Lloyd Blankfein'.

59 W.D. Cohan, 'The Rise and Fall of Jimmy Cayne'.

60 http://www.nytimes.com/2008/10/24/business/economy/24panel.html.

61 http://www.opensecrets.org/news/2010/04/goldman-sachs-congressional-inquisi.html.

62 http://www.vanityfair.com/society/features/2011/05/top-one-percent-201105.

63 'How the Bank Lobby Loosened US Reins on Derivatives', Bloomberg, 4 September 2013.

64 http://www.newyorker.com/reporting/2010/03/15/100315fa_fact_cassidy.

65 http://www.telegraph.co.uk/finance/financialcrisis/10684896/George-Soros-blasts-parasite-banks.html.

Conclusion

1 http://www.nytimes.com/2007/08/27/opinion/27mon4.html?_r=0.

2 http://blogs.ft.com/the-a-list/2012/02/07/western-capitalism-has-much-to-learn-from-asia/#axzz2vfYJABG9.

Bibliography

Abdulla, Abdul Khaleq, 'Dubai: The Journey of an Arab City from Localism to Cosmopolitanism', *al-Mustaqbal al-Arabi*, vol. 323 (2006)

Aburish, Said K., *The House of Saud* (Bloomsbury, 1994)

Adams, Julia, 'The Decay of Company Control in the Dutch East Indies', *American Sociological Review*, vol. 61, no. 1 (1996)

Adams, Julia, 'Principles, Agents, Colonists and Company Men: The Decay of Colonial Control in the Dutch East Indies', *American Sociological Review*, vol. 61, no. 1 (1996)

Adams, Tim, 'Sheikh Mohammad: The Ruler with Real Horsepower', *Observer*, 28 April 2013

Adcock, F.E., *Marcus Crassus: Millionaire* (W. Heffer & Sons, 1966)

Ade Ajayi, Jacob F. and Crowder, Michael, *A History of West Africa* (Columbia University Press, 1972)

Adelman, K.L., 'The Zairian Political Party as a Religious Surrogate', *Africa Today*, vol. 23, no. 4 (1976)

Anderson, Perry, 'Russia's Managed Democracy', *London Review of Books*, 25 January 2007

Appian, *The Roman History* (Loeb, 1913)

Aquino, Belinda, *Politics of Plunder: The Philippines under Marcos* (Great Books Trading, 1987)

Aquino, Belinda, *The Transnational Dynamics of the Marcos Plunder* (University of the Philippines, 1999)

Arlidge, Jon, 'The Excesses of the Filthy Rich', *The Times*, 21 September 2008

Arlidge, Jon, 'I'm Doing God's Work: Meet Mr Goldman Sachs', *Sunday Times*, 8 November 2009

Aronson, D., 'The Dead Help No One Living: A Return to the Congo', *World Policy Journal*, vol. 14, no. 4 (1997)

Assmann, Jan, *Of God and Gods: Egypt, Israel, and the Rise of Monotheism* (University of Wisconsin Press, 2008)

Augar, Philip, *The Death of Gentlemanly Capitalism: The Rise and Fall of London's Investment Banks* (Penguin, 2008)

Bakewell, Peter, *Miners of the Red Mountain: Indian Labour in Potosí* (University of New Mexico Press, 2010)

Batty, Peter, *The House of Krupp: The Steel Dynasty that Armed the Nazis* (Cooper Square, 2001)

Baxter, S. 'Lordship and Labour', in J. Crick and E. van Houts (eds), *A Social History of England 900–1200* (Cambridge University Press, 2011)

Bence-Jones, Mark, *Clive of India* (Constable & Company, 1974)

Berdrow, Wilhelm, *The Letters of Alfred Krupp* (Gollancz, 1930)

Beresford, Philip and Rubinstein, William, *The Richest of the Rich* (Harriman House, 2011)

Berg, Maxine and Eger, Elizabeth (eds), *Luxury in the 18th Century* (Palgrave Macmillan, 2002)

Berger, Stefan, *Social Democracy and the Working Class in Nineteenth and Twentieth Century Germany* (Routledge, 1999)

Bernstein, Peter L., *The Power of Gold: The History of an Obsession* (John Wiley & Sons, 2001)

Bernstein, William J., *A Splendid Exchange: How Trade Shaped the World* (Grove Press, 2009)

Bhatia, Shekhar, '500 Chefs, 4000 Lobsters, and Kylie – Recession Dubai Style', *Guardian*, 21 November 2008

Bhattacharya, Sukumar, *The East India Company and the Economy of Bengal* (Luzac, 1954)

Birrell, I., 'Bill Gates Preaches the Aid Gospel, but is He Just a Hypocrite?', *Guardian*, 6 January 2014

Bishop, Matthew and Green, Michael, *Philanthrocapitalism: How Giving Can Save the World* (A&C Black, 2008)

Blake McHam, Sarah, 'Donatello's Bronze "David" and "Judith" as Metaphors for Medici Rule in Florence', *Art Bulletin*, vol. 83 (2001)

Blanning, Timothy C.W., *The Culture of Power and the Power of Culture: Old Regime Europe 1660–1789* (Oxford University Press, 2002)

Blick, R., *Fascism in Germany* (Steyn Publications, 1975)

Blodget, H., 'Apple Had No Choice but to Oust Steve Jobs', *Business Insider*, 23 September 2013

Bovill, Edward William, *The Golden Trade of the Moors* (Markus Weiner, 2005)

Bowen, H.V., 'Lord Clive and Speculation in East India Company Stock, 1766', *Historical Journal*, vol. 30, no. 4 (1987)

Bowen, H.V., Lincoln, M. and Rigby, N. (eds), *The Worlds of the East India Company* (Boydell Press, 2011)

Boye, Alida May and Hunwick, John O., *The Hidden Treasures of Timbuktu* (Thames & Hudson, 2008)

Brad Faught, C., *Clive: Founder of British India* (Potomac Books, 2013)

Brandt, Richard L., *One Click: Jeff Bezos and the Rise of Amazon.com* (Penguin, 2011)

Brewer, Thomas B., *The Robber Barons: Saints or Sinners* (R.E. Krieger, 1976)

Bruijn, Jaap R., 'Between Batavia and the Cape: Shipping Patterns of the Dutch East India Company', *Journal of Southeast Asian Studies*, vol. 11, no. 2 (1980)

Burke, Peter, *The Fabrication of Louis XIV* (Yale University Press, 1992)

Carnegie, Andrew, *Triumphant Democracy* (Cosimo Classics, 2005 edition)

Carnegie, Andrew, *The Autobiography of Andrew Carnegie and the 'Gospel of Wealth'* (Signet, 2006)

Cashman, Sean Dennis, *America in the Gilded Age* (NYU Press, 1993)

Cassius Dio, *Roman History* (Loeb, 1914)

Center for Public Integrity, 'After the Meltdown: Ex-Wall Street Chieftains Living it Large in a Post-meltdown World' (2013)

Center for Public Integrity, 'After the Meltdown: Ex-SEC Chief Now Helps Companies Navigate Post-meltdown Reforms' (2013)

Chancey, Karen, 'The Amboyna Massacre in English Politics 1624–32', *Albion*, vol. 30, no. 4 (1998)

Chaudhuri, Nirad C., *Clive of India: A Political and Psychological Essay* (Barrie & Jenkins, 1975)

Chayka, Doug, 'The Misunderstood Robber Baron', *The Nation*, 11 November 2009

Chibnall, Marjorie, *Anglo-Norman England 1066–1166* (Blackwell, 1987)

Chibnall, Marjorie, *The Debate on the Norman Conquest* (Manchester University Press, 1999)

Chu, Daniel and Skinner, Elliott P., *A Glorious Age in Africa: The Story of Three Great African Empires* (Africa Research & Publications, 1996)

Close, William T., *Beyond the Storm: Treating the Powerless and the Powerful in Mobutu's Congo/Zaire* (Meadowlark Springs, 2006)

Cohan, W.D., 'The Rise and Fall of Jimmy Cayne,' *Fortune*, 25 August 2008

Conniff, Richard, *The Natural History of the Rich* (W.W. Norton, 2002)

Cook, Noble D., *Born to Die: Disease and the New World Conquest 1492–1650* (Cambridge University Press, 1998)

Crick, Julia and van Houts, Elisabeth (eds), *A Social History of England 900–1200* (Cambridge University Press, 2011)

Cringely, R.X., *Accidental Empires: How the Boys of Silicon Valley Make Their Millions, Battle Foreign Competition and Still Can't Get a Date* (Penguin, 1996)

Crosby, Alfred W. Jr, *The Columbian Exchange: Biological and Cultural Consequences of 1492* (Praeger, 2003)

Crossen, Cynthia, *The Rich and How They Got That Way* (Nicholas Brealey, 2001)

Crouch, David, *The Birth of Nobility: Constructing Aristocracy in England and France 900–1300* (Routledge, 2005)

da Bisticci, Vespasiano, *The Vespasiano Memoirs* (Renaissance Society of America, 1997)

Dalley, Jan, *The Black Hole: Money, Myth, and Empire* (Fig Tree, 2006)

Dalton, Paul, *Conquest, Anarchy, and Lordship: Yorkshire 1066–1154* (Cambridge University Press, 2002)

D'Auria, Sue H., 'Preparing for Eternity', in Rita E. Freed, Sue H. D'Auria and Yvonne J. Markowitz (eds), *Pharaohs of the Sun: Akhenaten, Nefertiti, and Tutankhamen* (Museum of Fine Arts, Boston, 1999)

Davidson, Christopher M., *Dubai: The Vulnerability of Success* (Hurst, 2008)

Davies, Norman, *The Isles: A History* (Macmillan, 1999)

Davis, R.H.C. and Chibnall, Marjorie, *The Gesta Guillelmi of William of Poitiers* (Oxford University Press, 1998)

Davis, William Stearns, 'The Influence of Wealth in Imperial Rome', *American Historical Review*, vol. 16, no. 3 (1911)

de Roover, Raymond, *The Rise and Decline of the Medici Bank 1397–1494* (Harvard University Press, 1963)

de Vries, J., 'Luxury in the Dutch Golden Age in Theory and Practice,' in Maxine Berg and Elizabeth Eger (eds), *Luxury in the 18th Century* (Palgrave Macmillan, 2002)

Demarest, David P. Jr, *The River Ran Red: Homestead 1892* (University of Pittsburgh Press, 1992)

Depelchin, J., 'Transformations of the Petite Bourgeoisie and the State in Post-Colonial Zaire', *Review of African Political Economy*, vol. 22 (1981)

Devlin, Larry, *Chief of Station, Congo: Fighting the Cold War in a Hot Zone* (Public Affairs, 2008)

Diallo, Siradiou, *Zaire Today* (Hippocrene Books, 1979)

Dougary, Ginny, 'Dasha's Next Move', *Financial Times*, 9 November 2012

Drelichman, Mauricio, 'All That Glitters: Precious Metals, Rent-seeking, and the Decline of Spain', *European Review of Economic History*, vol. 9, no. 3 (2005)

Duc de Saint-Simon, *The Memoirs of Louis XIV and his Court and of the Regency* (George Allen & Unwin, 1926)

Dunne, Dominick, 'Khashoggi's Fall', *Vanity Fair*, September 1989

Edge, L.B., *Andrew Carnegie: Industrial Philanthropist* (Lerner Publications Company, 2004)

Edwardes, Allen, *The Rape of India: A Biography of Robert Clive* (Julian Press, 1966)

Ehrenreich, Barbara, *Smile or Die: How Positive Thinking Fooled America* (Granta, 2010)

Eisenstadt, A.S., *Carnegie's Model Republic: Triumphant Democracy and the British–American Relationship* (State University of New York Press, 2008)

Elson, R.E., *Suharto: A Political Biography* (Cambridge University Press, 2008)

Farhi, P., '*Washington Post* Closes Sale to Amazon Founder Jeff Bezos', *Washington Post*, 1 October 2013

Feldenkirchen, W., 'Banking and Economic Growth: Banks and Industry in Germany in the Nineteenth Century' in W.R.Lee (ed.), *German Industry and German Industrialisation* (Routledge, 1991)

Ferguson, Niall, *The Ascent of Money: A Financial History of the World* (Penguin, 2009)

Findlay, Ronald and O'Rourke, Kevin H., *Power and Plenty: Trade, War, and the World Economy in the Second Millennium* (Princeton University Press, 2009)

Fleming, Robin, *Kings and Lords in Conquest England* (Cambridge University Press, 2004)

Fleming, Robin, 'Land and People', in J. Crick and E. van Houts (eds), *A Social History of England 900–1200* (Cambridge University Press, 2011)

Flinders Petrie, W.M., *History of Egypt* (Methuen & Co., 1894)

Foster, L.J., 'The New Religion', in Rita E. Freed, Sue H. D'Auria and Yvonne J. Markowitz (eds), *Pharaohs of the Sun: Akhenaten, Nefertiti, and Tutankhamen* (Museum of Fine Arts, Boston, 1999)

Frank, Robert, *Richistan: A Journey through the American Wealth Boom and the Lives of the New Rich* (Three Rivers, 2008)

Freed, Rita E., D'Auria, Sue H. and Markowitz, Yvonne J. (eds), *Pharaohs of the Sun: Akhenaten, Nefertiti, and Tutankhamen* (Museum of Fine Arts, Boston, 1999)

Freeland, Chrystia, *Plutocrats: The Rise of the New Global Super Rich and the Fall of Everyone Else* (Penguin, 2013)

Friedman, Thomas L., *The World is Flat: A Brief History of the 21st Century* (Farrar Straus Giroux, 2005)

Fukuyama, Francis, *The End of History and the Last Man* (Penguin, 1992)

Gaastra, F.S., *The Dutch East India Company: Expansion and Decline* (Walburg, 2003)

Gaastra, F.S., 'War, Competition and Collaboration: Relations between the English and Dutch East India Companies in the 17th and 18th Centuries', in H.V. Bowen, M. Lincoln and N. Rigby (eds), *The Worlds of the East India Company* (Boydell Press, 2011)

Gangewere, Robert J., *Palace of Culture: Andrew Carnegie's Museums and Library in Pittsburgh* (University of Pittsburgh Press, 2011)

Garrard, Timothy F., *African Gold* (Prestel, 2011)

Gates, B., 'A New Approach to Capitalism', in Michael Kinsley (ed.), *Creative Capitalism* (Simon & Schuster, 2009)

Gluckman, Ron, 'Hong Kong of the Desert?', *Asia Inc.*, 12 April 2012

Golding, Brian, *Conquest and Colonisation: The Normans in Britain 1066–1100*, 2nd edn (Palgrave Macmillan, 2013)

Goodway, N., 'My Regrets, by Goldman Sachs Boss Lloyd Blankfein', *London Evening Standard*, 13 November 2013

Gordon, Stewart, *When Asia was the World* (Da Capo Press, 2008)

Graeber, David, *Debt: The First 5,000 Years (*Melville House, 2011)

Green, Joshua, 'Where is Dick Fuld Now? Finding Lehman Brothers' Last CEO', *Businessweek*, 12 September 2013

Green, Judith A., *The Aristocracy of Norman England* (Cambridge University Press, 2002)

Greenspan, Alan, *The Age of Turbulence* (Penguin, 2008)

Grossman, R.S., *Unsettled Account: The Evolution of Banking in the Industrialized World since 1800* (Princeton University Press, 2010)

Grubb, Ben, 'Gates on Tax, Giving his Kids Only $10m – and Still Doing the Dishes', *Sydney Morning Herald*, 28 May 2013

Hadley, D.M., 'Ethnicity and Acculturation', in J. Crick and E. van Houts (eds), *A Social History of England 900–1200* (Cambridge University Press, 2011)

Hancock, Matthew and Zahawi, Nadhim, *Masters of Nothing: How the Crash Will Happen Again unless We Understand Human Nature* (Biteback, 2011)

Harrington, Jack, *Sir John Malcolm and the Making of British India* (Palgrave Macmillan, 2010)

Harvey, Robert, *Clive: The Life and Death of a British Emperor* (St Martin's, 2000)

Haskin, Jeanne M., *The Tragic State of the Congo: From Decolonisation to Dictatorship* (Algora, 2005)

Hemming, John, *The Conquest of the Incas* (Pan, 2004)

Henson, Donald, *The English Elite in 1066: Gone but not Forgotten* (Anglo-Saxon, 2001)

Hibbert, Christopher, *Florence: The Biography of a City* (Penguin, 1993)

Hibbert, Christopher, *The House of Medici: Its Rise and Fall* (Morrow, 1974)

Hills, John, *Inequality and the State* (Oxford University Press, 2004)

Ho, Karen, *Liquidated: An Ethnography of Wall Street* (Duke University Press, 2009)

Hochstrasser, J.B., *Still Life and Trade in the Dutch Golden Age* (Yale University Press, 2007)

Hoffman, David E., *The Oligarchs: Wealth and Power in the New Russia* (Public Affairs, 2003)

Hofstadter, R., 'The Pervasive Influence of Social Darwinism', in Thomas B. Brewer (ed.), *The Robber Barons: Saints or Sinners?* (Holt, Rinehart and Winston, 1970)

Holland, Tom, *Rubicon: The Triumph and Tragedy of the Roman Republic* (Abacus, 2005)

Hollingsworth, Mark and Lansley, Stewart, *Londongrad, from Russia with Cash: The Inside Story of the Oligarchs* (Fourth Estate, 2010)

Holt, J.C., *Colonial England 1066–1215* (Hambledon, 1997)

Holt, J.C. (ed.), *Domesday Studies* (Boydell, 1987)

Hornung, Erik, *Akhenaten and the Religion of Light* (Cornell University Press, 2001)

Hosenball, M., 'Here's Who's Backing Glenn Greenwald's New Website', *Reuters*, 15 October 2013

Hovey, Carl, *The Life Story of J. Pierpont Morgan* (Kessinger, 2006)

Human Rights Watch, 'UAE: Address Abuse of Migrant Workers', 29 March 2006

Hunwick, J.O., 'The Mid-fourteenth Century Capital of Mali', *Journal of African History*, vol. 14, no. 2 (1973)

Ikambana, Peta, *Mobutu's Totalitarian Political System: An Afrocentric Analysis* (Taylor & Francis, 2006)

Inglis, Fred, *A Short History of Celebrity* (Princeton University Press, 2010)

Israel, Jonathan, *The Dutch Republic: Its Rise, Greatness, and Fall* (Oxford University Press, 1998)

James, Harold, *Krupp: A History of the Legendary German Firm* (Princeton University Press, 2012)

Jones, D., 'Facebook CEO is Youngest Self-made Billionaire', *USA Today*, 5 March 2008

Josephson, Matthew, *The Robber Barons* (Mariner, 1962)

Kahney, L., 'Jobs vs Gates: Who's the Star?', *Wired*, 25 January 2006

Kalb, Madeleine, *The Congo Cables* (Macmillan, 1982)

Kampfner, John, *Freedom for Sale: How We Made Money and Lost our Liberty* (Simon & Schuster, 2009)

Kampfner, John, *Inside Yeltsin's Russia: Corruption, Conflict, Capitalism* (Cassell, 1994)

Kapelle, William E., *The Norman Conquest of the North* (Croom Helm, 1979)

Kelly, Sean, *America's Tyrant* (American University Press, 1993)

Kemp, Barry J., *Ancient Egypt: Anatomy of a Civilisation* (Routledge, 2006)

Kinsley, Michael (ed.), *Creative Capitalism* (Simon & Schuster, 2009)

Kirkpatrick, David, *The Facebook Effect* (Simon & Schuster, 2011)

Kramer, Andrew E., 'Midas Touch in St Petersburg: Friends of Putin Glow Brightly', *New York Times*, 1 March 2012

Krause, Paul, *The Battle for Homestead, 1880–1892* (University of Pittsburgh Press, 1992)

Krugman, Paul, *The Return of Depression Economics and the Crisis of 2008* (Penguin, 2008)

The Krupp Trial Before the French Court Martial (Sueddeutsche Monatshefte, 1923)

Kruppische Gustahlfabrik, *Krupp: A Century's History of the Krupp Works* (Krupp, 1912)

La Roche, J., 'Ex-Bear Stearns CEO is Selling His Apartment for $14.95m', *Business Insider*, 16 August 2013

La Roche, J., 'Lloyd Blankfein's Advice to Interns – Relax', *Business Insider*, 10 October 2013

La Roche, J., 'What Lloyd Blankfein Does All Weekend', *Business Insider*, 10 October 2013

Lacovara, Peter, 'The City of Amarna', in Rita E. Freed, Sue H. D'Auria and Yvonne J. Markowitz (eds), *Pharaohs of the Sun: Akhenaten, Nefertiti, and Tutankhamen* (Museum of Fine Arts, Boston, 1999)

Landes, David S., *The Wealth and Poverty of Nations* (Abacus, 1999)

Lane, Randall, 'Bill Gates and Bono on Their Alliance of Fortune, Fame and Giving', *Forbes*, 2 December 2013

Lawford, James P., *Clive: Proconsul of India* (Allen & Unwin, 1972)

Lawson, P. and Phillips, J., 'Our Execrable Banditti: Perceptions of Nabobs in Mid-18th Century Britain', *Albion*, vol. 16, no. 3 (1984)

Lee, W.R. (ed.), *German Industry and German Industrialisation* (Routledge, 1991)

Lenman, B. and Lawson, P., 'Robert Clive, the Black *Jagir* and British Politics', *Historical Journal*, vol. 26, no. 4 (1983)

Levy, Steven, *Hackers: Heroes of the Computer Revolution* (Doubleday, 1984)

Leyne, Jon, 'Dubai Ruler in Vast Charity Gift', BBC, 19 May 2007

Lindsay, Samuel M., 'Social Work at the Krupp Foundries, Essen', *Annals of the American Academy of Political and Social Science*, vol. 3 (1892)

Livesay, Harold C., *Andrew Carnegie and the Rise of Big Business* (Pearson, 2006)

Livingstone, Grace, *America's Back Yard: The United States and Latin America from the Monroe Doctrine to the War on Terror* (Zed Books, 2009)

Lockhart, James, *The Men of Cajamarca* (University of Texas Press, 1972)

Lockhart, James, *Spanish Peru* (University of Wisconsin Press, 1994)

Losse, Katherine, *The Boy Kings: A Journey into the Heart of the Social Network* (Free Press, 2012)

Loth, V.C., 'Armed Incidents and Unpaid Bills: Anglo-Dutch Rivalry in the Banda Islands in the 17th Century', *Modern Asian Studies*, vol. 29, no. 4 (1995)

Lucas, Ed, *The New Cold War: How the Kremlin Menaces both Russia and the West* (Bloomsbury, 2008)

Lucassen, J., 'A Multinational and its Labour Force: The Dutch East India Company 1595–1795', *International Labor and Working-Class History*, vol. 66 (2004)

Machiavelli, Niccolò, *History of Florence and the Affairs of Italy from the Earliest Times to the Death of Lorenzo the Magnificent* (Dunne, 1901)

Mahbubani, Kishore, *The Great Convergence: Asia, the West, and the Logic of One World* (Public Affairs, 2013)

Mahbubani, Kishore, *The New Asian Hemisphere: The Irresistible Shift of Global Power to the East* (Public Affairs, 2008)

Malleson, G.B., *Lord Clive* (Lancer Publishers, 2008 edition)

Maltby, William S., *The Rise and Fall of the Spanish Empire* (Palgrave Macmillan, 2009)

Manapat, Ricardo, *Some are Smarter than Others: The History of Marcos' Crony Capitalism* (Aletheia, 1991)

Manchester, William, *The Arms of Krupp* (Little, Brown, 1968)

Martin, Iain, *Making it Happen: Fred Goodwin, RBS, and the Men who Blew up the British Economy* (Simon & Schuster, 2013)

Martinez, Amy, 'Amazon.com's Bezos to Invest in Space Travel, Time', *Seattle Times*, 31 March 2012

Mason, Paul, *Meltdown: The End of the Age of Greed* (Verso, 2010)

Mason Ward, Allen, *Marcus Crassus and the Late Roman Republic* (University of Missouri Press, 1977)

McCabe, Joseph, *Crises in the History of the Papacy* (Kessinger, 2003)

McCreary, E.C., 'Social Welfare and Business: The Krupp Welfare Programme 1860–1914', *Business History Review*, vol. 42, no. 1 (1968)

McGregor, Richard, *The Party: The Secret World of China's Communist Rulers* (Allen Lane, 2010)

McGurk, Patrick, *The Chronicle of John of Worcester* (Oxford University Press, 1998)

McNaughton, Patrick R., 'Malian Antiquities and Contemporary Desire', *African Arts*, vol. 28, no. 4 (1995)

McQuaig, Linda and Brooks, Neil, *The Trouble with Billionaires: How the Super-rich Hijacked the World, and How we Can Take it Back* (Oneworld, 2013)

Menne, Bernhard, *Blood and Steel: The Rise of the House of Krupp* (Menne Press, 2008)

Metcalf, Barbara D. and Metcalf, Thomas R., *A Concise History of Modern India*, 3rd edn (Cambridge University Press, 2006)

Milanovic, Branko, *The Haves and the Have-nots, A Brief and Idiosyncratic History of Global Inequality* (Basic Books, 2011)

Milanovic, Branko, Lindert, Peter and Williamson, Jeffrey, *Pre-industrial Equality* (SFI Working Paper, 2009)

Milton, Giles, *Nathaniel's Nutmeg: How One Man's Courage Changed the Course of History* (Sceptre, 2000)

Moore, Malcolm, 'The Rise and Rise of Wang Jianlin, China's Richest Man', *Daily Telegraph*, 21 September 2013

Morris, David, *The Honour of Richmond: A History of the Lords, Earls and Dukes of Richmond* (William Sessions, 2000)

Morris, Marc, *The Norman Conquest* (Windmill, 2013)

Mouritsen, Henrik, *Plebs and Politics in the Late Roman Republic* (Cambridge University Press, 2001)

Nasaw, David, *Andrew Carnegie* (Penguin, 2007)

O'Brien, B., 'Authority and Community', in J. Crick and E. van Houts (eds), *A Social History of England 900–1200* (Cambridge University Press, 2011)

Ochoa, José María Gonzalez, *Francisco Pizarro* (Palacio de Los Barrantes-Cervantes, 2009)

Osborn, J., 'India and the East India Company in the Public Sphere in 18th Century Britain', in H.V. Bowen, M. Lincoln and N. Rigby (eds), *The Worlds of the East India Company* (Boydell Press, 2011)

Parks, Tim, *Medici Money: Banking, Metaphysics and Arts in Fifteenth Century Florence* (Atlas, 2006)

Parthasarathi, Prasannan, *Why Europe Grew Rich and Asia Did Not: Global Economic Divergence 1600–1850* (Cambridge University Press, 2011)

Peston, Robert, *Who Runs Britain? How the Super-rich are Changing our Lives* (Hodder & Stoughton, 2008)

Pierenkemper, T., 'Pre-1900 Industrial White Collar Employees at the Krupp Steel Casting Works: A New Occupational Category in Germany', *Business History Review*, vol. 58, no. 3 (1984)

Piketty, Thomas, *Capital in the 21st Century* (Harvard University Press, 2014)

Plutarch, *Parallel Lives* (Loeb, 1916)

Quinn, James, 'Dick Fuld of Collapsed Bank Lehman Brothers Says his Mother Loves Him', *Daily Telegraph*, 8 September 2009

Rachman, Gideon, *Zero-sum World: Politics, Power and Prosperity after the Crash* (Atlantic, 2010)

Rajan, Raghuram, *Fault Lines: How Hidden Fractures Still Threaten the World Economy* (Princeton University Press, 2011)

Redford, D.B., 'The Beginning of the Heresy', in Rita E. Freed, Sue H. D'Auria and Yvonne J. Markowitz (eds), *Pharaohs of the Sun: Akhenaten, Nefertiti, and Tutankhamen* (Museum of Fine Arts, Boston, 1999)

Reeves, Nicholas, *Akhenaten: Egypt's False Prophet* (Thames & Hudson, 2005)

Reich, Robert, *Supercapitalism: The Battle for Democracy in an Age of Big Business* (Icon, 2008)

Reinhart, Carmen M. and Rogoff, Kenneth, *This Time is Different: Eight Centuries of Financial Folly* (Princeton University Press, 2011)

Riemersma, J.C., 'Government Influence on Company Organisation in Holland and England 1550–1650', *Journal of Economic History*, vol. 10 (1950)

Roberts, Keith, *The Origins of Business, Money, and Markets* (Columbia University Press, 2011)

Rubinstein, William D., *Men of Property: The Very Wealthy in Britain since the Industrial Revolution* (The Social Affairs Unit, 2006)

Rubinstein, William D., *Who Were the Rich? A Biographical Directory of British Wealth-holders* (The Social Affairs Unit, 2009)

Ruggie, John G. (ed.), *Embedding Global Markets: An Enduring Challenge* (Ashgate, 2008)

Sampson, Anthony, *Who Runs This Place? The Anatomy of Britain in the 21st Century* (John Murray, 2005)

Sampson, Gareth C., *The Defeat of Rome: Crassus, Carrhae, and the Invasion of the East* (Pen & Sword, 2008)

Saxena, Anil, *East India Company* (Anmol, 2007)

Schama, Simon, *The Embarrassment of Riches: An Interpretation of Dutch Culture in the Modern Age* (Harper Perennial, 2004)

Schatzberg, Michael G., *The Dialectics of Oppression in Zaire* (Indiana University Press, 1991)

Schatzberg, Michael G., *Mobutu or Chaos?* (University Press of America, 1991)

Scheidel, Walter and Friesen, Steven J., 'The Size of the Economy and the Distribution of Income in the Roman Empire', *Journal of Roman Studies*, vol. 99 (2009)

Schmitz, David F., *The United States and Right Wing Dictatorships 1965–89* (Cambridge University Press, 2006)

Shevtsova, Lilia, *Putin's Russia* (Carnegie Endowment, 2003)

Singleton, Brent D., 'African Bibliophiles: Books and Libraries in Medieval Timbuktu', *Libraries and Culture*, vol. 39, no. 1 (2004)

Skrabec, Quentin R., *The Carnegie Boys: The Lieutenants of Andrew Carnegie that Changed America* (McFarland, 2012)

Slaughter, Anne-Marie, *A New World Order* (Princeton University Press, 2004)

Sorkin, Andrew Ross, *Too Big to Fail: Inside the Battle to Save Wall Street* (Penguin, 2010)

Stearns, Jason, *Dancing in the Glory of Monsters: The Collapse of the Congo and the Great War of Africa* (Public Affairs, 2012)

Stewart, H. and Goodley, S. 'Big Bang's Shockwaves Left us with Today's Big Bust', *Guardian*, 9 October 2011

Strathern, Paul, *The Medici: Godfathers of the Renaissance* (Jonathan Cape, 2003)

Surk, Barbara, 'Meet Dubai's Billionaire Ruler, Sheikh Mohammad bin Rashid al Maktoum', *Huffington Post*, 12 April 2009

Swanton, Michael, *The Anglo-Saxon Chronicle* (Phoenix Press, 2000)

Thomas, Hugh, *The Golden Age: The Spanish Empire of Charles V* (Penguin, 2011)

Thomas, Hugh, *Rivers of Gold: The Rise of the Spanish Empire, from Columbus to Magellan* (Random House, 2005)

Thomas, Hugh M., *The English and the Normans: Ethnic Hostility, Assimilation, and Identity 1066–1220* (Oxford University Press, 2003)

Thomas, Landon, 'A $31 Billion Gift between Friends', *New York Times*, 27 June 2006

Thomas, Landon, 'Distinct Culture at Bear Stearns Helps it Surmount a Grim Market', *New York Times*, 28 March 2003

Traynor, Ian, 'Putin Urged to Apply the Pinochet Stick', *Guardian*, 31 March 2000

Tweedie, N., 'Bill Gates Interview: I Have no Use for Money. This is God's Work', *Daily Telegraph*, 18 January 2013

Unoki, Ko, *Mergers, Acquisitions, and Global Empires* (Routledge, 2013)

van Houts, Elisabeth, *The Gesta Normannorum Ducum of William of Jumièges, Orderic Vitalis, and Robert of Torigni* (Oxford University Press, 1995)

van Reybrouck, David, *Congo: The Epic History of a People* (Ecco, 2014)

Varon Gabai, Rafael, *Francisco Pizarro and his Brothers: The Illusion of Power* (University of Oklahoma Press, 1997)

Varon Gabai, R. and Jacobs, A.P., 'Peruvian Wealth and Spanish Investments: The Pizarro Family during the 16th Century', *Hispanic American Historical Review*, vol. 67, no. 4 (1987)

Ververka, M., 'Richard Branson's Otherworldly Space Quest', *USA Today*, 27 May 2013

Walker, Peter, 'Nat Rothschild Loses Libel Case against *Daily Mail* over Mandelson Trip', *Guardian*, 10 February 2012

Walker, T., 'Pierre Omidyar: The Reclusive eBay Founder Will Battle with the *Washington Post* Owner and Amazon Founder Jeff Bezos to Create the Future of News', *Independent*, 18 October 2013

Ward, Kerry, *Networks of Empire: Forced Migration in the Dutch East India Company* (Cambridge University Press, 2008)

Warner, Isabel, *Steel and Sovereignty: The Deconcentration of the West German Steel Industry 1949–1954* (Phillip von Zarben, 1996)

Waters, R., 'An Exclusive Interview with Bill Gates', *Financial Times*, 1 November 2013

Webster, Anthony, *The Twilight of the East India Company* (Boydell Press, 2009)

Wedeman, A., 'Looters, Rent-scrapers, and Dividend Collectors', *Journal of Developing Areas*, vol. 31 (1997)

Werth, Barry, *Banquet at Delmonico's: Great Minds, the Gilded Age, and the Triumph of Evolution in America* (Random House, 2009)

Whoriskey, P., 'Record Thin on Steve Jobs' Philanthropy', *Washington Post*, 7 October 2011

William of Malmesbury, *History of the Norman Kings* (Llanerch Press, 1989)

Williamson, Jeffrey G., 'History without Evidence: Latin American Inequality since 1491', National Bureau of Economic Research Paper No. 14766 (2009)

Wolverton, T., 'Amazon, Barnes & Noble Settle Patent Suit', *CNET*, 6 March 2002

Wong, Edward, 'Bloomberg Code Keeps Articles from Chinese Eyes', *New York Times*, 28 November 2013

Wong, Edward, 'Bloomberg News is Said to Curb Articles that Might Anger China', *New York Times*, 8 November 2013

Wrong, Michela, *In the Footsteps of Mr Kurtz* (Fourth Estate, 2001)

Wrong, Michela, 'The Mystery of Mobutu's Millions', *New Statesman*, 26 July 2007

Young, Crawford and Turner, Thomas, *The Rise and Decline of the Zairian State* (University of Wisconsin Press, 2012)

Zagorin, Adam, 'Leaving Fire in his Wake', *Time*, 22 February 1993

Index